... ist of British Parli... ...ooks

Occasional Pu...ication Number 4

Edited by John Sims

General Editor: Aubrey Newman
University of Leicester
History Department

First published in 1984 by

University of Leicester History Department
and University of California, Riverside

Distributed by

Aubrey Newman
Department of History
University of Leicester

Department of History
University of California, Riverside
Riverside, CA 92521
United States of America

British Library Cataloguing in Publication Data

Sims, John

A Handlist of British Parliamentary poll books.
—(Occasional publications / University of Leicester.
History Department, ISSN 0144—3739; no. 4)
1. Great Britain—Voting Registers—Bibliography
I. Title II. Newman, Aubrey III. Series
016.324941 Z7164. V/
ISBN 0-906696-04-6

INTRODUCTION

The purpose of this handlist is to provide a record of all known printed poll books for English parliamentary elections. It is based on the unpublished "Draft register of poll books" compiled by the History of Parliament Trust in 1953 and also includes those which have been traced since then. Irish poll books have been omitted as a list has already been published![1] No systematic survey has yet been made of Scottish and Welsh poll books but a small number which have been identified are included in an appendix.

Before the introduction of the secret ballot in 1872 the normal procedure at contested elections was for the names of voters and the candidates for whom they polled to be entered in a poll book. The development of this practice is obscure, but it was first given official recognition in an Act of 1696 for regulating parliamentary elections (7 & 8 Will 3 c.25). This laid down that at county elections the sheriff or his representative should "set down the names of each freeholder and the place of his freehold and for whom he shall poll." The Act also required the returning officers of all constituencies to "forthwith deliver to such person or persons as shall desire the same a copy of the poll," implying that it was expected that boroughs as well as counties would have a written poll. No provision was made for the permanent retention of the poll books and the difficulty found to result from this omission in the determination of disputed returns led to a further Act in 1711 (10 Anne c.23). In addition to requiring the poll clerk to enter the elector's place of residence as well as his freehold, this Act ordered county poll books to be handed over to the Clerk of the Peace within twenty days of the declaration "to be carefully kept and preserved among the records of the sessions of the peace." It was not until 1843, however, that any statutory measures were taken for the preservation of borough poll books. An Act of that year (35 & 36 Vict. c.33), observing that "no adequate provision has been made for the safe custody and production of poll books" required that after the declaration at all parliamentary elections the poll books should be deposited with the Clerk of the Crown in Chancery. The Crown Office was to "keep and preserve the said several poll books and shall deliver to any party applying for the same an office copy...and shall also permit any party to inspect such poll books." Unfortunately the historical value of these documents was not fully appreciated and the entire collection of original poll books in the Crown Office was destroyed in 1907.

This legislation, with its consistent if sporadic concern with the preservation and availability of poll books, provided a framework favourable to publication. It is significant that, with a single exception, the earliest printed poll books are those for the general election in 1702, the first to be held after the enactment of the 1696 legislation. Unlike the originals, printed poll books are not official documents and must be treated with a certain amount of caution. They were usually published by local printers or newspaper offices and, while in many cases it is clear that the compiler had access to the original poll book and made every effort to produce an accurate record, the need for rapid publication must have resulted in a significant number of errors. In other cases, the poll book was openly published on behalf of the committee of one or other of the candidates, using the figures of their own check clerk which were likely to be at variance with those of the official return. Nevertheless, their value as source material for local history, genealogy and the study of voting patterns is widely recognized and has been exploited by historians of both the eighteenth and nineteenth centuries.[2]

About 2000 printed poll books have so far been traced, representing approximately one-third of the contested elections between 1700 and 1872. The earliest one known is for the Essex by-election of 1694 and the last for a county or borough seat is that of the Bedfordshire by-election of June 1872.[3] The university seats were exempted from the provisions of the 1872 Ballot Act and as a result there are later poll books of 1878, 1880 and 1882 for Oxford, London and Cambridge Universities respectively. County poll books tend to dominate the early eighteenth century, with 64 for the forty counties of England before 1760 compared to 58 for nearly two hundred boroughs. This reflects the pattern of contested county elections, which are numerous until 1740 but then decline sharply until 1832. From the mid-eighteenth century there is a marked increase in the number of borough poll books, particularly in those boroughs of medium size which had a comparatively wide franchise. An excessively large electorate could be as much of a deterrent to the publication of poll books as the opposite extreme. It is notable that no Middlesex poll book later than 1802 was published and that there are only two printed for Manchester compared to regular runs for Oldham and Bolton.

Since the publication of poll books continued undiminished right up to the abolition of open voting, it is clear that there was always a ready market. This is borne out further by the number of instances in which rival printers each brought out their own edition, and on some occasions a second edition was issued or a poll originally published in a newspaper was reprinted in pamphlet form. Publication was sometimes presented as performing a public service, as when the compiler of the Cambridge University poll book of 1780 urged his readers "to guard against corruption, patronage, and undue and secret influence in the electors and elected. To give some small check to this last seems to be a sufficient reason why all polls should be published...It has been suggested that the publication of this poll might offend some persons in the University...[the writer] neither fears the resentment nor values the friendship of any elector who is ashamed that the world should know in what manner he voted." A more partisan purpose is suggested by the extract from the hustings speech of the defeated candidate at Banbury in 1835 which is printed as an epigraph in the poll book: "If I sell the shirt off my back...I will publish a *black book* in which the name of every voter shall be entered, his residence and his trade, that every farmer may know with whom he ought or ought not to deal." That this was no empty threat is borne out by the Liberal candidate at Colchester in 1852 who recalled later how "the morning after the poll-book was published, the farmers of the neighbourhood came into the town and, going round the small tradesmen of the borough with that poll-book in their hands, said one to another—'No, you voted for Wingrove Cooke; we will never darken your doors again.'"[4]

This handlist includes all printed polls, whether issued as separate pamphlets or appearing in newspapers or as part of another publication, which were published at the time of the election or so soon afterwards that their purpose may be recognized as political rather than historical. It therefore excludes a number of editions of manuscript poll books which have been published at a later date since they belong more properly to the bibliography of manuscript poll books, an area which still awaits exhaustive investigation.[5] Also excluded are the electoral registers which were published annually from 1832 and which are often confused with poll books. The registers give a complete list of eligible voters with addresses but do not record votes cast at an election. Some copies of registers are known which have indications of voting added in manuscript and these would have to be included in any survey of manuscript polls.

Many people have contributed to the preparation of the handlist. Credit is due in the first place to Mr. George Cunningham, the results of whose expeditions in search of poll books were incorporated in the History of Parliament Trust's draft register, and whose research notes led me to some of the details in this introduction. Mr. E. L. C. Mullins placed the Trust's card index at my disposal and gave me much help and advice. Dr. David Armstrong, in addition to other discoveries, carried out a systematic search of newspapers and located a significant number of polls which were not published in any other form. My former colleagues at the Institute of Historical Research have given me every assistance and encouragement, and Clyve Jones kindly volunteered to prepare the appendix of Welsh and Scottish poll books. I am also indebted to numerous librarians, archivists and researchers for information and it is also appropriate to take this opportunity to thank all those institutions which have generously co-operated with the Institute of Historical Research in its acquisition of photocopies of poll books, since without such a collection compilation of the handlist would not have been possible.

Finally, it is inevitable that the list as it stands at present is incomplete. I shall be glad to hear of any additions or corrections which can be incorporated in a supplementary list.

J. M. Sims
India Office Library and Records
British Library

Note on Arrangement

The poll books are listed in alphabetical order of county with boroughs and universities following the county constituencies in each case. Monmouthshire has been treated as an English county and London is placed under Middlesex. By-elections are denoted by an asterisk and in cases when two elections occurred in the same year the month is given. Titles have been abbreviated to the minimum necessary for identification as they tend to follow a more or less standard form. Where no date of publication is shown in the poll book it has been supplied in square brackets, but the place of publication has only rarely been attributed as it is usually less certain. Publication in the form of a single sheet which is not part of a newspaper has been indicated by the term broadsheet.

Each entry gives a brief description of the arrangement of the voters' names and the extent of the information provided. Alphabetical order is not specified if it is already stated in the title. Place of residence denotes a town or village and address a more specific location such as a street. The term electors was used to distinguish those enfranchised by the Reform Act of 1832 from the old electorate. Tendered votes were recorded at the poll but were held in abeyance while their validity was examined. Candidates' names are given but party affiliations, which seldom occur in poll books, are not included. Voting figures have been omitted as those given in poll books are often in conflict with those of the official return and reproduction would risk giving them a spurious authority.[6]

Whenever possible one London and one local location have been supplied, but it must be emphasised that they are selective and do not in any way represent all known copies. For London locations priority has been given to the Institute of Historical Research as it has, including photocopies, the most complete single collection and it is where the handlist was compiled. Many of the poll books at the Institute are also in the Guildhall Library to which there is unrestricted access and which has published a complete list of its collection?[7] The British Library, the Bodleian Library, Cambridge University Library and the Society of Genealogists also have substantial collections which are not fully represented by the locations in the handlist. In a few cases I have not been able to see a poll book of whose existence there is firm evidence and these have been recorded as "untraced" at the end of the constituency list.

Notes to Introduction

1. B. M. Walker and K. T. Hoppen, "Irish Election Poll Books, 1832-1872," *Irish Booklore* 3 (1976); 4 (1980).

2. E.g. W. A. Speck and W. A. Grey, "Computer Analysis of Poll Books: an Initial Report," *Bulletin of the Institute of Historical Research* 43 (1970); Speck, Grey and R. Hopkinson, "Computer Analysis of Poll Books: a Further Report," ibid. 48 (1975); J. R. Vincent, *Pollbooks: How Victorians Voted* (Cambridge, 1967).

3. It has been suggested that the reason for the publication of the 1694 Essex poll book was the public interest in the election on account of its having been caused by the suicide of the sitting member. G. Holmes, *The Electorate and the National Will in the First Age of Party* (Lancaster, 1976).

4. *Essex Standard*, 19 April 1861, quoted in A. F. J. Brown, *Colchester 1815-1914* (Chelmsford, 1980).

5. The bibliography in W. A. Speck, *Tory and Whig: the Struggle in the Constituencies 1701-1715* (1970) includes manuscript as well as printed poll books for that period.

6. Voting figures are available in R. Sedgwick (ed.), *The History of Parliament: The House of Commons 1715-1754* (1970); Sir L. Namier and J. Brooke (eds.), *The History of Parliament: The House of Commons 1754-1790 (1964); F. W. S. Craig, British Parliamentary Election Results 1832-1885* (1977); H. Stooks Smith, *The Register of Parliamentary Contested Elections*, 2d edn. (1842).

7. *A Handlist of Poll Books and Registers of Electors in Guildhall Library* (1970).

List of Abbreviations

Archaeol	Archaeological
Bodl	Bodleian Library
Brit Lib	British Library
Brit Lib (News)	British Library Newspaper Library
Inst Hist Res	Institute of Historical Research
n.p.	no place of publication known
Natl Lib Scot	National Library of Scotland
Natl Lib Wales	National Library of Wales
Pub Lib	Public Library
Rec Off	Record Office
Soc Geneal	Society of Genealogists
Univ Lib	University Library
*	by-election

POLL BOOKS AND ENGLISH ELECTORAL BEHAVIOR

Poll Books

During the first session of William III's third parliament, the House of Commons considered four measures intended to remedy some of the deficiencies in parliamentary election procedures. The often acrimonious election disputes common after general elections and by-elections demanded attention and required correction. Both houses passed all four measures; three became statutes with William's signature.[1] The first Act failed dismally to accomplish its intended goal of preventing charges and expenses at elections. The second somewhat more successfully prevented false and double returns of MPs. The third may not have completely achieved its goal of preventing ''irregular proceedings of sheriffs and other officers,'' at contested elections, but it certainly provided a lasting record of English elections in the attempt.[2] The act did not require publication of polling lists, but its provision requiring copies of any county poll to be available upon request resulted almost immediately in the publication of poll books. Once begun the practice spread rapidly, and the result is measured in part by the large number of poll books listed in this register.

The earliest poll books usually contained nothing more than a list of voters and their votes, but poll books soon included more information about those wielding the franchise. County poll books soon included each voter's address as a matter of course, either specifically or by parish or hundred, and sometimes both. Borough poll books typically included more. The occupation and residence (usually by street) of each voter became two commonly recorded pieces of information in borough poll books. In freeman boroughs, resident voters often are distinguished from non-resident voters along with the addresses of the non-residents. Beyond these rules of thumb, however, generalizations about the contents of poll books cannot be made easily. Variations in the borough lists include the allocation of each voter by street and parish address, the identification of freeholders and freemen in those towns with county status (like Norwich), and even notations of the actual sequence in which each voter cast his vote. After 1832, poll book publishers often listed the new £10 householders apart from the remaining freemen who retained their franchises in the old freeman boroughs. Nonconformists were identified very rarely in the earliest decades of poll book publication.

The greatest similarity in the poll books is found not in the information they contain (beyond the names of voters and their votes), but in the convention quickly adopted for reporting the votes cast at each election. Originally most poll books simply listed separately the names of those individuals voting for each candidate. This method was used as late as the Northampton borough election of 1841 (see Figure 1), but it soon gave way to a convention in both manuscript and printed poll books of reporting the votes cast by each voter on a single line by marking a series of columns designating each of the candidates standing for election. (see Figure 2) Virtually every poll book in this list except for those of the late seventeenth and very early eighteenth centuries conforms to this model.[3] Except for the earliest poll books, then, which can require a considerable effort to analyze even a single election involving several candidates since each elector's voting record must be reconstructed from separate listings, the three and four-candidate contests of the eighteenth and nineteenth centuries are not difficult to interpret.

The chronological distribution of the existing printed poll books is skewed slightly toward the end of the period covered by poll book publication. Sims notes that poll books exist for one-third of all contests between 1700 and 1832, but a higher proportion have survived for the later years. In fact, Vincent has estimated that poll books exist for fully half the contests between 1830 and 1872. Nevertheless, the number surviving for all periods is impressive; Vincent's 1967 estimate of approximately 2,000 existing printed poll books has proven remarkably accurate.

Printed poll books are by no means the only potential source of information available for an examination of the English electorate. Unprinted poll books may exist in the absence of printed poll books, and apparent gaps in the printed record after 1696 may on occasion be filled with surviving manuscript copies. A polling record of the Maidstone parliamentary election of 1796, for example, exists only in manuscript, as does the Bristol poll book for the contested election of 1820.[4] Nor are the years prior to the 1696 Act which resulted in so many printed lists of voters totally bereft of poll books, printed or otherwise. A printed poll book exists for an election in 1694, and manuscript poll books for elections before 1696 have survived as well. Derek Hirst cited nine manuscript poll books in describing voting behavior and electoral politics under the early Stuarts.[5]

Poll books for by-elections seem to have been left unprinted more often than those for general elections. The 1816 Lewes poll for the by-election at which James Scarlett stood against Sir John Shelley to replace Thomas Read Kemp was never printed, but it has survived in manuscript.[6] Nevertheless, by-elections were potentially as divisive as regular elections and were printed when political considerations warranted; this register lists more than 350 printed by-election pollbooks. Polls resulting from nineteenth-century by-elections do seem to have been printed with some regularity. Printed poll books not included in this listing probably exist as well. The Liverpool poll book for 1831, for example, may exist in printed or manuscript form, though it has been missing for the last thirty years.[7]

Surviving printed and manuscript poll books for *municipal* elections also supplement the printed parliamentary poll books. A great many municipal elections for Common Council seats in later-eighteenth century Maidstone survive in manuscript and can reveal as much about local political behavior as the printed parliamentary poll books. The 1819 published poll for the election of a Recorder in Colchester and the 1821 poll for the election of Colchester's Headmen can be compared profitably to the printed poll books for the parliamentary elections of 1818 and 1820.[8] Printed parliamentary poll books frequently provide extensive information for various borough and county constituencies, but the addition of manuscript parliamentary poll books and both manuscript and printed lists from local elections may complete, or significantly augment, the record. While this register provides no guide to either type of ancillary record, it does allow the identification of those constituencies for which such supplementary material is essential due to deficiencies in the printed poll book record.

Poll Books and the Historians

Just over two decades ago, John Cannon described Britain's surviving parliamentary poll books in *History's* "Short Guide to the Records" series.[9] Though far from unknown in 1962, a very short list of publications appended to Cannon's brief description encompassed the principal works in which poll books had played a part. Except for George Rudé's imaginative and innovative research concerning John Wilkes and the Middlesex voters which had just appeared and Cannon's own look at Wiltshire, poll book analysis had precious little to do with the arguments and conclusions of many of the works cited. The majority, as Cannon himself noted, were useful for their explanations of the complicated mechanisms of the electoral system rather than for anything bearing directly on electoral behavior.[10]

Given the original purpose of the poll books, it is less than surprising that most poll book research has focused almost exclusively on politics, albeit broaching social, economic, and religious issues along the way. The mining of poll books for "fruitful" information (to use Eric Allardt's term) regarding England's political history has yielded ore of impressively high quality, though much of it has been left in a relatively unrefined state![11]

The Reformed Electorate: Electoral Behavior After the Great Reform Act

D.C. Moore's now famous "The Other Face of Reform," for example, identified "block-voting" in the English countryside in the era of the passage of the Great Reform Act, and opened a heated, persistent debate over the objectives of the framers of the first Reform Bill as well as over the effects of the Act, particularly in rural areas. Moore's work examined very few poll books in detail and considered county electorates exclusively, but his provocative interpretation of reform as a vehicle for reinforcing "deference communities" and continuing the domination of the "politics of deference" challenged the standard Whiggish interpretation of the Reform Act with such apparent success that it could hardly be ignored.

Moreover, much of Moore's thesis could be tested only with recourse to the very evidence he used, poll books. The range of Moore's work has been expanded by Patrick Joyce and challenged by a number of scholars including Richard Davis, John Milton-Smith, and J.R. Fisher; the debate is far from concluded![12]

The principal examination of nineteenth-century poll books, however, though published well after Moore's article, was neither provoked by it nor directly concerned with it. In fact, John Vincent's *Poll Books: How Victorians Voted* accepted without comment Moore's arguments about the nature of the county electorates. On the other hand, Vincent's *Poll Books* clearly disagreed with Moore's contention that "the use of borough poll books for a study analagous to ['The Other Face of Reform'] could hardly be contemplated."[13] Of the nearly 200 poll books from almost 90 different constituencies examined by Vincent, most described borough elections. Vincent set a mere handful of county elections against dozens of urban contests to pose a multitude of hypotheses concerning urban and rural voters which remain to be tested by further "careful analysis of voting habits." The poll books may not have shed much "light on the politics of the great cities," but they revealed much regarding urban politics in general. Vincent's identification of the solitary Roman Catholic Tory priest at Ipswich in 1865, for example, or the Roman Catholic voting a split-ticket at Tamworth in 1837, raise key issues regarding the place of religion in Victorian Britain which can be addressed only through detailed analyses of poll books![14]

The other descriptions of the occupations of groups of voters in *Poll Books* reveal the votes of "selected categories" of occupations for constituency after constituency. These descriptions pose questions about the relationships, if any, between socio-economic characteristics and political preferences which must be examined thoroughly and systematically across the electorate. These "door-to-door interviews with the dead," if conducted systematically to allow comparisons across constituencies, can reveal in remarkable detail the political realities of a large segment of English society.

A variety of important nineteenth century projects *not* involved in the debate over "deference communities" have been conducted as well. Michael Drake's first "psephological" foray exhibited the potential rewards of systematic analysis without reference to the overreaching question of the place of the electorate in the nineteenth century constitution![15] Quite unlike Vincent's look at Victorian voters, Drake limited his examination to a single constituency. More importantly, he also differed from Vincent by comparing the behavior of Ashford's electors from election to election. Those men who voted for Sir Edward Dering in 1852 were traced to the election of 1857, just as Dering's supporters in 1857 were followed at the election of 1863. By thus examining "panels" of voters instead of limiting his focus to electors at a single election, Drake addressed directly many of the analytical questions either included only by implication or completely overlooked in *Poll Books*. Combining the electoral registers available after 1832 with the poll books, Drake measured voter turnout precisely. He also reported the persistence of voters over successive elections, identified residential and occupational characteristics of the Ashford voting public, and described their recruitment into the electorate. Having thus confronted many of the most important basic issues facing any analysis of a relatively uncharted electorate, Drake assessed the strength of the Ashford electorate's partisan support at specific elections by measuring their willingness to "plump" (cast a single vote) instead of using their full allotment of two votes to support two candidates.

A single constituency also served as the focal point for another analysis of voters that proved to be even more systematic and specifically concerned with the analytical possibilities posed by poll book analysis![16] Jeremy Mitchell and James Cornford examined Cambridge voters between the first and second reform acts, and in doing so considered many of the questions which had concerned Drake such as recruitment into the electorate. They also measured "cohort decay," voter registration and participation, and the actual voting patterns of the electors over time. No other analysis prior to theirs had tackled so bluntly so many questions of fundamental importance to any discussion of English voting behavior, and no other study before or since has dealt with the questions more satisfactorily.

The Unreformed Electorate

J.H. Plumb boosted interest in poll books at the other chronological extreme of poll book coverage with his seminal 1969 *Past and Present* article, "The Growth of the Electorate in England from 1600 to 1715." Unconvinced that Lewis Namier justifiably dismissed the electorate as a body in which not one in twenty exercised his franchise freely, and in which voters slavishly obeyed the political dictates of landlords, Plumb argued for a more discriminating assessment of the political nation. His own creative and ingenious look at a sequence of Suffolk poll books for elections in the reign of Anne suggested the inadequacies inherent in many Namierite interpretations of the era.[17]

W.A. Speck and W.A. Gray took up Plumb's important questions in an equally ingenious examination of the Hampshire poll books of 1705 and 1710. Speck already had revealed something of the nature and scope of the electoral frenzies of the early eighteenth century in *Tory and Whig* (1970). The publication of "Computer Analysis of Poll Books: An Initial Report," by Speck and Gray in the same year further demonstrated the benefits of systematic analysis as well as the advantages of computer assistance in dealing with large numbers of individual voters. Even when considering the electorate at only two elections (separated by an interval of five years), a computer enabled Speck and Gray to examine electoral behavior by assisting in "linking" the records of the individual voters contained in the two poll books.[18] Although it was a rudimentary analysis unaugmented by supplementary data concerning the voters of Hampshire, the Speck-Gray report could hardly have been more illuminating. It suggested, albeit briefly, the means of resolving some of the methodological problems encountered in trying to trace and combine (link) the records of the votes of thousands of Englishmen. In addition to, and partly because of, its longitudinal focus, this examination of two Hampshire elections also broached questions similar to those raised the following year in Drake's analysis of Ashford such as the level of voter turnout, recurrent participation by electors, split-ticket voting, straight-party voting, "floating" voters (those who changed their partisan support from one election to the next), and the impact of religion on voting choice (through a separate look at the behavior of the 61 identifiable clergymen in these contests.)[19]

Five years after their "Initial Report," Speck and Gray (along with R. Hopkinson) published a "Further Report" in which they argued persuasively in favor of a "participatory" model of electoral behavior in the Augustan era and against the "deference" model posed so often at least by implication in other studies of the period. Their "Further Report" examined a much expanded base of fourteen elections distributed among five county constituencies (including the original pair of elections in Hampshire), and its more sophisticated presentation of results encompassed a much more direct discussion of individual voting patterns at the elections in question.[20] Three of the five counties permitted only two elections to be considered, and a fourth allowed the examination of three contests. The politically hyperactive Buckinghamshire voters permitted a lengthier focus since they contested all but one of the general elections of Anne's reign, but the conclusions drawn rested on the analysis of all of the boroughs, whether frequently contested or not.

The two articles by Speck and Gray and those by Drake, Mitchell, and Cornford elevated the discussion of English electoral behavior to a much higher plane. The debate has continued there with considerable animation and covers the entire range of years between the solitary rule of William III to the introduction of the secret ballot in 1872. Individual historians have, on occasion, ventured into the fray without exhibiting an awareness of the new level upon which the debate has taken place since the pioneering work of the early 1970s, but on the whole recent work has maintained the standard. Unfortunately, with the exception of the examination of Cambridge by Mitchell and Cornford, each of these reports suffered from one potentially severe methodological limitation; in each, comparative examinations of electoral behavior were limited to pairs of elections. The remainder of this essay will consider both the means to overcome this limitation and the reasons for doing so.

Panels And Poll Books

The lack of published parliamentary poll books as a result of either uncontested or unpolled elections poses a potentially severe barrier to the analysis of electoral behavior which, given their rarity, usually cannot be overcome with poll books for local elections or even manuscript poll books for parliamentary elections. "Panels" of voters whose behavior can be examined over relatively long periods are required for extensive analysis. The barrier imposed by missing poll books or unpolled elections may well eliminate a particular constituency from consideration, for the extremely limited value of isolated poll books increases only "if they can be analyzed as part of a series."[21] Fortunately, many constituencies contested a sufficient number of elections to allow this sort of extended analysis. Longitudinal analyses of voting behavior remain extremely rare, but the rapid improvement of nominal record linkage techniques (those procedures used to merge the records of these individual English voters) and the proliferation of computer software that facilites linkage should result in a substantial increase in the numbers of constituencies examined over several elections. Moreover, once a "panel" has been created by a researcher, almost any data analysis required, from simple cross-tabulations to complicated analyses of variance and covariance, can be accomplished with widely available statistical packages.[22]

Speck's research illustrated the immeasureable value of a "panel survey" in examinations of electoral behavior.[23] The value of a panel, through which the behavior of voters could be compared across elections, had not passed unnoticed prior to Speck's work, but too often accounts of voting behavior had relied exclusively on cross-sectional analytical techniques. As early as 1835, James Ackland published a *Comparative Poll Book* for Hull in which he compared the choices of each voter over three elections (1832, 1835, and 1835-by), but the severe difficulties encountered in "linking" the information contained in poll books from election to election deterred almost all emulation before Speck's report.[24] Unfortunately, even since the publication of Speck and Gray's initial report the typical focus has remained cross-sectional, although researchers are willing increasingly to compare two elections.[25]

Drake's look at Ashford is an excellent case in point. The value of Drake's analysis cannot be denied, but rather than an extended focus across all five Ashford elections in the period from 1852 to 1865, Drake's analysis was limited to pairs of elections. Drake could not examine a single "panel" of voters since his data were linked only from one election to the next. Accordingly, he was forced to consider four different panels. The voters in 1852 could be traced in the election of 1857, but their behavior at the subsequent election could not be determined. Similarly, the voters in 1865 could be observed again in 1868 if they reappeared at the hustings, but their inclusion in a separate panel containing voters from only these two elections rather than as part of an extended panel containing *all* Ashford voters at the five elections under review prevented additional comparisons over several contests and severely limited the value of the "psephological trees" Drake constructed.

The limitations imposed by data sets linked across only two elections also prevented other than the simplest "longitudinal" analysis in the Speck-Gray "Further Report." Each election and set of electors was compared only to the one immediately following. But where Speck and Gray's analysis of Augustan voters and Drake's analysis of Victorian voters proved deficient in the creation of panels, the work by Jeremy Mitchell and James Cornford excels.[26] In fact, of all the work published for any era, theirs is among the most methodologically sophisticated. Their careful explanation of the data used and descriptions of the techniques through which the data were both assembled and analyzed is a model of quantitative research reporting. Their actual creation of a single linked file of electors from which to take precise measures of the electoral process is a model of quantitative analysis.

Panels from Poll Books: Nominal Record Linkage

Using the printed poll books or any other existing data pertaining to the electorate of any period poses an almost identical set of problems regardless of variations in the data examined. In fact, unbeknownst to most of them, historians have long dealt with these same problems of nominal record linkage. The only differences distinguishing the more commonly encountered task of tracing the records of an individual for a biographical study and that of linking the records of thousands of voters over time (or linking several sets of records for a single year) are (1) the relative number of "identifiers" contained in the available data which permit the information for a specific individual to be kept separate from the information regarding others, and (2) the scale of the task. A large data set requires clearly defined linkage rules to allow computer assistance. Name spelling variations may loom much larger in linking two files of 10,000 names than in sorting through papers looking for references to John Spencer, Lord Althorp, but the processes are in essence identical. Spelling variations pose a much less pronounced problem in either case for examinations of the later eighteenth and nineteenth centuries than for studies of earlier periods, but relatively standard spelling does not alter the need to compensate for apparent differences in recorded given names or surnames which might prevent the linkage of two or more records regarding the same individual.[27] A reference to Lord Spenser instead of Lord Spencer is unlikely to lead to much confusion, but the problem is exactly the same as the possibly more difficult one created by a reference in one poll book to a Geoffrey Braythwayte and a reference in another to a Geoffrey Braithwaite.

Nominal record linkage is of such general concern that many discussions of problems and remedies now provide a reasonable guide for the researcher approaching poll books for the first time. Wrigley's *Identifying People in the Past*, published a decade ago, contains considerations of a variety of data bases and research objectives, and the publications of the Canadian Social History Project also serve as excellent introductions to the field.[28] The now widespread availability of sorting and merging software packages for virtually every computer system has improved matters even further and greatly facilitated this kind of research. Problems may still require relatively sophisticated, project-specific programming, but standard sort-merge packages may greatly assist the process, even in the face of significant variations in the data. With adequate identifiers such as the occupations of voters and/or their addresses (which poll books tended increasingly to contain after the very early eighteenth century), nominal record linkage is less difficult than it is simply laborious.

Other developments also have reduced substantially the work required to analyze a series of poll books. Random sampling and nominal record linkage are incompatible. Thus random sampling cannot be used to reduce the potentially Herculean task of data entry when poll books from larger constituencies are to be examined. Conversely, other sampling techniques are compatible with nominal record linkage and can reduce data requirements substantially. Letter-cluster sampling, in combination with random sampling, successfully shrank to manageable proportions the data base required for an examination of several nineteenth-century borough constituencies in one recent study; the resulting analyses of sampled constituencies were both compatible with and comparable to the results obtained in constituencies for which entire electorates comprised the data pool.[29] Even massive constituencies like nineteenth-century Liverpool or Bristol need not result in impossibly large investments of labor before analyses can be undertaken.

One aspect of the linkage process, deserves closer attention despite a brief description of it already in print.[30] Files of names of voters must be linked across elections in order to create panels, and this linkage, even in the presence of adequate identifiers which allow similarly named individuals to be distinguished, frequently involves linking data in the face of less than perfect matches and some uncertainty. As Speck has noted, "the compilation of completely accurate lists [from two or more original lists] is beyond the ingenuity of man or machine."[31] Nevertheless, decisions concerning those names which pose problems may be facilitated by constructing "maps" of the linkages already accomplished. Two or more absolutely identical entries on a single voting list or any other list usually present an insoluble dilemma; linkages involving duplicate entries are possible only under certain conditions. If two identical entries on one list are matched exactly by two identical entries on a second list, the four records can be merged into two sets safely. Two John Smiths of identical occupations and street addresses voting in Bristol in 1818 for the same candidates might be linked to two identically described John Smiths voting in the 1820 Bristol election if the second pair of Smiths also voted in exactly the same way as well, but a third entry for yet another John Smith for either election would prevent a link, as would the slightest difference in the voting choices of the original pairs of Smiths. Much more commonly, however, entries which may be unique to a particular list involve names (and other data) not unique across lists, and linkages may well be impossible when such similar entries are encountered. Even more commonly, similar or even identical names contained in two or more lists may appear to refer to the same individual, but the similarities in the records may be offset by discrepancies which prevent automatic linkage. The success of linkage in the face of less than perfect matches across lists depends upon the success with which other information concerning the individuals can be reconciled. Linkage decisions in some cases may be resolved by modifying the specified linkage rules applied and thus accomplished automatically. Others defy categorization. In more difficult instances in which completely systematic linkage rules cannot be applied, reliance on computer-assisted manual linkage rather than computer-directed automatic linkage may prove the most reasonable recourse. In either case, linkage maps are extremely beneficial.

The utility of linkage maps can be described best through example. In linking records for the town of Northampton over its six polled elections during the last half of the eighteenth century, a fairly sophisticated computerized linkage program accomplished the linkage of all perfect matches and also allowed otherwise identical records to be linked if the recorded residence of an individual voter changed no more than once over the period being examined. Such a program produced three separate linked records for the single name, Abraham Botterell. The first set recorded two appearances of Botterell (in 1761 and 1784) in which his address was listed as Bridge Street. Another contained three records of Botterell's appearances (1768, 1774, and 1796) listing Kingswell Lane as his address. The computer program did not link these two sets of records because of yet another entry for Botterell in 1790 with the address, Woolmonger Street. Yet, at each of these Northampton elections only one Abraham Botterell appeared, and at each the Botterell whose vote was recorded called himself a currier. With this relatively unusual and, more importantly for the linkage programs, list-unique name, along with a more common yet still not ordinary occupation, the odds in favor of all of these records referring to one man were excellent, but creating a linkage map clarified the matter. By assigning a series of columns to be completed by the computer appropriately for each election examined, a summary of the linked files was created to assist further consideration. Each column referred to one election only, and each contained either 1, indicating data for that election, or 0, indicating no data. Abraham Botterell's summary assumed this form:

Years of election	**1761**	**1768**	**1774**	**1784**	**1790**	**1796**
Abraham Botterell #1	1	0	0	0	1	0
Abraham Botterell #2	0	1	1	0	0	1
Abraham Botterell #3	0	0	0	1	0	0

Clearly, these columns, if compressed into one, would mesh exactly. On the other hand, if the 1774 column for the third Abraham Botterell contained a 1, indicating data for 1774, the maps would not mesh since 1774 data exists for the second Botterell; two 1774 records would indicate more than one Botterell in the electorate and a link could not be made on the basis of this information alone. Thus the columns arranged in this fashion created a shortcut through the maze created by Abraham Botterell's apparently peripatetic nature. For files containing thousands of names, mapping columns such as these are valuable both in checking automated linkage and in assisting manual linkage.

Another example of the usefulness of the mapping columns is provided by David Dady, one of the hundreds of worsted weavers who voted in Norwich elections between 1761 and 1802. Dady's record of residential stability was even worse than Botterell's; he gave four different parish addresses for his seven votes, apparently indicating six moves. A program written to flag similar records when automated linkage proved impossible given the linkage rules in effect printed the following map of Dady's linked records:

David Dady #1—00000100 Parish of Michael Coslany
David Dady #2—00010000 Parish of St. Mary
David Dady #3—01000001 Parish of St. Martin at Oak
David Dady #4—10001010 Parish of St. Augustine

The linkage map permitted a linkage decision to be made without much difficulty. As in the example of the three records for Abraham Botterell, the mapping columns for all four sets of records meshed perfectly, and since only one Dady appeared as a worsted weaver at each of these elections, a merging of the four sets of records into one extended record seemed justifiable, particularly since all four of the parishes recorded as places of residence were in Norwich's Great Northern Ward across the Wensum River from the center of town. These links could have been made without the assistance of linkage maps, but the decisions would have been much more difficult and quite probably less accurate.

Aggregate and Individual-Level Data Analysis: The Value of Poll Book Data

The creation of panels of elector for each constituency to be examined may require an intensive effort and possibly the expenditure of not inconsiderable sums. Data entry, preparation, and computing time can all require a substantial investment. Certainly problems and costs will far exceed the requirements of a comparable study relying solely on aggregate data analysis, and a discussion of the reasons for adopting these linkage techniques and examining individual-level data with some care seems particularly appropriate accordingly.[32]

A lengthy argument considering the relative merits of aggregate and individual-level data would be needlessly repetitious since the proponents of both types of data analysis have written copiously in their own defense. Both aggregate and individual-level data are useful, and *either* used exclusively raises problems for any analysis. It is undeniably the case that "areal units are more than the sum of the individuals that comprise them," and that "the unit of interest may be the ecological unit" itself.[33] Certainly the analogy between aggregate data analysts and Sisyphus drawn by Hayward Alker undoubtedly underestimates the value of aggregate data.[34] Even if individuals are to comprise the units of analysis rather than areal (ecological) units, the individuals themselves may be examined in several ways. The distinction between the unique individual measured in terms of "attributes and variables," and the individual in aggregation measured with rates, averages, is an important one. The relationship between individuals in populations (variously termed structural or contextual variables) is equally important. Finally, global properties (the characteristics of the group itself, unrelated to the individuals who comprise it), are legitimate foci.

Nevertheless, unaugmented aggregate data encounter a problem not normally faced with individual-level data: measurement across levels of inference. County-level voting statistics, for example, will not reveal easily the political behavior of particular segments of the population for which voting data are available. Knowing the proportion of Irish-born in each of a group of counties and the aggregate Tory vote in those same counties will not allow a simple measurement of the voting preferences of the Irish-born. Yet aggregate data often have been put to exactly this task of explaining the behavior of groups within a given population. Direct comparisons of the variations in the Irish proportion of several counties and the proportionate Tory vote in those counties may reveal information of some interest, but the ecological correlations which have been employed by generations of scholars in order to make individual-level arguments with aggregate data do *not* constitute legitimate inferences. Aggregate data of this sort used to draw individual-level inferences engender the "ecological fallacy;" straight-forward inferences across levels of measurement simply cannot be made.

Unfortunately, awareness of the "ecological fallacy" inherent in this practice of using simple ecological correlations to infer individual-level behavior has spread slowly despite W.S. Robinson's article, written more than thirty years ago, revealing the potential inequality of ecological and individual-level correlations. While noting the three possible levels of measurement in studies of populations (ecological, individual, and within-areas), Robinson focused on the obstacles blocking the then common practice of relying on simple ecological correlations to infer individual-level relationships. His first example was striking; the strong +.946 ecological correlation between race and illiteracy in the United States grossly overstated the actual individual-level correlation of only +.203. His second example was devastating. The positive ecological correlation (+.118) between foreign birth and illiteracy completely misrepresented the actual negative individual-level correlation (−.619). After revealing these startling discrepancies, Robinson argued that although it was theoretically possible for ecological correlations to approximate individual-level correlations, the only reasonable assumption was inequality. Only in very specific and, Robinson asserted, infrequent situations would an ecological correlation equal an individual-level correlation.[35]

Robinson has since been accused of academic overkill and an excessive desire for rigor. Parts of Robinson's argument are also demonstrably inaccurate, but his article identified a genuine and continuing problem.[36] While his complete rejection of ecological correlation may not have been warranted since there are circumstances in which ecological correlations may be used to create acceptable estimates of individual-level correlations, it is undoubtedly the case that reliable individual-level correlations can seldom, if ever, be obtained directly. Aggregate data will simply not yield individual-level inferences readily, if at all.

Two basic approaches have been taken by those determined to avoid the ecological fallacy while continuing to use aggregate data. The first approach was suggested within three years of Robinson's 1950 article. O.D. Duncan and B. Davis proposed a method of ecological inference through which "unimpeachable limits" could be established around the true value of the individual-level relationships in question. The Duncan-Davis technique required no assumptions regarding the data, but the limits their method set often proved too broad to be valuable. Moreover, the limits set by Duncan-Davis ecological analysis could yield a range including a positive maximum and a negative minimum. However useful it might have been in certain circumstances, therefore, its limitations prevented its general applicability.[37] Hubert Blalock's proposed remedy, ecological regression, though more refined, was restricted to data measured intervally (precise numerical measurements with distances between categories defined in terms of fixed and equal lengths, such as income or height) at both the aggregate and individual level. Many of the variables of interest to historians, notably voting decisions, are measured nominally at the individual-level (Whig double-vote, Tory double-vote, Whig-Tory split vote, Whig single, etc.), thus eliminating the potential utility of Blalock's method for much historical research.[38]

Much recent research has relied on L.A. Goodman's method of ecological regression which is appropriate for either nominal or interval data, or some combination of both. Goodman's regression can be applied to diverse data sets and allows the use of a variety of models (eg. bivariate or multivariate).[39] The validity of the method rests largely on attributes of the data to be examined and the appropriateness of the regression model, but a bivariate model most easily illustrates Goodman's basic approach. If an analysis is to attempt estimates of two qualitative, dichotomous (nominal) variable X and Y, representing individual behavior, and the only data available are interval-level figures for aggregates of the dichotomous values of the X and Y variables for a number of ecological units, Goodman's technique is appropriate. The objective of the regression is the derivation of estimates of individual cell entries in a standard cross-tabulation in spite of the fact that only marginal totals for the table are known. The desired estimates are not actually estimates of individual behavior, since it is impossible to discern the behavior of specific individuals from aggregate data, but estimates of aggregates of individuals and therefore ecological by definition.

This bivariate ecological regression is an effort to complete a matrix in which the desired proportions of the X variable are indicated by P, Q, R, and S. If it can be assumed that these unknown proportions remain constant for each ecological unit under consideration, the various cell entries can be obtained by applying the standard regression formula $Y=a+bX$.

$P \cdot X_1$	$Q \cdot X_1$	X_1
$R \cdot X_2$	$S \cdot X_2$	X_2
Y_1	Y_2	

Before considering the regression itself, however, a slight restructuring of the matrix facilitates conceptualization of the method by which the estimates are derived. By substituting other symbols in the matrix for the unknown proportions (P,Q,R, and S) which emphasize the fact that both rows total 100% of one of the dichotomous subtotals, the original matrix is transformed but not actually changed into the following:

p	(1-p)	X_1 (100%)
r	(1-r)	X_2 (100%)
Y_1	Y_2	

In the resulting matrix, r is the proportion of X_2 who are also Y_1, and p is the proportion of X_1 who are Y_1, just as (1-r) and (1-p) are the proportions of X_1 and X_2 who are also Y_2. If several conditions are assumed to have been met, such as linearity, the intercept, a, of the regression line $Y=a+bX$ will equal the proportion of X_1 individuals who are also Y_2 (r in matrix 2), and the slope of the regression, b, will equal (p-r). Thus in place of the standard regression formula, the new regression equation emerges as $Y_1=r+(p-r)X_1$. Since it can be shown that $b=(p-r)$, it follows that $p=b+r$. Thus the computations of the slope and intercept in the regression of X against Y provide the figures with which two of the cells in the matrix can be filled. The proportion of X_2 who are also Y_1 is the value of the intercept multipled by the total number (or percentage) of X_2, and the proportion of X_1 who are Y_1 is the value of the slope added to the intercept and multiplied by the total of X_1. After deriving these two cell entries, completing the matrix is a simple enough matter.

The real problems with ecological regression lie not in the method itself, nor even necessarily in the assumptions made regarding the data. The derivation of entries for individual cells in a 2X2 or 2XN matrix is straightforward, if rather complicated. The problems posed by some of the assumptions necessary before any confidence can be placed in regression estimates derived from these formulae may be severe, though not invariably insurmountable. Unwarranted assumptions lead at best to biased estimates and at worst to completely unacceptable estimates. Several of the necessary assumptions are applicable to regression analysis generally, and others are specific to ecological regression. Ignoring either jeopardizes the resulting correlations. For example, simple regression assumes linearity; by definition the relationship between the two variables X and Y is linear.[40] Non-linear data may be used in both regression and ecological regression by altering the regression equation (or model), but failure to make the necessary adjustment would prove fatal to the exercise immediately, even though the fatal error might well remain invisible to the researcher.

A possible exception of potentially greater importance to the general utility of ecological regression is the manner in which the data are grouped (aggregated). Data upon which ecological regression is to be applied should have been aggregated independently and should be randomly distributed. At the very least, the aggregation must be unrelated to the dependent variable.[41] Historians, unfortunately, are seldom afforded the luxury of choosing the means through which the data to be examined are aggregated. In fact, much historical research involves data analysis in which it is difficult to know and/or demonstrate how the data have been aggregated, at least in relationship to the dependent variable.

The real obstacle to successful ecological regression in most historical research, however, is not statistical, but theoretical. Moreover, this problem, model misspecification, frequently assumes insurmountable proportions.[42] Whatever the level of measurement, and regardless of the degree to which the data can be shown to meet the necessary assumptions underlying regression, the exclusion of one or more relevant variables from the regression model introduces a level of bias which cannot be overcome except by the inclusion of the missing variable(s). The more severe the model misspecification, the less likely the estimates obtained through ecological regression will closely approximate actual relationships. The data to which historians have access is seldom, if ever, all that it might be; rarely are all the data possibly needed available. An examination of voting behavior, for example, which postulated the influence of seven discreet variables such as socio-economic status and religious affiliation to explain voting choices adequately using a regression model could not be persuasive without a consideration of all seven. In the absence of data for one or two of the pertinent variables, a properly specified model is impossible, and estimates derived from ecological regression are unlikely to be satisfactory because they will fail to be persuasive. Worst of all, in the absence of at least some corroborative data for the purposes of testing, it is impossible to determine whether or not the regression model is yielding acceptable estimates. Faced with the usual paucity of available variables and the potentially overwhelming problems even when the desired variables are available, it is difficult to believe that historical models incorporating all relevant variables can be specified and appropriately measured at the aggregate level.[43] One analysis of voting patterns which compared ecological regression estimates with individual-level figures achieved "some direct hits, some near misses, and some duds." Without supporting data, distinguishing one from the other is impossible; a "dud" appears as real as a "hit."[44]

The other approach to the resolution of the ecological fallacy is the adoption of "geographic areas rather than individual as the units of analysis." The resulting ecological analysis thus avoids all problems raised by the effort to achieve cross-level inference. According to one of the most recent practitioners of this technique, though it was "once regarded as a second-best kind of approach, clearly inferior to modes of analysis based on individual-level data, ecological analysis has recently come into its own."[45] For an analysis of voting behavior well after the introduction of secret ballot, Kenneth Wald has focused on constituencies rather than individual voters in an effort to measure the political effects of religion and social class. Unfortunately, the geographic boundaries for the available aggregate data do not coincide. Data regarding religious affiliations (as rare as such data are), were collected for geographic units which were unrelated and unrelateable to the units for which data for social class in the censuses (flawed as they are prior to 1911) were collected. Neither of these, moreover, conformed to the boundaries of parliamentary constituencies. Wald was forced, therefore, to construct "surrogate constituencies," reducing in the process Britain's 537 parliamentary districts to 115. His efforts also were hampered by the existence of two-member constituencies and plural voters, but the lack of coterminous boundaries and the resulting obliteration of actual constituencies in favor of "surrogates" would seem to have eliminated effectively most of the potential ecological analysis might have held for an electoral analysis of British voters. Examining voting patterns outside their local contexts is quite simply impermissible. Very few "contextual" effects are more telling and more fatal to an analysis when ignored than those involved in England's parliamentary elections. An aggregately measured correlation +.98 for the two major English parties in the general elections of 1964 and 1966, for example, actually masked a substantial regional effect rather than indicating uniformity of voting behavior across the country.[46] Even individual-level data, examined without reference to local contexts, would yield little of value. Certainly aggregate data cannot be examined successfully in such an isolated, sterile fashion.

Aggregate data analysis can, of course, yield highly significant results in some circumstances, and contains merits other than mere ease of access.[47] Nevertheless, the obstacles barring the way to effective aggregate analysis place the effort expended to create panels of individual voters in a somewhat different light. The potential benefits of individual-level data analysis employing poll books as a principal focus are great enough to justify the requisite effort, particularly with the advances of the last decade in the analysis of nominal data.

The "rage of party" in Augustan England, the era of Tory proscription under Walpole, the renewed partisan rancors of the later eighteenth century, the struggles over reform, and the popular politics of Victorian England all await further delineation through poll book analysis.

J. A. Phillips
Department of History
University of California, Riverside

Notes

1. *Journals of the House of Commons*, XI, pp.338-407, 345-416, 394-555, 410-556. After William's refusal to give his assent to the last bill, which entailed at one point a discussion of accepting a clause calling for the ballot (XI,427), the Commons rejected on a vote of 70 to 219 a resolution calling for the condemnation of those who advised William's refusal as enemies of the King and the Kingdom. *Commons Journal*, XI, 460.

2. 7/8 William III, c.25.

3. The Bath pollbook of 1855 and the Banbury polls of 1859 and 1865 have been published by the Open University for the third level course, "Historical Data and the Social Sciences."

4. Kent Record Office, Maidstone Municipal Records, VII, c, 1 (Temporary Box 356); Bristol Central Library, B4419. A number of other manuscript sources such as local poor rate lists, land tax assessments, nonconformist registers of births and burials, and canvass books supplement the poll books, as well as some printed sources such as local registers.

5. Derek Hirst, *Representative of the People?*, (Cambridge, 1975): 122-29, 197-212, 223-28.

6. East Sussex Record Office, Lewes Borough Records.

7. The handlist kept by the History of Parliament Trust listed the Liverpool poll book as "missing" in 1953. Also see, Corporation of London, *A Handlist of Poll Books and Registers of Electors in Guildhall Library*, (London, 1970); L.W.L. Edwards, (ed.) *A New and Revised Catalogue of Poll Books in the Possession of the Society of Genealogists* (London, 1974).

8. *The Poll for the Election of Headmen of the Borough of Colchester,* (Colchester, 1821); *The Poll for the Election of a Recorder of Colchester,* (Colchester, 1819). Swinborne and Walter printed both of these municipal poll books and also printed the 1820 parliamentary pollbook, as well as several in later years after the firm became Swinborne, Walter, and Taylor.

9. John Cannon, "Poll Books," *History*, 47 (1962):166-69.

10. One major additional study in which poll books played a central role had appeared in print prior to Cannon's 1962 description, but D.C. Moore's "Other Face of Reform" appeared too far afield and too near the time of publication of "Poll Books" to be included on Cannon's list. D.C. Moore, "The Other Face of Reform," *Victorian Studies* 5 (1961):7-34.

11. E. Allardt, "Aggregate Analysis: The Problem of Its Informational Value," in M. Doggan and S. Rokkan (eds.), *Quantitative Ecological Analysis in the Social Sciences* (Cambridge, Mass., 1969) p.68.

12. D.C. Moore, *The Politics of Deference*, (Hassocks, 1976); Patrick Joyce, *Work, Society, and Politics*, (New Brunswick, NJ, 1980); Richard Davis, "Toryism to Tamworth: The Triumph of Reform, 1827-1835," Albion, 12(1980):132-46; J.R. Fisher, "Issues and Influence: Two By-Elections in South Nottinghamshire in the Mid-Nineteenth Century," *Historical Journal*, 24(1981):155-65; J.R. Fisher, "The Limits of Deference," *Journal of British Studies*, 21 (1981):90-105; John Milton-Smith, "Earl Grey's Cabinet and the Objects of Parliamentary Reform," *Historical Journal*, 15(1972): 55-74.

13. Moore, "Other Face," p.11; John Vincent, *Pollbooks: How Victorians Voted* (Cambridge, 1967).

14. Vincent, *Pollbooks*, pp.4, 57.

15. Michael Drake, "The Mid-Victorian Voter," *Journal of Interdisciplinary History*, 1(1971):473-90. David Butler coined the new word "psephology" to describe the study of electoral behavior.

16. Jeremy Mitchell and James Cornford, "The Political Demography of Cambridge, 1832-1868," *Albion*, 9 (1977):242-65.

17. J.H. Plumb, "The Growth of the Electorate in England from 1600-1715," *Past and Present*, 45(1969):90-116.

18. W.A. Speck, *Tory and Whig*, (London, 1969); W.A. Speck and W.A. Gray, "Computer Analysis of Poll Books: An Initial Report," *Bulletin of the Institute of Historical Research*, 43(1970):105-12.

19. For a discussion of the permutations resulting from the double vote, see Jeremy Mitchell, "Electoral Strategy Under Open Voting: Evidence from England, 1832-1880," *Public Choice*, 28(1976):17-35.

20. Speck and Gray, "Computer Analysis of Poll Books: A Further Report," *Bulletin of the Institute of Historical Research*, 48(1975):64-90.

21. Cannon, "Poll Books," p.168.

22. Basic sort/merge utilities are available on most computer systems. See also Norman Nie, et al, *Statistical Package for the Social Sciences-X*, (New York, 1983).

23. The value of "panels" for social-scientific research is well known and well documented. See, for example, Charles Blackstrom and G.D. Hursch-Cesar, *Survey Research*, (New York, 1981); James S. Coleman, *Longitudinal Data Analysis*, (New York, 1981).

24. James Ackland, *Ackland's Comparative Poll Book*, (Hull, 1835).

25. For example, Thomas R. Knox, "Popular Politics and Provincial Radicalism," *Albion*, 11 (1979):224-41. Knox examined Newcastle voters in 1777 and 1780 with some reference to the election of 1774.

26. Mitchell and Cornford, "Political Demography," pp.242-65.

27. A project currently examining voting behavior and religious affiliation in the eighteenth century has linked the existing eighteenth-century Liverpool pollbooks. The 1734 Liverpool poll presented a much greater challenge to record linage because of variant spellings than those of 1761, 1780 and 1784. For discussion, though unrelated to the project mentioned, see Gloria Guth, "Surname Spellings and Computerized Record Linkage," *Historical Methods*, 10(1976):10-19.

28. E.A. Wrigley, *Identifying People in the Past*, (London, 1973); Michael Katz, *The People of Hamilton, Canada West*, (Cambridge, Mass., 1975).

29. John Phillips, "Achieving a Critical Mass While Avoiding an Explosion," *Journal of Interdisciplinary History*, 9(1979):493-508; John Phillips, "The Many Faces of Reform," *Parliamentary History*, 1(1982):115-35.

30. John Phillips, "Nominal Record Linkage and the Study of Electoral Behavior," *Laboratory for Political Research*, (Iowa City, 1976) pp.1-17.

31. Speck and Gray, "Initial Report," p.109.

32. Kenneth Wald, *Crosses on the Ballot*, (Princeton, 1983).

33. R. Retzlaff, "The Use of Aggregate Data in Comparative Political Analysis," in C.L. Taylor (ed.), *Aggregate Data Analysis*, (Paris, 1967).

34. H. Alker, "Research Possibilities Using Aggregate Political and Social Data," in Taylor, *Aggregate Data.*

35. W.S. Robinson, "Ecological Correlation and the Behavior of Individuals," *American Sociological Review*, 15(1950):351-57; Edward Thorndike, "On the Fallacy of Imputing the Correlations Found for Groups to the Individuals or Smaller Groups Composing Them," *American Journal of Psychology*, 52(1939):122-24. Also see D. Price, "Micro- and Macro-Politics: Notes on Research Strategy," in Oliver Garceau (ed.) *Political Research and Political Theory*, (Cambridge, 1968):102-40. Also see David Jackson, *Aggregate Data: Analysis and Interpretation*, (Beverly Hills, 1980).

36. Price, "Micro- and Macro-," p.126.

37. O.D. Duncan and B. Davis, "An Alternative to Ecological Correlation," *American Sociological Review*, 18(1953):665-66.

38. H. Blalock, *Causal Inferences in Nonexperimental Research*, (Chapel Hill, 1964), pp.97-107.

39. L.A. Goodman, "Ecological Regression and the Behavior of Individuals," *American Journal of Sociology*, 64(1959):610-25. Also see Laura Langbein and Alan Lichtman, *Ecological Regression*, (Beverly Hills, 1978).

40. Linearity is assumed, but multicollinearity must be avoided. A strong linear relationship is a necessary but not sufficient characteristic of the data to be used in the ecological regression. J.M. Kousser, "Ecological Regression and the Analysis of Past Politics," *Journal of Interdisciplinary History*, 4 (1973):237-62; D. Stokes, "Cross Level Inferences as a Game Against Nature," in J.L. Bernd (ed.), *Mathematical Application in Political Science*, 4(1969):62-83.

41. J. Shover and J. Kushma, "Retrieval of Individual Data from Aggregate Units of Analysis," in Joel Silbey, et al, *The History of American Electoral Behavior*, (Princeton, 1978):327-39.

42. E. Hanushek, J. Jackson, and J. Kain, "Model Specification, the Use of Aggregate Data, and the Ecological Correlation Fallacy," *Political Methodology*, 1(1974):87-106. Also see J. Morgan Kousser and Allan J. Lichtman, "New Political History: Some Statistical Questions Answered," *Social Science History*, 7 (1983):321-44.

43. T. Falkonen, "Individual and Structural Effects in Ecological Research," in M. Doggan and S. Rokkan (eds.), *Quantitative Ecological Analysis in the Social Sciences*, (Cambridge, 1969), p.68.

44. Terrence Jones, "Ecological Inference and Electoral Analysis," *Journal of Interdisciplinary History*, 2(1972):249-62; Allan J. Lichtman, "Correlation, Regression, and the Ecological Fallacy," *Journal of Interdisciplinary History*, 4(1974):417-33. With limited data, a condition typical in historical research, a researcher may be "virtually unlimited in the interpretation that he may choose." Angus Campbell (ed.), *Legislative Systems and Party Voting*, (New York, 1966), p.1.

45. Wald, *Crosses on the Ballot*, p.75.

46. Stokes, "Cross Level Inference," pp.76-83. James Cornford's review of Wald's book in the TLS (July 22, 1983) argued that answers to important questions are "not going to emerge from the analysis of aggregate national data, because, contrary to the received wisdom, Britain was not (and is not) a homogenous country."

47. An excellent example is William O. Aydelotte, "Constituency Influence in the British House of Commons," in W.O. Aydelotte (ed.), *The History of Parliamentary Behavior*, (Princeton, 1977):225-46. A radically different approach to the use of aggregate data, see Daniel Calhoun's treatment of multidimensional scaling. Daniel Calhoun, "From Collinearity to Structure: San Francisco and Pittsburgh, 1860," *Historical Methods*, 14(1981):107-21. Yet another approach of particular interest to students of voting behavior is: John L. McCarthy and John W. Tukey, "Exploratory Analysis of Aggregate Voting Behavior," *Social Science History*, 2(1978):292-331.

Figure 1: Northampton Poll Book, 1841

Ashby Joseph, gold street, ironmonger
s Ashby Wm., Hewitt's yd., horse mkt., blacksmith
s Ashby Edward, yard, Abington street, bricklayer
Ashby Thomas, newland, shoemaker
Atkins Benjamin, mercer's row, upholder
s Atkins Edward, Iliff, mercer's row, upholder
Atkins Thomas Iliff, Augustin street, gentleman
m Atkins Richard, woolmonger street, servant
Auld Henry, drapery, shoe manufacturer

B.

m Bacchus Edmund, bridge street, pork butcher
s Bailey John, castle terrace, groom
Balaam Thos. wood hill, hair dresser
Ball Wm. Kingswell-street, hawker
Bamford Wm. court 10, bridge street, labourer
Barrett John, woolmonger street, carrier
Barry George, parade, druggist
Bason George, court 4, bridge street, labourer
Battershill John, King's street, tailor
Banks Geo. Mellows's row, shoemaker
s Banks Joseph, brier-lane, carpenter
Banks Wm. St. Edmund's terrace, carpenter
m Barlow Robt. wood street, woolstapler
Barlow Rev. T. W. Waterloo terrace, clerk
Barnes Wm. fish street, hair dresser
Barnsley Jos. cow lane, file cutter
Baseley William, brier lane, labourer
Baucutt Jos. lower mounts, servant
Bagley John, church lane, labourer
m Baker Wm. St. Andrew's gardens, yeoman
Balderson John, union place, shoemaker
c Ball Charles, upper mounts, tailor
Barley Abraham, church lane, shoemaker
Barringer Edward, yard, sheep street, labourer
Barron James, regent's square, shoemaker
Barwell James, Mayorhold, shoefactor
Barwell Wm. regent street, shoefactor
Baseley John, silver-street, innkeeper
m Bason John, lady's lane, tailor
Bayes Richd. silver street, chimney sweeper
Bayes William, yard, sheep street, labourer
Beckwith Wm. court, college street, labourer
Bennett Wm. gas street, foundryman
Beckwith Jas. St. Giles' street, yeoman
Begley Matthias, church lane, chimney sweeper
Bennett S. P. St. George's street, rate collector
Bentley Thos. St. George's street, builder
Berwick Thos. newland, labourer
Bickerstaffe Henry, woolmonger st., yeoman
m Billingham Abraham, St. Mary's street, mason
Billingham Thos. King's street, shoemaker
Bird Richd. gold street, innkeeper
Birdsall Wm. St. Giles' square, surgeon
Bing John, Gardiner's row, labourer
Billingham Thos. upper mounts, rate collector
s Birdsall Richard, wood street, bookbinder
Bissell Robert, bridge street, cork cutter
Blithrey Wm., square, No. 2, Todd's lane, labourer
Blunt Delina, sheep street, watchmaker
Blunt Delina, jun., sheep street, watchmaker

m Blunt John, bridge street, yeoman
Blencowe George, albion place, solicitor
Blick Francis, cow lane, butcher
Blunsom William, St. Giles' street, farrier
s Bland Richard, Todd's lane, shoemaker
Bodeley William, green lane, glover
Bolter James, Alfred place, labourer
m Bond John, bridge street, foundryman
Bond Charles, abington street, painter
Boteler James Wade, parade, bookseller
Boyal John Bowman, gold street, grocer
Boyal William Bowman, bridge street, innkeeper
Bonham Henry, bearward street, baker
Boodger William, Bath street, sawyer
Botterill George, bearward street, labourer
Braine William, fetter street, yeoman
s Bratt Nathaniel, horsemarket, gunmaker
Brawn Jonathan, cow lane, carpenter
Brettell John, Mercer's row, ironmonger
Briggs William, horse-shoe street, shoemaker
Brown William, wharf yard, bridge st., coal dealer
Brown William, mount pleasant, labourer
Bryan John Morgan, mare fair, surgeon
Brice Thomas, abington street, yeoman
Britten Charles, albion terrace, solicitor
Bromley Wm. St. John's terrace, shoemaker
Bromwell John, St. Edmund's row, carpenter
Brasher William, sheep street, gunmaker
m Briggs Allen, Leicester terrace, gent.
c Brown James, Hope's place, beerseller
Brown Joseph, Wellington place, shoemaker
c Bryan Mark, Hind yard, sheep street, turner
Bull John, drapery, grocer
s Bull James, phoenix place, currier
m Burgess Joseph, St. Mary's street, brewer
Burrows John, bridge street, eating-house keeper
Bush William, drum lane, shoe factor
Buswell William, gold st., straw bonnet manftr.
m Butcher Robert, conduit lane, beerseller
Butcher William, St. Edmund's end, victualler
Buzzard James, Kingswell st., tailor
Bull Richard, cow lane, labourer
m Bull Thomas, chapel court, shoemaker
Butlin Thomas, Wellington street, brewer
c Bullock William, scarlet well street, shoemaker
m Burnaby Charles, regent street, carpenter
Butcher Thomas, wood street, printer
m Butterfield James, Wellington place, apothecary.

C.

m Campion John Samuel, gold street, auctioneer
Carpenter Wm., court 6, bridge street, waterman
m Carter William, angel street, beerseller
Cave Paul Warren, bridge street, shoemaker
Campion William, court, St. Giles's st., labourer
Carr D., court 2, Wellington street, shoemaker
Cartwright John, riding, carpenter
m Carver Thomas, brier lane, beerseller
Cattle George, St. Giles street, law stationer
c Caulcutt J., St. Edmund's square, shoemaker
Campbell George, Bearward street, carpenter

Figure 2: Northampton Poll Book, 1837

6

Persons' Names.	Occupations.	Places of Abode.	S.	C.	R.
Ager William	Currier	Gas street	1	1	
Ager William	Merchant	Castle street	1	1	
Alderman Stephen	Shoemaker	Bridge street			1
Aldridge John	Brickmaker	Green lane	1	1	
Albright John	Foundryman	Navigation row, Bridge st.			1
Albright Thomas	Labourer	Backside Weston's			1
Alchin William	Foundryman	Weston place	1	1	
Allen John	Gardener	Horseshoe lane	1	1	
Allen Robert	Victualler	Bridge street			1
Alliston Benjamin	Shoemaker	Court 4, Bridge street			1
Alliston George	Shoemaker	Roberts's court, Bridge st.	1	1	
Alliston John	Shoemaker	Bridge street			1
Amerson John	Coachman	Marefair			1
Andrews J. Norris	Cornfactor	Gold street	1	1	
Anstie Edward	Shoemaker	St. Mary's street			1
Armfield F. Barlow	Draper	Parade			1
Armitt T. Burbidge	Druggist	Drapery			1
Ashby Joseph	Ironmonger	Gold street			1
Ashby William	Blacksmith	Hewitt's yard, Horsemarket	1		1
Atkins Benjamin	Gentleman	Cow lane			1
Atkins James	Nurseryman	Drapery	1	1	
Atkins Richard	Groom	Woolmonger street			1
Atkins T. Iliffe	Upholsterer	Mercers' row			1
Auld Henry	Manufacturer	Drapery			1
Bacon John	Druggist	Parade	1	1	
Bailey John	Shoemaker	New court, Horsemarket	1	1	
Bailey John	Cutler	Castle terrace			1
Baines William	Dyer	Gas street	1	1	
Baker George	Carver&Gilder	Silver street			1
Baker William	Victualler	Kingshead lane			1
Balaam Thomas	Hairdresser	Wood Hill			1
Ball William	Draper	Kingswell street			1
Barker Thomas	Labourer	Court 2, Bridge street	1	1	
Barnes Joseph	Butcher	Castle street	1	1	
Barratt John	Carrier	Woolmonger street	1		1
Barry George	Druggist	Parade			1
Bartram Robert	Hosier	Drapery	1	1	
Baseley John	Victualler	Kingshead lane			1
Basford James	Shoemaker	Court, St. Mary's place	1		1
Bason George	Labourer	Court 4, Bridge street			1
Bates Charles	Grocer	Horsemarket	1	1	
Beckwith William	Labourer	College street			1
Beck Henry	Solicitor	George row	1	1	
Bellfield Thomas	Waiter	Angel lane	1	1	
Beale John	Grocer	Bridge street	1	1	
Bennett William	Foundryman	Gas street	1	1	
Bennett Rev. John	Dissenting Minister	St. Mary's street	1	1	
Benton Thomas	Shoemaker	Silver street	1	1	

ENGLISH POLL BOOKS

BEDFORDSHIRE

1705—A copy of the poll... London, 1705
By parish.

Sir Pynsent Chernock Sir William Gostwick Lord Edward Russell John Harvey

Beds Rec Off Inst Hist Res

1715—A copy of the poll... London, 1715
By parish. Place of residence.

John Harvey William Hillersden John Cater Sir Pynsent Chernock

Beds Rec Off Inst Hist Res

1722—A copy of the poll... London, 1722
By parish. Place of residence. A few notes on qualifications.

Charles Leigh Sir Rowland Alston William Hillersden

Beds Rec Off Inst Hist Res

1774—A copy of the poll... Bedford: Bartholemew Hyatt, 1775
By hundred and parish. Place of residence, nature and occupier of freehold.

Earl of Upper Ossory Robert Henley Ongley Thomas Hampden

Beds Rec Off Inst Hist Res

1784—A copy of the poll... n.p., [1784]
By hundred and parish. Place of residence, nature and occupier of freehold. Rejected voters with reasons. Index.

Earl of Upper Ossory St. Andrew St. John Lord Ongley

Beds Rec Off Inst Hist Res

1807—A copy of the poll... Bedford: J. Webb, 1808
Alphabetical by hundred and parish. Place of residence, nature and occupier of freehold. List of out-voters by county and parish of residence. Rejected voters with reasons and voting intentions. Index.

Francis Pym Richard Fitzpatrick John Osborn

Beds Rec Off Inst Hist Res

1820—A copy of the poll... Bedford: C. B. Merry, 1820
Alphabetical by hundred and parish. Place of residence, nature and occupier of freehold. List of out-voters by county and parish of residence. Rejected voters with reasons and voting intentions. Index.

Marquess of Tavistock Francis Pym Sir John Osborn

Beds Rec Off Inst Hist Res

1826—A copy of the poll... Bedford: C. B. Merry, 1826
Alphabetical by hundred and parish. Place of residence, nature and occupier of freehold. List of out-voters by county and parish of residence. Rejected and undetermined voters with reasons and voting intentions. Index.

Thomas Potter Macqueen Marquess of Tavistock Francis Pym

Beds Rec Off Inst Hist Res

1831—A copy of the poll... Bedford: W. White, 1831
Alphabetical by hundred and parish. Place of residence, nature and occupier of freehold. Rejected and undetermined voters with reasons and voting intentions. Index.

Marquess of Tavistock   Sir Peter Payne   William Stuart

Beds Rec Off   Guildhall Lib

1857—General election, 1857. The poll for the election... Bedford: F. Thompson, 1857
Alphabetical by polling district and parish. Place of residence and qualification.

Francis Charles Hastings Russell Richard Thomas Gilpin W. B. Higgins William Stuart

Beds Rec Off   Inst Hist Res

1859—General election, 1859. The poll... Bedford: Frederick Thompson, 1859
Alphabetical by polling district and parish. Place of residence and qualification. Non-voters. Index.

Richard Thomas Gilpin   Francis Charles   Hastings Russell   W. B. Higgins

Guildhall Lib

1872*—Beds. County election, Tuesday, June 25th, 1872. The poll... Bedford: C. F. Timaeus, [1872]
Alphabetical by polling district, parish and candidate.

Francis Bassett   William Stuart

Beds Rec Off   Inst Hist Res

BEDFORD

1790—The poll for the election... Bedford: W. Smith, [1790]
Alphabetical by residents and out-voters by county. Address or place of residence. Rejected voters.

William Colhoun   Samuel Whitbread, Jr.   John Payne

Beds Rec Off   Inst Hist Res

1830—General election, 1830. A copy of the poll... Bedford: C. B. Merry, 1830
Alphabetical by qualification and parish or place of residence. Occupation. Rejected voters with reasons and voting intentions.

William Henry Whitbread   Frederic Polhill   Lord John Russell

Bedford Town Hall   Inst Hist Res

1835—General election, 1835. The poll for the election... Bedford: J. S. Merry, 1835
Alphabetical by parish and out-voters. Address. Non-voters.

Frederic Polhill   Samuel Crawley   William Henry Whitbread

Beds Rec Off   Inst Hist Res

1837—General election, 1837. The poll for the election... Bedford: C. B. Merry, 1837
Alphabetical by parish and out-voters. Occupation and address. Non-voters.

Frederic Polhill   Henry Stuart   Samuel Crawley

Beds Rec Off   Inst Hist Res

1841—General election, 1841. The poll for the election... Bedford: C. B. Merry, 1841
Alphabetical by parish and out-voters. Occupation and address. Non-voters.
Frederic Polhill Henry Stuart William Henry Whitbread
Beds Rec Off Inst Hist Res

1847—General election, 1847. The poll for the election... Bedford: C. B. Merry, 1847
Alphabetical by parish and out-voters. Occupation and address. Non-voters.
Sir Harry Verney Henry Stuart Frederic Polhill
Beds Rec Off Inst Hist Res

1852—General election, 1852. The poll for the election... Bedford: F. Thompson, 1852
Alphabetical by parish and out-voters. Occupation and address. Dead and non-voters.
Henry Stuart Samuel Whitbread T. Chisholm Anstey
Bedford Town Hall Inst Hist Res

1854*—The poll taken at the Bedford election... *Bedford Times*, 9 December 1854
Alphabetical by qualification. Address. Non-voters.
William Stuart J. S. Trelawny
Brit Lib (News) Inst Hist Res

1857—Published by request. Bedford borough election... Bedford: Rowland Hill [Reprinted from *Bedford Mercury*, 28 March 1857]
Alphabetical by candidate. Occupation and address. Non-voters.
Samuel Whitbread Thomas Barnard William Stuart Edward Tyrrell Smith
Bedford Town Hall Inst Hist Res

1859 (April)—General election, 1859. The poll for the election... Bedford: Frederic Thompson, 1859
Alphabetical by parish and out-voters. Occupation and address. Dead and non-voters.
Samuel Whitbread William Stuart Frederick Charles Polhill-Turner Thomas Barnard
Bedford Town Hall Inst Hist Res

1859* (June)—The poll. Bedford borough election... *Bedfordshire Mercury* Supplement, 2 July 1859.
Alphabetical by candidate and parish. Address. Non-voters.
Samuel Whitbread Frederick Charles Polhill-Turner
Bedford Town Hall Inst Hist Res

1865—Bedford borough election... The poll... *Bedfordshire Mercury*, 15 July 1865
Alphabetical by candidate and parish. Address. Freemen distinguished. Non-voters.
Samuel Whitbread William Stuart Montagu Chambers
Bedford Town Hall Inst Hist Res

1868—Supplement to the *Bedford Times*, 24 November 1868. Bedford borough election... Bedford: C. F. Timaeus, [1868]
Alphabetical by candidate. Address. Non-voters.

James Howard Samuel Whitbread Frederick Charles Polhill-Turner E. L. O'Malley

Bedford Town Hall Inst Hist Res

BERKSHIRE

1722—The poll of the freeholders... London, 1722
By parish. Place of residence.

Sir John Stonehouse Robert Packer Henry Grey

Guildhall Lib

1727—The poll of the freeholders... London, 1727
By parish. Place of residence.

Robert Packer Sir John Stonehouse Viscount Fane

Oxford Rec Off Inst Hist Res

1768—The copy of the poll... Reading: J. Carnan, [1768]
Alphabetical by groups of hundreds. Place of residence, place, nature and occupier of freehold.

Arthur Vansittart Thomas Craven John Stone

Berks Rec Off Inst Hist Res

1796—The copy of the poll... Reading: Smart & Cowslade, [1796]
Alphabetical. Place of residence, place, nature and occupier of freehold.

George Vansittart Charles Dundas Edward Loveden Loveden

Berks Rec Off Inst Hist Res

1812—The poll of the freeholders... Abingdon: J. King, [1812]
Alphabetical by parish. Place of residence.

Charles Dundas Richard Neville William Hallett

Berks Rec Off Inst Hist Res

1818—The poll of the freeholders... Windsor: C. Knight, [1818]
Alphabetical by parish. Place of residence.

Richard Neville Charles Dundas William Hallett

Berks Rec Off Inst Hist Res

ABINGDON

1734—An exact list of those who poll'd... n.p., [1734]
Alphabetical by candidate. Occupation. Dissenters distinguished.

Robert Hucks John Jennings

Bodl Inst Hist Res

1734—An exact list of those who voted... n.p., [1734]
Alphabetical by candidate and religion. Occupation. Principal burgesses, governors of Christ's Hospital, and Jennings voters promised to Hucks distinguished.

Robert Hucks John Jennings

Bodl Inst Hist Res

1754—An exact list of those who poll'd... [Title page missing] n.p., [1754]
Alphabetical by candidate. Occupation. Principal and secondary burgesses, dissenters and Thrale voters promised to Moreton distinguished.

John Moreton Henry Thrale

Oxford Rec Off Inst Hist Res

1768—A true copy of the poll... n.p., [1768]
Alphabetical by candidate. Occupation. Frequent recipients of poor relief, members of the corporation, dissenters, Moreton voters promised to Bayly and recently admitted ratepayers distinguished.

John Moreton Nathaniel Bayly

Bodl Guildhall Lib (typed copy)

1830—A full report of the speeches... also the names of the electors... Abingdon: C. Evans, [1830]
Poll order. Occupation and address. Account of proceedings.

John Maberley Ebenezer Fuller Maitland

Bodl Inst Hist Res

1854*—Abingdon election, 1854. John Tomkins, Esq., Mayor. Poll book... Reading: H. & W. Cowslade, [1854]
Alphabetical. Occupation and address. Non-voters and disqualified. Candidates' addresses.

Joseph Haythorne Reed John Thomas Norris

Berks Rec Off Inst Hist Res

1868—Abingdon election, 1868. The following gentlemen were the General Committee to promote the re-election of Col. the Hon. C. H. Lindsay... [Abingdon: J. G. Davis, 1868]
Alphabetical by qualification and parish.

Charles Hugh Lindsay Godfrey Lushington

Inst Hist Res

NEW WINDSOR

1757*—A copy of the poll... n.p., [1757]
Alphabetical by candidate. Occupation.

Henry Fox Charles Bowles

Berks Rec Off Inst Hist Res

1780—A copy of the poll... J. Fote, 1780
Alphabetical. Occupation.

John Montagu   Penyston Portlock Powney   Augustus Keppell

Windsor Guildhall   Inst Hist Res

1794*—A copy of the poll... Windsor: Knight, [1794]
Alphabetical. Occupation. Oath takers distinguished. Non-voters. Contested voters with reasons and decisions. Account of proceedings.

William Grant   Henry Isherwood

Berks Rec Off   Inst Hist Res

1802—A copy of the poll... Windsor: C. Knight, 1802 [Two editions known]
Alphabetical. Occupation. Non-voters. Contested voters with reasons and list of those rejected. Account of proceedings.

John Williams   Robert Fulk Greville   Richard Ramsbottom

Berks Rec Off   Inst Hist Res

1804*—A copy of the poll... Windsor: C. Knight, 1804
Alphabetical. Occupation. Non-voters. Contested voters with reasons and decisions. Account of the 1802 election and subsequent proceedings.

Arthur Vansittart   Anthony Bacon

Windsor Guildhall   Inst Hist Res

1806—A copy of the poll... Windsor: C. Knight, [1806]
Alphabetical. Occupation. Oath takers distinguished. Non-voters. Contested voters with reasons and decisions. Account of proceedings.

Edward Disbrowe   Richard Ramsbottom   Arthur Vansittart

Windsor Guildhall   Inst Hist Res

1832—Windsor election. A list of the electors who voted... Windsor: R. Oxley, [1832]
Alphabetical by parish and district. Address. Rejected and non-voters distinguished. Account of proceedings.

Johm Ramsbottom   Sir Samuel John Brooke Pechell   Sir John Edmond De Beauvoir

Berks Rec Off   Inst Hist Res

1835—Windsor election. January 1835. A list of electors...
Windsor: Oxley & Brown, [1835]
Alphabetical by parish and district. Address. Rejected, dead and non-voters distinguished. Account of proceedings.

John Ramsbottom   Sir John Edmond De Beauvoir   Sir John Elley

Berks Rec Off   Inst Hist Res

1857—Borough of New Windsor. Poll book of the Windsor election...
Windsor: J. R. Brown, [1857]
Alphabetical by parish. Address. Non-voters distinguished.

William Vansittart   Charles William Grenfell   Samson Ricardo

Berks Rec Off   Inst Hist Res

1863*—Borough of New Windsor. Poll book of the Windsor election...
Windsor: Charles Provest, [1863]
Alphabetical by parish. Address. Non-voters and dead distinguished.

Richard Howard Vyse   Arthur Divett Hayter

Berks Rec Off   Inst Hist Res

1865—Borough of New Windsor. Poll book of the Windsor election...
Windsor: S. Collier, [1865]
Alphabetical by parish. Address. Non-voters, dead and duplicates distinguished.

Sir Henry Ainslie Hoare   Henry Labouchere   William Vansittart   Richard Howard Vyse

Berks Rec Off   Inst Hist Res

1868—Windsor election, 1868. The correct poll book...   Windsor: Medhurst, [1868]
Alphabetical by parish and qualification. Address. Tendered, dead, duplicate and non-voters distinguished.

Roger Eykyn   Robert Richardson-Gardner

Windsor Guildhall   Inst Hist Res

READING

1740*—The borough of Reading in the county of Berks. The names of such persons...
n.p., [1740] [Broadsheet]
Alphabetical by candidate.

William Strode   John Dodd

Reading Pub Lib   Inst Hist Res

1754—An exact list of the voters...   Reading: C. Micklewright, [1754] [Broadsheet]
Alphabetical by candidate. Occupation. Non-voters.

William Strode   Lord Fane   John Dodd

Reading Pub Lib   Inst Hist Res

1754—An exact list of the voters...   n.p., [1754] [Broadsheet]
Alphabetical by parish.

William Strode   Lord Fane   John Dodd

Bodl   Inst Hist Res

1768—An exact list of the voters...   Reading: J. Carnan, [1768] [Broadsheet]
Alphabetical. Occupation. Non-voters.

Henry Vansittart   John Dodd   John Bindley

Reading Pub Lib   Inst Hist Res

1774—A correct list of the voters...   Reading: J. Carnan, [1774] [Broadsheet]
Alphabetical by candidate. Occupation. Non-voters.

Francis Annesley   John Dodd   John Walter

Reading Pub Lib   Inst Hist Res

1780—A correct list of the voters... Reading: Carnan & Smart, [1780]
Alphabetical by candidate. Occupation. Non-voters.
Francis Annesley John Dodd Temple Luttrell
Reading Pub Lib Inst Hist Res

1782*—A correct list of the voters... n.p., [1782] [Broadsheet]
Alphabetical by candidate. Occupation. Non-voters.
Richard Aldworth Neville John Simeon
Reading Pub Lib Inst Hist Res

1790—A correct list of the voters... Reading: Smart & Cowslade, [1790] [Broadsheet]
Alphabetical by candidate. Occupation. Non-voters.
Francis Annesley Richard Aldworth Neville Lord Barrymore
Berks Rec Off Inst Hist Res

1802—A correct list of the voters... Reading: Smart & Cowslade, [1802] [Broadsheet]
Alphabetical by candidate. Occupation. Non-voters.
Francis Annesley Charles Shaw Lefevre John Simeon
Reading Pub Lib Inst Hist Res

1812—A correct list of the voters... Reading: M. Cowslade, [1812] [Broadsheet]
Alphabetical. Occupation and address. Non-voters distinguished.
Charles Shaw Lefevre John Simeon John Berkeley Monck
Reading Pub Lib Inst Hist Res

1820—A correct list of the voters... Reading: M. Cowslade, [1820]
Alphabetical. Occupation and address. Non-voters.
John Berkeley Monck Charles Fyshe Palmer John Weyland, Jr.
Reading Pub Lib

1820—A correct list of the voters... Reading: Cowslade, [1820] [Broadsheet]
Alphabetical. Occupation and address. Non-voters.
John Berkeley Monck Charles Fyshe Palmer John Weyland, Jr.
Guildhall Lib

1826—A correct list of the voters... Reading: M. Cowslade, 1827
Alphabetical. Occupation and address. Non-voters. Account of petition with lists of voters struck off and added by the Select Committee.
John Berkeley Monck George Spence Charles Fyshe Palmer Edward Wakefield
Reading Pub Lib Inst Hist Res

1826—A correct list of the voters... Reading: William Drysdale, [1826]
Alphabetical by candidate. Occupation and address. Non-voters.
John Berkeley Monck George Spence Charles Fyshe Palmer Edward Wakefield
Reading Pub Lib Guildhall Lib

1826—Reading election. A correct list of the voters... Reading: Drysdale, [1826] [Broadsheet]
Alphabetical by candidate. Occupation and address. Non-voters.
John Berkeley Monck George Spence Charles Fyshe Palmer Edward Wakefield
Reading Pub Lib Inst Hist Res

1835—A correct list of the voters... Reading: W. Swallow, 1835
Alphabetical. Address. Rejected and non-voters.
Thomas Noon Talfourd Charles Russell Benjamin Oliveira
Reading Pub Lib Guildhall Lib

1837—A correct list of the voters... Reading: J. Snare, 1837
Alphabetical. Occupation and address. Rejected and non-voters.
Thomas Noon Talfourd Charles Fyshe Palmer Charles Russell
Reading Pub Lib

1837—Reading election. A list of voters... Reading: R. Welch, [1837]
Alphabetical by candidate. Occupation and address. Non-voters.
Thomas Noon Talfourd Charles Fyshe Palmer Charles Russell
Reading Pub Lib Guildhall Lib

1841—A correct list of the voters... Reading: John Snare, 1841
Alphabetical. Occupation and address. Rejected and non-voters.
Charles Russell Viscount Chelsea Thomas Mills William Tooke
Reading Pub Lib Inst Hist Res

1847—Reading election. The official list... Reading: R. Welch, [1847]
Alphabetical by candidate. Occupation and address. Non-voters.
Francis Pigott Thomas Noon Talfourd Charles Russell Viscount Chelsea
Reading Pub Lib Inst Hist Res

1849*—Reading election—a list of voters. *Berkshire Chronicle* Supplement, 18 August 1849
Alphabetical by candidate. Occupation and address. Non-voters.
John Frederick Stanford George Bowyer Thomas Norton
Brit Lib (News) Inst Hist Res

1852—A correct poll list, and register of voters... Reading: *Mercury* Office, [1852]
Alphabetical. Address. Non-voters.
Francis Pigott Henry Singer Keating Samuel A. Dickson
Reading Pub Lib Inst Hist Res

1859—Reading election—poll list. *Berkshire Chronicle,* 14 May 1859
Alphabetical by candidate. Occupation and address. Non-voters.
Francis Pigott Sir Henry Singer Keating Ralph Benson
Brit Lib (News) Inst Hist Res

1860*—Reading election—poll list. *Berkshire Chronicle*, 21 January 1860
Alphabetical by candidate. Occupation and address. Non-voters.

Sir Francis Henry Goldsmid   Ralph Benson

Brit Lib (News)   Inst Hist Res

1865—A correct poll list of the voters... Reading: T. Barcham, 1865
Alphabetical. Address. Dead, disqualified, moved and non-voters.

Sir Francis Henry Goldsmid   George John Shaw Lefevre   Stephen Tucker

Reading Pub Lib   Inst Hist Res

WALLINGFORD

1820—An alphabetical list of voters... Wallingford: Bradford, [1820] [Broadsheet]
Alphabetical. Occupation.

William Lewis Hughes   George James Robarts   Ebenezer Fuller Maitland

Berks Rec Off   Inst Hist Res

1832—Triumph of independence. A list of the names... Wallingford: J. Bradford, [1832]
Alphabetical by parish, qualification and candidate. Members of the corporation distinguished. Non-voters.

William Seymour Blackstone   Charles Eyston

Berks Rec Off   Inst Hist Res

1847—Wallingford election. Triumph of independence. A list of the names... Wallingford: J. Bradford, [1847]
Alphabetical by candidate and district. Occupation and address or place of residence. Members of the corporation distinguished. Non-voters.

William Seymour Blackstone   Alfred Morrison

Reading Pub Lib   Inst Hist Res

BUCKINGHAMSHIRE

1705—A copy of the poll... n.p., [1705]
By hundred and parish.

Robert Dormer   Sir Richard Temple   Viscount Cheyne

Bodl   Guildhall Lib

1710—A list of the names... London, 1711
By parish.

Viscount Fermanagh   Sir Edmund Denton   Richard Hampden   Sir Henry Seymour

Bucks Archaeol Soc   Inst Hist Res

1713—A list of the names... London, 1714
By hundred and parish. Place of residence.

John Fletewode   Viscount Fermanagh   Richard Hampden   Sir Edmund Denton

Bucks Rec Off   Inst Hist Res

1722—A list of the names... London, 1722
By hundred and parish. Place of residence.
Montagu Garrard Drake Sir Thomas Lee Fleetwood Dormer
Bucks Rec Off Inst Hist Res

1784—An alphabetical list of the names... Aylesbury: W. Nicholls, 1785
Alphabetical by hundred and parish. Place of residence.
William Wyndham Grenville John Aubrey Earl Verney
Bucks Rec Off Inst Hist Res

1784—A copy of the poll... n.p., [1784]
Alphabetical by hundred, division and parish. Place of residence, nature and occupier of freehold.
William Wyndham Grenville John Aubrey Earl Verney
Bucks Archaeol Soc Inst Hist Res

1831—A poll of the freeholders... Aylesbury: J. H. Marshall, 1831
Alphabetical by hundred and parish. Place of residence.
Lord Chandos John Smith Pascoe Grenfell
Bucks Archaeol Soc Inst Hist Res

1841—A poll book of the combined forces of Whig, Radical, and Liberal electors... n.p., [1841]
Alphabetical by parish of residence. Voters for Lee and Vane only.
Sir William Lawrence Young Caledon George Du Pre
Charles Robert Scott Murray John Lee Henry Morgan Vane
Bucks Archaeol Soc Inst Hist Res

AYLESBURY

1804*—A poll of the electors... London: T. Wheeler, [1804]
Alphabetical by householders, and Aylesbury Hundreds freeholders by parish. Occupation and address of householders, place of residence of freeholders.
William Cavendish Thomas Grenville
Bucks Archaeol Soc Inst Hist Res

1804*—A poll of the electors... Buckingham: Seeley, [1804]
Alphabetical by householders, and Aylesbury Hundreds freeholders by parish. Occupation and address of householders, place of residence of freeholders.
William Cavendish Thomas Grenville
Bucks Rec Off Guildhall Lib

1818—A poll of the electors... Aylesbury: W. Woodman, [1818]
Alphabetical by householders, and Aylesbury Hundreds freeholders by parish. Occupation and address of householders, place of residence of freeholders.
Lord Nugent William Rickford Charles Compton Cavendish
Bucks Archaeol Soc Inst Hist Res

1831—A poll of the electors... Aylesbury: J. May, [1831]
Alphabetical by householders, and Aylesbury Hundreds freeholders by parish. Occupation and address of householders, place of residence of freeholders.

William Rickford   Lord Nugent   Lord Kirkwall

Bucks Archaeol Soc   Inst Hist Res

1832—A poll of the electors... Aylesbury: James May, [1832]
Alphabetical by parish. Occupation and address for Aylesbury, place of residence for other parishes.

William Rickford   Henry Hanmer   Thomas B. Hobhouse

Bucks Rec Off   Inst Hist Res

1835—Poll of the electors... Aylesbury: James May, [1835]
Alphabetical by parish. Occupation and address or place of residence.

William Rickford   Henry Hanmer   Thomas B. Hobhouse   John Lee

Bucks Archaeol Soc   Inst Hist Res

1839*—A poll of the electors... Aylesbury: James May, [1839]
Alphabetical by parish. Occupation and address or place of residence.

Charles John Baillie Hamilton   John Ingram Lockhart   Lord Nugent

Bucks Rec Off   Inst Hist Res

1847—Copy of the poll of the electors... Aylesbury: R. Gibbs, [1847]
Alphabetical by parish. Occupation for Aylesbury, address for other parishes.

John Peter Deering   Lord Nugent   Rice Richard Clayton

Bucks Rec Off   Inst Hist Res

1848*—Copy of the poll of the electors... Aylesbury: R. Gibbs, 1848
Alphabetical by parish. Occupation for Aylesbury, address for other parishes.

Quintin Dick   John Houghton

Bucks Rec Off   Inst Hist Res

1850*—Copy of the poll of the electors... Aylesbury: G. De Fraine, [1850]
Alphabetical by parish. Occupation and a few addresses.

Frederick Calvert   John Houghton

Bucks Rec Off   Inst Hist Res

1851*—Copy of the poll of the electors... Aylesbury: G. De Fraine, [1851]
Alphabetical by parish. Occupation or address.

Richard Bethell   William Busfield Ferrand

Bucks Rec Off   Inst Hist Res

1852—A copy of the poll... Aylesbury: R. Gibbs, [1852]
Alphabetical by parish. Occupation or place of residence. Non-voters.

Sir Harry Verney   Sir Thomas Francis Fremantle

Bucks Archaeol Soc   Inst Hist Res

1852—Copy of the poll of the electors... Aylesbury: G. De Fraine, [1852]
Alphabetical by parish. Occupation or place of residence.

Austen Henry Layard Richard Bethell Augustus Frederick Bayford John Temple West

Bucks Archaeol Soc Inst Hist Res

1857—Copy of the register of electors... showing the poll... Aylesbury: James Pickburn, 1857
Alphabetical by parish. Address. Non-voters included.

Thomas Tyringham Bernard Sir Richard Bethell Austen Henry Layard

Bucks Rec Off Inst Hist Res

1859—Copy of the register of electors... shewing the poll... Aylesbury: James Pickburn, 1859
Alphabetical by parish. Address. Non-voters included.

Thomas Tyringham Bernard Samuel George Smith
Thomas Frederick Charles Vernon Wentworth

Bucks Archaeol Soc Inst Hist Res

1868—A revised copy of the poll of electors... Aylesbury: De Fraine, [1868]
Alphabetical by polling district and parish. Address. Non-voters included.

Nathaniel Mayer De Rothschild Samuel George Smith George Howell

Bucks Archaeol Soc Inst Hist Res

BUCKINGHAM

1832—A poll of the electors... Buckingham: R. Chandler, 1833
Alphabetical by parish and township. Non-voters included. Signatories of the invitation to Morgan to stand distinguished. Notes on voters.

Sir Harry Verney Sir Thomas Francis Fremantle George Morgan

Bucks Rec Off Inst Hist Res

GREAT MARLOW

1784—A copy of the original poll... Great Marlow: John How, [1784] [Broadsheet]
Poll order. Non-voters included.

William Clayton Sir Thomas Rich Thomas Keating

Bucks Archaeol Soc Inst Hist Res

1847—Copy of the poll taken at the election... n.p., [1847] [Broadsheet]
Alphabetical by candidate. Occupation and address. Voters promised not to vote against Clayton distinguished. Non-voters promised to Clayton. Tendered votes.

Thomas Peers Williams Brownlow Knox Sir William Robert Clayton

Bucks Rec Off Inst Hist Res

HIGH WYCOMBE

1832—A poll of the electors... [High Wycombe]: W. T. Butler, 1832
Alphabetical. Address.
Robert John Smith   Charles Grey   Benjamin Disraeli
High Wycombe Pub Lib   Inst Hist Res

1868—Copy of the poll... [High Wycombe]: 1868
Alphabetical by borough district and parish. Address.
William Carrington   John Remington Mills
High Wycombe Pub Lib   Inst Hist Res

CAMBRIDGESHIRE

1705—A copy of the poll... n.p., [1705]
By parish.
Sir Rushout Cullen   Sir Roger Jenyns   Granado Piggott   John Bromley
Guildhall Lib

1722—A copy of the poll... London, 1722
By parish. Place of residence.
Sir John Hinde Cotton   Lord Harley   Sir Francis Whitchcot   Sir Robert Clarke
Cambridge Pub Lib   Inst Hist Res

1724*—A copy of the poll... n.p., [1724]
Alphabetical by parish of residence. Place of freehold.
Samuel Shepheard   Francis Pemberton
Cambridge Pub Lib   Inst Hist Res

1780—The poll for the election... Cambridge: Francis Hodson, [1780]
Alphabetical by hundred and parish. Place of residence and nature of freehold.
Lord Robert Manners   Philip Yorke   Sir Sampson Gideon
Cambridge Pub Lib   Inst Hist Res

1802* (May)—A state of the polls... Cambridge: F. Hodson, [1802]
Alphabetical by hundred and parish. Place of residence and nature of freehold. Votes in general and by-election.
Sir Henry Peyton   Lord Charles Somerset Manners
Cambridge Pub Lib   Inst Hist Res

1802 (July)—A state of the polls... Cambridge: F. Hodson, [1802]
Alphabetical by hundred and parish. Place of residence and nature of freehold. Votes in general and by-election.
Lord Charles Somerset Manners   Charles Yorke   Thomas Brand
Cambridge Pub Lib   Inst Hist Res

1826—A copy of the poll... Cambridge: Weston Hatfield, [1826]
Alphabetical by hundred and parish of residence. Place, nature and occupier of freehold. Out-voters alphabetical by county.

Lord Charles Somerset Manners Lord Francis Godolphin Osborne Henry John Adeane

Cambridge Pub Lib Inst Hist Res

1830—The poll for two knights... arranged . . . by Thomas Allen. Cambridge: Weston Hatfield, [1830]
Alphabetical by hundred and parish. Place of residence, nature and occupier of freehold. Index.

Lord Francis Godolphin Osborne Henry John Adeane Lord Charles Somerset Manners

Cambridge Pub Lib Inst Hist Res

1831*—The poll on the election of a representative... by Charles Henry Cooper. Cambridge: Benjamin Bridges, 1831
Alphabetical by parish of residence.

Richard Greaves Townley Charles Philip Yorke

Cambridge Pub Lib Inst Hist Res

1831*—The poll for a knight of the shire... Cambridge: J. Hodson, 1831
Alphabetical by hundred and parish. Place of residence, nature and occupier of freehold. Index.

Richard Greaves Townley Charles Philip Yorke

Cambridge Pub Lib Guildhall Lib

1832—The poll on the election of three knights... London: Pelham Richardson, 1833
Alphabetical by hundred and parish.

Charles Philip Yorke Richard Greaves Townley John Walbanke Childers
Henry John Adeane

Cambridge Pub Lib Inst Hist Res

1835—The poll on the election of three knights... Cambridge: John Hall, 1835
Alphabetical by hundred and parish. Place of residence. Index.

Eliot Thomas Yorke Richard Jefferson Eaton Richard Greaves Townley
John Walbanke Childers

Cambridge Pub Lib Inst Hist Res

1857—The poll taken at the election... Cambridge: C. W. Naylor, [1857]
Alphabetical by polling district. Address or place of residence.

Edward Ball Henry John Adeane Eliot Thomas Yorke Lord George Manners

Cambridge Pub Lib Guildhall Lib

1857—The poll taken at the election... Cambridge: Henry Smith, [1857]
Alphabetical by polling district. Address or place of residence.

Edward Ball Henry John Adeane Eliot Thomas Yorke Lord George Manners

Inst Hist Res

1868—The poll taken at the election... Cambridge: C. W. Naylor, [1868]
Alphabetical by polling district. Address or place of residence. Tendered and non-voters.

Lord George John Manners Viscount Royston Henry Bouverie William Brand Richard Young

Cambridge Pub Lib Inst Hist Res

CAMBRIDGE

1774—The poll for representatives in Parliament... n.p., [1774]
Poll order. Occupation and place of residence. Rejected voters.

Soames Jenyns Charles Sloane Cadogan Thomas Plumer Byde Samuel Meeke

Cambridge Pub Lib Inst Hist Res

1776*—A copy of the poll... n.p., [1776]
Alphabetical. Occupation and place of residence.

Benjamin Keene Thomas Plumer Byde

Cambridge Pub Lib Guildhall Lib

1780—The poll for the election... Cambridge: Francis Hodson, [1780]
By rank. Occupation and place of residence of esquires and freemen. Non-voting aldermen and common councilmen included. Explanatory note on Mortlock's candidacy.

John Whorwood Adeane Benjamin Keene Christopher Potter John Mortlock

Cambridge Pub Lib Guildhall Lib

1832—The poll on the election... by Charles Henry Cooper. Cambridge: W. Metcalfe, 1833
Alphabetical. Occupation and address. Tendered votes.

George Pryme Thomas Spring Rice Sir Edward Burtenshaw Sugden

Cambridge Pub Lib Inst Hist Res

1832—Copy of the poll... Cambridge: Hodson & Brown, 1833
Alphabetical. Occupation and address. Non-voters.

George Pryme Thomas Spring Rice Sir Edward Burtenshaw Sugden

St. John's, Cambridge Inst Hist Res

1834*—The poll on the election... by Charles Henry Cooper. Cambridge: W. Metcalfe, 1834
Alphabetical. Occupation and address. Tendered votes.

Thomas Spring Rice Sir Edward Burtenshaw Sugden

Cambridge Pub Lib Inst Hist Res

1835—The poll on the election... by Charles Henry Cooper. Cambridge: W. Metcalfe, [1835]
Alphabetical. Occupation and address. Rejected voters.

Thomas Spring Rice George Pryme James Lewis Knight

Cambridge Pub Lib Guildhall Lib

1837—The poll on the election... by Charles Henry Cooper... Cambridge: Henry Wallis, 1837
Alphabetical. Occupation and address. Tendered votes.

Thomas Spring Rice George Pryme James Lewis Knight Henry Manners Sutton

Cambridge Pub Lib Inst Hist Res

1837—The poll at the election... Cambridge: C. E. Brown, 1837
Alphabetical by candidate. Occupation and address.

Thomas Spring Rice George Pryme James Lewis Knight Henry Manners Sutton

Brit Lib

1839*—The poll on the election... [Cambridge, 1839]
Alphabetical by street.

Henry Manners Sutton Thomas Milner Gibson

Cambridge Pub Lib Inst Hist Res

1840*—The poll on the election... London: Geo. Nichols, 1840
Alphabetical by parish and candidate. Occupation and address.

Sir Alexander Cray Grant Thomas Starkie

Cambridge Pub Lib Guildhall Lib

1841—The poll on the election... Cambridge: Metcalfe & Palmer, 1841
Alphabetical. Occupation and address. Tendered vote.

Henry Manners Sutton Sir Alexander Cray Grant Richard Foster, Jr.
Lord Cosmo George Russell

Cambridge Pub Lib Inst Hist Res

1843*—The poll at the election... Cambridge: C. E. Brown, [1843]
Alphabetical by candidate. Occupation and address.

Fitzroy Kelly Richard Foster

Cambridge Pub Lib Inst Hist Res

1845*—The poll on the election... Cambridge: Henry Smith, 1845
Alphabetical. Occupation and address. Rejected voters.

Fitzroy Kelly Robert Alexander Shafto Adair

Cambridge Pub Lib Guildhall Lib

1847—The poll on the election... by William Cockerell. Cambridge: Henry Smith, 1847
Alphabetical. Occupation and address. Tendered votes.

Robert Alexander Shafto Adair William Frederick Campbell
John Henry Thomas Manners Sutton

Cambridge Pub Lib Inst Hist Res

1852—The poll on the election... Cambridge: Naylor & Co., 1852
Alphabetical by qualification. Occupation of householders and address. Non-voters.

Kenneth Macaulay   John Harvey Astell
Robert Alexander Shafto Adair   Francis Mowatt

Cambridge Pub Lib   Inst Hist Res

1854*—The poll on the election... by William Cockerell. Cambridge: Henry Smith, 1854
Alphabetical. Occupation and address.

Robert Alexander Shafto Adair   Francis Mowatt   Viscount Maidstone
Frederick William Slade

Cambridge Pub Lib   Inst Hist Res

1854*—The poll on the election... Cambridge: C. W. Naylor, 1854
Alphabetical by candidate. Tendered votes and non-voters.

Robert Alexander Shafto Adair   Francis Mowatt   Viscount Maidstone
Frederick William Slade

Cambridge Pub Lib   Inst Hist Res

1857—The poll on the election... Cambridge: Naylor, 1857
Alphabetical. Occupation and address. Non-voters.

Kenneth Macaulay   Andrew Steuart   Robert Alexander Shafto Adair   John Hibbert

Cambridge Pub Lib   Guildhall Lib

1859—The poll on the election... Cambridge: Naylor, 1859
Alphabetical. Occupation and address. Non-voters.

Kenneth Macaulay   Andrew Steuart   Edward Turner Boyd Twistleton   Francis Mowatt

Cambridge Pub Lib   Guildhall Lib

1863*—The poll on the election... Cambridge: C. W. Naylor, 1863
Alphabetical. Occupation and address. Non-voters.

Francis Sharp Powell   Henry Fawcett

Cambridge Pub Lib   Inst Hist Res

1865—The poll on the election... Cambridge: C. W. Naylor, 1865
Alphabetical. Occupation and address. Non-voters.

William Forsyth   Francis Sharp Powell   Robert Richard Torrens   William Dougal Christie

Cambridge Pub Lib   Guildhall Lib

1866*—The poll on the election... Cambridge: C. W. Naylor, 1866
Alphabetical. Occupation and address. Non-voters.

John Eldon Gorst   Robert Richard Torrens

Cambridge Pub Lib   Guildhall Lib

1868—The poll on the election... Cambridge: C. W. Naylor, 1868
Alphabetical. Occupation and address. Tendered votes and non-voters.

Robert Richard Torrens William Fowler Francis Sharp Powell John Eldon Gorst

Inst Hist Res

1868—The poll at the election... Cambridge: Hatfield & Tofts, 1869
Alphabetical. Occupation and address. Non-voters.

Robert Richard Torrens William Fowler Francis Sharp Powell John Eldon Gorst

Cambridge Pub Lib Guildhall Lib

CAMBRIDGE UNIVERSITY

1727—A copy of the poll... London, 1727
By college. Pairs and non-voters included.

Edmund Finch Thomas Townshend Dixey Windsor

Cambridge Univ Lib Inst Hist Res

1780—The poll for the election... Cambridge: Francis Hodson, [1780]
Alphabetical by college. Non-voters.

James Mansfield John Townshend Lord Hyde Richard Crofts William Pitt

Cambridge Pub Lib Inst Hist Res

1784—The poll for the election... by John Beverley. Cambridge:
Francis Hodson, [1784]
Alphabetical by college. Objected voters distinguished. Non-voters.

William Pitt Lord Euston John Townshend James Mansfield

Cambridge Pub Lib Inst Hist Res

1790—The poll for the election... by John Beverley. Cambridge:
John Archdeacon, [1790]
Alphabetical by college. Objected voters distinguished. Non-voters.

William Pitt Lord Euston Lawrence Dundas

Cambridge Pub Lib Inst Hist Res

1806*—The poll for the election... by John Beverley. Cambridge:
Francis Hodson, [1806]
Alphabetical by college. Objected voters distinguished. Non-voters.

Lord Henry Petty Lord Althorp Viscount Palmerston

Cambridge Univ Lib Inst Hist Res

1807—The poll for the election... by John Beverley. Cambridge:
Francis Hodson, [1807]
Alphabetical by college. Non-voters included.

Lord Euston Sir Vicary Gibbs Viscount Palmerston Lord Henry Petty

Cambridge Univ Lib Inst Hist Res

1811*—The polls for the election of Chancellor... and that of representative in Parliament... Cambridge: University Press, 1811
Alphabetical by college. Objected voters distinguished and also listed separately.

Viscount Palmerston　　John Henry Smyth

Cambridge Univ Lib　Guildhall Lib

1822*—The poll for the election... by Henry Gunning. Cambridge: James Hodson, [1822]
Alphabetical by college.

William John Bankes　　Lord Hervey　　James Scarlett

Cambridge Univ Lib　Inst Hist Res

1826—The poll for the election... by Henry Gunning. Cambridge: J. Smith, 1826
Alphabetical by college. Objected voters.

Sir John Singleton Copley　Viscount Palmerston　William John Bankes　Henry Goulburn

Cambridge Univ Lib　Inst Hist Res

1827*—The poll for the election... by Henry Gunning. Cambridge: J. Smith, [1827]
Alphabetical by college.

Sir Nicholas Conyngham Tindal　　William John Bankes

Cambridge Univ Lib　Inst Hist Res

1829*—The poll for the election... by Henry Gunning. Cambridge: J. Smith, 1829
Alphabetical by college.

William Cavendish　　George Bankes

Cambridge Univ Lib　Inst Hist Res

1831—The poll for the election... by Henry Gunning. Cambridge: J. Smith, 1831
Alphabetical by college.

Henry Goulburn　William Yates Peel　William Cavendish　Viscount Palmerston

Cambridge Univ Lib　Inst Hist Res

1847—The poll for the election... Cambridge: J. & J. J. Deighton, 1847
Alphabetical by college.

Charles Ewan Law　Henry Goulburn　Viscount Feilding　John George Shaw Lefevre

Cambridge Univ Lib　Inst Hist Res

1847—The poll taken at the election... Cambridge: C. E. Brown, 1847
Alphabetical by college. Committee lists showing voting.

Charles Ewan Law　Henry Goulburn　Viscount Feilding　John George Shaw Lefevre

Cambridge Univ Lib　Inst Hist Res

1856*—The poll for the election... Cambridge: Naylor, 1856
Alphabetical by college.

Spencer Horatio Walpole　　George Denman

Cambridge Univ Lib　Inst Hist Res

1868*—The poll for the election... Cambridge: University Press, 1868
Alphabetical by college.

Alexander James Beresford Beresford Hope Anthony Cleasby

Cambridge Univ Lib Inst Hist Res

1882*—The poll for the election... Cambridge: C. J. Clay at the University Press, 1883
Alphabetical by college. Rejected votes.

Henry Cecil Raikes James Stuart

Cambridge Univ Lib Inst Hist Res

CHESHIRE

1705—A copy of the poll... n.p., [1705]
By township.

Sir George Warburton John Crew Offley Sir Roger Mostyn Langham Booth

Bangor Univ College (Mostyn MSS) Inst Hist Res

SOUTH CHESHIRE

1832—A poll book for the southern division... Chester: J. Dixon, 1833
Alphabetical by hundred and parish. Place of residence. Non-voters included.

George Wilbraham Earl Grosvenor Sir Philip Grey Egerton

Birkenhead Pub Lib Inst Hist Res

1837—The poll book for the southern division... Chester: T. Griffith, [1837]
Alphabetical by hundred and parish. Place of residence. Non-voters included. Tendered votes, votes recorded for persons not on the register and persons voting twice.

Sir Philip Grey Egerton George Wilbraham Edwin Corbett

Birkenhead Pub Lib Inst Hist Res

1841—A poll book for the Southern Division... Chester: J. Topham, 1842
Alphabetical by hundred and parish. Place of residence.

Sir Philip Grey Egerton John Tollemache George Wilbraham

Birkenhead Pub Lib Inst Hist Res

CHESTER

1733*—An alphabetical list of the names... Chester: Roger Adams, for John Page, 1733
Alphabetical. Occupation and place of residence. Includes voting in mayoral election of October 1732.

Robert Grosvenor Richard Manley

Guildhall Lib

1747—An alphabetical list... Chester: Eliz. Adams, for John Page, [1747]
Alphabetical by first letter. Occupation and place of residence. Mainwaring plumpers distinguished.

Sir Robert Grosvenor   Philip Henry Warburton   James Mainwaring, Jr.

Chester Pub Lib   Inst Hist Res

1747—An alphabetical list... Chester: John Rowley, 1747
Alphabetical by first letter and candidate. Occupation and place of residence.

Sir Robert Grosvenor   Philip Henry Warburton   James Mainwaring, Jr.

Inst Hist Res

1784—An alphabetical list... Chester: John Monk, [1784]
Occupation and address. Election literature.

Thomas Grosvenor   Richard Wilbraham Bootle   John Crewe   Roger Barnston

Chester Pub Lib   Inst Hist Res

1784—An alphabetical list of the names... Chester: J. Fletcher, 1784
Occupation and address.

Thomas Grosvenor   Richard Wilbraham Bootle   John Crewe   Roger Barnston

Chester Pub Lib   Guildhall Lib

1812—The Chester poll book: containing the names of the voters... Chester: J. Fletcher, 1812
Alphabetical. Occupation and address. Account of proceedings and election literature.

Thomas Grosvenor   John Egerton   Sir Richard Brooke   Edward Venables Townsend

Chester Pub Lib   Guildhall Lib

1812—The poll book, corrected and revised... Chester: M. Cutter, [1812]
Alphabetical. Occupation and address.

Thomas Grosvenor   John Egerton   Sir Richard Brooke   Edward Venables Townsend

Guildhall Lib

1812—History of the contested election... Chester: John Monk, [1812]
Alphabetical by first letter and candidate. Occupation and address. Account of proceedings and election literature.

Thomas Grosvenor   John Egerton   Sir Richard Brooke   Edward Venables Townsend

Chester Pub Lib   Inst Hist Res

1818—Chester election, 1818. The complete poll book... Chester: J. Fletcher, 1818
Alphabetical. Occupation and address. Electoral history since 1807 and account of proceedings. Election literature.

Viscount Belgrave   Thomas Grosvenor   Sir John Grey Egerton   John Williams

Chester Pub Lib   Guildhall Lib

1818—History of the contested election... Chester: M. Monk, [1818]
Alphabetical by first letter and candidate. Occupation and address. Account of proceedings and election literature.

Viscount Belgrave   Thomas Grosvenor   Sir John Grey Egerton   John Williams

Birkenhead Pub Lib   Inst Hist Res

1820—Poll book for the general election. List of voters... Chester: J. Fletcher, [1820]
Alphabetical. Occupation and address. Account of proceedings and election literature.

Viscount Belgrave   Thomas Grosvenor   Sir John Grey Egerton
Edward Venables Townshend

Chester Pub Lib   Brit Lib

1820—List of voters, who polled for General Grosvenor... Chester: M. Monk, [1820]
Alphabetical by first letter. Occupation and address.

Viscount Belgrave   Thomas Grosvenor   Sir John Grey Egerton
Edward Venables Townshend

Inst Hist Res

1826—Chester election, 1826. The complete poll book... Chester: John Fletcher, [1826]
Alphabetical. Occupation and address. Rejected voters. Account of proceedings and election literature.

Viscount Belgrave   Robert Grosvenor   Charles Bulkeley Egerton
Edward Venables Townshend

Chester Pub Lib   Guildhall Lib

1826—A narrative of the proceedings... Chester: M. Monk, [1826]
Alphabetical by candidate. Occupation and address. Rejected voters distinguished. Account of proceedings.

Viscount Belgrave   Robert Grosvenor   Charles Bulkeley Egerton
Edward Venables Townshend

Chester Pub Lib   Inst Hist Res

1837—The city of Chester poll book... Chester: T. Griffith, [1837]
Alphabetical by qualification. Occupation and address of freemen, address and qualification of householders. Non-voters included. Votes recorded for those not on the register.

Lord Robert Grosvenor   John Jervis   Frederick D. Ryder

Birkenhead Pub Lib   Inst Hist Res

1850*—List of the electors who polled... *Chester Courant,* 7 August 1850
Alphabetical by candidate. Occupation and address.

William Owen Stanley   Edward Christopher Egerton

Chester Pub Lib   Inst Hist Res

1857—City of Chester election, 1857. The poll book... Chester: *Chronicle* Office, [1857]
Alphabetical by qualification and parish. Occupation and address for freemen, address for householders.

Earl Grosvenor   Enoch Gibbon Salisbury   Henry Riversdale Grenfell

Chester Pub Lib   Inst Hist Res

1859—Chester election. List of the freemen... Chester: *Courant Office*, [1859]
Alphabetical by qualification and parish. Occupation and address of freemen, address of householders.

Earl Grosvenor   Enoch Gibbon Salisbury   Philip Stapleton Humberston

Chester Pub Lib   Guildhall Lib

1865—Chester election, 1865. Poll Book... [Chester, 1865]
Alphabetical by qualification and parish. Occupation and address of freemen, address of householders.

Earl Grosvenor   William Henry Gladstone   W. Fenton   Henry Cecil Raikes

Chester Pub Lib   Inst Hist Res

MACCLESFIELD

1835—The poll at an election of representatives... Macclesfield: J. Swinnerton, [1835]
Alphabetical by township. Place and nature of qualification. Dead, rejected and non-voters.

John Ryle   John Brocklehurst   Thomas Grimsditch

Brit Lib

STOCKPORT

1835—A list of the electors who voted... Second edition with corrections... Broadsheet [Stockport]: Lambert & Blackshaw, [1835]
Alphabetical by district and street. Additions and corrections to the first edition distinguished.

Henry Marsland   Thomas Marsland   Edward D. Davenport

Stockport Pub Lib   Inst Hist Res

Untraced: 1847

CORNWALL, TRURO

1832—Truro. Farther account of election proceedings in this borough... together with a copy of the poll... Truro: G. Clyma, 1833
Alphabetical. Parish. Voters for Tooke only. Account of proceedings and Tooke's addresses.

Sir Hussey Vivian   William Tooke   Ennis Vivian

Guildhall Lib

CUMBERLAND

1831—The poll for knights... Cockermouth: Thomas Bailey, 1831
Alphabetical by ward. Place of residence and freehold. Objected voters. Account of proceedings.

Sir James Robert George Graham   William Blamire   Viscount Lowther

Carlisle Pub Lib   Inst Hist Res

EAST CUMBERLAND

1841—The polling book for the eastern division... Carlisle: Charles Thurnam, 1843
Alphabetical by polling district. Place of residence and qualification.

Charles Wentworth George Howard   William James   W. W. Stephenson

Carlisle Pub Lib   Inst Hist Res

1868—Poll book for the eastern division... Carlisle: Charles Thurnam, [1868]
Alphabetical by parish and qualification. Address. Non-voters included.

William Nicholson Hodgson   Charles Wentworth George Howard   William Marshall

Carlisle Pub Lib   Inst Hist Res

WEST CUMBERLAND

1857—Poll book of the election... Whitehaven: R. Gibson, [1857]
Alphabetical by ward and parish. Address. Non-voters included.

Henry Wyndham   Henry Lowther   Wilfrid Lawson

Carlisle Pub Lib   Inst Hist Res

CARLISLE

1774—A political history of the city of Carlisle... Carlisle: F. & J. Jollie, 1820
Alphabetical. Voters for George Musgrave and Robert Milbourn only. Political history of Carlisle since 1700.

Fletcher Norton   Anthony Storer   George Musgrave   Robert Milbourn

Carlisle Pub Lib   Inst Hist Res

1786* (April)—Boletarium: or a collection of papers, squibs... Carlisle, 1786
Alphabetical by candidate. Voters for Lowther divided into freemen and those "elected to the Freedom . . . without any Title by Birth or Servitude." Guild of freemen, place of residence and occasional occupation or description of Lowther voters. Common councillors distinguished. Election literature.

John Lowther   John Christian

Carlisle Pub Lib   Inst Hist Res

1786* (December)—Supplement to Boletarium... Carlisle, 1787
Alphabetical by candidate. "Mushroom" voters [newly created freemen] for Knubley not given. Place of residence and guild. Common councillors, Stephenson voters who abstained in April and Knubley voters who did not vote for Lowther in April distinguished. Election literature.

Edward Knubley   Rowland Stephenson

Carlisle Pub Lib   Inst Hist Res

1816*—Carlisle election for 1816. The proceedings... Newcastle-on-Tyne: J. Mitchell, [1816]
Poll order. Place of residence and occupation. Objected voters distinguished. Account of Carlisle elections since 1786, account of proceedings and election literature.

John Christian Curwen   Sir Philip Musgrave

Carlisle Pub Lib   Inst Hist Res

1816*—A political history of the city of Carlisle... Carlisle: F. & J. Jollie, 1820
Alphabetical by candidate. Place of residence and occupation. Political history of Carlisle since 1700.

John Christian Curwen   Sir Philip Musgrave

Carlisle Pub Lib   Inst Hist Res

1820*—A political history of the city of Carlisle... Carlisle: F. & J. Jollie, 1820
Alphabetical by candidate. Place of residence, occupation and guild. Voters at 1816 election alphabetically by candidate with place of residence and occupation. Alphabetical list of voters for George Musgrave and Robert Milbourn at the 1774 election. Political history of Carlisle since 1700.

William James   Sir Philip Musgrave

Carlisle Pub Lib   Inst Hist Res

1847—The poll book for the borough of Carlisle... Carlisle: C. Thurnam, 1847
Alphabetical by qualification and ward. Address.

John Dixon   William Nicholson Hodgson   Philip Henry Howard

Carlisle Pub Lib   Guildhall Lib

1847—Poll book for the city and borough... Carlisle: James Steel, 1847
Alphabetical by candidate, qualification and ward. Occupation and address. Non-voters.

John Dixon   William Nicholson Hodgson   Philip Henry Howard

Carlisle Pub Lib   Inst Hist Res

1848*—The poll book for the borough... Carlisle: C. Thurnam, 1848
Alphabetical by qualification and ward. Address. Non-voters included.

William Nicholson Hodgson Philip Henry Howard John Dixon Peter Murray McDougall

Carlisle Pub Lib   Inst Hist Res

1852—The poll book for the city... Carlisle: J. & R. Steel, 1852
Alphabetical by qualification and ward. Address. Non-voters included.

Sir James Robert George Graham   Joseph Ferguson   William Nicholson Hodgson

Carlisle Pub Lib   Inst Hist Res

1857—The poll book for the borough... Second edition. Carlisle: Charles Thurnam, 1857
Alphabetical by qualification and ward. Address. Non-voters included.

William Nicholson Hodgson   Sir James Robert George Graham   Joseph Ferguson

Carlisle Pub Lib   Inst Hist Res

1859—The poll book for the city... Carlisle: John Irving Lonsdale, 1859
Alphabetical by qualification and ward. Address. Non-voters included.

Sir James Robert George Graham Wilfrid Lawson William Nicholson Hodgson

Carlisle Pub Lib Inst Hist Res

1861—The poll book for the city... Carlisle: John Irving Lonsdale, 1861
Alphabetical by qualification and ward. Address. Non-voters included.

Edmund Potter William Nicholson Hodgson

Carlisle Pub Lib Inst Hist Res

1861—The poll book for the city... Carlisle: Charles Thurnam, 1861
Alphabetical by qualification and ward. Address. Non-voters included.

Edmund Potter William Nicholson Hodgson

Carlisle Pub Lib Inst Hist Res

1865—The poll book for the city... Carlisle: *Express* Office, 1865
Alphabetical by qualification and ward. Address. Non-voters included.

William Nicholson Hodgson Edmund Potter Wilfrid Lawson

Carlisle Pub Lib Inst Hist Res

1868—The poll book for the city... Carlisle: R. & J. Steel, 1868
Alphabetical by qualification and ward. Address. Non-voters included.

Sir Wilfrid Lawson Edmund Potter William Nicholson Hodgson William Slater

Carlisle Pub Lib Inst Hist Res

COCKERMOUTH

1852—A list of the voters of the borough... Cockermouth: D. Fidler, 1852
Alphabetical by candidate and occupation. Place of residence. Non-voters. Unqualified voters. Voters for Aglionby and Horsman in 1841 who voted against them on this occasion.

Henry Wyndham Henry Aglionby Aglionby Edward Horsman

Carlisle Pub Lib Inst Hist Res

1852—The poll book of the election... published in commemoration of the first Conservative victory since the passing of the Reform Bill... Cockermouth: J. Naisbit, 1852
Alphabetical by township. Address. Splits with Wyndham. Voters failing to fulfill various promises to Wyndham. Non-voters. Election literature.

Henry Wyndham Henry Aglionby Aglionby Edward Horsman

Carlisle Pub Lib Inst Hist Res

1868—Borough of Cockermouth. Particulars of poll at election... Cockermouth: D. Fidler, [1868]
Alphabetical by township. Address. Non-voters.

Isaac Fletcher Henry Lorton Bourke

Carlisle Pub Lib Inst Hist Res

WHITEHAVEN

1832—The poll book of the election... Whitehaven: R. Gibson, 1832
Alphabetical by township. Address. Tendered and objected votes and non-voters included. Election literature, including 1832 register.

Matthias Attwood   Isaac Littledale

Carlisle Pub Lib   Inst Hist Res

1868—Poll book of the election... Whitehaven: William Smith, [1868]
Alphabetical. Address of residence and of qualification. Non-voters included.

George Augustus Frederick Cavendish Bentinck   Anthony Benn Steward

Carlisle Pub Lib   Inst Hist Res

DERBYSHIRE

1734—A copy of the poll... Nottingham: Henry Alestree, [1734]
Alphabetical by hundred. Place of residence and freehold.

Lord Charles Cavendish   Sir Nathaniel Curzon   Henry Harpur

Bodl Guildhall Lib

1734—A copy of a poll... Derby: Jer. Roe, [1734]
Alphabetical by hundred and parish of residence. Place of freehold. Out-voters alphabetical by county and parish of residence.

Lord Charles Cavendish   Sir Nathaniel Curzon   Henry Harpur

Derby Pub Lib   Inst Hist Res

EAST DERBYSHIRE

1868—Copy of the poll book... Chesterfield: J. B. White, [1868]
Alphabetical by polling district, parish and qualification. Place of residence.

Francis Egerton   Henry Strutt   Gladwin Turbutt   William Overend

Derby Pub Lib   Inst Hist Res

NORTH DERBYSHIRE

1832—Poll book for the northern division... Chesterfield: J. Roberts, [1832]
Alphabetical by polling district and parish. Qualification. Non-voters included. Account of proceedings.

Lord Cavendish   Thomas Gisborne   Sir George Sitwell

Derby Pub Lib   Guildhall Lib

1837—Poll book for the northern division... Chesterfield: J. Roberts, [1837]
Alphabetical by polling district and parish. Place of residence and qualification. Non-voters included. Rejected voters distinguished. Account of proceedings.

George Henry Cavendish   William Evans   George Arkwright

Derby Pub Lib   Inst Hist Res

1853*—Poll book for the northern division... Derby: W. & W. Pike, [1853]
By polling district and booth. Place of residence.

William Pole Thornhill   Thomas William Evans

Derby Pub Lib   Inst Hist Res

1868—Copy of the poll book... Chesterfield: J. B. White, [1868]
Alphabetical by polling district and parish. Place of residence.

Lord George Henry Cavendish   Augustus Peter Arkwright   William Jackson

Derby Pub Lib   Inst Hist Res

SOUTH DERBYSHIRE

1832—A list of the electors... Derby: W. & W. Pike, [1832]
Alphabetical by polling district and parish. Place of residence and nature, place and occupier of qualification. Non-voters included.

George John Vernon   Lord Waterpark   Sir Roger Greisley

Inst Hist Res

1835—List of electors for the southern division... Derby: William Bemrose, 1835
Alphabetical by polling district and parish. Place of residence. Non-voters included.

Sir George Crewe   Sir Roger Greisley   George John Vernon   Lord Waterpark

Derby Pub Lib   Guildhall Lib

1841—Poll book for the southern division... Derby: William Bemrose, 1841
Alphabetical by polling district and parish. Place of residence. Non-voters included. Account of elections since 1832.

Edward Miller Mundy   Charles Robert Colvile   Matthew Gisborne   Lord Waterpark

Derby Pub Lib   Inst Hist Res

1857—Poll book for the southern division... Derby: W. Bemrose, 1857
Alphabetical by polling district and parish. Place of residence. Non-voters included.

Thomas William Evans   Charles Robert Colvile   Samuel William Clowes   Lord Stanhope

Derby Pub Lib   Guildhall Lib

1859—Poll book for the southern division... Derby: W. Bemrose, 1859
Alphabetical by polling district and parish. Place of residence or address. Non-voters included.

Thomas William Evans   William Mundy   Augustus Henry Vernon

Derby Pub Lib   Inst Hist Res

1865—Poll book for the southern division... London: Bemrose, 1865
Alphabetical by polling district and parish. Place of residence or address. Non-voters included.

Thomas William Evans   Charles Robert Colvile   William Mundy

Derby Pub Lib   Inst Hist Res

1868—Poll book for the southern division... at the contested elections, November 19, 1868, and January 14, 1869... London: Bemrose, 1869
Alphabetical by polling district and parish. Place of residence or address. Non-voters included. Single list for both elections.

Rowland Smith Sir Thomas Gresley Thomas William Evans Charles Robert Colvile

Derby Pub Lib Inst Hist Res

1869*—Poll book for the southern division... at the contested elections, November 19, 1868, and January 14, 1869... London: Bemrose, 1869
Alphabetical by polling district and parish. Place of residence or address. Non-voters included. Single list for both elections.

Henry Wilmot Thomas William Evans

Derby Pub Lib Inst Hist Res

DERBY

1710—Poll taken October the 9th... London, [1710]
Alphabetical. Some occupations and places of residence. Non-voters. London voters (also in the main list).

Sir Richard Leeving John Harpur Richard Pye Lord Cavendish

Derby Pub Lib Inst Hist Res

1727—A poll of the burgesses... Nottingham: Anne Ayscough, 1727
Poll order. Some occupations and places of residence of out-voters. Non-voters and disenfranchised.

Lord James Cavendish William Stanhope Thomas Bayly

Derby Pub Lib Inst Hist Res

1734—A list of the poll... London: Henry Allestree, [1734]
Alphabetical. Some occupations and places of residence.

Lord James Cavendish Charles Stanhope William Curzon Richard Harpur

Derby Pub Lib Inst Hist Res

1742*—A true copy of the poll... Derby: Sam. Drewry, 1741
Poll order. Some occupations of residents and places of residence of out-voters. Index.

Viscount Duncannon German Pole

Derby Pub Lib Inst Hist Res

1742*—A true list of the persons... Coventry: J. Jopson for S. Trimer, Derby, [1742]
Alphabetical. Occupation.

Viscount Duncannon German Pole

Inst Hist Res (typescript)

1748*—A copy of the poll... Derby: S. Drewry, 1748
Poll order. Occupation of residents and place of residence of out-voters. Non-voters. Index.

Thomas Rivett Thomas Stanhope

Derby Pub Lib Inst Hist Res

1775*—Copy of a poll... Derby: T. Trimmer, 1775
Poll order. Occupation and place of residence. Non-voters.

John Gisborne Daniel Parker Coke

Derby Pub Lib Inst Hist Res

1775*—An alphabetical list of the burgesses... Derby: John Drewry, [1775]
Occupation and place of residence. Rejected and non-voters.

John Gisborne Daniel Parker Coke

Bodl Inst Hist Res

1832—A correct list of the electors... published by Stephen Glover. Derby: Ward & Probert, 1832
Alphabetical by qualification and parish. Place of residence.

Edward Strutt Frederick Compton Cavendish Sir Charles Henry Colvile

Derby Pub Lib Inst Hist Res

1837—The poll taken on the 25th day of July... Derby: William Bemrose, [1837]
Alphabetical by qualification and parish. Address of freemen, nature and address of qualification for householders. Non-voters included.

Edward Strutt John George Brabazon Ponsonby Francis Curzon Charles Robert Colvile

Derby Pub Lib Guildhall Lib

1841—The poll taken on the 25th day of July... Derby: Wm. Bemrose, [1841]
Alphabetical by qualification and parish. Address of freemen, nature and address of qualification for householders. Non-voters included.

Edward Strutt John George Brabazon Ponsonby E. S. Chandos-Pole

Derby Pub Lib Guildhall Lib

1847—Poll book for the borough... Derby: Wm. Bemrose, [1847]
Alphabetical by qualification and parish. Address. Non-voters included. Electoral history from 1775.

Edward Strutt Frederick Leveson Gower Henry Raikes Philip McGrath

Derby Pub Lib Inst Hist Res

1848*—Poll book for the borough... Derby: W. Bemrose, 1848
Alphabetical by qualification and parish. Address. Non-voters included.

Michael Thomas Bass Lawrence Heyworth James William Freshfield James Lord

Derby Pub Lib Inst Hist Res

1852—Poll book for the borough... Derby: W. Bemrose, 1852
Alphabetical by qualification and parish. Address. Non-voters included. Brief review of the political state of the borough.

Michael Thomas Bass Thomas Berry Horsfall Lawrence Heyworth

Derby Pub Lib Inst Hist Res

1859—Poll book for the borough... Derby: W. Bemrose, 1859
Alphabetical by qualification and parish. Address. Non-voters included.

Michael Thomas Bass Samuel Beale William Melbourne James Henry Raikes

Guildhall Lib

1865—Poll book for the borough... London: W. Bemrose & Son, 1865
Alphabetical by qualification and parish. Address. Non-voters included.

William Thomas Cox   Michael Thomas Bass   Samuel Plimsoll   Samuel Beale

Bodl   Inst Hist Res

DEVON, BARNSTAPLE

1832—A collection of the addresses... Barnstaple: T. Cornish, 1833
Alphabetical. Freemen distinguished. Election literature.

John Palmer Bruce Chichester   Charles St. John Fancourt   Thomas Northmore
Lord George Hervey

North Devon Athenaeum   Inst Hist Res

1837—List of voters... *County and North Devon Advertiser*, 11 August 1837
Alphabetical. Address.

John Palmer Bruce Chichester   Frederick Hodgson   W. S. Best

Brit Lib (News)   Inst Hist Res

1841—List of persons who voted... *County and North Devon Advertiser*, 30 July 1841
Alphabetical.

Frederick Hodgson   Montague Gore   John William Fortescue
John Palmer Bruce Chichester

Brit Lib (News)   Inst Hist Res

1847—A list of the voters... Barnstaple: W. Avery, 1847
Alphabetical by qualification. Occupation and address.

Richard Brembridge   John William Fortescue   Frederick Hodgson

North Devon Athenaeum   Inst Hist Res

1847—A list of the voters... *County and Devon Advertiser*, 27 August 1847
Alphabetical. Address. Signatories of the requisition to Hodgson who voted against him distinguished.

Richard Brembridge   John William Fortescue   Frederick Hodgson

Brit Lib (News)   Inst Hist Res

1852—A list of the voters... Barnstaple: T. Hearson, 1852
Alphabetical by qualification. Occupation and address.

Sir William Augustus Fraser   Richard Brembridge   Viscount Ebrington

North Devon Athenaeum   Inst Hist Res

1852—The list of the voters... *Western Standard and North Devon General Advertiser*, 23 July 1852
Alphabetical by qualification and parish. Occupation and address.

Sir William Augustus Fraser   Richard Brembridge   Viscount Ebrington

Brit Lib (News)   Inst Hist Res

1852—Barnstaple general election. The poll book... *North Devon Journal,* 22 July 1852
Alphabetical by candidate, qualification and address. Occupation.
Sir William Augustus Fraser Richard Brembridge Viscount Ebrington
Brit Lib (News) Inst Hist Res

1854*—A list of the voters... Barnstaple: S. Searle, 1854
Alphabetical. Occupation and address.
John Laurie Richard Samuel Guinness William Tite
North Devon Athenaeum Inst Hist Res

1857—A list of the voters... Barnstaple: A. P. Wood, 1857
By voters for Fraser with each other candidate and other voters. Occupation and address.
Sir William Augustus Fraser John Laurie James Taylor George Potts Henry Thoby Prinsep
North Devon Athenaeum Inst Hist Res

1859—A list of the voters who polled... Barnstaple: S. Searle, 1859
Alphabetical by candidate. Address.
John Davie Ferguson Davie George Potts Sir George Stucley Stucley Sir William Augustus Fraser
Yale Univ Lib Inst Hist Res

1863*—A list of the voters... Barnstaple: S. Searle, 1863
Alphabetical by candidate. Address.
Thomas Lloyd Richard Brembridge
North Devon Athenaeum Inst Hist Res

1865—Corrected edition. A list of the voters... Barnstaple: E. J. Arnold, 1865
Alphabetical by qualification. Address.
Sir George Stucley Stucley Thomas Cave Howel Gwyn Henry Hawkins
North Devon Athenaeum Inst Hist Res

1865—The poll book... *North Devon Journal,* 20 July 1865
Alphabetical by qualification. Address.
Sir George Stucley Stucley Thomas Cave Howel Gwyn Henry Hawkins
Brit Lib (News) Inst Hist Res

1868—A list of the voters... Barnstaple: S. Searle, 1868
Alphabetical by candidate. Address. Non-voters.
Thomas Cave Charles Henry Williams William Herbert Evans
North Devon Athenaeum Inst Hist Res

1868—Copy of the poll book. *North Devon Journal,* 26 November and 3 December 1868
Alphabetical by candidate. Occupation and address.
Thomas Cave Charles Henry Williams William Herbert Evans
Brit Lib (News) Inst Hist Res

EXETER

1761—A list of the freemen and freeholders... Exeter: Andrew Brice, [1761] [Broadsheet]
Alphabetical by candidate. Occupation. Freeholders distinguished. Pairs.
John Tuckfield John Rolle Walter William Mackworth Praed Thomas Sewell
Cornwall Rec Off Inst Hist Res

1776*—A list of the freemen and freeholders who voted... Exeter: R. Trewman, [1776] [Broadsheet]
Alphabetical by candidate and qualification. Occupation. Pairs.
John Baring John Burridge Cholwich
Exeter Pub Lib Inst Hist Res

1784—A list of the freemen and freeholders who voted... [Exeter, 1784] [Broadsheet]
Alphabetical by candidate. Occupation. Freeholders and plumpers distinguished.
John Baring Sir Charles Warwick Bampfylde John Buller
Exeter Pub Lib Inst Hist Res

1790—A list of the freemen and freeholders who voted... [Exeter, 1790] [Broadsheet]
Alphabetical. Occupation. Freeholders distinguished.
James Buller John Baring Sir Charles Warwick Bampfylde
Exeter Pub Lib Inst Hist Res

1802—An alphabetical list of the freemen and freeholders who voted... Exeter: Trewman, [1802] [Broadsheet]
Occupation. Freeholders distinguished.
James Buller Sir Charles Warwick Bampfylde Edmund Granger
Exeter Pub Lib Inst Hist Res

1818—The addresses, speeches... likewise a correct list of the names... Exeter: R. Cullum, [1818]
Alphabetical. Occupation. Freeholders distinguished. Election literature of this and the Devon elections of 1816 and 1818.
William Courtenay Robert William Newton Thomas Northmore
Exeter Pub Lib Inst Hist Res

1818—An alphabetical list of the freemen and freeholders... [Exeter, 1818] [Broadsheet]
Occupation. Freeholders distinguished.
William Courtenay Robert William Newton Thomas Northmore
Exeter Pub Lib Inst Hist Res

1831—List of voters in the several parishes... *Exeter Itinerary and General Directory,* July 1831, (Exeter: T. & H. Besley), pp. 223-235
Alphabetical by parish. Occupation. Freeholders distinguished. Place of residence of out-voters.

James Wentworth Buller   Lewis William Buck   Edward Divett

Exeter Pub Lib   Inst Hist Res

1835—List of voters polled... *Besley's Exeter Directory* for 1835, (Exeter: Henry Besley), pp. 121-139
Alphabetical. Occupation and parish of residence.

Sir William Webb Follett   Edward Divett   James Wentworth Buller

Exeter Pub Lib   Inst Hist Res

1845*—The list of voters... Exeter: T. Latimer, [1845]
Alphabetical by qualification and parish. Address. Non-voters included.

Sir John Thomas Buller Duckworth   John Briggs

Devon Rec Off   Inst Hist Res

1852—The list of persons entitled to vote... Exeter: Woolmer, [1852]
Alphabetical. Occupation and address. Freemen distinguished. Non-voters included.

Sir John Thomas Buller Duckworth   Edward Divett   George Stucley Buck

Exeter Pub Lib   Inst Hist Res

1864*—The list of persons . . . who voted... Exeter: William Clifford, 1864
Alphabetical. Occupation and address. Freemen distinguished. Non-voters included.

Edward Baldwin Courtenay   John Duke Coleridge

Exeter Pub Lib   Inst Hist Res

1868—A complete list of the persons . . . who voted... Exeter: *Devon Weekly Times,* 1868
Alphabetical. Occupation and address. Freemen distinguished. Non-voters included.

John Duke Coleridge   Edgar Alfred Bowring   Sir John Burgess Karslake   Arthur Mills

Exeter Pub Lib   Inst Hist Res

HONITON

1763*—A poll taken the 21st day of November, 1763... n.p., [1763] [Broadsheet]
By Candidate. Occupation.

Sir George Yonge   Anthony Bacon

Guildhall Lib

TOTNES

1812—Totnes general election, October the 9th, 1812... n.p., [1812] [Broadsheet]
By candidate.

Thomas Peregrine Courtenay   Ayshford Wise   J. P. Anderson   F. G. Seymour

Devon Rec Off   Inst Hist Res

1837—A list of the voters polled . . . Totnes: S. Hannaford, [1837]
By candidate. Occupation and address.

Lord Seymour   Jasper Parrott   Sir George Pownall Adams

Devon Rec Off   Inst Hist Res

1859—[Incomplete copy lacking title page] Booth 2: persons voting in respect of property situated in the parish of Totnes only.
Address.

Earl of Gifford   Thomas Mills   John Dunn

Devon Rec Off   Inst Hist Res

DORSET

1727*—The poll taken at the election... Exeter: E. Farley, 1727
By division. Place of freehold and residence. Oathtakers distinguished.

George Pitt   Thomas Horner

Weymouth Pub Lib   Inst Hist Res

1806—The poll taken at the election... Dorchester: G. Frampton, 1807
Alphabetical by division, hundred, parish and place. Place of residence, place, nature and occupier of freehold. Oathtakers distinguished. Rejected voters with reasons included. Account of proceedings.

William Morton Pitt   Edward Berkeley Portman   Henry Bankes

Weymouth Pub Lib   Inst Hist Res

1807—The poll taken... Dorchester: G. Frampton, 1807
Alphabetical by division, hundred, parish and place. Place of residence, place, nature and occupier of freehold. Oathtakers distinguished. Rejected voters with reasons included.

William Morton Pitt   Edward Berkeley Portman   Henry Bankes

Dorset Rec Off   Inst Hist Res

1831 (May)—Dorset election, 1831. The poll taken... Dorchester: Weston, Simonds and Sydenham, 1831
By division and tithing. Occupation and place of residence, nature and occupier of freehold. Oathtakers distinguished. Rejected voters with reasons and voting intentions included. Index.

Edward Berkeley Portman   John Calcraft   Henry Bankes

Weymouth Pub Lib   Guildhall Lib

1831* (September)—Dorset election... The poll taken... Dorchester: Weston, Simonds & Sydenham, 1832
Alphabetical by tithing or place. Place of residence, nature and occupier of freehold. Oathtakers distinguished. Objected and rejected voters with reasons included. Index.

Lord Ashley   William Francis Spencer Ponsonby

Inst Hist Res

1857—The poll book for the county of Dorset... Dorchester: *Dorset County Chronicle,* 1857
By district and polling booth. Place of residence and qualification. Account of 1831 and 1857 elections.

Henry Ker Seymour Henry Gerard Sturt William Henry Berkeley Portman John Floyer

Weymouth Pub Lib Guildhall Lib

BRIDPORT

1841—The poll taken before William Colfox, Esq.... Bridport: J. Prince, 1841
Alphabetical. Occupation or address where necessary to distinguish two or more of the same name. Non-voters included.

Henry Warburton Thomas Alexander Mitchell
Alexander Dundas Ross Wishart Baillie Cochrane

Dorset Rec Off Inst Hist Res

1847—The poll taken before J. Pike Stephens... Bridport: J. Prince, 1847
Alphabetical. Occupation or address where necessary to distinguish two or more of the same name. Non-voters included, dead distinguished.

Alexander Dundas Ross Wishart Baillie Cochrane Thomas Alexander Mitchell
Edward R. Petre R. M. Martin

Dorset Rec Off Inst Hist Res

1859—The poll book; an account of the poll... Bridport: F. Tucker, 1859
Alphabetical. Non-voters included, dead distinguished.

Thomas Alexander Mitchell Kirkman Daniel Hodgson Henry Hyde Nugent Bankes

Yale Univ Lib Inst Hist Res

1859—The poll at the Bridport election. *Bridport News & General Advertiser,* 7 May 1859
Alphabetical. Non-voters.

Thomas Alexander Mitchell Kirkman Daniel Hodgson Henry Hyde Nugent Bankes

Brit Lib (News) Inst Hist Res

LYME REGIS

1837—A list of persons who voted for the Conservative candidate, B. Hampden, Esq.... Lyme: Landray, [1837] [Broadsheet]
Alphabetical. Occupation.

William Pinney Benn Hampden

Lyme Regis Museum

1841—Borough of Lyme Regis. The following persons voted for Thomas Hussey, Esq., the Conservative candidate... Lyme: Locke, [1841] [Broadsheet]
Alphabetical by parish.

William Pinney Thomas Hussey

Lyme Regis Museum

1865—Borough of Lyme Regis & Charmouth. A list of persons who voted... Lyme: H. Locke, [1865]
Alphabetical by candidate. Non-voters, dead distinguished.

John Wright Treeby   John C. Hawkshaw

Dorset Rec Off   Inst Hist Res

Untraced: 1859

POOLE

1835—An account of the election... Poole: J. Lankester, 1835
Alphabetical. Place of residence. Burgesses and non-voters distinguished. Electoral history since 1831 and account of proceedings.

Sir John Byng   John Irving   Charles Augustus Tulk   James Bonar

Poole Pub Lib   Guildhall Lib

1841—Poole. The poll taken at the election... Poole: J. Lankester, 1841
Alphabetical. Address. Non-voters distinguished.

Charles Frederick Ashley Ponsonby   George Richard Philips   George Pitt Rose

Brit Lib   Poole PL   Inst Hist Res

1847—Poole election, 1847. The poll taken at the election... Poole: John Sydenham, [1847]
Alphabetical. Address.

George Richard Robinson   George Richard Philips   Edward John Hutchins

Brit Lib   Inst Hist Res

1850*—Poole election. September 1850. The poll taken... Poole: J. R. Justican, [1850]
Alphabetical. Occupation and address. Absent non-voters included, others listed separately, distinguishing those who voted for Robinson in 1847.

Henry Danby Seymour   John Savage

Brit Lib   Inst Hist Res

1857—Poole. The poll taken at the election... Poole: J. Lankester, 1857
Alphabetical. Address. Non-voters distinguished.

Henry Danby Seymour   George Woodroffe Franklyn   William Taylor Haly

Brit Lib   Inst Hist Res

1859—Poole election, April 1859. The poll taken... Poole: S. Kinsman, 1859
Alphabetical. Occupation and address.

George Woodroffe Franklyn   Henry Danby Seymour   William Taylor Haly

Poole Pub Lib   Inst Hist Res

1865—The poll taken at the election... Poole: J. Lankester, 1865
Alphabetical. Non-voters distinguished.

Henry Danby Seymour   Charles Waring   Stephen Lewin

Poole Pub Lib   Inst Hist Res

Untraced: 1837

SHAFTESBURY

1830—History of the Shaftesbury election, 1830... Shaftesbury: George Adams, [1830]
Alphabetical. Rejected voters with reasons and voting intentions included. Abstract of notes of evidence on 26 rejected voters. Account of proceedings and election literature.

Edward Penrhyn William Stratford Dugdale Francis C. Knowles

Guildhall Lib

WEYMOUTH AND MELCOMBE REGIS

1727—The copy of the poll... n.p., [1727]
Poll order. Queried and rejected voters. Account of proceedings.

Edward Tucker William Betts Thomas Pearse Sir John Thornhill Knox Ward
Henry Neale Edward Seymour Richard Bury

Dorset Rec Off Inst Hist Res

1847—Borough and town of Weymouth, Melcombe Regis. A poll taken... Weymouth: Benson & Barling, [1847]
Alphabetical by parish. Address. Dead and non-voters.

William Dougal Christie William Lockyer Freestun Frederick William Child Villiers
George Medd Butt

Weymouth Pub Lib Inst Hist Res

1852—Weymouth election, July 9, 1852. The poll book analysed... Weymouth: J. Sherren, [1852]
Alphabetical by candidate and parish. Address. Non-voters.

George Medd Butt William Lockyer Freestun Alexander Oswald

Soc Geneal Inst Hist Res

COUNTY DURHAM

1761—The poll for knights... Newcastle: I. Thompson, 1761
Alphabetical by ward. Place of residence, place, nature and occupier of freehold. Oathtakers distinguished. Rejected voters.

Robert Shafto Frederick Vane Sir Thomas Clavering

Durham Univ Lib Inst Hist Res

1790—The general election poll... Newcastle: D. Akenhead, 1790
Alphabetical by ward. Place of residence, place, nature and occupier of freehold. Oathtakers distinguished. Rejected and postponed voters with reasons.

Rowland Burdon Ralph Milbanke Sir John Eden

Durham County Lib Inst Hist Res

1820—The general election poll... Durham: G. Walker, 1820
Alphabetical by ward. Place of residence, place, nature and occupier of freehold. Oathtakers distinguished. Rejected and postponed voters with reasons in some cases.

John George Lambton William John Frederick Powlett Richard Wharton

Durham County Lib Inst Hist Res

NORTH DURHAM

1832—The poll for two knights... Durham: George Walker, 1833
Alphabetical by polling district. Address, nature and place of qualification.

Hedworth Lambton   Sir Hedworth Williamson   Edward Richmond Gale Braddyll

Durham County Lib   Inst Hist Res

1837—The proceedings and poll at the election... Durham: George Walker, Jr., 1837
Alphabetical by polling district. Address, place and nature of qualification. Account of proceedings.

Hedworth Lambton   Henry Thomas Liddell   Sir William Chaytor

Durham County Lib   Guildhall Lib

1865—North Durham election, 1865. The poll... Durham: George Walker, 1865
Alphabetical by polling district. Address.

Sir Hedworth Williamson   Robert Duncombe Shafto   George William Barrington

Durham Univ Lib   Inst Hist Res

1868—Register of voters for the northern division... Sunderland: printed for Richard Laurence Pemberton, 1869
Alphabetical by polling district, township and qualification. Place of residence. Dead and non-voters included. Objected voters distinguished. Tendered voters.

George Elliot   Sir Hedworth Williamson   Isaac Lowthian Bell

Durham County Lib   Inst Hist Res

1868—North Durham election, 1868. The poll... Durham: Ainsley, [1868]
Alphabetical by polling district, township and qualification. Place of residence. Non-voters included.

George Elliot   Sir Hedworth Williamson   Isaac Lowthian Bell

Durham County Lib   Inst Hist Res

SOUTH DURHAM

1832—The poll for two knights... Durham: George Walker, 1833
Alphabetical by polling district. Place of residence, place and nature of qualification.

Joseph Pease, Jr.   John Bowes   Robert Duncombe Shafto

Durham County Lib   Guildhall Lib

1841—The proceedings and the poll at the election... Durham: George Walker, Jr., 1841
Alphabetical by polling district. Place of residence, nature and place or occupier of qualification. Tendered votes. Account of proceedings.

Lord Harry Vane   John Bowes   James Farrer

Durham County Lib   Inst Hist Res

1857—South Durham election, 1857. The poll... Darlington: *Times* Office, 1857
Alphabetical by polling district and township. Place of residence. Account of proceedings.

Lord Harry Vane James Farrer Henry Pease

Newcastle-upon-Tyne Pub Lib Inst Hist Res

1865—South Durham election, 1865. The poll... Hartlepool: Mercury Steam Printing Offices, [1865]
Alphabetical by polling district and township. Place of residence.

Joseph Whitwell Pease Charles Freville Surtees Frederick Blackett Beaumont

Durham County Lib Inst Hist Res

1868—South Durham election. The poll, 1868... Darlington: *Telegraph* Office, [1868]
Alphabetical by polling district, township and qualification. Place of residence. Non-voters included.

Joseph Whitwell Pease Frederick Blackett Beaumont Charles Freville Surtees
Gustavus Hamilton Russell

Inst Hist Res

1868—Register of voters for the southern division... Sunderland: Thomas Reed, 1869
Alphabetical by polling district, township and qualification. Place of residence. Non-voters included. Tendered votes.

Joseph Whitwell Pease Frederick Blackett Beaumont Charles Freville Surtees
Gustavus Hamilton Russell

Durham County Lib Inst Hist Res

DARLINGTON

1868—Darlington borough election, 1868. The poll... Darlington: *Times* Office, 1868
Alphabetical by polling district. Address.

Edmund Backhouse Henry King Spark

Darlington Pub Lib Inst Hist Res

DURHAM CITY

1761 (March-April)—The poll for the election of members... Durham: I. Lane, [1761]
Alphabetical by company.

John Tempest Henry Lambton Ralph Gowland

Guildhall Lib

1761* (December)—The poll at the election... Newcastle: John White, 1762
Alphabetical. Company and place of residence or address. Oathtakers distinguished. Rejected voters. Separate list of occasional freemen who voted for Gowland with place of residence, occupation and company.

Ralph Gowland John Lambton

Sunderland Pub Lib Inst Hist Res

1774—The poll at the election... Durham: G. Sowler, [1774]
Alphabetical by company. Address or place of residence.

John Tempest   John Lambton   Mark Milbanke

Guildhall Lib

1774—The poll at the election... Durham: P. Barwick, [1774]
Alphabetical. Company and address or place of residence. Objected voters distinguished.

John Tempest   John Lambton   Mark Milbanke

Durham Univ Lib   Guildhall Lib

1800*—The poll at the election... Stockton: Christopher & Jennett, 1800
Alphabetical. Company and place of residence. Oathtakers distinguished. Rejected voters.

Michael Angelo Taylor   Matthew Russell   George Baker

Sunderland Pub Lib   Inst Hist Res

1800*—The poll at the election of one citizen... Durham: G. Walker, [1800]
Alphabetical. Company and place of residence. Oathtakers, recipients of relief and rejected voters distinguished.

Michael Angelo Taylor   Matthew Russell   George Baker

Durham County Lib   Guildhall Lib

1802—The poll for the election... Durham: G. Walker, [1802]
Alphabetical. Company and place of residence. Oathtakers distinguished. Rejected voters.

Richard Wharton   Ralph John Lambton   Michael Angelo Taylor

Manchester Pub Lib   Inst Hist Res

1802—The poll at the election... Durham: L. Pennington, 1802
Alphabetical. Company and place of residence. Oathtakers, rejected and postponed voters distinguished.

Richard Wharton   Ralph John Lambton   Michael Angelo Taylor

Sunderland Pub Lib   Guildhall Lib

1804*—The poll at the election of a citizen... Durham: R. Brockett, [1804]
Alphabetical. Company and place of residence. Oathtakers distinguished.

Robert Eden Duncombe Shafto   Francis Tweddell   Charles Spearman

Durham Univ Lib   Inst Hist Res

1813*—The poll at the election... Durham: L. Pennington, 1813
Alphabetical. Company and place of residence. Oathtakers distinguished. Rejected voters with reasons. Non-voters.

George Allan   George Baker

Durham Univ Lib   Inst Hist Res

1830—Proceedings at the Durham City election... Durham: George Walker, 1830
Poll order and alphabetical by company within each letter. Company and place of residence. Account of proceedings and candidates' addresses.

Michael Angelo Taylor Sir Roger Gresley William Richard Carter Chaytor

Bodl Inst Hist Res

1830—Proceedings and addresses at the Durham City election . . . 2nd edition. Durham: George Walker, 1830
Poll order and alphabetical by company within each letter. Company and place of residence. Account of proceedings and candidates' addresses.

Michael Angelo Taylor Sir Roger Gresley William Richard Carter Chaytor

Durham County Lib Guildhall Lib

1831*—The poll at the election... Durham: George Walker, 1831
Alphabetical by polling day. Company and place of residence. Freemen arrived too late to vote.

William Richard Carter Chaytor Arthur Trevor John Clervaux Chaytor

Durham County Lib Inst Hist Res

1832—The poll of the freemen and householders... Durham: George Waalker, 1832
Alphabetical by qualification and parish. Occupation and address.

William Charles Harland William Richard Carter Chaytor Arthur Trevor

Durham County Lib Guildhall Lib

1835—Proceedings and poll at the Durham City election... Durham: George Walker, Jr., 1835
Alphabetical by qualification. Occupation and address or place of residence. Account of proceedings.

Arthur Trevor William Charles Harland Thomas Colpitts Granger

Durham Univ Lib Inst Hist Res

1837—Proceedings and poll at the Durham City election... Durham: George Walker, Jr., 1837
Alphabetical by qualification. Occupation and address or place of residence. Account of proceedings.

Arthur Trevor William Charles Harland Thomas Colpitts Granger

Durham County Lib Guildhall Lib

1843* (April)—The proceedings and poll at the Durham City election... Durham: George Walker, Jr., 1843
Alphabetical by qualification. Occupation for freemen and address or place of residence. Account of proceedings and election literature.

Arthur Trevor Viscount Dungannon John Bright

Durham Univ Lib Guildhall Lib

1843* (July)—The poll at the election of one citizen... Durham: George Walker, Jr., 1843
Alphabetical by qualification. Occupation of freemen and address. Non-voters. Candidates' addresses.

John Bright   Thomas Purvis

Durham County Lib   Inst Hist Res

1847—The proceedings and poll... Durham: George Walker, Jr., [1847]
Alphabetical by qualification and parish. Address. Non-voters. Account of proceedings.

Thomas Colpitts Granger   Henry John Spearman   David Edward Wood

Durham Univ Lib   Guildhall Lib

1852 (July)—The proceedings and poll... Durham: George Walker, 1852
Alphabetical by qualification and parish. Address. Non-voters and pairs. Account of proceedings.

Thomas Colpitts Granger   William Atherton   Lord Adolphus Vane

Durham Univ Lib   Inst Hist Res

1852* (December)—The proceedings and poll... Durham: George Walker, 1852
Alphabetical by qualification and parish. Address. Non-voters. Account of proceedings.

Lord Adolphus Vane   Henry Fenwick

Durham Univ Lib   Inst Hist Res

1853*—The poll at the contested election... Durham: George Walker, 1853
Alphabetical by qualification and parish. Address. Non-voters.

John Robert Mowbray   Sir Charles Eurwicke Douglas

Durham Univ Lib   Inst Hist Res

1868—The poll at the Durham City election... *Durham Chronicle,* 20 November 1868
Alphabetical by qualification and parish. Address. Non- voters.

John Henderson   John Robert Davison   John Lloyd Wharton

Darlington Pub Lib   Inst Hist Res

1871*—Register of voters . . . and poll... Durham: George Walker, [1871]
Alphabetical by qualification and parish. Address. Dead and non-voters distinguished.

John Lloyd Wharton   Thomas Charles Thompson

Durham Univ Lib   Inst Hist Res

GATESHEAD

1837—The poll book of the first contested election... Gateshead: Lowthin & Douglas, 1837
Alphabetical. Address. Non-voters included.

Cuthbert Rippon   John William Williamson

Newcastle-upon-Tyne Pub Lib   Inst Hist Res

1852—[The Gateshead poll, July 9, 1852] Gateshead: William L. Douglas, [1852]
Alphabetical by candidate. Address.

William Hutt A. F. O. Liddell Ralph Walters

Newcastle-upon-Tyne Pub Lib Inst Hist Res

HARTLEPOOLS

1868—First election for the Hartlepools. Who supported the Tories? *South Durham & Cleveland Mercury,* 5 December 1868
Alphabetical by township. Conservative voters only.

Ralph Ward Jackson Thomas Richardson

Brit Lib (News) Inst Hist Res

SOUTH SHIELDS

1832—The electors' scrap book; or a complete collection of the addresses, speeches, and squibs... South Shields: B. G. Sharp, 1833
Alphabetical. Account of proceedings and election literature.

Robert Ingham George Palmer William Gowan Russell Bowlby

Guildhall Lib

1852—Poll for South Shields election, July 8, 1852. *North & South Shields Gazette,* 16 July 1852
Alphabetical by candidate. Address.

Robert Ingham H. T. Liddell

Tynemouth Pub Lib Guildhall Lib

STOCKTON

1868—Records of the first parliamentary election . . . , edited by H. G. Reid. Stockton: *Gazette* Office, 1869
Alphabetical by polling district and qualification. Address for householders, occupation for lodgers. Account of proceedings.

Joseph Dodds Ernest Vane Tempest

South Shields Pub Lib Inst Hist Res

SUNDERLAND

1832—Poll book. A list of the names... Sunderland: Thomas Marwood, Jr., 1833
Alphabetical by district. Place of qualification.

Sir William Chaytor George Barrington William Thompson David Barclay

Sunderland Pub Lib Guildhall Lib

1837—Poll book of the Sunderland borough election... Sunderland: Thomas Marwood, Jr., [1837]
Alphabetical by district. Place of qualification.

William Thompson David Barclay Andrew White

Sunderland Pub Lib Guildhall Lib

1841*—Copy of the poll in the election... Gateshead: William Douglas, 1841
Alphabetical by candidate and district. Place of qualification.

Viscount Howick   Matthias Wolverly Attwood

Sunderland Pub Lib   Guildhall Lib

1845*—Borough of Sunderland poll. *Sunderland & Durham County Herald,* 22 August 1845
Alphabetical by candidate and district. Occupation.

George Hudson   Thomas Perronet Thompson

Brit Lib (News)   Inst Hist Res

1847 (August)—Poll for Sunderland election. *Sunderland & Durham County Herald,* 6 August 1847
Alphabetical by polling booth. Address. Non-voters included.

George Hudson   David Barclay   William Arthur Wilkinson

Brit Lib (News)   Inst Hist Res

1847* (December)—Copy of the poll... *Sunderland Herald,* 24 December 1847
By candidate and district. Address. Non-voters.

Sir Hedworth Williamson   William Arthur Wilkinson

Brit Lib (News)   Inst Hist Res

1852—Poll for Sunderland election. *Sunderland Herald,* 9 July 1852
Alphabetical by district and candidate. Address.

George Hudson   William Digby Seymour   Henry Fenwick

Brit Lib (News)   Inst Hist Res

1852—Poll for Sunderland election. *Sunderland Times,* 10 July 1852
Alphabetical by district and candidate. Address. Non-voters.

George Hudson   William Digby Seymour   Henry Fenwick

Brit Lib (News)   Inst Hist Res

1855*—Poll for Sunderland election. *Sunderland Herald,* 5 January 1855
Alphabetical by district. Address.

Henry Fenwick   William Digby Seymour

Brit Lib (News)   Inst Hist Res

1857—Sunderland election. List of the poll. *Sunderland Herald,* 3 April 1857
Alphabetical by candidate and district. Address.

Henry Fenwick   George Hudson   Ralph Walters

Brit Lib (News)   Inst Hist Res

1859—Copy of the poll... Sunderland: R. Vint & Carr, 1859
Alphabetical by district. Address.

Henry Fenwick   William Scaw Lindsay   George Hudson

Brit Lib

1865—Sunderland election. List of the poll. *Sunderland Herald,* 14 July 1865
Alphabetical by district. Address.

Henry Fenwick James Hartley John Candlish

Brit Lib (News) Inst Hist Res

1866*—Sunderland election. List of the poll. *Sunderland Herald,* 2 March 1866
Alphabetical by district. Address.

John Candlish Henry Fenwick

Brit Lib (News) Inst Hist Res

ESSEX

1694*—A true and exact catalogue... n.p., [1694]
By parish of residence in separately paginated lists for each candidate. Out-voters arranged by Suffolk and others.

Sir Charles Barrington Benjamin Mildmay

Colchester Pub Lib Inst Hist Res

1702—A true and exact list of the names... London: 1702
By parish. Place of residence.

Sir Charles Barrington Sir John Marshall Sir Francis Masham Edward Bullock

Guildhall Lib

1710—List of the names... London, 1711
By parish.

Sir Richard Child Thomas Middleton Sir Francis Masham

Essex Rec Off Inst Hist Res

1715*—An exact list... London, 1715
By parish. Place of residence. Oathtakers distinguished.

William Harvey Robert Honywood

Essex Rec Off Inst Hist Res

1722—An exact list of names... London, 1724
Alphabetical by parish. Place of residence. Oathtakers distinguished.

William Harvey Robert Honywood Lord Castlemaine

Colchester Pub Lib Inst Hist Res

1734—The poll for knights of the shire... London: M. Downing, 1734
By parish of residence. Place of freehold. Out-voters by county and parish. Non-voters.

Sir Robert Abdy Thomas Bramston Lord Castlemaine

Essex Rec Off Inst Hist Res

1763*—The poll for knights [sic] of the shire... London: Charles Bathurst, 1764
By hundred. Place of residence, nature and occupier of freehold.

John Luther John Conyers

Essex Rec Off Inst Hist Res

1763*—The poll for a knight of the shire... Chelmsford: T. Toft, 1764
By hundred and parish. Place of residence.

John Luther — John Conyers

Essex Rec Off — Inst Hist Res

1768—The poll for knights of the shire... Chelmsford: T. Toft & R. Lobb, 1768
Alphabetical by hundred and parish of residence. Place of freehold. Out-voters alphabetical by county.

John Luther — Sir William Maynard — Jacob Houblon — Eliab Harvey

Essex Rec Off — Inst Hist Res

1774—The poll for knights of the shire... Chelmsford: W. Clachar & C. Frost, 1775
Alphabetical by hundred and parish of residence. Place of freehold. Out-voters alphabetical by county.

John Luther — John Conyers — Lord Waltham

Colchester Pub Lib — Inst Hist Res

1810*—The poll for a knight... Chelmsford: Meggy, Chalk & Stanes, 1810
Alphabetical by polling division. Place of residence and of freehold.

John Archer Houblon — Montagu Burgoyne

Essex Rec Off — Guildhall Lib

1812—A true copy of the poll... Harlow: B. Flower, 1812
Alphabetical by polling division. Place of freehold. Includes votes at 1810 election. Introduction by Burgoyne.

John Archer Houblon — Charles Callis Western — Montagu Burgoyne

Colchester Pub Lib — Guildhall Lib

1830* (March)—The poll for a knight of the shire... Chelmsford: Meggy & Chalk, 1830
Alphabetical by polling division. Place of residence and of freehold.

Thomas Gardiner Bramston — Henry John Conyers

Colchester Pub Lib — Inst Hist Res

1830 (August)—The poll for two knights of the shire... Chelmsford: Meggy & Chalk, 1830
Alphabetical by polling division and parish of residence when they coincide. Place, nature and occupier of freehold. Out-voters, including those resident in a different Essex division, alphabetical by county within the polling division containing the freehold.

John Tyssen Tyrell — Charles Callis Western — William Pole Tylney Long Wellesley

Essex Rec Off — Inst Hist Res

EAST ESSEX

1868—Eastern division of Essex. The poll... Colchester: *Essex & West Suffolk Gazette*, [1868]
Alphabetical by polling district, parish and qualification. Place of residence. Non-voters included. Tendered votes.

James Round   Samuel Brise Ruggles-Brise   Sir Thomas Burch Western
Sir Thomas Neville Abdy

Inst Hist Res

NORTH ESSEX

1847—North Essex election. The poll... Colchester: John Taylor, Jr., [1847]
Alphabetical by polling district and parish.

Sir John Tyssen Tyrell   William Beresford   John Gurdon Rebow
Fyske Goodeve Fyske Harrison

Essex Rec Off   Inst Hist Res

SOUTH ESSEX

1857—The poll for two knights... Chelmsford: T. B. Arthy; London: Simpkin, Marshall, 1857
Alphabetical by polling district and parish.

Thomas William Bramston   Richard Baker Wingfield   Sir William Bowyer Smijth

Essex Rec Off   Inst Hist Res

1859—South Essex election. The poll... Chelmsford: *Chronicle & Herald* Steam Press, [1859]
Alphabetical by polling district and parish.

Thomas William Bramston   John Watlington Perry Watlington   Richard Baker Baker

Essex Rec Off   Inst Hist Res

1865—South Essex election. The poll... Chelmsford: *Chronicle & Herald* Steam Press, [1865]
Alphabetical by polling district and parish.

Henry John Selwyn   Lord Eustace Gascoyne Cecil   Richard Baker Wingfield Baker

Essex Rec Off   Inst Hist Res

COLCHESTER

1741—The poll for members... Ipswich: W. C. for John Kendall, 1741
Alphabetical by place of residence. Honorary freemen and objected or rejected voters distinguished.

Charles Gray   Samuel Savill   John Olmius   Matthew Martin

Colchester Pub Lib   Inst Hist Res

1741—The poll for representatives... Colchester: John Pilborough, 1741
Alphabetical by place of residence.

Charles Gray   Samuel Savill   John Olmius   Matthew Martin

Essex Archaeol Soc   Inst Hist Res

1747—The poll for members... Colchester: J. Pilborough for J. Kendall, [1747]
Alphabetical by place of residence.
Richard Savage Nassau   Charles Gray   John Olmius
Colchester Pub Lib   Inst Hist Res

1768—The poll for members... London: W. Richardson & S. Clark for John Kendall, 1768
Alphabetical by place of residence. Occupation.
Charles Gray   Isaac Martin Rebow   Alexander Fordyce
Colchester Pub Lib   Inst Hist Res

1780—[No title page. Begins:] A poll for members... [Colchester, 1780]
Alphabetical by place of residence. Occupation.
Isaac Martin Rebow   Sir Robert Smyth   Alexander Fordyce   Robert Mayne
Colchester Pub Lib   Inst Hist Res

1781*—A poll for members [sic] . . . n.p., [1781]
Alphabetical. Occupation and place of residence. Non-voters included.
Christopher Potter   Edmund Affleck
Colchester Pub Lib   Guildhall Lib

1781*—[No title page. Begins] Poll for the borough of Colchester... [Colchester, 1781]
Alphabetical. Resident voters only. Occupation.
Christopher Potter   Edmund Affleck
Essex Archaeol Soc

1781*—A poll for members [sic] . . . n.p., [1781]
Alphabetical by place of residence. Out-voters only. Occupation.
Christopher Potter   Edmund Affleck
Colchester Pub Lib   Inst Hist Res

1784 (April)—The poll for members... Colchester: J. Fenno, [1784]
Alphabetical by place of residence.
Sir Edmund Affleck   Christopher Potter   Sir Robert Smyth
Essex Archaeol Soc   Inst Hist Res

1784 (April)—The poll for members... Colchester: W. Keymer, 1784
Alphabetical by place of residence. Occupation.
Sir Edmund Affleck   Christopher Potter   Sir Robert Smyth
Colchester Pub Lib   Inst Hist Res

1784* (July)—The poll for a member... Colchester: W. Keymer, 1784
Alphabetical by place of residence. Occupation.
Sir Robert Smyth   Christopher Potter   Samuel Tyssen
Colchester Pub Lib   Inst Hist Res

1788*—The poll for a member... Colchester: J. Fenno, 1788
Alphabetical. Occupation and place of residence.

George Jackson George Tierney

Essex Archaeol Soc Inst Hist Res

1788*—The poll for a member... Colchester: W. Keymer, [1788]
Alphabetical by place of residence. Occupation.

George Jackson George Tierney

Colchester Pub Lib Inst Hist Res

1790—The poll for members... Colchester: W. Keymer, [1790]
Alphabetical by place of residence. Occupation.

Robert Thornton George Jackson George Tierney

Colchester Pub Lib Inst Hist Res

1796—The poll for members... Colchester: W. Keymer, Jr., [1796]
Alphabetical by place of residence. Occupation.

Robert Thornton Lord Muncaster Richard Shepley

Colchester Pub Lib Inst Hist Res

1806—The poll for members... Colchester: W. Keymer, [1806]
Alphabetical by place of residence or regiment. Occupation.

Robert Thornton William Tufnell John Prinsep

Colchester Pub Lib Inst Hist Res

1806—The poll for members... Colchester: I. Marsden, [1806]
Alphabetical by place of residence or regiment. Occupation.

Robert Thornton William Tufnell John Prinsep

Colchester Pub Lib Inst Hist Res

[Same printing as preceding entry with different title page]

1807—The poll for members... Colchester: W. Keymer, [1807]
Alphabetical by place of residence or regiment. Occupation.

Robert Thornton Richard Hart Davis John Charles Tufnell

Colchester Pub Lib Inst Hist Res

1812—The poll for members... Colchester: W. Keymer, [1812]
Alphabetical by place of residence or regiment. Occupation.

Richard Hart Davis Robert Thornton Daniel Whittle Harvey

Colchester Pub Lib Inst Hist Res

1818* (February)—The poll for a member... [Colchester:] W. Keymer, [1818]
Alphabetical by place of residence. Occupation.

James Beckford Wildman Daniel Whittle Harvey

Colchester Pub Lib Inst Hist Res

1818 (June)—The poll for members... [Colchester:] W. Keymer, [1818]
Alphabetical by place of residence. Occupation.

James Beckford Wildman   Daniel Whittle Harvey   Peter Wright

Colchester Pub Lib   Inst Hist Res

1820—The poll for members... Colchester: Swinborne & Walter, 1820
Alphabetical by place of residence. Occupation.

Daniel Whittle Harvey   James Beckford Wildman   Sir Henry Russell

Colchester Pub Lib   Inst Hist Res

1830—The poll for members... Colchester: Swinborne, Walter & Taylor, [1830]
Alphabetical by place of residence. Occupation.

Daniel Whittle Harvey   Andrew Spottiswoode   William Mayhew

Colchester Pub Lib   Inst Hist Res

1831* (April)—The poll for a member... Colchester: Swinborne, Walter & Taylor, 1831]
Alphabetical by place of residence. Occupation.

William Mayhew   Sir William Curtis

Colchester Pub Lib   Inst Hist Res

1831 (May)—The poll for members... Colchester: Swinborne, Walter & Taylor, [1831]
Alphabetical by place of residence. Occupation.

Daniel Whittle Harvey   William Mayhew   Richard Sanderson

Colchester Pub Lib   Inst Hist Res

1831 (May)—Haddon's poll book. The poll... [Colchester:] S. Haddon, [1831]
Out-voters alphabetical by place of residence. Voters (resident and out-voters) at the Committee Room, Angel Inn. Occupation. Intending and rejected voters.

Daniel Whittle Harvey   William Mayhew   Richard Sanderson

Essex Archaeol Soc   Inst Hist Res

[Only known copy is defective
and lacks pp. 1-18]

1832—The poll for members... Colchester: Swinborne, Walter & Taylor, [1832]
Alphabetical by qualification and parish. Place of residence.

Richard Sanderson   Daniel Whittle Harvey   William Mayhew

Colchester Pub Lib   Inst Hist Res

1835—The poll for members... Colchester: John Taylor, Jr., [1835]
Alphabetical by qualification and parish. Place of residence. Non-voters distinguished.

Richard Sanderson   Sir George Henry Smyth   Henry Tufnell

Colchester Pub Lib   Inst Hist Res

1837—Borough of Colchester. The poll... Colchester: John Taylor, Jr., 1837
Alphabetical by qualification and parish. Non-voters, dead and those voting after the close of the poll distinguished.

Richard Sanderson Sir George Henry Smyth James Ruddell Todd

Colchester Pub Lib Inst Hist Res

1847—Borough of Colchester. The poll... Colchester: John Taylor, Jr., 1847
Alphabetical by qualification and parish. Address or place of residence. Non-voters distinguished.

Sir George Henry Smyth Joseph Alfred Hardcastle Richard Sanderson

Colchester Pub Lib Inst Hist Res

1850*—Borough of Colchester. The poll... Colchester: John Taylor, Jr., [1850]
Alphabetical by qualification and parish. Non-voters, dead and removed distinguished.

Lord John James Robert Manners George Wingrove Cooke

Colchester Pub Lib Inst Hist Res

1852—Borough of Colchester. The poll... Colchester: John Taylor, Jr., 1852
Alphabetical by qualification and parish. Address. Non-voters distinguished.

William Warwick Hawkins Lord John James Robert Manners Joseph Alfred Hardcastle Henry Thoby Prinsep

Colchester Pub Lib Inst Hist Res

1852—Borough of Colchester. The poll... Colchester: *Essex & West Suffolk Gazette*, [1852]
Alphabetical by qualification and parish. Address. Non-voters, dead and removed distinguished.

William Warwick Hawkins Lord John James Robert Manners Joseph Alfred Hardcastle Henry Thoby Prinsep

Colchester Pub Lib Inst Hist Res

1857* (February)—The poll for a member... *Essex Standard* Supplement, 27 February 1857
Alphabetical by qualification. Address. Non-voters distinguished.

John Gurdon Rebow Taverner John Miller William Rawdon Havens

Brit Lib (News) Inst Hist Res

1857 (March)—The poll for members... *Essex Standard* Supplement, 3 April 1857
Alphabetical by qualification. Address. Non-voters distinguished.

Taverner John Miller John Gurdon Rebow William Rawdon Havens

Brit Lib (News) Inst Hist Res

1859—The poll for members... *Essex Standard* Supplement, 4 May 1859
Alphabetical by qualification. Address. Non-voters distinguished.

Taverner John Miller Philip Oxenden Papillon John Gurdon Rebow

Brit Lib (News) Inst Hist Res

1865—The poll for members... Colchester: J. B. Harvey, [1865]
Alphabetical by qualification and parish. Address. Non-voters distinguished.
John Gurdon Rebow   Taverner John Miller   Philip Oxenden Papillon
Essex Rec Off   Inst Hist Res

1865—The poll for members... *Essex Telegraph* Supplement 22 August 1865
Alphabetical by qualification and parish. Address. Non-voters distinguished.
John Gurdon Rebow   Taverner John Miller   Philip Oxenden Papillon
Colchester Pub Lib   Inst Hist Res

1865—Colchester election, 1865. The poll... [Colchester, 1865]
Alphabetical by qualification and parish. Address. Non-voters distinguished.
John Gurdon Rebow   Taverner John Miller   Philip Oxenden Papillon
Colchester Pub Lib   Inst Hist Res

1867*—Borough of Colchester. The poll... Colchester: *Essex & West Suffolk Gazette*, [1867]
Alphabetical by qualification and parish. Address. Non-voters distinguished.
Edward Kent Karslake   William Brewer
Colchester Pub Lib   Inst Hist Res

1868—Colchester election, 1868. The poll... Colchester: *Essex Standard*, [1868]
Alphabetical by qualification and parish. Address. Non-voters distinguished.
John Gurdon Rebow   William Brewer   Edward Kent Karslake   Alexander Learmonth
Colchester Pub Lib   Inst Hist Res

1870*—Colchester election, 1870. The poll... Colchester: *Essex Standard* Office, [1870]
Alphabetical by qualification, ward and parish. Address. Non-voters.
Alexander Learmonth   Sir Henry Knight Storks
Colchester Pub Lib   Inst Hist Res

[Also issued with *Essex and West Suffolk Gazette* Office imprint.]

HARWICH

1859—The poll for two burgesses... Harwich: J. Smith, [1859]
Alphabetical by parish. Non-voters, absent and dead distinguished.
Henry Jervis White Jervis   William Frederick Campbell   Richard Thomas Rowley
John Clarke Marshman
Yale Univ Lib   Inst Hist Res

MALDON

1807—The poll for members... Witham: P. Youngman, [1807]
Alphabetical. Occupation, place of residence and qualification. Rejected voters.
John Holden Strutt   Charles Callis Western   Benjamin Gaskell
Essex Rec Off   Inst Hist Res

1826—The poll for members... Maldon: P. H. Youngman, 1826
Alphabetical by (a) Maldon and district, (b) London and environs. Occupation and place of residence. Rejected voters distinguished. Index of places with number of voters.

George Mark Arthur Way Allanson Winn Thomas Barrett Lennard Quintin Dick

Essex Rec Off Inst Hist Res

1847—The poll for members... Maldon: P. H. Youngman, 1847
Alphabetical. Occupation and parish or place of residence. Occupiers distinguished. Non-voters, distinguishing dead.

David Waddington Thomas Barrett Lennard Quintin Dick

Essex Rec Off Inst Hist Res

1852—The poll for members... Maldon: P. H. Youngman, 1852
Alphabetical. Occupation and parish or place of residence. Occupiers distinguished. Non-voters, distinguishing dead.

Charles Du Cane Taverner John Miller Thomas Barrett Lennard Quintin Dick

Essex Rec Off Inst Hist Res

1859—The poll for members... Authorised edition. Maldon: P. H. Youngman, [1859]
Alphabetical by parish of residence. Occupiers distinguished. Non-voters included.

George Warren Montagu Peacocke Thomas Sutton Western A. W. H. Meyrick

Essex Rec Off Inst Hist Res

1865—The poll for members... Maldon: Bridge, [1865]
Alphabetical by parish of residence. Occupiers and ''radical admissions'' distinguished. Non-voters included.

George Warren Montagu Peacocke Ralph Anstruther Earle Thomas Sutton Western

Essex Rec Off Inst Hist Res

Untraced: 1761, 1841, 1854, 1857

GLOUCESTERSHIRE

1715—Gloucester. February the 9th, 1714. Alphabetically digested... London, 1714
Alphabetical by parish of residence, and by parish of freehold for out-voters. Place of freehold or place of residence.

Thomas Stephens Matthew Ducie Morton John Berkeley John Howe, Jr.

Guildhall Lib

1776*—The poll at the election... London, 1776
Alphabetical by hundred and parish. Place of residence, nature and occupier of freehold. Index.

William Bromley Chester George Cranfield Berkeley

Gloucester Pub Lib Guildhall Lib

1776*—(By authority) An accurate copy of the poll... Gloucester: R. Raikes, [1776]
Alphabetical by polling booth. Place of residence and place of freehold.

William Bromley Chester   George Cranfield Berkeley

Gloucester Pub Lib Inst Hist Res

1811*—Copied from the sheriff's books. The poll at the election... Gloucester: D. Walker, 1811
Alphabetical by hundred and parish. Place of residence, nature and occupier of freehold.

John Dutton   Sir Berkeley William Guise

Gloucester Pub Lib Guildhall Lib

EAST GLOUCESTERSHIRE

1832—The poll at the election... Gloucester: A. & D. M. Walker, 1833
Alphabetical by polling district and parish. Address, nature and place of qualification. Account of proceedings.

Sir Berkeley William Guise   Henry George Francis Moreton
Christopher William Codrington

Gloucester Pub Lib Inst Hist Res

1834*—The poll at the election... Gloucester: *Gloucestershire Chronicle*, [1834]
Alphabetical by polling district and parish. Address, nature and place of qualification.

Christopher William Codrington   Charles Hanbury Tracy Leigh

Gloucester Pub Lib Inst Hist Res

1854*—A correct list of the poll... arranged under the direction... of Mr. Richard Helps. Gloucester: Edmund Waring, [1854]
Alphabetical by polling district and parish. Address. Non-voters included. Account of proceedings.

Sir Michael Hicks Hicks Beach   Edward Holland

Gloucester Pub Lib Inst Hist Res

BRISTOL

1715—A true and exact list of the inhabitants... who poll'd for Philip Freke and Thomas Edwards... Bristol: W. Bonny, 1715
Alphabetical by parish. Occupation. Freeholders distinguished.

Thomas Edwards   Philip Freke   Sir William Davies Joseph Earle

College of Arms Inst Hist Res (Typescript)
Bristol Record Office (Photocopy of typescript)

1722—The list of the votes... Bristol: Joseph Penn, 1722
Alphabetical by parish. Occupation of freemen. Freeholders distinguished. Clergy and out-voters listed separately.

Joseph Earle Sir   Abraham Elton   William Hart

Bristol Pub Lib Brit Lib Inst Hist Res (Facsimile)

1734—A list of the freeholders and freemen... Bristol: Felix Farley, [1734]
Alphabetical by parish. Occupation of freemen. Freeholders distinguished. Clergy and out-voters listed separately.

Sir Abraham Elton   Thomas Coster   John Scrope

Bristol Pub Lib   Inst Hist Res

1734—An alphabetical list of the freeholders... London, 1734
Alphabetical by parish. Occupation. Separate list of out-voters with place of residence.

Sir Abraham Elton   Thomas Coster   John Scrope

Bristol Pub Lib   Inst Hist Res

1739*—The poll book. Being a list of the freeholders and freemen... Bristol: Felix Farley, [1739]
Alphabetical by qualification and parish. Corporation, clergy and out-voters listed separately. Parish of freeholders, occupation of freemen. Non-voters. Election literature.

Edward Southwell   Henry Combe

Bristol Pub Lib   Inst Hist Res

1754—The Bristol poll book... Bristol: E. Farley, [1754]
Alphabetical by parish. Corporation, clergy and out-voters listed separately. Occupation and place of freehold. Freeholders distinguished. Non-voters.

Robert Nugent   Richard Beckford   Sir John Philipps

Bristol Pub Lib   Inst Hist Res

1754—A genuine list of the freeholders and freemen... Bristol: T. Cadell & E. Ward, 1755
Alphabetical by parish. Corporation, clergy and out-voters listed separately. Occupation, and place of residence of out-voters. Freeholders distinguished.

Robert Nugent   Richard Beckford   Sir John Philipps

Bristol Pub Lib   Guildhall Lib

1774—The Bristol poll book... n.p., [1774]
Alphabetical by parish. Corporation, clergy and out-voters by county and parish listed separately. Occupation and address of London voters. Freeholders distinguished. Non-voting corporation and clergy.

Henry Cruger   Edmund Burke   Matthew Brickdale   Viscount Clare

Bristol Pub Lib   Guildhall Lib

1774—The Bristol poll book... Bristol: W. Pine, [1774]
Alphabetical by parish. Corporation, clergy and out-voters listed separately. Occupation, and place of residence of out-voters. Freeholders distinguished. Account of proceedings. Proceedings on the election petition.

Henry Cruger   Edmund Burke   Matthew Brickdale   Viscount Clare

Bristol Pub Lib   Inst Hist Res

1781*—The Bristol poll book... n.p., [1781]
Alphabetical by parish. Corporation, clergy, and out-voters by county and parish listed separately. Occupation and place of freehold. Freeholders distinguished. Non-voting corporation and clergy. Election petition.

George Daubeney   Henry Cruger

Bristol Pub Lib   Inst Hist Res

1784—The Bristol poll book... Bristol: William Pine, [1784]
Alphabetical by parish. Corporation, and out-voters by county and parish listed separately. Occupation and place of freehold. Freeholders distinguished. Non-voting corporation.

Matthew Brickdale   Henry Cruger   George Daubeney   Samuel Peach

Bristol Pub Lib   Inst Hist Res

1812—The Bristol poll book... Bristol: J. Mills, 1818
Alphabetical by parish. Occupation, place of residence and place of freehold. Freeholders distinguished. Out-voters by county and by parish for Gloucestershire and Somerset.

Richard Hart Davis   Edward Protheroe   Sir Samuel Romilly   Henry Hunt

Bristol Pub Lib   Inst Hist Res

1830—The Bristol poll book... Bristol: Philip Rose, 1830
Alphabetical by parish. Occupation, address and qualification. Out-voters by county. Account of proceedings and candidates' addresses.

Richard Hart Davis   James Evan Baillie   Edward Protheroe   James Acland

Bristol Pub Lib   Inst Hist Res

1832—The poll book of the electors... Bristol: T. J. Manchee, 1833
Alphabetical by parish and qualification. Occupation and address. Account of proceedings.

Sir Richard Rawlinson Vyvyan   James Evan Baillie   Edward Protheroe   John Williams

Bristol Pub Lib   Inst Hist Res

1832—The Bristol poll book... Bristol: J. Wansbrough, 1833
Alphabetical by parish and by qualification within each letter. Occupation and address. Out-voters by county. Report of speeches.

Sir Richard Rawlinson Vyvyan   James Evan Baillie   Edward Protheroe   John Williams

Bristol Pub Lib   Inst Hist Res

1835—The Bristol poll book... Bristol: J. Wansbrough, 1835
Alphabetical by parish. Occupation and address. Account of proceedings.

Sir Richard Rawlinson Vyvyan   Philip John Miles   James Evan Baillie
Sir John Cam Hobhouse

Bristol Pub Lib   Guildhall Lib

1837—The Bristol poll book... Bristol: John Wansbrough, 1837
Alphabetical by parish. Occupation and address.

Philip William Skinner Miles   Francis Henry Fitzhardinge Berkeley   William Fripp

Bristol Pub Lib   Inst Hist Res

1837—[No title page. Privately printed for Mr. Berkeley's committee in connection with the election petition] n.p., [1837]
Alphabetical by parish and street. Qualification. Multiple voters distinguished. Out-voters by county and parish.

Philip William Skinner Miles Francis Henry Fitzhardinge Berkeley William Fripp

Bristol Pub Lib Inst Hist Res

1841—The Bristol poll book... Bristol: H. & A. Hill, 1841
Alphabetical by parish. Occupation, address and qualification. Those voting twice or personated distinguished.

Philip William Skinner Miles Francis Henry Fitzhardinge Berkeley William Fripp

Bristol Pub Lib Inst Hist Res

1847—The Bristol poll book... Bristol: J. W. Newcombe, 1848
Alphabetical by parish and qualification. Address. Those voting twice or personated distinguished. Account of proceedings.

Francis Henry Fitzhardinge Berkeley Philip William Skinner Miles William Fripp
Apsley Pellatt

Bristol Pub Lib Inst Hist Res

1852—The Bristol poll book... Bristol: Henry & Alfred Hill, 1853
Alphabetical by parish. Occupation, address and qualification. Out-voters by county.

Francis Henry Fitzhardinge Berkeley William Henry Gore Langton
Forster Alleyne McGeachy

Bristol Pub Lib Inst Hist Res

CHELTENHAM

1841—Cheltenham election, June 30th, 1841. A list of the electors... Cheltenham: J. J. Hadley, [1841]
Alphabetical by candidate and occupation. Address. Berkeley voters who signed the request to Gardner to stand.

Craven Fitzhardinge Berkeley James Agg Gardner Thomas Perronet Thompson

Gloucester Pub Lib Inst Hist Res

1847—The Cheltenham poll book: being an alphabetical list... Cheltenham: J. J. Hadley, 1847
Alphabetical by district and candidate. Occupation and address.

Sir Willoughby Jones Craven Fitzhardinge Berkeley Carrington Smith

Gloucester Pub Lib Inst Hist Res

1848*—Cheltenham election, 1848. The poll book... Cheltenham: Harper, 1848
Alphabetical. Occupation and address. Non-voters included.

Craven Fitzhardinge Berkeley James Agg Gardner

Gloucester Pub Lib Inst Hist Res

1852—Cheltenham election, July 9th, 1852. (Corrected and revised by the poll books). The poll book... Cheltenham: W. Paine, [1852]
Alphabetical by candidate. Occupation and address. Non-voters.

Craven Fitzhardinge Berkeley   Sir Willoughby Jones

Gloucester Pub Lib   Inst Hist Res

1852—Cheltenham election, 1852. The poll book, or alphabetical list of the tradesmen... Cheltenham: C. Neale, [1852]
Alphabetical by candidate and occupation. Address. Berkeley voters who signed the requisition to Jones distinguished. Non-voters who signed the requisition with reason in a few cases.

Craven Fitzhardinge Berkeley   Sir Willoughby Jones

Gloucester Pub Lib   Inst Hist Res

1856*—Cheltenham election, 1856. The poll book... Cheltenham: John Lowe, [1856]
Alphabetical. Address.

Francis William Fitzhardinge Berkeley   E. G. Hallewell

Gloucester Pub Lib   Inst Hist Res

1859—Cheltenham election, 1859. The correct poll book... revised by the Cheltenham Reform Club... Cheltenham: Alfred Harper, [1859],
Alphabetical by ward. Address. Dead and non-voters.

Francis William Fitzhardinge Berkeley   Charles Schreiber

Gloucester Pub Lib   Inst Hist Res

[Two editions known]

1865—Cheltenham election, 1865. The poll book... Cheltenham: H. Davies, [1865]
Alphabetical by ward. Address. Non-voters.

Charles Schreiber   Francis William Fitzhardinge Berkeley

Gloucester Pub Lib   Inst Hist Res

1865—The poll book of the Cheltenham election... Cheltenham: Alfred Harper, [1865]
Alphabetical by ward. Address. Non-voters. Includes dead and paired.

Charles Schreiber   Francis William Fitzhardinge Berkeley

Gloucester Pub Lib   Inst Hist Res

1868—Cheltenham election, 1868. The poll book... Cheltenham: Hailing & Poole, [1868]
Alphabetical by ward. Address. Non-voters. Lodgers.

Henry Bernhard Samuelson   James Tynte Agg-Gardner

Gloucester Pub Lib   Inst Hist Res

CIRENCESTER

1768—The poll of the borough... Cirencester: S. Rudder, [1768]
Alphabetical. Occupation. Rejected voters, some with reason or place of residence, and with voting intentions.

Estcourt Cresswell   James Whitshed   Samuel Blackwell

Gloucester Pub Lib   Inst Hist Res

1790—The book of the poll... Cirencester: S. Rudder, [1790]
Alphabetical. Occupation and ward.

Lord Apsley   Richard Masters   Robert Preston

Gloucester Pub Lib   Inst Hist Res

1802—The book of the poll... Cirencester: J. Turner, [1802]
Alphabetical. Occupation and ward of residence. Rejected and non-voters.

Michael Hicks Beach   Sir Robert Preston   Thomas Bayley Howell

Cirencester Pub Lib   Gloucester Pub Lib   Guildhall Lib

1802—The book of the poll... Cirencester: T. Stevens, [1802]
Alphabetical. Occupation.

Michael Hicks Beach   Sir Robert Preston   Thomas Bayley Howell

Cirencester Pub Lib   Gloucester Pub Lib   Inst Hist Res

1812—The book of the poll... Cirencester: P. Watkins, 1812
Alphabetical. Occupation and ward. Non-voters and rejected voters with reasons.

Lord Apsley   Michael Hicks Beach   Joseph Cripps

Cirencester Pub Lib   Gloucester Pub Lib   Inst Hist Res

1848*—The poll book. Cirencester borough election... Cirencester: Henry Smith, [1848]
Alphabetical by qualification. Occupation and address. Paired, dead, disqualified and non-voters distinguished.

Joseph Randolph Mullings   Charles Ponsonby

Cirencester Pub Lib   Inst Hist Res

1852—The poll book of the election... Cirencester: H. G. Keyworth, 1852
Alphabetical. Address. Non-voters included, dead distinguished.

Joseph Randolph Mullings   Ashley George John Ponsonby   Viscount Villiers

Cirencester Pub Lib   Inst Hist Res

1857—The poll book. Cirencester borough election, 1857. Cirencester: Charles H. Savory, [1857]
Alphabetical by qualification. Address. Non-voters included.

Allen Alexander Bathurst   Joseph Randolph Mullings   Ashley George John Ponsonby

Cirencester Pub Lib

1857—A classified poll book... Cirencester: H. G. Keyworth, [1857]
Alphabetical by candidate. Address, qualification and 1852 voting. Dead and non-voters.

Allen Alexander Bathurst   Joseph Randolph Mullings   Ashley George John Ponsonby

Cirencester Pub Lib   Gloucester Pub Lib   Inst Hist Res

1859—A sheet of the poll... Cirencester: C. H. Savory, [1859] [Broadsheet]
Alphabetical by qualification. Address. Non-voters included.

Allen Alexander Bathurst Ashley George John Ponsonby Bret Spencer Follett

Cirencester Pub Lib

[Two editions known]

1859—The classified poll book... Cirencester: H. G. Keyworth, [1859]
Alphabetical by candidate. Address, qualification and 1852 and 1857 voting. Dead and non-voters.

Allen Alexander Bathurst Ashley George John Ponsonby Bret Spencer Follett

Cirencester Pub Lib Gloucester Pub Lib Inst Hist Res

1865—Cirencter election. The poll... *Wilts and Gloucestershire Standard* Supplement, 15 July 1865
Alphabetical by qualification. Non-voters included. Account of proceedings.

Allen Alexander Bathurst Ralph Dutton Julian Goldsmid

Cirencester Pub Lib Inst Hist Res

1865—Cirencester election. The poll book... Cirencester: H. G. Keyworth, [1865]
Alphabetical by qualification. Address. Non-voters included.

Allen Alexander Bathurst Ralph Dutton Julian Goldsmid

Cirencester Pub Lib Gloucester Pub Lib Inst Hist Res

1865—The poll book of the Cirencester borough election... Cirencester: C. H. Savory, [1865]
Alphabetical by qualification. Address. Non-voters included.

Allen Alexander Bathurst Ralph Dutton Julian Goldsmid

Cirencester Pub Lib Gloucester Pub Lib Inst Hist Res

1868—[Cirencester election. The poll . . .] *Wilts and Gloucestershire Standard* Supplement, 21 November 1868
Alphabetical by candidate and qualification. Address. Non-voters. Account of proceedings.

Allen Alexander Bathurst Frederick Andrew Inderwick

Cirencester Pub Lib Inst Hist Res

[The issue of 17 November has an incomplete list of non-voters.]

1868—The poll book of the election... Cirencester: C. H. Savory, [1868]
Alphabetical by qualification. Address. Non-voters included.

Allen Alexander Bathurst Frederick Andrew Inderwick

Cirencester Pub Lib Gloucester Pub Lib Inst Hist Res

1868—*Cotswold Almanack 1869*, pp. 24-32
Alphabetical by candidate and qualification. Address. Non-voters.

Allen Alexander Bathurst Frederick Andrew Inderwick

Gloucester Pub Lib Inst Hist Res

GLOUCESTER

1741—An alphabet of the poll... London, 1741
Alphabetical. Occupation and place of residence. New freemen and voters promised to Bathurst and Selwyn distinguished. Rejected and objected voters with reasons.

John Selwyn   Benjamin Bathurst   Benjamin Hyett

Gloucester Pub Lib   Inst Hist Res

1816*—Gloucester city election, 1816. List of the poll... Gloucester: Walker & Sons, [1816]
Alphabetical. Occupation and place of residence. Rejected and postponed voters, distinguishing paupers.

Edward Webb   Robert Bransby Cooper

Gloucester Pub Lib   Inst Hist Res

1816*—Gloucester election. A list of the freemen... Gloucester: J. Roberts, 1816
Alphabetical by poll order within each letter. Occupation and place of residence.

Edward Webb   Robert Bransby Cooper

Gloucester Pub Lib   Inst Hist Res

1818—Gloucester city election, 1818. Local arrangement of the poll... Gloucester: J. Roberts, 1826
Alphabetical by residents and out-voters by county and place of residence. Occupation and place of residence, address for Londoners. Rejected voters, distinguishing paupers.

Edward Webb   Robert Bransby Cooper   Frederick Berkeley

Gloucester Pub Lib   Guildhall Lib

1818—Gloucester city election, 1818. Alphabetical list of the poll... Gloucester: J. Roberts, [1818]
Alphabetical. Occupation and place of residence. Rejected and postponed voters, distinguishing paupers.

Edward Webb   Robert Bransby Cooper   Frederick Berkeley

Gloucester Pub Lib   Inst Hist Res

1818—Gloucester city election, 1818. Alphabetical list of the poll... Gloucester: Walker & Sons, [1818]
Alphabetical. Occupation and place of residence. Rejected and postponed voters, distinguishing paupers.

Edward Webb   Robert Bransby Cooper   Frederick Berkeley

Gloucester Pub Lib   Inst Hist Res

[Same printing as preceding entry
with different title page.]

1830—Gloucester city election, 1830. List of the poll... Gloucester: D. Walker, [1830]
Alphabetical by residents and out-voters by county and parish. Occupation and place of residence, address for Londoners.

Edward Webb John Phillpotts Robert Bransby Cooper

Gloucester Pub Lib Guildhall Lib

1830— Alphabetical list of the poll... Gloucester: Joseph Roberts, [1830]
Occupation and place of residence.

Edward Webb John Phillpotts Robert Bransby Cooper

Bristol & Glos Archaeol Soc Inst Hist Res

1832— Alphabetical list of the poll... Gloucester: A. & D. M. Walker, 1833
Alphabetical by residents and out-voters. Address, nature and parish of qualification for residents, place of residence for out-voters. Speeches.

Frederic Berkeley John Phillpotts Henry Thomas Hope

Gloucester Pub Lib Inst Hist Res

1833*— Alphabetical list of the poll... Gloucester: Jew & Wingate, 1833
Alphabetical by residents and out-voters. Address or place of residence, nature and parish of qualification.

Henry Thomas Hope Frederic Berkeley

Gloucester Pub Lib Inst Hist Res

1835—A list of the poll... Gloucester: *Gloucestershire Chronicle*, 1835
Alphabetical by qualification and parish. Address. Non-voters.

Maurice Frederick Fitzhardinge Berkeley Henry Thomas Hope John Phillpotts William Cother

Gloucester Pub Lib Inst Hist Res

1837—A list of the poll... Gloucester: Lewis Bryant, 1837
Alphabetical. Address and qualification. Non-voters distinguished.

Henry Thomas Hope Maurice Frederick Fitzhardinge Berkeley John Phillpotts

Gloucester Pub Lib Inst Hist Res

1838*—A list of the poll... Gloucester: Lewis Bryant, 1838
Alphabetical. Address and qualification. Non-voters distinguished.

Henry Thomas Hope Edward Webb

Gloucester Pub Lib Inst Hist Res

1841—A list of the poll... Gloucester: J. E. Lea, 1841
Alphabetical. Address and qualification. Non-voters distinguished.

John Phillpotts Maurice Frederick Fitzhardinge Berkeley Henry Thomas Hope Viscount Loftus

Gloucester Pub Lib Inst Hist Res

1852—A list of the poll... Gloucester: William Henley, [1852]
Alphabetical by qualification and parish. Address. Non-voters. Price's speech at nomination.

William Philip Price Maurice Frederick Fitzhardinge Berkeley Henry Thomas Hope

Gloucester Pub Lib Inst Hist Res

[Two editions known]

1853*—A list of the poll... Gloucester: W. Henley, [1853]
Alphabetical by qualification and parish. Address. Non-voters.

Maurice Frederick Fitzhardinge Berkeley Henry Thomas Hope

Gloucester Pub Lib Inst Hist Res

1857—A list of the poll... Gloucester: W. Henley, [1857]
Alphabetical. Occupation and address. Dead and non-voters. Account of proceedings.

Sir Robert Walter Carden William Philip Price Maurice Frederick Fitzhardinge Berkeley

Gloucester Pub Lib Inst Hist Res

1859—A list of the poll... Gloucester: W. Henley, [1859]
Alphabetical by qualification and parish. Occupation and address. Dead and non-voters. Account of proceedings.

William Philip Price Charles James Monk Sir Robert Walter Carden

Gloucester Pub Lib Inst Hist Res

1862*—A list of the poll... Gloucester: William Henley, [1862]
Alphabetical by qualification and parish. Occupation and address. Dead and non-voters. Account of proceedings.

Charles Paget Fitzhardinge Berkeley John Joseph Powell Richard Potter

Gloucester Pub Lib Inst Hist Res

1865—A list of the poll at the contested election... Gloucester: Liberal Registration Agents, [1865]
Alphabetical by qualification and parish. Occupation and address. Dead and non-voters. Speeches.

William Philip Price Charles James Monk Adam S. Kennard

Gloucester Pub Lib Inst Hist Res

1868—City of Gloucester. Copy of the register of voters with a list of the poll... *Gloucester Mercury,* 20 March-10 April 1869
Alphabetical by qualification and parish. Occupation and address. Non-voters included.

William Philip Price Charles James Monk Nassau W. Lees Edward J. Brennan

Gloucester Pub Lib Inst Hist Res

STROUD

1832—The poll book at the first election... Stroud: W. Harmer, 1833
Alphabetical by parish. Occupation. Non-voters included.

William Henry Hyett David Ricardo George Poulett Scrope

Gloucester Pub Lib Inst Hist Res

1841—The poll at the election... Stroud: R. Bucknall, 1841
Alphabetical by parish. Address. Non-voters included.

William Henry Stanton George Poulett Scrope Sir William Lascelles Wraxall

Gloucester Pub Lib Inst Hist Res

1841—Stroud election, 1841. A list of the poll... Stroud: J. P. Brisley, [1841]
Alphabetical by parish. Nature and situation of qualification. Non-voters included.

William Henry Stanton George Poulett Scrope Sir William Lascelles Wraxall

Gloucester Pub Lib Inst Hist Res

1852—The poll at the election... Stroud: F. W. Harmer, [1852]
Alphabetical by parish. Address. Non-voters included.

George Poulett Scrope Lord Moreton Samuel Baker John Norton

Gloucester Pub Lib Inst Hist Res

1867*—List of the poll... *Stroud Journal,* 31 August 1867
Alphabetical by candidate and parish. Address. Non-voters.

Henry Seife Page Winterbotham John Edward Dorington

Brit Lib (News) Inst Hist Res

1868—Stroud election, 1868. The poll book... Stroud: *Stroud News,* [1868]
Alphabetical by polling district and parish. Address. Non-voters included.

Sebastian Stewart Dickinson Henry Seife Page Winterbotham John Edward Dorington

Gloucester Pub Lib Inst Hist Res

TEWKESBURY

1831—Tewkesbury election, 1831. A list of the poll... Tewkesbury: James Bennett, [1831]
Alphabetical by residents, and out-voters by county. Occupation, place of residence of out-voters, and qualification. Rejected and suspended voters with voting intentions. Non-voters. Candidates' addresses.

John Edmund Dowdeswell John Martin Charles Hanbury Tracy

Gloucester Pub Lib Guildhall Lib

1832—An alphabetical list of the poll... Tewkesbury: James Bennett, 1832
Place of residence of out-voters and qualification. Non-voters distinguished.

Charles Hanbury Tracy John Martin William Dowdeswell

Gloucester Pub Lib Guildhall Lib

1835—An alphabetical list of the poll... Tewkesbury: James Bennett, 1835
Place of residence of out-voters and qualification. Non-voters distinguished.

Charles Hanbury Tracy — William Dowdeswell — John Martin

Gloucester Pub Lib — Guildhall Lib

1837—An alphabetical list of the poll... Tewkesbury: I. Jenner, 1837
Place of residence. Non-voters.

William Dowdeswell — John Martin — Joseph Peel

Gloucester Pub Lib — Guildhall Lib

1841—A list of the poll... Tewkesbury: Joseph Okell, 1841
Alphabetical. Occupation and place of residence of out-voters. Non-voters distinguished. Account of proceedings.

William Dowdeswell — John Martin — John Easthope

Gloucester Pub Lib — Guildhall Lib

1852—A list of the poll... Tewkesbury: John Lawler, 1852
Alphabetical. Place of residence of out-voters and qualification. Non-voters distinguished. Account of proceedings.

Humphrey Brown — John Martin — Edward William Cox

Brit Lib

HAMPSHIRE

1705—A true copy of the poll... London, 1705
By parish.

Thomas Jervoise — Richard Chaundler — Thomas Lewis

Southampton Univ Lib — Inst Hist Res

1710—The poll at the election... London: Geo. James, 1714
By parish.

George Pitt — Sir Simeon Stuart — Thomas Jervoise — Marquess of Winchester

Bodl — Inst Hist Res

1713—A true copy of the poll... London: Thomas Lewis, 1714
By division, hundred and parish. Place of residence. Oathtakers distinguished.

Thomas Lewis — Sir Anthony Sturt — Marquess of Winchester — John Wallop

Hants Rec Off — Inst Hist Res

1734—An exact list of the names... London, 1736
By division and parish. Place of residence.

Edward Lisle — Lord Harry Powlett — Sir Simeon Stewart — Anthony Chute

Winchester Pub Lib — Guildhall Lib

1779*—County of Southampton. A true copy of the poll book... London, 1780
By division. Place of residence and freehold.

Jervoise Clarke Jervoise — Sir Richard Worsley

Hants Rec Off — Guildhall Lib

1790—The poll for the election... Romsey: J. S. Hollis, [1790]
By division and parish. Place of residence.

Sir William Heathcote William Chute Lord John Russell Jervoise Clarke Jervoise

Hants Rec Off Inst Hist Res

1806—The poll for the election... Romsey & Winchester: J. S. Hollis & W. Jacob, [1806]
Alphabetical by division and parish. Place of residence.

Thomas Thistlethwayte William Herbert William Chute
Sir Henry Paulett St. John Mildmay

Hants Rec Off Inst Hist Res

1807—The poll for the election... Winchester: W. Jacob, [1807]
Alphabetical by division and parish. Place of residence.

Sir Henry Paulett St. John Mildmay William Chute William Herbert

Southampton Univ Lib Inst Hist Res

ANDOVER

1859—Classified list of votes. *Andover Advertiser,* 6 May 1859
Alphabetical by candidate. Non-voters.

William Cubitt Dudley Francis Fortescue R. W. Johnson

Brit Lib (News) Inst Hist Res

1863*—[List of the electors]. *Andover Advertiser,* 27 November 1863
Alphabetical by candidate. Address. Non-voters.

William Henry Humphery John Hawkshaw

Brit Lib (News) Inst Hist Res

CHRISTCHURCH

1727—A poll taken... *The case of Mr. Richard Holoway* . . . , [1727], pp. [24-25]
Rejected voters distinguished.

Edward Hooper Jacob Bancks Charles Wither Joseph Hinxman

Southampton Univ Lib Inst Hist Res

LYMINGTON

1859—A correct alphabetical list of the voters... Lymington: Edward King, 1859
Alphabetical by parish. Non-voters distinguished.

William Alexander Mackinnon Sir John Rivett-Carnac John Bramley-Moore

Yale Univ Lib Inst Hist Res

PORTSMOUTH

1835—List of persons who voted... *Portsmouth, Portsea, Gosport & Chichester Herald,* 21 March and 28 March, 1835
Alphabetical by district. Address.

John Bonham Carter Francis Thornhill Baring Sir Charles Rowley Charles Napier

Brit Lib (News) Inst Hist Res

SOUTHAMPTON

1774—A true copy of the poll... Southampton: T. Baker, 1774
Poll order. Occupation.

Hans Stanley John Fleming Lord Charles Montagu

Southampton Univ Lib Inst Hist Res

1790—Copy of the poll... Southampton: A. Cunningham, [1790]
Poll order. Occupation. Burgesses distinguished.

James Amyatt Henry Martin George Hay Dawkins

Southampton Univ Lib Inst Hist Res

1790—An alphabetical list of the voters... Southampton: T. Baker, [1790]
By qualification. Occupation.

James Amyatt Henry Martin George Hay Dawkins

Southampton Pub Lib Inst Hist Res

1790—Independence: or a correct list of the independent commercial gentlemen tradesmen who voted for Mr. Dawkins... Copied from the printed poll book. n.p., [1790]
Alphabetical. Occupation. Members of the Select Committee of Independence distinguished. Plumpers for Amyatt. Omits burgesses.

James Amyatt Henry Martin George Hay Dawkins

Southampton Univ Lib Inst Hist Res

1794*—An alphabetical list of the voters... Southampton: T. Skelton, [1794]
Occupation.

George Henry Rose Bryan Edwards

Southampton Univ Lib Inst Hist Res

1794*—A copy of the poll... Baker, [1794]
Poll order. Occupation. Burgesses distinguished.

George Henry Rose Bryan Edwards

Southampton Univ Lib Inst Hist Res

1802—An alphabetical list of the voters... Southampton: T. Skelton, [1802]
Occupation.

George Henry Rose James Amyatt William Scott

Southampton Univ Lib Inst Hist Res

1806—An alphabetical list of the voters... Southampton: T. Skelton, [1806]
Occupation.

Arthur Atherley, Jr. George Henry Rose Josias Jackson

Southampton Pub Lib Inst Hist Res

1806—Copy of the poll... Baker & Fletcher, [1806]
Poll order. Occupation.

Arthur Atherley, Jr. George Henry Rose Josias Jackson

Southampton Univ Lib Inst Hist Res

1812—An alphabetical list of the voters... Southampton: T. Skelton, [1812]
Occupation.

Arthur Atherley, Jr. George Henry Rose William Chamberlayne

Southampton Univ Lib Inst Hist Res

1812—Copy of the poll... T. Baker, for I. Fletcher, [1812]
Poll order. Occupation.

Arthur Atherley, Jr. George Henry Rose William Chamberlayne

Southampton Univ Lib Inst Hist Res

1818—Alphabetical list of the voters... Southampton: E. Skelton, [1818]
Occupation. Burgesses distinguished.

William Chamberlayne Sir William Champion De Crespigny Lord Ashtown

Southampton Univ Lib Inst Hist Res

1818—Copy of the poll... T. Baker, [1818]
Poll order. Occupation.

William Chamberlayne Sir William Champion De Crespigny Lord Ashtown

Southampton Univ Lib Inst Hist Res

1820—Alphabetical list of the voters... Southampton: P. Barnfield, [1820]
Occupation. Honorary burgesses distinguished.

Sir William Champion De Crespigny William Chamberlayne Abel Rous Dottin

Southampton Pub Lib Inst Hist Res

1820—Alphabetical list of the voters... Southampton: T. Baker, for I. Fletcher, [1820]
Occupation.

Sir William Champion De Crespigny William Chamberlayne Abel Rous Dottin

Southampton Univ Lib Inst Hist Res

1831—Alphabetical list of the voters... Southampton: Thomas King, [1831]
Occupation. Burgesses distinguished.

Arthur Atherley John Story Penleaze James Barlow Hoy

Southampton Univ Lib Inst Hist Res

1831—List of the voters... Southampton: John Fletcher, [1831]
Poll order. Occupation. Burgesses distinguished.

Arthur Atherley John Story Penleaze James Barlow Hoy

Southampton Univ Lib Inst Hist Res

1832—Alphabetical list of the voters... Southampton: Fletcher & Sons, 1833
By candidate. Address.

Arthur Atherley James Barlow Hoy John Story Penleaze James Mackillop

Southampton Univ Lib Inst Hist Res

1835—Lists of the voters who polled... Southampton: J. Coupland, [1835]
Alphabetical by candidate. Occupation and address.

James Barlow Hoy Abel Rous Dottin John Easthope Peregrine Bingham

Southampton Univ Lib Inst Hist Res

1837—Alphabetical list of the voters... Southampton: J. Coupland, [1837]
By candidate. Occupation and address.

Abel Rous Dottin Lord Duncan Charles Cecil Martyn Lord Henry Paget

Southampton Univ Lib Inst Hist Res

1841—Alphabetical lists of the voters... Southampton: H. Couzens, 1841
By candidate. Occupation and address.

Lord Bruce Charles Cecil Martyn Edward John Hutchins Charles Edward Mangles

Southampton Pub Lib Inst Hist Res

1841—1841. List of the voters who polled... Southampton: Best & Snowden, [1841]
Alphabetical. Occupation and address.

Lord Bruce Charles Cecil Martyn Edward John Hutchins Charles Edward Mangles

Southampton Univ Lib Inst Hist Res

1842*—1842. List of the voters who polled... Southampton: Best & Snowden, [1842]
Alphabetical. Occupation and address.

Humphrey St. John Mildmay George William Hope Lord Nugent George Thompson

Southampton Univ Lib Inst Hist Res

1852—1852. List of the voters... Southampton: R. B. King, [1852]
Alphabetical. Occupation and address.

Brodie McGhie Willcox Sir Alexander James Edmund Cockburn
Alexander Baillie Cochrane Augustus Arthur Vansittart

Southampton Pub Lib Inst Hist Res

1852—1852. List of the voters... Southampton: James R. Canaway, [1852]
Alphabetical. Occupation and address.

Brodie McGhie Willcox Sir Alexander James Edmund Cockburn
Alexander Baillie Cochrane Augustus Arthur Vansittart

Southampton Pub Lib Inst Hist Res

1857* (February)—Voters who polled at the election... *Hampshire Advertiser* Supplement, 21 February 1857
By polling booth. Address.
Thomas Matthias Weguelin   Sir Edward Butler   Richard Andrews
Brit Lib (News)   Inst Hist Res

1865—1865. List of the voters who polled... Southampton: R. B. King, [1865]
Alphabetical. Address.
Russell Gurney George Moffatt William Anderson Rose T. M. Mackay Digby Seymour
Guildhall Lib

WINCHESTER

1835—A list of the voters who polled... Winchester: Jacob Jacob, [1835]
Alphabetical by qualification and parish. Occupation. Non-voters included.
James Buller East   William Bingham Baring   Paulet St. John Mildmay
Winchester Pub Lib   Inst Hist Res

1835—An alphabetical list of persons who voted... Winchester: Jacob & Johnson, [1835]
Address and parish. Freemen distinguished.
James Buller East   William Bingham Baring   Paulet St. John Mildmay
Winchester Pub Lib   Inst Hist Res

1837—[Title page missing. Begins:] List of voters... Winchester: Jacob Jacob, [1837]
Alphabetical by qualification and parish. Non-voters included.
James Buller East   Paulet St. John Mildmay   Bickham Escott
Winchester Pub Lib   Inst Hist Res

1837—An alphabetical list of persons who voted... Winchester: N. Warren, [1837]
Address. Freemen distinguished. Non-voters.
James Buller East   Paulet St. John Mildmay   Bickham Escott
Winchester Pub Lib   Inst Hist Res

1841—An alphabetical list of persons who voted... Winchester: D. E. Gilmour, [1841]
Occupation and address. Freemen distinguished. Non-voters, distinguishing those disqualified by removal or government appointment.
James Buller East   Bickham Escott   Richard Budden Crowder   Francis Pigott
Hants Rec Off   Inst Hist Res

1847—An alphabetical list of persons who voted... Winchester: W. Tanner, [1847]
Address. Freemen distinguished. Non-voters.
John Bonham Carter   Sir James Buller East   Bickham Escott
Winchester Pub Lib   Inst Hist Res

1852—An alphabetical list of persons who voted... Winchester: W. Tanner, [1852]
Address. Non-voters.
John Bonham Carter   Sir James Buller East   William Whitear Bulphett
Winchester Pub Lib   Inst Hist Res

1852—Winchester election. MDCCCLII. The list of persons who voted... Winchester: N. Warren, [1852]
Alphabetical. Address. Freemen and non-voters distinguished.
John Bonham Carter Sir James Buller East William Whitear Bulphett
Winchester Pub Lib Inst Hist Res

1857—Winchester election, 1857. The list of persons who voted... Winchester: N. Warren, [1857]
Alphabetical. Address. Freemen and non-voters distinguished.
John Bonham Carter Sir James Buller East Wyndham Spencer Portal
Winchester Pub Lib Inst Hist Res

1859—Winchester election, 1859. The list of persons who voted... Winchester: W. Tanner, [1859]
Alphabetical. Address. Freemen distinguished. Non-voters.
Sir James Buller East John Bonham Carter Thomas Willis Fleming George Shaw Lefevre
Winchester Pub Lib Inst Hist Res

1859—Winchester election, 1859. The list of persons who voted... Winchester: Warren, [1859]
Alphabetical. Address. Freemen and non-voters distinguished.
Sir James Buller East John Bonham Carter Thomas Willis Fleming George Shaw Lefevre
Winchester Pub Lib Inst Hist Res

1865—Winchester election, 1865. The list of persons who voted... Winchester: Warren, [1865]
Alphabetical. Address. Freemen and non-voters distinguished.
John Bonham Carter William Barrow Simonds Thomas Willis Fleming
Winchester Pub Lib Inst Hist Res

1868—Winchester election, 1868. The list of voters... Winchester: Warren & Son, [1868]
Alphabetical. Address. Tendered votes distinguished. Non-voters.
William Barrow Simonds John Bonham Carter Arthur Jervoise Scott
Winchester Pub Lib Inst Hist Res

1868—Winchester election, 1868. The list of voters... Winchester: J. Pamplin, [1868]
Alphabetical. Address. Tendered votes distinguished. Non-voters.
William Barrow Simonds John Bonham Carter Arthur Jervoise Scott
Hants Rec Off Inst Hist Res

[Same printing as preceding entry
with different imprint.]

HEREFORDSHIRE

1722—A copy of the poll... Hereford: W. Parks, [1722]
By parish. Place of residence.

Velters Cornewall   Sir Edward Goodere   Sir Hungerford Hoskins

Hereford Pub Lib   Guildhall Lib

1754—A copy of the poll... Gloucester: 1754
By hundred. Place of residence and of freehold.

Velters Cornewall   Lord Harley   Robert Price

Hereford Pub Lib   Inst Hist Res

1774—An alphabetical list of the poll... Hereford: C. Pugh, 1774
By hundred. Place of residence and of freehold.

Thomas Foley   Sir George Cornewall   Thomas Harley

Hereford Pub Lib   Guildhall Lib

1796—An alphabetical list of the poll... Hereford: D. Walker, 1796
By hundred. Place of residence and place and occupier of freehold.

Thomas Harley   Sir George Cornewall   Robert Biddulph

Hereford Pub Lib   Guildhall Lib

1802—An alphabetical list of the poll... Hereford: W. H. Parker, 1802
By hundred. Place of residence and place and occupier of freehold.

John Geers Cotterell   Sir George Cornewall   Robert Myddleton Biddulph

Hereford Pub Lib   Inst Hist Res

1818—Published by authority of the High Sheriff. A list of the poll... Hereford: Watking & Wright, 1818
Alphabetical by hundred. Place of residence and place and occupier of freehold. Day of voting.

Sir John Geers Cotterell   Robert Price   Col. Cornewall

Hereford Pub Lib   Inst Hist Res

1835—Published by authority of the High Sheriff. A list of the freeholders and electors... Hereford: John Parker & Charles Anthony, 1835
Alphabetical by polling district. Place of residence, place and nature of qualification.

Kedgwin Hoskins   Edward Thomas Foley   Sir Robert Price   Edward Poole

Hereford Pub Lib   Inst Hist Res

1852—A copy of the poll... Hereford:
William Phillips, 1852
Alphabetical by polling district and parish. Place of residence.

George Cornewall Lewis   Thomas William Booker   James King King
Charles Spencer Bateman Hanbury

Herefod Pub Lib   Inst Hist Res

1857—A copy of the poll... Hereford: John Parker, William Phillips & Joseph Jones, Jr., for the election committees, 1857
Alphabetical by polling district and parish. Place of residence.

Sir Henry Geers Cotterell Thomas William Booker Blakemore James King King Charles Spencer Bateman Hanbury

Hereford Pub Lib Inst Hist Res

1868—A copy of the poll... Hereford: *Journal* Office, 1868
Alphabetical by polling district, parish and qualification. Address.

Sir Herbert Croft Sir Joseph Russell Bailey Michael Biddulph Thomas Blake

Hereford Pub Lib Inst Hist Res

HEREFORD

1741—An alphabetical copy of the poll... Gloucester: R. Wilde, [1741]
Occupation and place of residence of out-voters.

Edward Cope Hopton Thomas Winford Herbert Westfaling Henry Cornewall William Brydges

Hereford Pub Lib Inst Hist Res

1747—An alphabetical copy of the poll... Hereford: R. Wilde, 1747
Occupation and place of residence of out-voters.

Henry Cornewall Daniel Leighton Herbert Westfaling

Hereford Pub Lib Inst Hist Res

1754—The names of the freemen... who voted for James Peachy... n.p., [1754] [Broadsheet]
Alphabetical. Occupation and place of residence or address. Second votes also shown.

Charles Fitzroy Scudamore John Symons James Peachy

Hereford Pub Lib Inst Hist Res

1761—An alphabetical copy of the poll... n.p., [1761]
Occupation and place of residence of out-voters.

Charles Fitzroy Scudamore John Symonds William Hussey

Hereford Pub Lib Inst Hist Res

1818—Published by authority of the Worshipful the Mayor. A list of the poll... Hereford: Watkins & Wright, 1818
Alphabetical. Occupation and place of residence. Day of voting.

John Somers Cocks Thomas Powell Symonds Richard Philip Scudamore

Hereford Pub Lib Inst Hist Res

1818—An alphabetical list of the poll... Hereford: E. G. Wright, [1818]
Occupation and place of residence.

John Somers Cocks Thomas Powell Symonds Richard Philip Scudamore

Hereford Pub Lib Inst Hist Res

1826—Published by authority of the Worshipful the Mayor. A list of the freemen... Hereford: W. H. & J. Parker, [1826]
Alphabetical. Occupation and place of residence. Day of voting.
Viscount Eastnor Edward Bolton Clive Richard Blakemore
Hereford Pub Lib Inst Hist Res

1826—A list of the poll... Hereford: Davies & Son, [1826]
Alphabetical. Occupation and place of residence.
Viscount Eastnor Edward Bolton Clive Richard Blakemore
Hereford Pub Lib Inst Hist Res

1832—Published by authority of the Worshipful the Mayor. A list of the freemen and electors... Hereford: John Parker, [1832]
Alphabetical. Occupation and address. Freemen and those voting on the second day distinguished.
Edward Bolton Clive Robert Biddulph Richard Blakemore
Hereford Pub Lib Inst Hist Res

1835—Published by authority of the Worshipful the Mayor. A list of the freemen and electors... Hereford: John Parker, [1835]
Alphabetical by qualification. Occupation and address.
Edward Bolton Clive Robert Biddulph Richard Blakemore
Hereford Pub Lib Inst Hist Res

1837—Published by permission of the Worshipful the Mayor. A list of the freemen and electors... Hereford: John Parker, [1837]
Alphabetical by qualification. Occupation and address.
Edward Bolton Clive Daniel Higford Daval Burr Robert Biddulph
Hereford Pub Lib Inst Hist Res

1841 (July)—Published by permission of the Worshipful the Mayor. A list of the freemen and electors... Hereford: F. & A. Merrick, [1841]
Alphabetical by qualification. Occupation and address.
Edward Bolton Clive Henry William Hobhouse Daniel Higford Daval Burr
Hereford Pub Lib Inst Hist Res

1841* (October)—Published by authority of the Worshipful the Mayor. A list of the freemen and electors... Hereford: F. & A. Merrick, [1841]
Alphabetical by polling booth and candidate. Occupation and address.
Robert Pulsford Edward Griffiths
Hereford Pub Lib Inst Hist Res

1852—A list of the freemen and electors... Hereford: J. Head, [1852]
Alphabetical by qualification. Occupation and address.
Sir Robert Price Henry Morgan Clifford A. W. H. Merrick
Hereford Pub Lib Inst Hist Res

1865—Hereford City election, 1865. List of electors... Hereford: William Phillips, [1865]
Alphabetical. Occupation and address. Non-voters.

Richard Baggallay George Clive Henry Morgan Clifford

Hereford Pub Lib Inst Hist Res

1868—Hereford City election, 1868. List of electors... Hereford: William Prosser, [1868]
Alphabetical. Occupation and address. Non-voters. Account of elections since 1826. Candidates' addresses.

George Clive John Shaw Wyllie Richard Baggallay George Arbuthnot

Hereford Pub Lib Inst Hist Res

1869*—An alphabetical list of the poll... [Hereford, 1869]
Occupation and address. Non-voters. Account of proceedings.

Henry Edward Clive Chandos Wren Hoskyns Sir Richard Baggallay George Arbuthnot

Hereford Pub Lib Inst Hist Res

1871*—Hereford City election, February 1871. List of freemen and electors... Hereford: E. K. Jakeman, [1871]
Alphabetical by candidate. Occupation and address. Non-voters. Account of proceedings.

George Arbuthnot Arthur Divett Hayter

Hereford Pub Lib Inst Hist Res

LEOMINSTER

1741—An exact copy of the poll... [n.p., 1741] [Broadsheet]
Alphabetical. Occupation.

Capel Hanbury John Caswall Robert Harley Bryan Crowther

Brit Lib

1742*—An alphabetical list of the poll... [n.p., 1742] [Broadsheet]
Occupation to distinguish voters of identical name.

Robert Harley Sir Robert Cornwall John Price William Bach

Natl Lib Wales Inst Hist Res

1796—An alphabetical state of the poll... Hereford: W. H. Parker, [1796]
Occupation. Rejected voters.

John Hunter George Augustus Pollen

Hereford Pub Lib Inst Hist Res

1797*—An alphabetical state of the poll... Hereford: W. H. Parker, [1797]
Occupation. Non-voters.

William Taylor Sir Henry Tempest

Hereford Pub Lib Guildhall Lib

1802—An alphabetical state of the poll... Leominster: J. Barrell, 1802
Occupation. Rejected voters with reasons and voting intentions. Non-voters.

John Lubbock Charles Kinnaird William Taylor

Hereford Pub Lib Inst Hist Res

1812—An alphabetical list of the electors... Leominster: F. Went, 1813
Occupation.

John William Lubbock John Harcourt Earl of Meath

Hereford Pub Lib Inst Hist Res

1818—An alphabetical list of the poll... Leominster: F. J. Burlton, 1819
Occupation. Rejected voters with reasons. Account of proceedings and of the election petition.

Sir John William Lubbock Sir William Cunningham Fairlie John Harcourt

Hereford Pub Lib Inst Hist Res

1820—An alphabetical list of the poll... Leominster: Burlton, [1820]
Occupation. Rejected voters with reasons and voting intentions.

Lord Hotham Sir William Cunningham Fairlie John Harcourt

Hereford Pub Lib Inst Hist Res

1826—An alphabetical list of the poll... Leominster: Burlton, [1826]
Occupation.

Lord Hotham Thomas Bish Rowland Stephenson Frederic Cuthbert

Hereford Pub Lib Inst Hist Res

1831—An alphabetical list of the poll... Leominster: J. V. Chilcott, [1831]
Occupation. Rejected voters with reasons. Non-voters. Account of proceedings.

William Bertram Evans Thomas Brayen Lord Hotham

Hereford Pub Lib Inst Hist Res

1837—An alphabetical list of the poll... Leominster: J. V. Chilcott, [1837]
Address. Nomination speeches.

Lord Hotham Charles Greenway James Wigram

Hereford Pub Lib Inst Hist Res

1852—A copy of the poll... Leominster: John Woolley, [1852]
Alphabetical by qualification. Occupation and address or place of residence.

George Arkwright John George Phillimore John Pollard Willoughby

Hereford Pub Lib Inst Hist Res

1868—A copy of the poll... Leominster: S. Partridge, [1868]
Alphabetical by residents and out-voters. Address. Non-voters.

Richard Arkwright Thomas Spinks

Hereford Pub Lib Inst Hist Res

HERTFORDSHIRE

1705—A copy of the poll... n.p., [1705]
By parish.

Sir John Spencer   Ralph Freman   Thomas Halsey   Sir John Bucknall

Inst Hist Res

1722—A copy of the poll... London, 1722
By hundred and parish. Place of residence.

Ralph Freman   Sir Thomas Saunders Seabright   Charles Caesar

Herts Rec Off   Inst Hist Res

1727—A copy of the poll... n.p., [1727]
By hundred and parish. Place of residence.

Charles Caesar   Sir Thomas Saunders Seabright   Ralph Freman

Herts Rec Off   Inst Hist Res

1734—A copy of the poll... London, 1734
By hundred and parish. Place of residence.

William Plumer   Sir Thomas Saunders Seabright   Charles Caesar

Herts Rec Off   Inst Hist Res

1754—A copy of the poll... London: Thomas Trye, 1754
By hundred and parish. Place of residence, nature and occupier of freehold.

Paggen Hale   Charles Gore   Edward Gardiner

Herts Rec Off   Inst Hist Res

1761—A copy of the poll... London: C. Bathurst, 1761
By hundred and parish. Place of residence, nature and occupier of freehold.

Charles Gore   Jacob Houblon   Thomas Plumer Byde

Herts Rec Off   Inst Hist Res

1774—A copy of the poll... Hertford: Stephen Austin, 1775
By hundred and parish. Place of residence, nature and occupier of freehold.

William Plumer   Thomas Halsey   Viscount Grimston

Herts Rec Off   Inst Hist Res

1784—A copy of the poll... Hertford: Stephen Austin, 1784
By hundred and parish. Place of residence, nature and occupier of freehold.

William Plumer   Viscount Grimston   Thomas Halsey

Herts Rec Off   Inst Hist Res

1790—A copy of the poll... Hertford: Stephen Austin, 1790
By hundred and parish. Place of residence, nature and occupier of freehold.

William Plumer   William Baker   William Hale, Jr.

Herts Rec Off   Inst Hist Res

1796—A copy of the poll... Hertford: Stephen Austin, 1796
By hundred and parish. Place of residence, nature and occupier of freehold.
William Plumer   William Baker   Samuel Ferrand Waddington
Herts Rec Off   Guildhall Lib

1802—A copy of the poll... Hertford: St. Austin, 1802
By hundred and parish. Place of residence, nature and occupier of freehold.
William Plumer   Peniston Lamb   William Baker
Herts Rec Off   Inst Hist Res

1805*—A copy of the poll... Hertford: Austin, [1805]
By hundred and parish. Place of residence, nature and occupier of freehold.
William Baker   Thomas Brand
Herts Rec Off   Inst Hist Res

1832—A copy of the register of electors... and the poll... Hertford: St. Austin, 1833
Alphabetical by polling district and parish. Place of residence, nature and situation or occupier of qualification. Non-voters included.
Sir John Saunders Sebright   Nicolson Calvert   Viscount Grimston   Rowland Alston
Herts Rec Off   Guildhall Lib

HERTFORD

1835—An alphabetical copy of the poll... Hertford: St. Austin, 1835
Occupation, address and qualification. Tendered votes. Non-voters.
Viscount Mahon   William Cowper   Viscount Ingestre
Inst Hist Res

Untraced: 1831, 1857, 1868

ST. ALBANS

1807—A copy of the poll... London: W. M'Dowall, 1807
Alphabetical. Occupation, place of residence and qualification. Rejected voters included.
Joseph Halsey   James Walter Grimston   Lord Duncannon
Bodl   Inst Hist Res

1820—An alphabetical copy of the poll... Hertford & Ware: Shaw, [1820]
Occupation, place of residence and qualification. Rejected voters included.
Christopher Smith   William Tierney Robarts   Sir Henry Wright Wilson
St. Albans Pub Lib   Inst Hist Res

1821*—An alphabetical copy of the poll... St. Albans: Briggs, [1821]
Occupation, place of residence and qualification. Rejected voters included.
Sir Henry Wright Wilson   Charles Ross   John Easthope
St. Albans Pub Lib   Inst Hist Res

1830—An alphabetical copy of the poll... St. Albans: W. Langley, [1830]
Occupation, place of residence and qualification. Rejected voters included.

Viscount Grimston Charles Tennant Henry Gally Knight

St. Albans Pub Lib Inst Hist Res

1831—An alphabetical copy of the poll... St. Albans: W. Langley, [1831]
Occupation, place of residence and qualification. Rejected voters included.

Sir Francis Vincent Richard Godson Viscount Grimston

St. Albans Pub Lib Inst Hist Res

1832—An alphabetical copy of the poll... St. Albans: W. Langley, [1832]
Address and qualification. Non-voters included.

Sir Francis Vincent Henry George Ward W. Turner

St. Albans Pub Lib Inst Hist Res

1832—An alphabetical copy of the poll... St. Albans: Nicholls, [1832]
Address and qualification. Non-voters included.

Sir Francis Vincent Henry George Ward W. Turner

St. Albans Pub Lib Inst Hist Res

1835—An alphabetical copy of the registration of 1834, and of the poll... St. Albans: W. Langley, [1835]
Address and qualification. Non-voters included.

Edward Harbottle Grimston Henry George Ward W. H. Beresford

St. Albans Pub Lib Inst Hist Res

1841*—An alphabetical copy of the poll... St. Albans: W. Langley, [1841]
Address and qualification. Non-voters included.

Earl of Listowel Benjamin Bond Cabbell

St. Albans Pub Lib Inst Hist Res

1847—An alphabetical copy of the poll... *Report of the Commissioners to Inquire into the Existence of Bribery in the Borough of St. Albans...* , pp. 455-63 (Parliamentary Papers, 1852 [1431], XXVII)
Alphabetical. Address.

Alexander Raphael George William John Repton John Wilks Frederick K. Craven

Inst Hist Res

HUNTINGDONSHIRE

1768—A poll taken before Edward Leeds... Cambridge: Fletcher & Hodson, [1768]
Alphabetical by hundred and parish. Place of residence.

Viscount Hinchingbrooke Earl Ludlow Sir Robert Bernard

Cambs (Huntingdon) Rec Off Inst Hist Res

1807—A state of the poll... Cambridge: F. Hodson, [1807]
Alphabetical by hundred and parish. Place of residence and nature of freehold.

Viscount Hinchingbrooke William Henry Fellowes Viscount Proby

Cambs (Huntingdon) Rec Off Inst Hist Res

1818—A state of the poll... Huntingdon: Thomas Lovell, 1818
Alphabetical by hundred and parish. Place of residence and nature of freehold.

Lord Frederick Montagu William Henry Fellowes William Wells

Cambs (Huntingdon) Rec Off Guildhall Lib

1826—A copy of the poll... Huntingdon: A. P. Wood, [1826]
Alphabetical by hundred and parish of residence. Place, nature and occupier of freehold. Out-voters by county with place of residence.

Lord Mandeville William Henry Fellowes Lord John Russell

Cambs (Huntingdon) Rec Off Inst Hist Res

1830—A copy of the poll... London: G. Taylor, [1830]
Alphabetical by hundred and parish of residence. Place, nature and occupier of freehold. Out-voters by county with place of residence. Index.

Viscount Mandeville Viscount Strathavon John Bonfoy Rooper

Cambs (Huntingdon) Rec Off Inst Hist Res

1831—The poll for two knights... Cambridge: Weston Hatfield, [1831]
Alphabetical by hundred and parish of residence. Place, nature and occupier of freehold. Out-voters by county and parish. Index.

John Bonfoy Rooper Viscount Mandeville Viscount Strathavon

Guildhall Lib

1837—A copy of the poll... Huntingdon: Robert Edis, 1837
Alphabetical by hundred and parish. Place of residence. Index.

Edward Fellowes George Thornhill John Bonfoy Rooper

Cambs (Huntingdon) Rec Off Guildhall Lib

1857—The poll taken at the election... Huntingdon: Robert Edis, 1857
Alphabetical by polling district and parish. Place of residence. Index.

James Rust Edward Fellowes John Moyer Heathcote

Cambs (Huntingdon) Rec Off Inst Hist Res

1859—General election, 1859. The poll taken... St. Neots: David R. Tomson, 1859
Alphabetical by polling district and parish. Place of residence.

Edward Fellowes Lord Robert Montagu John Moyer Heathcote

Cambs (Huntingdon) Rec Off Guildhall Lib

HUNTINGDON

1832—Copy of the poll... Huntingdon: A. P. Wood, [1832]
Alphabetical by Huntingdon and Godmanchester. Occupation. Burgesses distinguished.

Jonathan Peel Frederick Pollock James Duberley Edward Maltby

Inst Hist Res

KENT

1734—The poll for knights of the shire... London: Stephen Austen, 1734
Alphabetical by parish of residence. Place of freehold. Index.

Sir Edward Dering Viscount Vane Earl of Middlesex Sir George Oxenden

Maidstone Pub Lib Inst Hist Res

1754—The poll for knights of the shire... London & Tunbridge Wells: Paul Vaillent & Edmund Baker, 1754
Alphabetical by parish of residence. Place, nature and occupier of freehold. Index.

Lewis Watson Robert Fairfax Sir Edward Dering

Maidstone Pub Lib Inst Hist Res

1790—The poll for knights of the shire... Rochester: Webster Gillman, 1791
By parish of residence. Place, nature and occupier of freehold. Out-voters by county. Index.

Sir Edward Knatchbull Filmer Honywood Charles Marsham

Maidstone Pub Lib Inst Hist Res

1802—The poll for knights of the shire... Canterbury: W. Bristow, 1803
By lathe and parish of residence. Out-voters by county. Index. Abstract of 1796 poll.

Filmer Honywood Sir William Geary Sir Edward Knatchbull

Maidstone Pub Lib Inst Hist Res

1802—The poll for knights of the shire... Canterbury: W. Bristow, 1804
By lathe and parish of residence. Place, nature and occupier of freehold. Out-voters by county and place of residence. Index.

Filmer Honywood Sir William Geary Sir Edward Knatchbull

Kent Archives Office Inst Hist Res

EAST KENT

1832—The poll for knights of the shire... Canterbury: Henry Ward, 1833
Alphabetical by lathe and parish. Place of residence. Non-voters distinguished. Tendered votes. Index.

John Pemberton Plumtre Sir Edward Knatchbull Sir William Richard Cosway
Sir William Percy Honywood Courtenay

Maidstone Pub Lib Inst Hist Res

1837—The poll for the knights... Canterbury: Henry Ward, 1837
Alphabetical by polling district, booth and parish. Place of residence. Non-voters distinguished. Index.

Sir Edward Knatchbull John Pemberton Plumtre Thomas Rider

Maidstone Pub Lib Inst Hist Res

1852* (February)—The poll for a knight... Canterbury: H. Chivers, 1852
Alphabetical by polling district. Place of residence. Non-voters included.

Sir Brook William Bridges Sir Edward Cholmeley Dering

Maidstone Pub Lib Guildhall Lib

1852 (July)—The poll for the knights... Canterbury: Henry U. Ward, 1852
Alphabetical by polling district and parish. Place of residence. Non-voters distinguished. Index.

Sir Edward Cholmeley Dering William Deedes Sir Brook William Bridges

Maidstone Pub Lib Inst Hist Res

1857—The poll for the knights... Canterbury: Thomas Ashenden, 1857
Alphabetical by polling district and parish. Place of residence. Non-voters distinguished. Index.

Sir Brook William Bridges Sir Edward Cholmeley Dering William Deedes
E. A. Acheson

Maidstone Pub Lib Inst Hist Res

1863*—The poll for a knight... Canterbury: Thomas Ashenden, 1863
Alphabetical by polling district and parish. Place of residence. Non-voters distinguished. Index.

Sir Edward Cholmeley Dering Sir Norton Joseph Knatchbull

Maidstone Pub Lib Guildhall Lib

1863*—The poll for a knight... by William Hall... Canterbury: William Davey, [1863]
Alphabetical by polling district and parish. Place of residence. Non-voters distinguished. Index.

Sir Edward Cholmeley Dering Sir Norton Joseph Knatchbull

Kent Archives Office Inst Hist Res

1865—The poll for two knights... Canterbury: William Davey, [1865]
Alphabetical by polling district and parish. Non-voters distinguished. Index.

Sir Edward Cholmeley Dering Sir Brook William Bridges Sir Norton Joseph Knatchbull

Folkestone Pub Lib Guildhall Lib

1865—The poll for two knights... Canterbury: *Kentish Observer* Office, 1866
Alphabetical by polling district and parish. Address. Non-voters distinguished. Index.

Sir Edward Cholmeley Dering Sir Brook William Bridges Sir Norton Joseph Knatchbull

Maidstone Pub Lib Inst Hist Res

1868* (April)—The poll of the electors... [compiled by James William Pilcher] Canterbury: Hal Drury, [1868]
Alphabetical by polling district and parish. Address. Non-voters distinguished. Index.

Edward Leigh Pemberton   Henry James Tufton

Maidstone Pub Lib   Inst Hist Res

1868 (November)—The poll of the electors... [compiled by James William Pilcher] Canterbury: Hal Drury, [1868]
Alphabetical by polling district, parish and qualification. Address. Non-voters distinguished. Index.

Edward Leigh Pemberton   George Watson Milles   Henry James Tufton
Sir John Frederick Croft

Maidstone Pub Lib   Inst Hist Res

MID-KENT

1868—The poll for two knights... Maidstone: *Journal* Office, [1868]
Alphabetical by polling district, parish and qualification. Address. Non-voters included.

Viscount Holmesdale   William Hart Dyke   Lord John Hervey   Francis S. Head

Dover Pub Lib   Guildhall Lib

WEST KENT

1835—The poll for the knights... Maidstone: J. Smith, [1835]
Alphabetical by polling district and parish. Place of residence or address. Non-voters included. Index.

Sir William Richard Powlett Geary   Thomas Law Hodges   Thomas Rider

Maidstone Pub Lib   Inst Hist Res

1837—The poll for the knights... Maidstone: J. Smith, [1837]
Alphabetical by polling district and parish. Address. Non-voters included. Index.

Sir William Richard Powlett Geary   Thomas Law Hodges   Sir Edmund Filmer

Maidstone Pub Lib   Inst Hist Res

1847—The poll for the knights... Maidstone: J. Smith, [1847]
Alphabetical by polling district and parish. Address. Non-voters included. Index.

Sir Edmund Filmer   Thomas Law Hodges   Thomas Austen

Maidstone Pub Lib   Inst Hist Res

1852—The poll for the knights... Maidstone: Smith & Son, [1852]
Alphabetical by polling district and parish. Address. Non-voters included. Index.

Sir Edmund Filmer   William Masters Smith   Thomas Law Hodges

Maidstone Pub Lib   Inst Hist Res

1857* (February)—The poll for the knights... at a bye election... and at a general election... collated and arranged by Robert Pearson, election agent. Maidstone: *Journal* Office, [1857]
Alphabetical by polling district and parish. Address. Non-voters included. Index.

Charles Wykeham Martin   Sir Walter Buchanan Riddell

Maidstone Pub Lib   Inst Hist Res

1857* (February)—The poll for a knight... and the poll for two knights... compiled... by Thomas Nicolls Roberts, Secretary to the West Kent Liberal Registration Association... London: Effingham Wilson, [1857]
Alphabetical by polling district and parish. Address. Non-voters included. Index. Voting for February by-election and April general election.

Charles Wykeham Martin   Sir Walter Buchanan Riddell

Maidstone Pub Lib   Inst Hist Res

1857 (April)—The poll for the knights... at a bye election... and at a general election... collated and arranged by Robert Pearson, election agent. Maidstone: *Journal* Office, [1857]
Alphabetical by polling district and parish. Address. Non-voters included. Index.

Charles Wykeham Martin   James Whatman   William Masters Smith

Maidstone Pub Lib   Inst Hist Res

1857 (April)—The poll for a knight... and the poll for two knights... compiled... by Thomas Nicolls Roberts, Secretary to the West Kent Liberal Registration Association... London: Effingham Wilson, [1857]
Alphabetical by polling district and parish. Address. Non-voters included. Index. Voting for February by-election and April general election.

Charles Wykeham Martin   James Whatman   William Masters Smith

Maidstone Pub Lib   Inst Hist Res

1859—The poll for two knights... compiled by Thomas Nicolls Roberts... London: Effingham Wilson, [1859]
Alphabetical by polling district and parish. Address. Non-voters included. Index.

Viscount Holmesdale   Sir Edmund Filmer   Charles Wykeham Martin   James Whatman

Maidstone Pub Lib   Inst Hist Res

1865—The poll for two knights... compiled . . . by William Hall, Secretary to the Liberal Registration Associations of East and West Kent... London: Haverson & Harding, [1866]
Alphabetical by polling district and parish. Address. Non-voters distinguished. Index.

Viscount Holmesdale   William Hart Dyke   Sir John Lubbock   William Angerstein

Maidstone Pub Lib   Inst Hist Res

1868—The poll for two knights... compiled by Edward Hughes... Secretary to the West Kent Conservative Registration Society... Woolwich: H. Pryce, [1869]
Alphabetical by polling district, parish and qualification. Address. Non-voters included. Index.

Charles Henry Mills John Gilbert Talbot Sir John Lubbock William Angerstein

Kent Archives Office Inst Hist Res

CANTERBURY

1790—The poll of the electors... Simmons & Kirby, [1790]
Poll order and alphabetical by parish of residence. Occupation and address or place of residence. Rejected voters with reasons. Index.

George Gipps Sir John Honywood Lord Daer Lewis Thomas Watson

Canterbury Pub Lib Inst Hist Res

1796—The poll of the electors... Canterbury: W. Bristow, [1796]
Poll order and alphabetical by parish of residence or regiment. Occupation and address or place of residence. Objected voters and those in receipt of parish relief. Non-voters. Index. Appendix on the voting right of those in receipt of parish relief.

John Baker Samuel Elias Sawbridge George Gipps Sir John Honywood

Canterbury Pub Lib Inst Hist Res

1818—The poll of the electors... Canterbury: Cowtan & Colegate, 1818
Poll order. Occupation and address or place of residence. Non-voters. Index.

Stephen Rumbold Lushington Lord Clifton John Baker Joseph Royle Edward Taylor

Canterbury Pub Lib Inst Hist Res

1826—The poll of the electors... Canterbury: T. Mathers, 1826
Alphabetical. Occupation and address or place of residence. Candidates' addresses.

Stephen Rumbold Lushington Lord Clifton Richard Watson

Woolwich Pub Lib Inst Hist Res

1830—The poll of the electors... Canterbury: Elizabeth Wood, 1830
Poll order by division and alphabetical by place of residence. Occupation and address or place of residence. Non-voters included in alphabetical list. Index. Account of proceedings.

Richard Watson Viscount Fordwich Henry Bingham Baring Samuel Elias Sawbridge George John Milles

Canterbury Pub Lib Inst Hist Res

1832—The poll of the freemen and electors... Canterbury: Elizabeth Wood, 1832
Alphabetical. Address or place of residence. Non-voters. Account of proceedings.

Richard Watson Viscount Fordwich Sir William Percy Honywood Courtenay

Canterbury Pub Lib Inst Hist Res

1835—The poll of the freemen and electors... Canterbury: Henry Ward, 1835
Poll order by booth. Address or place of residence. Tendered votes. Non-voters. Index. Account of proceedings.

Lord Albert Denison Conyngham Frederic Villiers Stephen Rumbold Lushington
George Francis Robert Harris Sir Edward William Campbell Rich Owen

Canterbury Pub Lib Inst Hist Res

1837—The poll of the freemen and electors . . . Part I. Canterbury: Henry Ward, 1837
Alphabetical. Address, qualification and booth. Tendered votes. Non-voters distinguished with reasons.

James Bradshaw Lord Albert Denison Conyngham Henry Plumtre Gipps
Frederic Villiers

Woolwich Pub Lib Inst Hist Res

[Part II was issued later and contained a list
of the new Parliament and other information.]

1837—The poll of the freemen and electors... Canterbury: S. Prentice, 1837
Alphabetical by polling booth. Address and qualification. Tendered votes. Non-voters. Account of proceedings.

James Bradshaw Lord Albert Denison Conyngham Henry Plumtre GippsFrederic Villiers

Canterbury Pub Lib Inst Hist Res

1841* (February)—Poll of the freemen and electors... Canterbury: Henry Ward, 1841
Alphabetical. Address and qualification. Dead and removed distinguished. Non-voters. Brief account of proceedings.

George Percy Sydney Smythe John Wright Henniker Wilson Thomas Twisden Hodges

Canterbury Pub Lib Inst Hist Res

1841 (June)—Poll of the freemen and electors... Canterbury: Henry Ward, 1841
Alphabetical. Address and qualification. Dead and removed distinguished. Non-voters, distinguishing those who did not vote in the February by-election. Brief account of proceedings.

George Percy Sydney Smythe James Bradshaw Thomas Twisden Hodges

Woolwich Pub Lib Inst Hist Res

1847—Poll of the freemen and electors... Canterbury: Henry Ward, 1847
Alphabetical. Address and qualification. Non-voters included. Dead distinguished and also listed separately. Brief account of proceedings.

Lord Albert Denison Conyngham George Percy Sydney Smythe John Vance
Lord Thomas Pelham Clinton

Canterbury Pub Lib Guildhall Lib

1847—Poll of the freemen and electors... Canterbury: R. Smithson, 1847
Alphabetical. Address and qualification. Non-voters included. Dead and removed distinguished. Those voting Conservative in 1841 but not in 1847 distinguished. Brief account of proceedings.

Lord Albert Denison Conyngham George Percy Sydney Smythe John Vance
Lord Thomas Pelham Clinton

Woolwich Pub Lib Inst Hist Res

1852—Poll of the freemen and electors... Canterbury: Henry U. Ward, [1852]
Alphabetical. Address, qualification and booth. Non-voters. Brief account of proceedings.

Henry Plumtre Gipps Henry Butler Johnstone Sir William Somerville Frederick Romilly George Percy Sydney Smythe

Maidstone Pub Lib Inst Hist Res

1854*—Poll of the freemen and electors... Canterbury: *Kentish Gazette*, 1854
Alphabetical by qualification. Address. Non-voters. Account of proceedings.

Charles Manners Lushington Sir William Meredyth Somerville Charles Lennox Butler Charles Purton Cooper Edward Auchmuty Glover

Maidstone Pub Lib Guildhall Lib

1857—Poll of the freemen and electors... Canterbury: Thomas Ashenden, 1857
Alphabetical. Address, qualification and booth. Non-voters distinguished. Brief account of proceedings.

Henry Butler Johnstone Sir William Meredyth Somerville Charles Purton Cooper

Woolwich Pub Lib Inst Hist Res

1857—The poll of the freemen and electors... Canterbury: William Davey, [1857]
Alphabetical. Address. Non-voters.

Henry Butler Johnstone Sir William Meredyth Somerville Charles Purton Cooper

Canterbury Pub Lib Inst Hist Res

1862*—Poll of the freemen and electors... Canterbury: William Davey, [1862]
Alphabetical. Address. Non-voters. Brief account of proceedings.

Henry Alexander Butler Johnstone William Lyon

Maidstone Pub Lib Inst Hist Res

1862*—The poll of the freemen and electors... Canterbury: Jane Ward, 1862
Alphabetical by qualification and parish. Address. Non-voters distinguished.

Henry Alexander Butler Johnstone William Lyon

Woolwich Pub Lib Inst Hist Res

1865—The official poll of freemen and electors... Canterbury: *Kentish Observer*, [1865]
Alphabetical by qualification. Address. Brief account of proceedings.

Henry Alexander Butler Johnstone John Walter Huddleston William Lyon Alexander Shafto Adair

Kent County Lib Inst Hist Res

1865—The poll of the freemen and electors... Canterbury: William Davey, [1865]
Alphabetical by qualification. Address. Brief account of proceedings.

Henry Alexander Butler Johnstone John Walter Huddleston William Lyon Alexander Shafto Adair

Canterbury Pub Lib Inst Hist Res

1868—The poll of the freemen and electors... Canterbury: Wiliam Davey, [1868]
Alphabetical. Address. Non-voters distinguished. Tendered votes. Brief account of proceedings.

Henry Alexander Butler Johnstone John Walter Huddleston Theodore Henry Brinckman Henry Brydges Lee Warner

Canterbury Pub Lib   Inst Hist Res

CHATHAM

1832—The poll of the electors... Chatham: William Burrill, 1832
Alphabetical by district. Occupation and address. Tendered or claimed votes distinguished. Non-voters with dead and removed distinguished.

William Leader Maberley   Erskine Perry

Brit Lib

1834*—The poll of the electors... Chatham: William Burrill, 1834
Alphabetical by district. Occupation and address. Non-voters with dead and removed distinguished.

George Stevens Byng   William John Ching

Brit Lib

1852—The poll of the electors... Chatham: Windeyer & Cackett, 1852
Alphabetical by district. Occupation and address. Non-voters with dead distinguished.

Sir John Mark Frederic Smith   Sir James Stirling

Brit Lib

1853*—The poll of the electors... Chatham: G. H. Windeyer, 1853
Alphabetical by district. Occupation and address. Non-voters.

Leicester Viney Vernon   Sir James Stirling

Maidstone Pub Lib   Inst Hist Res

1857—The poll of the electors... Chatham: Robert Beck, 1857
Alphabetical by district. Occupation and address. Non-voters.

William Govett Romaine   Sir John Mark Frederic Smith

Guildhall Lib

1859—The poll of the electors... Chatham: Richard Taylor, 1859
Alphabetical by district. Occupation and address. Non-voters.

Sir John Mark Frederic Smith   Arthur John Otway

Guildhall Lib

1865—The poll of the electors... Chatham: George H. Windeyer, 1865
Alphabetical by district. Address. Non-voters.

Arthur John Otway   George Elliot

Guildhall Lib

1865—The poll of the electors... compiled from Mr. Otway's private poll book by J. R. Bennett... Chatham: R. Taylor, 1865
Alphabetical by district and poll order by booth. Address. Non-voters.

Arthur John Otway   George Elliot

Chatham Pub Lib   Inst Hist Res

1868—The poll of the electors... compiled from Mr. Otway's private poll book by S. W. Dadson... Chatham: G. S. Mullinger, 1868
Alphabetical by district. Address. Non-voters.

Arthur John Otway   George Elliot

Chatham Pub Lib   Inst Hist Res

DOVER

1826—The poll for two barons... Dover: Thomas Rigden, [1826]
Poll order. Occupation and place of residence. Tendered votes included. Non-voters. Index.

Edward Bootle Wilbraham   Charles Poulett Thomson   John Halcomb   Joseph Butterworth
George Finch   Michael Kingsford

Dover Pub Lib   Inst Hist Res

1828*—The poll for one baron... Dover: G. Chapman, [1828]
Poll order. Occupation and place of residence. Tendered votes included. Index.

William Henry Trant   John Halcomb

Dover Pub Lib   Inst Hist Res

1830—The poll for two barons... Dover: W. Batcheller, [1830]
Alphabetical. Occupation and place of residence. Tendered votes included.

Charles Poulett Thomson   Sir John Rae Reid   John Halcomb

Dover Pub Lib   Inst Hist Res

1832—The poll book for two barons... Dover: W. Batcheller, [1832]
Alphabetical by qualification and parish. Occupation and address of freemen, address and qualification of householders. Non-voters included.

Charles Poulett Thomson   Sir John Rae Reid   John Halcomb   R. H. Stanhope

Dover Pub Lib   Inst Hist Res

1833*—The poll book for one baron... Dover: W. Batcheller, [1833]
Alphabetical by qualification and parish. Occupation and address of freemen, address and qualification of householders. Non-voters included.

John Halcomb   R. H. Stanhope

Dover Pub Lib   Inst Hist Res

1835—The poll book for two barons... Dover: W. Batcheller, [1835]
Alphabetical by qualification and parish. Occupation and address of freemen, address and qualification of householders. Non-voters included. Account of proceedings.

John Minet Fector   Sir John Rae Reid   Edward Royd Rice

Dover Pub Lib   Inst Hist Res

1837—The poll book for two barons... Dover: W. Batcheller, [1837]
Alphabetical by qualification and parish. Occupation and address of freemen, address and qualification of householders. Non-voters included. Account of proceedings.

Edward Royd Rice   Sir John Rae Reid   John Minet Fector

Dover Pub Lib   Inst Hist Res

1841—The poll-book for two barons... Dover: W. Batcheller, 1841
Alphabetical by qualification and parish. Address. Non-voters included. Account of proceedings.

Sir John Rae Reid   Edward Royd Rice   John Halcombe   Alexander Galloway

Dover Pub Lib   Inst Hist Res

1847—The poll-book for two barons... Dover: W. Batcheller, 1847
Alphabetical by qualification and parish. Address. Non-voters included. Account of proceedings.

Edward Royd Rice   Sir George Clerk   Henry Thoby Prinsep

Dover Pub Lib   Inst Hist Res

1852—The poll-book for two barons... Dover: W. Batcheller, 1852
Alphabetical by qualification and parish. Address. Non-voters included. Account of proceedings.

Viscount Chelsea   Edward Royd Rice   Sir George Clerk

Dover Pub Lib   Inst Hist Res

1857—The poll-book for two barons... Dover: W. Batcheller, 1857
Alphabetical by qualification and parish. Address. Non-voters included. Account of proceedings.

Ralph Bernal Osborne   Sir William Russell   Sir George Clerk   George William Hope

Dover Pub Lib   Inst Hist Res

1859—The poll-book for two barons... Dover: King's Arms Library, 1859
Alphabetical by qualification and parish. Address. Non-voters included. Account of proceedings.

Sir Henry John Leake   William Nicol   Sir William Russell   Ralph Bernal Osborne

Maidstone Pub Lib   Inst Hist Res

1865—The poll-book for two barons... Dover: *Dover Telegraph*, 1865
Alphabetical by qualification and parish. Address. Non-voters included. Account of proceedings.

Alexander George Dickson   Charles Kaye Freshfield   Viscount Bury
Thomas Eustace Smith

Dover Pub Lib   Inst Hist Res

1868—The poll-book for two barons... Dover: *Dover Chronicle*, 1868
Alphabetical by polling district, qualification and parish. Address. Non-voters included. Account of proceedings.

Alexander George Dickson   George Jessel   Charles Freshfield   Israel Abrahams

Dover Pub Lib   Inst Hist Res

1868—1868. The poll for two barons... compiled by William Hall... Dover: J. T. Friend, [1868]
Alphabetical by polling district, qualification and parish. Address. Non-voters and duplicates distinguished. Index. Analysis of errors in the official figures.
Alexander George Dickson George Jessel Charles Freshfield Israel Abrahams
Dover Pub Lib Inst Hist Res

1871*—The poll for one baron... Dover: J. T. Friend, [1871]
Alphabetical by polling district, qualification and parish. Address. Non-voters distinguished. Account of proceedings. Index.
George Jessel Edward William Barnett
Dover Pub Lib Guildhall Lib

GREENWICH

1837—The poll taken at the election... Greenwich: Henry S. Richardson, [1837]
Alphabetical by parish and street. Non-voters included.
Matthias Wolverley Attwood Edward George Barnard Charles Napier
Greenwich Pub Lib Inst Hist Res

MAIDSTONE

1734—The poll for electing two burgesses... Maidstone: T. Edlin, 1734
Alphabetical. Occupation and place of residence. Out-voters distinguished.
John Finch William Turner Thomas Hope
Kent Archives Office Inst Hist Res

1761—The poll for electing two burgesses... Maidstone: W. Mercer, [1761]
Poll order. Occupation and place of residence. Index.
Rose Fuller William Northey Gabriel Hanger
Maidstone Pub Lib Guildhall Lib

1768—The poll for electing two burgesses... n.p., [1768]
Poll order. Occupation of residents and place of residence of out-voters. Index.
Charles Marsham Roert Gregory Arthur Annesley
Maidstone Pub Lib Guildhall Lib

1774—The poll for electing... Maidstone: W. Mercer, [1774]
Poll order. Occupation of residents and place of residence of out-voters.
Sir Horatio Mann Lord Guernsey Robert Gregory
Maidstone Pub Lib Inst Hist Res

1780—The poll for electing... Rochester: T. Fisher, [1780]
Poll order. Occupation of residents and place of residence of out-voters. Index including non-voters.
Sir Horace Mann Clement Taylor Charles Finch
Maidstone Pub Lib Inst Hist Res

1784—The poll for the election... Maidstone: J. Blake, [1784]
Poll order. Occupation of residents and place of residence of out-voters. Index.

Clement Taylor   Gerard Noel Edwards   William Geary

Maidstone Pub Lib   Inst Hist Res

1788*—The poll for electing a burgess... Rochester: Phoenix Printing Office, [1788]
Poll order. Occupation of residents and place of residence of out-voters. Index.

Matthew Bloxham   George Byng, Jr.

Maidstone Pub Lib   Guildhall Lib

1790—The poll for electing... Maidstone: D. Chalmers, [1790]
Poll order. Occupation of residents and place of residence of out-voters. Index.

Clement Taylor   Matthew Bloxham   Robert Parker

Maidstone Pub Lib   Inst Hist Res

1802—The poll for electing... Maidstone: J. Blake, [1802]
Poll order. Occupation. Index.

John Hodson Durand   Sir Matthew Bloxam   John Henniker Major

Maidstone Pub Lib   Inst Hist Res

1806—The poll for electing... Maidstone: J. Blake, [1806]
Poll order. Occupation and place of residence. Index.

George Simson   George Longman   Sir Matthew Bloxam

Maidstone Pub Lib   Guildhall Lib

1807—The poll for electing... Maidstone: J. Blake, [1807]
Poll order. Occupation and place of residence. Index.

George Simson   George Longman   Sir William Geary

Maidstone Pub Lib   Guildhall Lib

1812—The poll for electing... Maidstone: J. Blake, [1812]
Poll order. Occupation and place of residence. Index.

George Simson   Sir Samuel Egerton Brydges   George Longman

Maidstone Pub Lib   Guildhall Lib

1818—The poll for electing... Maidstone: J. V. Hall, [1818]
Poll order. Occupation and place of residence. Index.

Abraham Wildey Robarts   George Longman   John Wells

Maidstone Pub Lib   Guildhall Lib

1820—The poll for electing... Maidstone: Wickham & Cutbush, [1820]
Poll order. Occupation and place of residence. Non-voters. Index.

Abraham Wildey Robarts   John Wells   Richard Sharp

Maidstone Pub Lib   Guildhall Lib

1820—The poll for electing... Maidstone: J. Smith, [1820]
Poll order. Occupation and place of residence. Index.

Abraham Wildey Robarts   John Wells   Richard Sharp

Maidstone Pub Lib   Inst Hist Res

1826—The poll for electing... Maidstone: R. J. Cutbush, [1826]
Poll order. Occupation and place of residence. Non-voters. Index.

John Wells   Abraham Wildey Roberts   Wyndham Lewis

Maidstone Pub Lib   Inst Hist Res

1826—The poll for electing... Maidstone: A. Austen, [1826]
Poll order. Occupation and place of residence. Index.

John Wells   Abraham Wildey Roberts   Wyndham Lewis

Maidstone Pub Lib   Inst Hist Res

1830—The poll for electing... Maidstone: Cutbush, [1830]
Poll order. Occupation and place of residence. Non-voters. Index.

Abraham Wildey Robarts   Henry Winchester   Philip Rawlings   W. G. T. D. Tyssen

Maidstone Pub Lib   Inst Hist Res

1830—The poll for electing... Maidstone: Austen, [1830]
Poll order. Occupation and place of residence. Index.

Abraham Wildey Robarts   Henry Winchester   Philip Rawlings   W. G. T. D. Tyssen

Maidstone Pub Lib   Inst Hist Res

1831—The poll for electing... Maidstone: A. Austen, [1831]
Poll order. Occupation and place of residence. Index.

Abraham Wildey Robarts   James Charles Barnett   Henry Winchester   George Simson

Maidstone Pub Lib   Inst Hist Res

1832—The poll for electing... Maidstone: A. Austen, [1832]
Poll order by booth. Occupation and address. Non-voters. Index.

Abraham Wildey Robarts   Charles James Barnett   Wyndham Lewis

Maidstone Pub Lib   Inst Hist Res

1832—The poll for electing... Maidstone: J. Brown, [1832]
Poll order by booth. Occupation and address. Non-voters. Index.

Abraham Wildey Robarts   Charles James Barnett   Wyndham Lewis

Maidstone Pub Lib   Inst Hist Res

[Same printing as preceding entry
with different title page.]

1835—The poll for electing... Maidstone: J. Brown, [1835]
Alphabetical by booth. Occupation and address. Freemen distinguished.
Non-voters.

Wyndham Lewis   Abraham Wildey Robarts   Charles James Barnett   Alderman Lucas
E. Hilliard

Maidstone Pub Lib   Inst Hist Res

1837—The poll for electing... Maidstone: J. Brown, [1837]
Poll order by ward and booth. Occupation and address. Freemen distinguished. Non-voters.

Wyndham Lewis Benjamin Disraeli Thomas Perronet Thompson Erskine Perry

Maidstone Pub Lib Inst Hist Res

1837—The poll for electing... Maidstone: J. V. Hall, [1837]
Alphabetical by ward. Occupation and address. Freemen distinguished. Non-voters included.

Wyndham Lewis Benjamin Disraeli Thomas Perronet Thompson Erskine Perry

Maidstone Pub Lib Inst Hist Res

1838*—The poll for electing... Maidstone: J. Smith, 1838
Alphabetical by ward and booth. Occupation, address and order of polling. Freemen distinguished. Non-voters included.

John Minet Fector Abraham Wildey Robarts

Maidstone Pub Lib Inst Hist Res

1841—The poll for electing... Maidstone: J. V. Hall, 1841
Alphabetical by ward and booth. Occupation, address and order of polling. Freemen and disqualified distinguished. Non-voters included.

Alexander James Beresford Hope George Dodd David Salomons

Maidstone Pub Lib Inst Hist Res

1852—The poll for the election... Maidstone: Cutbush, Whiting & Cutbush, 1852
Alphabetical by ward. Address. Freemen distinguished. Non-voters.

James Whatman George Dodd William Lee

Maidstone Pub Lib Inst Hist Res

1853*—The poll for the election... Maidstone: F. W. & H. R. Cutbush, [1853]
Alphabetical by ward. Occupation and address. Freemen distinguished. Non-voters.

William Lee Charles Wykeham Martin

Maidstone Pub Lib Inst Hist Res

1857—The poll for the election... Maidstone: Wickham Library, [1857]
Alphabetical by ward. Occupation and address. Freemen distinguished. Non-voters.

Alexander James Beresford Hope Edward Scott William Lee Humphrey Mildmay

Maidstone Pub Lib Inst Hist Res

1859—Borough of Maidstone election. The poll... Maidstone: F. W. & H. R. Cutbush, [1859]
Alphabetical by ward. Occupation and address. Freemen distinguished. Non-voters.

William Lee Charles Buxton Egerton Vernon Harcourt John Wardlaw

Maidstone Pub Lib Inst Hist Res

1859—The poll for the election of two burgesses... Maidstone: Wickham, [1859]
Alphabetical by ward. Occupation and address. Freemen distinguished. Non-voters.

William Lee   Charles Buxton   Egerton Vernon Harcourt   John Wardlaw

Maidstone Pub Lib   Inst Hist Res

1865—Borough of Maidstone election. The poll... Maidstone: *South Eastern Gazette,* [1865]
Alphabetical by ward. Occupation and address. Freemen distinguished. Non-voters and tendered votes.

William Lee   James Whatman   Edward Ladd Betts   John Wardlaw

Maidstone Pub Lib   Inst Hist Res

1865—The poll for the election of two burgesses... Maidstone: Wickham, [1865]
Alphabetical by ward. Occupation and address. Freemen distinguished. Non-voters and tendered votes.

William Lee   James Whatman   Edward Ladd Betts   John Wardlaw

Maidstone Pub Lib   Inst Hist Res

1868—Compiled from the official returns. 1868. Borough of Maidstone election... Maidstone: *South Eastern Gazette,* [1868]
Alphabetical by ward. Occupation and address. Freemen and lodgers distinguished. Non-voters.

William Lee   James Whatman   William Foster White   G. Parbury

Maidstone Pub Lib   Guildhall Lib

1870*—Compiled from the official returns. 1870. Borough of Maidstone election... Maidstone: *South Eastern Gazette,* [1870]
Alphabetical by ward. Occupation and address. Freemen and lodgers distinguished. Non-voters.

Sir John Lubbock   William Foster White

Maidstone Pub Lib   Inst Hist Res

ROCHESTER

1768—The poll of the city of Rochester... Rochester: Thomas Fisher, 1768
Alphabetical. Occupation.

John Calcraft   William Gordon   Francis Geary

Rochester Pub Lib   Guildhall Lib

1771*—The poll of the city of Rochester... Rochester: T. Fisher, 1771
Poll order. Occupation. Non-voters. Index.

Thomas Pye   Richard Smith

Rochester Pub Lib   Guildhall Lib

1774—[Lacks title page. Begins: The poll of the freemen of the city of Rochester . . .]
[Rochester, 1774]
Poll order. Occupation. Index.

Robert Gregory   George Finch Hatton   Sir Thomas Pye

Rochester Pub Lib   Brit Lib

1780—The poll for the city of Rochester... Rochester: T. Fisher, [1780]
Poll order. Occupation. Index.

George Finch Hatton   Robert Gregory   Nathaniel Smith

Rochester Pub Lib   Guildhall Lib

1790—The poll for the city of Rochester... Rochester: W. Gillman, [1790]
Poll order. Occupation and place of residence. Index.

George Best   Sir Richard Bickerton   Marquess of Titchfield

Rochester Pub Lib   Inst Hist Res

1792*—The poll for the city of Rochester... Rochester: Gillman & Etherington, [1792]
Poll order. Occupation and place of residence. Index.

Nathaniel Smith   Sir Richard King

Rochester Pub Lib   Brit Lib

1802—The poll of the electors... Rochester: W. Epps, 1802
Poll order. Occupation and place of residence. Alphabetical list by place of residence. Non-voters, distinguishing disqualified. Index.

Sir William Sidney Smith   James Hulks   George Smith   James Roper Head

Rochester Pub Lib   Inst Hist Res

1806—The poll of the electors... Rochester: W. Epps, 1807
Poll order. Occupation and place of residence. Alphabetical list by place of residence. Non-voters, distinguishing disqualified. Index.
Petition proceedings.

John Calcraft   James Barnett   Sir William Sidney Smith

Rochester Pub Lib   Inst Hist Res

1807—The poll of the electors... Rochester: W. Epps, 1807
Poll order. Occupation and place of residence. Alphabetical list by place of residence. Non-voters, distinguishing disqualified. Index.

Sir Thomas Boulden Thompson   John Calcraft   Sir Thomas Trigge

Rochester Pub Lib   Inst Hist Res

1816*—The poll of the electors... Rochester: W. Epps, 1816
Poll order. Occupation and place of residence. Rejected voters distinguished. Alphabetical list by place of residence. Non-voters, distinguishing disqualified. Index.

James Barnett   Sir Thomas Boulden Thompson

Guildhall Lib

1816*—The poll of the electors... Rochester: W. Wildash, 1817
Poll order. Occupation and place of residence. Rejected voters distinguished. Alphabetical list by place of residence. Non-voters, distinguishing disqualified.

James Barnett   Sir Thomas Boulden Thompson

Rochester Pub Lib   Brit Lib

1818—The poll of the electors... Rochester: W. Epps, [1818]
Poll order. Occupation and place of residence. Index.

James Barnett   Lord Binning   Robert Torrens

Rochester Pub Lib   Brit Lib

1818—The poll of the electors... Rochester: W. Wildash, 1818
Poll order. Occupation and place of residence. Alphabetical list by place of residence. Non-voters, distinguishing disqualified. Index.

James Barnett   Lord Binning   Robert Torrens

Rochester Pub Lib   Guildhall Lib

1826—The poll of the electors... Rochester: Wm. Epps, 1826
Poll order. Occupation and place of residence. Non-voters, distinguishing disqualified. Index.

Henry Dundas   Ralph Bernal   William Armstrong

Rochester Pub Lib   Guildhall Lib

1830—The poll of the electors... Rochester: S. Caddel & G. H. Vidion, 1830
Poll order. Occupation and place of residence. Alphabetical list by place of residence. Rejected voters with reasons. Non-voters and disqualified. Index.

Ralph Bernal   Lord Villiers   John Mills

Rochester Pub Lib   Inst Hist Res

1835—The poll of the freemen and electors... Rochester: William Wildash, 1835
Alphabetical. Occupation and place of residence. Non-voters and disqualified.

Ralph Bernal   Thomas Twisden Hodges   Lord Charles Wellesley

Rochester Pub Lib   Guildhall Lib

1835—The poll of the electors... Rochester: S. Caddel & G. H. Vidion, 1835
Poll order by booth. Occupation and place of residence. Alphabetical list. Non-voters, distinguishing dead and disqualified.

Ralph Bernal   Thomas Twisden Hodges   Lord Charles Wellesley

Rochester Pub Lib   Brit Lib

1837—The poll of the electors... Strood: J. & W. H. Sweet, 1837
Poll order by booth. Occupation and place of residence. Alphabetical list. Tendered votes. Non-voters, distinguishing dead and disqualified.

Ralph Bernal   Thomas Benjamin Hobhouse   James Stoddart Douglas   Thomas Best

Rochester Pub Lib   Brit Lib

1841—The poll of the electors... Rochester: S. Caddell, 1841
Poll order by booth. Occupation and place of residence. Alphabetical list. Tendered votes. Non-voters, distinguishing dead and disqualified.

James Stoddart Douglas William Henry Bodkin Lord Melgund Francis Dashwood

Rochester Pub Lib Brit Lib

1847—The poll of the electors... Rochester: H. V. Scriven, 1847
Poll order by booth. Occupation and address. Non-voters, distinguishing dead. Index.

Ralph Bernal Thomas Twisden Hodges James Stoddart Douglas William Henry Bodkin

Rochester Pub Lib Inst Hist Res

1852—The poll of the electors... Rochester: W. Shadbolt, 1852
Poll order by booth. Occupation and address. Non-voters. Index.

Francis Villiers Sir Thomas Herbert Maddock Ralph Bernal Thomas Twisden Hodges

Rochester Pub Lib Guildhall Lib

1856*—The poll of the electors... Rochester: Caddell, 1856
Poll order by polling station. Occupation and address. Non-voters. Index.

Philip Wykeham Martin William Henry Bodkin

Rochester Pub Lib Guildhall Lib

1856*—The poll of the electors... Rochester: Joseph E. Macaulay, 1856
Poll order by polling station. Occupation and address. Non-voters. Index.

Philip Wykeham Martin William Henry Bodkin

Rochester Pub Lib Inst Hist Res

1859—The poll for two members... Rochester: Caddell, 1859
Poll order by polling station. Occupation and address. Alphabetical list by qualification and parish. Non-voters.

Philip Wykeham Martin John Alexander Kinglake George Henry Money George Mitchell

Rochester Pub Lib Guildhall Lib

1865—The poll for two members... Rochester: Caddell, 1866
Poll order by polling station. Occupation and address. Alphabetical list by qualification and parish. Non-voters.

Philip Wykeham Martin John Alexander Kinglake Alfred Smee

Rochester Pub Lib Guildhall Lib

1868—The poll for two members... Rochester: Caddell Bros., 1869
Poll order by polling station. Occupation and address. Alphabetical list by qualification and parish. Non-voters.

Philip Wykeham Martin John Alexander Kinglake Alfred Smee

Rochester Pub Lib Inst Hist Res

SANDWICH

1831—The poll for the election... Sandwich: T. E. Stow, [1831]
Poll order. Occupation and place of residence. Non-voters. Index.

Joseph Marryat Sir Edward Thomas Troubridge Samuel Grove Price

Deal Pub Lib Inst Hist Res

1832—The poll for the election... Deal: Hayward, [1832]
Poll order. Occupation and place of residence. Non-voters. Index.

Joseph Marryat Sir Edward Thomas Troubridge Samuel Grove Price
Sir Edward William Campbell Rich Owen

Kent Archives Office Inst Hist Res

1837—The poll for the election... Deal: Hayward, [1837]
Alphabetical by polling booth. Occupation, place of residence and qualification. Non-voters.

Sir Edward Thomas Troubridge Sir James Rivett Carnac Samuel Grove Price
Sir Brook William Bridges

Soc Geneal Inst Hist Res

1841*—The poll of the election of a baron... Deal: Deveson, [1841]
Alphabetical by polling booth. Occupation and place of residence. Householders distinguished. Non-voters with freemen distinguished.

Hugh Hamiton Lindsay Charles Richard Fox

Brit Lib

1847—The poll of the election... Sandwich: Hayward, [1847]
Alphabetical. Occupation and place of residence. Non-voters.

Lord Clarence Paget Charles William Grenfell Lord Charles Pelham Clinton

Guildhall Lib

1852*—The poll book of the election... Deal: E. F. Giraud, [1852]
Alphabetical by polling booth. Occupation and place of residence. Non-voters.

Lord Charles Pelham Clinton J. T. W. French

Brit Lib Guildhall Lib

1857—The poll of the election... Deal: T. Hayward, [1857]
Alphabetical by polling booth. Occupation and place of residence. Freemen distinguished. Non-voters.

Edward Hugessen Knatchbull Hugessen Lord Clarence Paget James MacGregor
John Lang

Kent Archives Office Guildhall Lib

1859 (April)—The poll for the election... Deal: Hayward, [1859]
Alphabetical by polling booth. Occupation and place of residence. Freemen distinguished. Non-voters.

Edward Hugessen Knatchbull Hugessen Lord Clarence Paget Sir James Fergusson
William David Lewis

Guildhall Lib

1859* (June)—The poll for the election of one baron... Deal: Thomas Hayward, [1859]
Alphabetical by polling booth. Occupation and place of residence. Non-voters.

Edward Hugessen Knatchbull Hugessen   Sir James Fergusson

Private Possession   Inst Hist Res

1865—The poll for the election... Sandwich: S. Prentice, [1865]
Alphabetical by polling booth. Occupation and place of residence. Non-voters.

Edward Hugessen Knatchbull Hugessen   Lord Clarence Paget   Charles Capper

Private Possession   Inst Hist Res

1868—The poll taken before Thomas Dorman... Deal: E. Hayward, [1868]
Alphabetical by qualification and candidate. Occupation and address. Non-voters.

Edward Hugessen Knatchbull Hugessen   Henry Arthur Brassey   Henry Worms

Deal Pub Lib   Guildhall Lib

LANCASHIRE, ASHTON-UNDER-LYME

1841—List of persons who voted for Charles Hindley... List of persons who voted for Jonah Harrop... Ashton: T. A. Phillips, [1841]
Alphabetical by candidate. Occupation and Address.

Charles Hindley   Jonah Harrop

Ashton Pub Lib   Inst Hist Res

BLACKBURN

1847—A list of persons who voted... *Blackburn Standard*, 4 August 1847
Alphabetical by candidate. Address. Rejected voters and non-voters.

John Hornby   James Pilkington   William Hargreaves   W. P. Roberts

Brit Lib (News)   Inst Hist Res

1852—A list of persons who voted... *Blackburn Standard*, 14 July 1852
Alphabetical by candidate. Address. Non-voters, dead and disqualified.

James Pilkington   William Eccles   John Hornby

Brit Lib (News)   Inst Hist Res

1853*—A list of persons who voted... *Blackburn Standard,* 30 March 1853
Alphabetical by candidate. Address. Non-voters.

Montague Joseph Feilden   William Henry Hornby

Brit Lib (News)   Inst Hist Res

1865—A list of persons who voted... Blackburn: J. Walkden, [1865]
Alphabetical by candidate. Address. Non-voters.

William Henry Hornby   Joseph Feilden   James Pilkington   J. Gerald Potter

Guildhall Lib

BOLTON

1832—A list of persons who voted... Bolton: R. Holden, 1832
Alphabetical by candidate. Occupation and address. Non-voters and rejected voters with nature and address of qualification.

Robert Torrens William Bolling J. Ashton Yates William Eagle

Bolton Pub Lib Inst Hist Res

1835—A list of persons who voted... Bolton: R. Holden, 1835
Alphabetical by candidate. Occupation and address. Rejected and non-voters, distinguishing dead and removed.

Robert Torrens William Bolling Peter Ainsworth

Bolton Pub Lib Guildhall Lib

1837—A list of persons who voted... Bolton: R. M. Holden, 1837
Alphabetical by candidate. Occupation and address. Non-voters, distinguishing dead and removed.

Peter Ainsworth William Bolling Andrew Knowles

Bolton Pub Lib Inst Hist Res

1841—A corrected list of persons who voted... *Bolton Chronicle*, 17 July 1841
Alphabetical by candidate. Occupation and address.

Peter Ainsworth John Bowring Peter Rothwell William Bolling

Bolton Pub Lib Inst Hist Res

1847—A list of the persons who voted... Bolton: William Bridge, 1847
Alphabetical by candidate. Address. Non-voters.

William Bolling John Bowring John Brooks

Bolton Pub Lib Inst Hist Res

1849*—The list of persons who voted... *Bolton Chronicle*, 10 February 1849
Alphabetical by candidate. Address. Dead and non-voters.

Sir Joshua Walmsley Thomas Ridgway Bridson

Bolton Pub Lib Inst Hist Res

1852—The list of persons who voted... Bolton: Jas. Hudsmith, 1852
Alphabetical by candidate. Address. Dead and non-voters.

Thomas Barnes Joseph Crook Stephen Blair Peter Ainsworth

Bolton Pub Lib Inst Hist Res

1857—The list of persons who voted... *Bolton Chronicle*, 1 April 1857
Alphabetical by candidate. Address. Dead and non-voters.

William Gray Joseph Crook Thomas Barnes

Bolton Pub Lib Inst Hist Res

1865—List of voters... Reprinted from the election supplement to the *Bolton Guardian*, July 15th, 1865. Bolton: Thomas Cunliffe, [1865]
Alphabetical by candidate. Address. Dead and non-voters.

William Gray   Thomas Barnes   Samuel Pope   William Gibb

Bolton Pub Lib   Inst Hist Res

BURY

1865—A list of persons who voted... *Bury Guardian*, 29 July 1865
Alphabetical by district and candidate. Occupation and address. Non-voters.

Robert Needham Philips   Frederick Peel

Brit Lib (News)   Inst Hist Res

1868—The Bury poll book... Bury: John Heap [1868]
Alphabetical by district and candidate. Address. Non-voters.

Robert Needham Philips   Viscount Chelsea

Bury Pub Lib   Inst Hist Res

LANCASTER

1784—An alphabetical list of the poll. Lancaster: H. Walmsley, etc., 1784
Occupation, place of residence, and father of freemen by patrimony.

Abram Rawlinson   Francis Reynolds   John Lowther

Lancaster Pub Lib   Inst Hist Res

1786*—An alphabetical list of the poll... Lancaster: Henry Walmsley, 1786
Occupation, place of residence, and father of freemen by patrimony.
1784 voting.

Sir George Warren   John Lowther

Lancaster Pub Lib   Inst Hist Res

1802—An alphabetical list of the freemen polled... Lancaster: C. Clark [1802]
Occupation, place of residence, and father of freemen by patrimony.

John Dent   Marquess of Douglas   John Fenton Cawthorne

Lancaster Pub Lib   Inst Hist Res

1818—An alphabetical list of the freemen... Lancaster: J. Jackson, 1818
Occupation, place of residence, and father of freemen by patrimony.

John Gladstone   Gabriel Doveton   John Fenton Cawthorne

Lancaster Pub Lib   Inst Hist Res

1837—Lancaster borough election, July 25th, 1837. The poll book... Lancaster: A. Milner, 1837
Alphabetical by qualification. Occupation and address of freemen, nature and address of property of householders.

Thomas Greene   George Marton   P.M. Stewart   W. Rathbone Greg

Lancaster Pub Lib   Inst Hist Res

1841—Lancaster borough election, July 1, 1841. The poll book... Lancaster: Barwick, 1841
Alphabetical by qualification. Occupation and address of freemen, nature and address of property of householders. Non-voters included.

Thomas Greene George Marton Robert Baynes Armstrong

Lancaster Pub Lib Inst Hist Res

1847—Lancaster borough election, July 29, 1847. The poll book... Lancaster: C. Barwick, 1847
Alphabetical by qualification and township. Occupation and address of freemen, address of householders. Non-voters included.

Samuel Gregson Thomas Greene Edward Dodson Salisbury

Lancaster Pub Lib Inst Hist Res

1847—Lancaster borough election. July 29, 1847. The poll book... Lancaster: A. Milner, [1847]
Alphabetical by qualification and township. Occupation and address of freemen, address of householders. Non-voters included.

Samuel Gregson Thomas Greene Edward Dodson Salisbury

Lancaster Pub Lib Inst Hist Res

1848*—Lancaster borough election, March 9, 1848. The poll book... Lancaster: C. Barwick, 1848
Alphabetical by qualification and township. Occupation and address of freemen, address of householders. Non-voters included.

Robert Baynes Armstrong Edward Henry Stanley

Lancaster Pub Lib Inst Hist Res

1848*—Lancaster borough election, March 9, 1848. The poll book... Lancaster: A. Milner, [1848]
Alphabetical by qualification and township. Occupation and address of freemen, address of householders. Non-voters included.

Robert Baynes Armstrong Edward Henry Stanley

Lancaster Pub Lib Inst Hist Res

1852—Lancaster borough election, July 9th 1852. List of voters... Lancaster: G. C. Clark. Reprinted from Supplement presented with the *Lancaster Gazette*, July 17th, 1852.
Alphabetical by qualification and township. Occupation and address of freemen, address of householders. Non-voters included.

Samuel Gregson Robert Baynes Armstrong Thomas Greene John Ellis

Lancaster Pub Lib Inst Hist Res

1853*—The polling list of the Lancaster election... Lancaster: A. Milner, 1853
Alphabetical by qualification and township. Occupation and address of freemen, address of householders. Non-voters included.

Thomas Greene John Armstrong

Lancaster Pub Lib Inst Hist Res

1857—The poll book of the Lancaster borough election... Lancaster: Milner, 1857
Alphabetical by qualification and township. Occupation and address of freemen, address of householders. Non-voters included.

Samuel Gregson   William James Garnett   Robert Gladstone

Lancaster Pub Lib   Inst Hist Res

1859—The polling list of the Lancaster election... Lancaster: Milner, 1859
Alphabetical by qualification and township. Occupation and address of freemen, address of householders. Non-voters included.

William James Garnett   Samuel Gregson   W.A.F. Saunders   Edward Matthew Fenwick

Lancaster Pub Lib   Inst Hist Res

1864*—The polling list of the Lancaster election... Lancaster: E. & J. L. Milner, 1864
Alphabetical by qualification and township. Occupation and address of freemen, address of householders. Non-voters included.

Edward Matthew Fenwick   W. A. F. Saunders

Lancaster Pub Lib   Inst Hist Res

1865—The polling list of the Lancaster election... Lancaster: E. & J. L. Milner, 1865
Alphabetical by qualification and township. Occupation and address of freemen, address of householders. Non-voters included.

Edward Matthew Fenwick   Henry William Schneider   E. Lawrence

Lancaster Pub Lib   Inst Hist Res

LIVERPOOL

1734—An exact list of the persons who polled... n.p., [1734]
Residents by candidate and occupation. Out-voters by candidate with occupation and place of residence. Recently created freemen by date of creation and candidate.

Thomas Brereton   Richard Geldard   Thomas Bootle   Foster Cunliffe

Liverpool Pub Lib   Inst Hist Res

1761—An entire and impartial collection of all the papers...to which is added a correct alphabetical list of the poll... Liverpool: John Sadler, 1761
Occupation and place of residence. Election literature.

Sir Ellis Cunliffe   Sir William Meredith   Charles Pole

Liverpool   Univ Lib   Guildhall Lib

1761—A genuine collection of all the papers... to which is added an alphabetical list of the poll... Liverpool: R. Williamson, 1761
Poll order by first letter. Occupation and address or place of residence. Election literature.

Sir Ellis Cunliffe   Sir William Meredith   Charles Pole

Liverpool Pub Lib   Guildhall Lib

1780—A collection of papers . . . to which is annexed an alphabetical list of the poll...
Liverpool: P. Johnson, 1780
Occupation. Election literature.

Bamber Gascoyne, Jr.   Henry Rawlinson   Richard Pennant

Liverpool Pub Lib   Inst Hist Res

1784—An alphabetical list of the freemen... Liverpool: Thomas Johnson, 1784
Occupation.

Bamber Gascoyne, Jr.   Lord Penrhyn   Banastre Tarleton   Sir William Meredith

Liverpool Pub Lib   Inst Hist Res

1790—The poll for the election... Liverpool: T. Johnson, [1790]
Alphabetical. Occupation. Election literature.

Banastre Tarleton   Bamber Gascoyne, Jr.   Lord Penrhyn   Thomas Townley Parker

Liverpool Pub Lib   Inst Hist Res

1796—The poll for the election... Liverpool: H. Hodgson, [1796]
Alphabetical. Occupation and address. Election literature.

Isaac Gascoyne   Banastre Tarleton   John Tarleton

Liverpool Pub Lib   Inst Hist Res

1802—A complete list of the 1425 burgesses... Liverpool: W. Jones, 1802
Alphabetical. Occupation and address. Voters for Chalmer listed separately. Election literature.

Isaac Gascoyne   Banastre Tarleton   Joseph Birch   Francis Chalmer

Liverpool Pub Lib   Inst Hist Res

1802—The poll for the election... Liverpool: Ferguson, Mackey, 1802
Alphabetical. Occupation and address. Election literature.

Isaac Gascoyne   Banastre Tarleton   Joseph Birch   Francis Chalmer

Liverpool Pub Lib   Inst Hist Res

1806—A compendious and impartial account of the election... Liverpool: Wright & Cruickshank, [1806]
Alphabetical. Occupation and address. Separate alphabetical arrangement by watchman's district and street. Political state of Liverpool and analysis of the election. Election literature.

William Roscoe   Isaac Gascoyne   Banastre Tarleton

Liverpool Pub Lib   Inst Hist Res

1806—History of the election... Liverpool: Jones & Wright, [1806]
Alphabetical. Occupation and address. History of representation and account of proceedings.

William Roscoe   Isaac Gascoyne   Banastre Tarleton

Liverpool Pub Lib   Inst Hist Res

1806—The poll for the election... Liverpool: J. Gore, [1806]
Alphabetical. Occupation and address.

William Roscoe   Isaac Gascoyne   Banastre Tarleton

Liverpool Pub Lib   Guildhall Lib

1807—The poll for the election... Liverpool: J. Gore, [1807]
Alphabetical. Occupation and address.

Banastre Tarleton   Isaac Gascoyne   William Roscoe   William Joseph Denison

Liverpool Pub Lib   Inst Hist Res

1812—A correct account of the poll... Liverpool: Wright & Cruickshank, [1812]
Alphabetical. Occupation and address. Electoral history from 1780 and account of proceedings.

George Canning   Isaac Gascoyne   Henry Brougham   Thomas Creevey   Banastre Tarleton

Liverpool Pub Lib   Inst Hist Res

1812—The poll for the election... Liverpool: J. Gore, [1812]
Alphabetical. Occupation and address.

George Canning   Isaac Gascoyne   Henry Brougham   Thomas Creevey   Banastre Tarleton

Liverpool Pub Lib   Guildhall Lib

1816*—The poll for the election... Liverpool: J. Gore, [1816]
Alphabetical. Occupation and address.

George Canning   Thomas Leyland

Manchester Pub Lib   Guildhall Lib

1818—The poll for the election... Liverpool: J. Gore, 1818
Alphabetical. Occupation and address. Analysis of voting by occupation.

George Canning   Isaac Gascoyne   Earl of Sefton

Liverpool Pub Lib   Inst Hist Res

1820—The poll for the election... Liverpool: J. Gore, 1820
Alphabetical. Occupation and address.

George Canning   Isaac Gascoyne   Peter Crompton   Thomas Leyland

Liverpool Pub Lib   Inst Hist Res

1830*—The poll for the election... Liverpool: J. Gore, 1830
Alphabetical. Occupation and address. Account of proceedings.

William Ewart   John Evelyn Denison

Liverpool Pub Lib   Inst Hist Res

1830*—Election for a member of parliament... Liverpool: Rockliff & Duckworth, 1831
Alphabetical. Occupation and address. Personated votes distinguished.

William Ewart   John Evelyn Denison

Liverpool Pub Lib   Inst Hist Res

1832—The poll for the election... Liverpool: J. & J. Mawdsley, 1833
Alphabetical by qualification. Occupation and address. Account of proceedings.

William Ewart Viscount Sandon Thomas Thornely

Liverpool Pub Lib Inst Hist Res

1835—The poll for the election... Liverpool: J. & J. Mawdsley, 1835
Alphabetical by qualification. Occupation and address. Account of proceedings.

Viscount Sandon William Ewart Sir Howard Douglas James Morris

Liverpool Pub Lib Inst Hist Res

1837—The poll for the election... Liverpool: J. & J. Mawdsley, 1837
Alphabetical by ward. Occupation and address. Freemen distinguished.

Viscount Sandon Cresswell Cresswell William Ewart Howard Elphinstone

Liverpool Pub Lib Inst Hist Res

1841—The poll for the election... Liverpool: J. Mawdsley, 1841
Alphabetical by ward. Occupation and address. Freemen distinguished.

Viscount Sandon Cresswell Cresswell Sir Joshua Walmsley Lord Palmerston

Liverpool Univ Lib Inst Hist Res

1857—Poll book: general election, 1857... Liverpool: Mail Office, [1857]
Alphabetical by polling station compartment half-hourly returns. Address.

Thomas Berry Horsfall Charles Turner Joseph Christopher Ewart

Liverpool Pub Lib Inst Hist Res

Untraced: 1852

MANCHESTER

1832—The electors' guide, containing a list of the names... who voted... Manchester: George Cave, 1833
Alphabetical by district. Address and qualification.

Mark Philips Charles Poulett Thomson Samuel Jones Loyd John Thomas Hope
William Cobbett

Manchester Pub Lib Inst Hist Res

1839*—Manchester poll book. The poll for the election... Manchester: Josiah Leicester, [1839]
Alphabetical by place and district. Nature and situation of qualification. Both polls on succeeding days given.

Robert Hyde Gregg Sir George Murray

Manchester Pub Lib Inst Hist Res

OLDHAM

1832—A list of the voters... Manchester: F. Looney for John Knight, [1832]
By district. Occupation and address. Address to non-electors.

William Cobbett John Fielden B. Heywood Bright William Burgh George Stephens

Oldham Pub Lib Inst Hist Res

1835*—Oldham election. The poll book... Oldham: J. Dodge, 1835
Alphabetical by district and candidate. Address. Non-voters. Prefatory note by Cobbett's committee.

John Frederick Lees John Morgan Cobbett Feargus O'Connor

Oldham Pub Lib Inst Hist Res

1847—The remembrancer, shewing how the electors... voted... Oldham: J. Dodge, 1847
Alphabetical by district and candidate. Address. Shopkeepers listed separately. Employers who voted against Fielden distinguishing Anti-Corn Law League contributors. Preface by committee of working men.

William Johnson Fox John Duncuft John Morgan Cobbett John Fielden

Oldham Pub Lib Inst Hist Res

1852 (July)—Election, 1852. The Oldham poll book... Oldham: Thomas Hayes, 1852
Alphabetical by district and candidate. Non-voters.

John Morgan Cobbett John Duncuft William Johnson Fox

Oldham Pub Lib Inst Hist Res

1852 (July)—The second remembrancer shewing how the electors... Oldham: J. Dodge, 1852
Alphabetical by district, candidate and occupation. Address. Non-voters. 1847 votes shown.

John Morgan Cobbett John Duncuft William Johnson Fox

Oldham Pub Lib Inst Hist Res

1852* (December)—Second election, 1852. The Oldham poll book... Oldham: Thomas Hayes, 1852
Alphabetical by district. Address. Non-voters included.

William Johnson Fox James Heald

Oldham Pub Lib Inst Hist Res

1852* (December)—The third remembrancer, shewing how the electors... Oldham: J. Dodge, 1852
Alphabetical by district, candidate and occupation. Address. Non-voters.

William Johnson Fox James Heald

Oldham Pub Lib Inst Hist Res

1857—Election, 1857. The Oldham poll book... Oldham: Thomas Hayes, [1857]
Alphabetical by district and candidate. Address. Non-voters.

John Morgan Cobbett James Platt William Johnson Fox

Oldham Pub Lib Inst Hist Res

1859—Election, 1859. The Oldham poll book... Oldham: John Hirst, [1859]
Alphabetical by district and candidate. Address. Dead and non-voters.

William Johnson Fox John Morgan Cobbett John Tomlinson Hibbert

Oldham Pub Lib Inst Hist Res

1865—Election, 1865. The Oldham poll book... Oldham: A. Morris, [1865]
Alphabetical by district and candidate. Occupation and address. Non-voters and dead.

John Tomlinson Hibbert John Platt John Morgan Cobbett Frederick Lowten Spinks

Oldham Pub Lib Inst Hist Res

1868—General election, 1868. Oldham borough poll book... Oldham: Jones, Tetlow & Stubbs, 1869
By polling district and booth. Queried and objected voters distinguished.

John Tomlinson Hibbert John Platt John Morgan Cobbett Frederick Lowten Spinks

Oldham Pub Lib Inst Hist Res

PRESTON

1807—An alphabetical list of the electors... Preston: W. Addison, [1807]
Occupation and address. Last day voters and Catholics distinguished. Last day voters also shown in poll order.

Lord Stanley Samuel Horrocks Joseph Hanson

Preston Pub Lib Inst Hist Res

1812—An alphabetical list of the electors... Preston: William Addison, [1812]
Occupation and address. Last day voters distinguished. Rejected voters with voting intentions.

Samuel Horrocks Edmund Hornby Edward Hanson

Lancs Rec Off Inst Hist Res

1818—An alphabetical list of the electors... Preston: William Addison, [1818]
Occupation and address. Rejected voters with voting intentions.

Samuel Horrocks Edmund Hornby Peter Crompton

Preston Pub Lib Inst Hist Res

1820—An alphabetical list of the electors... Preston: William Addison, [1820]
Occupation and address. Rejected voters with voting intentions.

Samuel Horrocks Edmund Hornby John Williams Henry Hunt

Preston Pub Lib Inst Hist Res

1830*—An alphabetical list of persons... Preston: L. Clarke, 1831
Occupation and address. Objected voters for Hunt distinguished.

Henry Hunt Edward Geoffrey Smith Stanley

Preston Pub Lib IHR

1832—A list of persons entitled to vote... Preston: L. Clarke, 1833
Alphabetical by qualification. Occupation, address and polling district. Non-voters included. Election regulations and list of districts and streets.

Peter Hesketh Fleetwood Henry Thomas Stanley Henry Hunt J. Forbes Charles Crompton

Preston Pub Lib Inst Hist Res

1835—A list of persons who voted... Preston: William Pritt, 1835
Alphabetical by place of qualification. Occupation, address and polling district. Non-voters included.

Peter Hesketh Fleetwood Henry Thomas Stanley Thomas Perronett Thompson Thomas Smith

Lancs Rec Off Inst Hist Res

1837—A list of persons who voted... Preston: William Pritt, 1838
Alphabetical by place of qualification. Occupation, address and ward. Non-voters included.

Peter Hesketh Fleetwood Robert Townley Parker J. Crawford

Preston Pub Lib Inst Hist Res

1841—A list of persons who voted... Preston: W. Bailey, 1841
Alphabetical by place of qualification. Occupation, address and ward. Non-voters included.

Sir Hesketh Fleetwood Sir George Strickland Robert Townley Parker Charles Swainson

Preston Pub Lib Inst Hist Res

1841—A list of persons who voted... Preston: W. Pollard, 1841
Alphabetical by place of qualification. Occupation, address and ward. Non-voters included.

Sir Hesketh Fleetwood Sir George Strickland Robert Townley Parker Charles Swainson

Lancs Rec Off Inst Hist Res

[Same printing as preceding entry with different imprint.]

1852—The poll list at Preston election... Preston: Worthington, 1853
Alphabetical. Occupation and address of old franchise, address of L10 voters. Non-voters included. Anti-Catholic election verses.

Robert Townley Parker Sir George Strickland Charles Pascoe Grenfell James German

Preston Pub Lib Inst Hist Res

1857—The poll list of Preston election... Preston: Edward Ambler, 1857
Alphabetical by qualification. Occupation and address of old franchise, address of L10 voters. Account of proceedings.

Charles Pascoe Grenfell Richard Assheton Cross Sir George Strickland

Lancs Rec Off Inst Hist Res

1859—The poll book of voters... Preston: E. Ambler, 1859
Alphabetical by qualification. Occupation and address of old franchise, address of L10 voters. Non-voters included. Account of proceedings.

Richard Assheton Cross   Charles Pascoe Grenfell   John Talbot Clifton

Preston Pub Lib   Inst Hist Res

1868—Preston election, 1868. The Herald poll list... Preston: *Herald* Steam Printing Office, [1868]
Alphabetical by qualification, ward and candidate. Address. Non-voters.

Edward Hermon Sir Thomas George Fermor HeskethJ. F. Leese Lord Edward Howard

Preston Rec Off   Guildhall Lib

Untraced: 1847, 1859 (Robinson), 1862

ROCHDALE

1837*—The Rochdale poll book... Rochdale: W. Butterworth, 1837
Alphabetical by township. Address and nature of qualification. Non-voters with dead and removed distinguished. Election literature.

John Fenton   Clement Royds

Rochdale Pub Lib   Inst Hist Res

1841—A copy of the poll of the electors... Rochdale: Jones & Crosskill, [1841]
By occupation and candidate. Address. Removed by candidate.

William Sharman Crawford   James Fenton

Rochdale Pub Lib   Inst Hist Res

1857—A copy of the poll of the electors... Rochdale: Felix Ashworth, [1857]
Alphabetical by township, occupation and candidate. Address. Non-voters.

Sir Alexander Ramsay   Edward Miall

Rochdale Pub Lib   Inst Hist Res

1857—A copy of the poll of the electors... Rochdale: Ormerod Bros., [1857]
Alphabetical by township, occupation and candidate. Address. Non-voters.

Sir Alexander Ramsay   Edward Miall

Rochdale Pub Lib   Inst Hist Res

SALFORD

1841—Salford poll book. Names of the persons who voted... Manchester: *Chronicle & Standard* Office, 1841
Alphabetical by polling district. Address. Voters for Brotherton disqualified by removal distinguished.

Joseph Brotherton   William Garnett

Manchester Pub Lib

WARRINGTON

1832—The poll for the election... Warrington: C. Malley, 1833
Alphabetical by township. Occupation and address.

Edward George Hornby   John Ireland Blackburne

Warrington Pub Lib   Inst Hist Res

1835—Poll book for the second election... [Warrington, 1835]
Alphabetical by candidate. Occupation and address. Rejected voters.

John Ireland Blackburne   Charles Hindley

Warrington Pub Lib   Inst Hist Res

1847—Poll book of the election... [Warrington, 1847]
Alphabetical by township and candidate. Occupation and address. Non-voters.

Gilbert Greenall   William Allcard

Warrington Pub Lib   Inst Hist Res

WIGAN

1830—An account of the origin of, and proceedings in the contested election... Wigan: J. Hilton, [1830]
Poll order. Occupation and place of residence. Objected and rejected voters distinguished.

James Hardcastle   Richard Potter   James Alexander Hodson   James Lindsay
John Hodson Kearsley

Brit Lib

1837—The Wigan election. *Wigan Gazette*, 8 September 1837
Alphabetical by qualification. Address. Non-voters included.

Charles Standish   Richard Potter   John Hodson Kearsley   Peter Grenfell

Brit Lib (News)   Inst Hist Res

1845*—Wigan election, 1845. A correct copy of the poll book... Wigan: T. Wall, 1845
Alphabetical. Address and nature of qualification. Non-voters included. Old burgesses and dead distinguished.

John Lindsay   Ralph Anthony Thicknesse

Wigan Pub Lib   Inst Hist Res

1852—An analytical copy of the poll book... Wigan: W. Strickland, 1852
Alphabetical by candidate. Address. Dead and non-voters.

Ralph Anthony Thicknesse   James Lindsay   Francis Sharpe Powell

Wigan Pub Lib   Inst Hist Res

1852—General election, 1852. A correct copy of the poll book... Wigan: Wall, 1852
Alphabetical. Address. Non-voters included. Old burgesses and dead distinguished. Separate lists of plumpers by candidate.

Ralph Anthony Thicknesse   James Lindsay   Francis Sharpe Powell

Wigan Pub Lib   Inst Hist Res

1852—Poll book of the election... Wigan: Birch & Pollard, 1852
Alphabetical. Address. Non-voters included. Old burgesses and dead distinguished. Separate lists of plumpers by candidate.

Ralph Anthony Thicknesse James Lindsay Francis Sharpe Powell

Wigan Pub Lib Inst Hist Res

1854*—[Title page missing. Begins 'Copy of the poll book of the borough of Wigan'] [Wigan, 1854]
Alphabetical. Address.

Joseph Acton Francis Sharpe Powell

Wigan Pub Lib Inst Hist Res (Typescript)

1857—General election, 1857. A correct copy of the poll book... Wigan: Wall, [1857]
Alphabetical. Address. Non-voters included. Burgesses and dead distinguished.

Francis Sharpe Powell Henry Woods James Lindsay

Wigan Pub Lib Inst Hist Res

1857—The late borough election. *Wigan Observer*, 5 April 1857
Alphabetical by candidate.

Francis Sharpe Powell Henry Woods James Lindsay

Brit Lib (News) Inst Hist Res

1859—The late borough election. *Wigan Observer & District Advertiser*, 6 May 1859
Alphabetical by candidate.

James Lindsay Henry Woods Francis Sharpe Powell

Brit Lib (News) Inst Hist Res

1866*—Poll book of the Wigan borough election... Wigan: Wall, [1866]
Alphabetical by candidate. Address. Non-voters.

Nathaniel Eckersley John Lancaster

Wigan Pub Lib Inst Hist Res

LEICESTERSHIRE

1719*—The Leicestershire poll... London: Simon Marten, 1720
Alphabetical by hundred and parish of residence. Place of freehold. Out-voters by county and parish.

Lord William Manners Francis Mundy

Leicester Pub Lib Inst Hist Res

1741—The poll for knights... London: James Bettenham, 1742
Alphabetical by hundred and parish of residence. Place of freehold. Out-voters by county and parish. Index.

Edward Smith Sir Thomas Cave Waring Ashby

Leicester Pub Lib Inst Hist Res

1775*—The poll for a knight... Leicester: John Gregory, 1775
Alphabetical by hundred and parish. Place of residence, nature and occupier of freehold.

John Peach Hungerford   William Pochin

Leicester Pub Lib   Inst Hist Res

1775*—An exact copy of the poll... Leicester: John Ireland, 1775
Alphabetical by hundred and parish of residence. Place of freehold. Out-voters by county and parish.

John Peach Hungerford   William Pochin

Leicester Pub Lib   Inst Hist Res

1830—The poll at the electing... Leicester: Thomas Combe, 1830
Alphabetical by hundred and parish. Occupation, place of residence and nature of freehold. Index.

George Anthony Legh Keck   Lord Robert Manners   Thomas Paget

Leicester Pub Lib   Inst Hist Res

1830—The poll as taken... Leicester: Albert Cockshaw, 1830
Alphabetical by hundred. Occupation and place of residence. Separate appendix listing voters alphabetically by hundred and parish of residence. Out-voters by county and parish.

George Anthony Legh Keck   Lord Robert Manners   Thomas Paget

Leicester Pub Lib   Inst Hist Res

NORTH LEICESTERSHIRE

1832—The poll as taken... Loughborough: S. Lee, 1833
Alphabetical by place of residence. Place and nature of qualification. Non-voters included.

Lord Robert Manners   Charles March Phillipps   William Augustus Johnson

Leicester Pub Lib   Inst Hist Res

1857—The poll taken on Friday, the 3rd of April... Leicester: T. Chapman Browne, [1857]
Alphabetical by polling district and parish. Place of residence. Non-voters by parish.

Edward Bazil Farnham   Lord John Manners   Charles Hay Frewen

Leicester Pub Lib   Guildhall Lib

1859—The poll taken on Friday, the 6th of May... Leicester: T. Chapman Browne, [1859]
Alphabetical by polling district and parish. Place of residence. Non-voters by parish.

Lord John Manners   Edward Bourchier Hartopp   Charles Hay Frewen

Leics Rec Off   Inst Hist Res

1865—The poll taken on Monday, the 24th July... Leicester: T. Chapman Browne,[1865]
Alphabetical by polling district and parish. Place of residence. Non-voters by parish.

Lord John Manners   Edward Bourchier Hartopp   Charles Hay Frewen

Leics Rec Off   Guildhall Lib

SOUTH LEICESTERSHIRE

1841—The poll for the election... Leicester: John S. Crossley, 1841
Alphabetical. Place of residence and qualification. Non-voters.

Henry Halford   Charles William Packe   Thomas Gisborne   Edward H. Cheney

Guildhall Lib   Inst Hist Res

1841—The poll taken... Leicester: J. G. & T. C. Brown, 1841
Alphabetical by polling district. Place of residence. Non-voters.

Henry Halford   Charles William Packe   Thomas Gisborne   Edward H. Cheney

Leicester Pub Lib   Inst Hist Res

1867*—The poll taken at the election... Leicester: F. Hewitt, [1867]
Alphabetical by polling district. Place of residence or qualification. Non-voters.

Thomas Tertius Paget   Albert Pell

Leicester Pub Lib   Guildhall Lib

1868—The poll taken on Tuesday, the 24th November... Leicester: T. Chapman Browne, [1868]
Alphabetical by polling district and parish. Place of residence. Non-voters by parish.

Viscount Curzon   Albert Pell   Thomas Tertius Paget

Leicester Pub Lib   Guildhall Lib

1870*—The poll taken on Friday, June 10th... Leicester: Wm. Penn Cox, [1870]
Alphabetical by polling district and parish. Place of residence. Non-voters by parish.

William Unwin Heygate   Thomas Tertius Paget

Leicester Pub Lib   Guildhall Lib

LEICESTER

1754—The poll for electing... Leicester: J. Gregory, [1754]
Poll order. Place of residence. Index of surnames.

James Wigley   George Wrighte   Robert Mitford

Leicester Pub Lib   Inst Hist Res

1768—A copy of the poll... Leicester: J. Gregory, 1768
Alphabetical. Place of residence. Scot and lot, disputed and rejected voters distinguished.

Booth Grey Eyre Coote John Darker Edward Palmer

Leicester Pub Lib Guildhall Lib

1768—An exact copy of the poll... Leicester: John Ireland, [1768]
Poll order. Place of residence. Index of surnames.

Booth Grey Eyre Coote John Darker Edward Palmer

Leicester Pub Lib Inst Hist Res

1796—An exact copy of the poll... Leicester: J. Throsby, 1796
Alphabetical. Address and day of polling.

Samuel Smith Lord Rancliff Bertie Greatheed Walter Ruding

Leicester Pub Lib Inst Hist Res

1800*—A copy of the poll... Leicester: Ireland, 1801
Alphabetical. Occupation and address.

Thomas Babington John Manners

Leicester Pub Lib Inst Hist Res

1826—The poll for the election... Leicester: Thomas Combe, 1826
Alphabetical by residents and out-voters. Occupation and address.

Sir Charles Abney Hastings Robert Otway Cave William Evans Thomas Denman

Leicester Pub Lib Guildhall Lib

1826—Cockshaw's edition. The poll for electing... Leicester: Albert Cockshaw, 1826
Alphabetical. Occupation, address and qualification. Electoral history since 1768 and account of proceedings.

Sir Charles Abney Hastings Robert Otway Cave William Evans Thomas Denman

Leicester Pub Lib Inst Hist Res

1832—The poll taken... Leicester: J. G. Brown, 1832
Alphabetical by residents and out-voters. Occupation and address. Non-voters.

William Evans Wynn Ellis Boughton Leigh

Leicester Pub Lib Guildhall Lib

1832—Cockshaw's edition. The poll for electing... Leicester: A. Cockshaw, 1833
Alphabetical. Address and qualification. Non-voters included.

William Evans Wynn Ellis Boughton Leigh

Leicester Pub Lib Inst Hist Res

1835—Cockshaw's edition, 1835. The poll for electing... Leicester: A. Cockshaw, 1835
Alphabetical by residents and out-voters. Occupation, address and qualification. Non-voters included.

William Evans Wynn Ellis Edward Gouldburn Thomas Gladstone

Leicester Pub Lib Guildhall Lib

1835—The poll taken on the 7th and 8th days of January... Leicester: J. G. Brown, 1835
Alphabetical by residents and out-voters. Occupation, address and qualification. Non-voters listed separately.

William Evans   Wynn Ellis   Edward Gouldburn   Thomas Gladstone

Leicester Pub Lib   Inst Hist Res

1837—The poll for electing... Leicester: J. G. Brown, 1837
Alphabetical by candidate and residents and out-voters. Occupation, address and qualification. Non-voters.

Samuel Duckworth   John Easthope   Edward Gouldburn   Thomas Gladstone

Leicester Pub Lib   Inst Hist Res

1837—Cockshaw's edition—1837. The poll for electing... Leicester: A. Cockshaw, 1837
Alphabetical by ward and out-voters. Occupation, address and qualification. Non-voters included.

Samuel Duckworth   John Easthope   Edward Gouldburn   Thomas Gladstone

Leicester Pub Lib   Inst Hist Res

1839*—The poll for the election... Leicester: J. F. Winks, 1839
Alphabetical by ward and out-voters. Occupation, address and qualification. Non-voters included.

Wynn Ellis   Charles Hay Frewen

Leicester Pub Lib   Inst Hist Res

1847—The poll taken at the election... Leicester: George Smallfield, 1848
Alphabetical by ward and street and out-voters. Occupation and qualification. Non-voters included.

Sir Joshua Walmsley   Richard Gardner   James Parker

Leicester Pub Lib   Inst Hist Res

1852—The poll taken at the election... Leicester: J. Burton, 1852
Alphabetical by ward and out-voters. Occupation, address and qualification. Non-voters distinguished. Liberal abstainers in 1847 and voters for Wilde and Palmer who voted for Walmsley and Gardner in 1847 distinguished. Votes of the corporation.

Sir Joshua Walmsley   Richard Gardner   James Wilde   Geoffrey Palmer

Leicester Pub Lib   Inst Hist Res

1857—The poll taken at the election... Leicester: Winks, [1857]
Alphabetical by ward and out-voters. Occupation, address and qualification. Non-voters distinguished.

John Dove Harris   John Biggs   Sir Joshua Walmsley

Leicester Pub Lib   Guildhall Lib

1857—The poll taken at the election... Leicester: J. Burton, [1857]
Alphabetical by ward and out-voters. Occupation, address and qualification. Non-voters distinguished.

John Dove Harris   John Biggs   Sir Joshua Walmsley

Leicester Pub Lib   Guildhall Lib

1859—The poll taken at the election... Leicester: J. Burton, 1859
Alphabetical by ward and out-voters. Occupation and address. Non-voters with reason in some cases.

John Biggs   John Dove Harris   Joseph William Noble   William Unwin Heygate

Leicester Pub Lib   Guildhall Lib

1861*—The poll taken at the election... Leicester: John Burton, 1861
Alphabetical by ward and out-voters. Occupation and address. Non-voters with reason in a few cases. Votes of the corporation.

John Dove Harris   Peter Alfred Taylor   William Unwin Heygate

Leicester Pub Lib   Guildhall Lib

1865—The poll taken at the election... Leicester: F. Hewitt, 1865
Alphabetical by ward and out-voters. Address. Votes of the corporation.

John Dove Harris   Peter Alfred Taylor   William Unwin Heygate

Leicester Pub Lib   Inst Hist Res

LINCOLNSHIRE

1724*—A copy of the poll for a knight . . . the 12th of February, 1723 n.p., [1724]
By division, wapentake and parish. Place of residence. Unqualified and doubtful voters distinguished.

Sir Nevile Hickman   Robert Viner

Lincs Archives Off   Inst Hist Res

1807—The poll for the county of Lincoln... Lincoln: William Brooke, 1807
Alphabetical. Place of residence and of freehold. Account of proceedings.

Charles Chaplin   Charles Anderson Pelham   Richard Ellison

Lincoln Pub Lib   Inst Hist Res

1818—The poll for the election... Lincoln: W. Brooke, 1818
Alphabetical by wapentake and parish of residence. Occupation and place of freehold. Out-voters by parish of freehold with place of residence given. Voters rejected as freeholders of Lincoln city. Account of proceedings.

Charles Anderson Pelham   Charles Chaplin   Sir Robert Heron

Lincoln Pub Lib   Inst Hist Res

1823*—The poll for the election... Lincoln: Bradbury & Dent, 1824
Alphabetical by wapentake and parish of residence. Occupation and place of freehold. Out-voters alphabetical with place of residence and freehold. Account of proceedings and election literature.

Sir William Amcotts Ingilby   Sir John Hayford Thorold

Lincoln Pub Lib   Inst Hist Res

NORTH LINCOLNSHIRE

1832—The poll for the election... Lincoln: Brooke, [1832]
Alphabetical by polling district and parish. Place of residence and qualification. Candidates' speeches.

Charles Anderson Pelham   Sir William Amcotts Ingilby   Sir Robert Sheffield

Lincoln Pub Lib   Guildhall Lib

1835—The poll book for the election... Stamford: T. Rawdon, [1835]
Alphabetical by polling district and parish. Occupation, place of residence and qualification. Account of proceedings.

Charles Anderson Pelham   Thomas George Corbett   Sir William Amcotts Ingilby

Lincoln Pub Lib   Inst Hist Res

1841—The poll book for the parts of Lindsey... Lincoln: James Drury, [1841]
Alphabetical by polling district and parish. Occupation (selectively), place of residence and qualification. Non-voters. Account of proceedings.

Lord Worsley   Robert Adam Christopher   C. H. Cust

Lincoln Pub Lib   Inst Hist Res

1852—General election, 1852. Poll book of the North Lincolnshire election . . . edited by Thomas Fricker. Boston: J. Morton, [1852]
Alphabetical by polling district and parish. Occupation, place of residence and qualification. Non-voters. Account of proceedings and election literature.

Robert Adam Christopher   James Banks Stanhope   Sir Montague Cholmeley

Lincoln Pub Lib   Inst Hist Res

SOUTH LINCOLNSHIRE

1841—The poll book for the election... Sleaford: James Creasey, [1841]
Alphabetical by polling district and parish. Place of residence and qualification. Account of proceedings and candidates' addresses.

Christopher Turner   Sir John Trollope   Henry Handley

Lincoln Pub Lib   Guildhall Lib

1841—The poll book for the election... Sleaford: J. Smedley, 1841
Alphabetical by polling district and parish. Place of residence. Account of proceedings and election literature.

Christopher Turner   Sir John Trollope   Henry Handley

Lincoln Pub Lib   Inst Hist Res

1857—The poll book for the election... Sleaford: William Fawcett, [1857]
Alphabetical by polling district and parish. Place of residence and qualification. Non-voters included. Account of proceedings and candidates' addresses.

Sir John Trollope   Anthony Willson   George Hussey Packe

Lincoln Pub Lib   Inst Hist Res

1868—The poll book for the election... Sleaford: William Fawcett, 1869
Alphabetical by polling district and parish. Place of residence and qualification. Non-voters included. Account of proceedings and candidates' addresses.

William Earle Welby Edmund Turnor George Hussey Packe

Lincoln Pub Lib Guildhall Lib

BOSTON

1802—A true and correct state of the poll... Boston: J. Hellaby, 1802
Alphabetical.

Thomas Fydell William Alexander Madocks John Ogle

Lincoln Pub Lib Guildhall Lib

1806—A correct state of the poll... Boston: J. Hellaby, 1806
Alphabetical. Rejected and tendered votes with reasons.

Thomas Fydell William Alexander Madocks John Cartwright

Guildhall Lib

1807—A correct state of the poll... Boston: J. Hellaby, 1807
Alphabetical. Rejected voters with reasons.

Thomas Fydell William Alexander Madocks Peter Robert Burrell John Cartwright

Spalding Gentlemen's Soc Inst Hist Res

1812*—A correct state of the poll... Boston: J. Hellaby, 1812
Alphabetical. Note on the conduct of the poll.

Peter Robert Drummond Burrell Sir Abraham Hume

Guildhall Lib

1812—A correct state of the poll... Boston: J. Hellaby, 1812
Alphabetical.

Peter Robert Drummond Burrell William Alexander Madocks Sir Abraham Hume

Bodl Inst Hist Res

1818—History of the Boston election... Boston: Noble, 1818
Alphabetical. Occupation. Rejected voters with voting intentions and reasons. Account of elections from 1796 and election literature.

Peter Robert Drummond Burrell William Alexander Madocks Henry Ellis

Lincs Archives Off Guildhall Lib

1818—A correct and alphabetical state of the poll... Boston: Kelsey, [1818]
Occupation and address. Rejected voters with voting intentions and reasons.

Peter Robert Drummond Burrell William Alexander Madocks Henry Ellis

Bodl Inst Hist Res

1820—The addresses, squibs, and other publications... Boston: Jackson, 1820
Alphabetical. Occupation. Rejected voters with voting intentions and reasons. Election literature.

Gilbert John Heathcote Henry Ellis Colonel Johnson

Lincs Archives Off Guildhall Lib

1820—A correct and alphabetical state of the poll... Boston: Kelsey, [1820]
Occupation and address. Rejected voters with voting intentions and reasons.

Gilbert John Heathcote Henry Ellis Colonel Johnson

Bodl Inst Hist Res

1826—The poll book (alphabetically arranged) together with the addresses... Boston: W. Bontoft, 1826
Occupation. Election literature.

Gilbert John Heathcote Neill Malcolm John Wilks

Lincoln Pub Lib Inst Hist Res

1826—A correct and alphabetical state of the poll... Boston: Kelsey, [1826]
Occupation and address. Rejected voters with voting intentions and reasons.

Gilbert John Heathcote Neill Malcolm John Wilks

Bodl Inst Hist Res

1830—A sketch of the Boston election... Boston: John Noble & Joseph Clark, 1830
Alphabetical. Occupation and address. Account of proceedings and election literature.

Neill Malcolm, Jr. John Wilks Charles Keightley Tunnard

Lincoln Pub Lib Guildhall Lib

1830—A correct and alphabetical state of the poll... Boston: Kelsey, [1830]
Occupation and address.

Neil Malcolm, Jr. John Wilks Charles Keightley Tunnard

Bodl Inst Hist Res

1832—A correct list of the poll... Boston: William Bontoft, 1832
Alphabetical by qualification. Address.

John Wilks Benjamin Handley John Stanhope Brownrigg

Lincoln Pub Lib Inst Hist Res

1835—An alphabetical list of the poll... Boston: William Bontoft, 1835
By qualification. Address.

John Studholme Brownrigg John Wilks Benjamin Handley

Lincoln Pub Lib Inst Hist Res

1837—An alphabetical list of the poll... Boston: John Noble, 1837
By qualification. Address.

John Studholme Brownrigg Sir James Duke Benjamin Handley William Rickford Collett

Lincoln Pub Lib Inst Hist Res

1841—The poll book, together with the addresses... Boston: William Bontoft, [1841]
Alphabetical by qualification. Address. Account of proceedings and election literature.

John Studholme Brownrigg Sir James Duke Charles Alexander Wood

Bodl Inst Hist Res

1841—An alphabetical list of the poll... Boston: T. N. Morton, [1841]
Alphabetical by qualification. Address. Account of proceedings and election literature.

John Studholme Brownrigg Sir James Duke Charles Alexander Wood

Bodl Inst Hist Res

1847—A record of the Boston election... Boston: J. Noble; C. Bontoft & Son, 1847
Alphabetical by qualification. Address. Non-voters distinguishing dead. Election literature.

Sir James Duke Benjamin Bond Cabbell David Williams Wire

Boston Pub Lib Inst Hist Res

1847—Borough of Boston—poll book. *Boston, Stamford & Lincolnshire Herald,* 3 August, 1847
Alphabetical by qualification. Address.

Sir James Duke Benjamin Bond Cabbell David Williams Wire

Brit Lib (News) Inst Hist Res

1849*—The poll book... Boston: C. Bontoft & Son, 1849
Alphabetical by candidate and qualification. Address. Non-voters. Election literature.

Dudley Anderson Pelham David Williams Wire

Lincs Archives Off Inst Hist Res

1851*—Poll book. *Boston, Stamford & Lincolnshire Herald,* 29 April, 1851
Alphabetical by candidate and qualification. Address. 1849 votes. Non-voters.

James William Freshfield David William Wire

Brit Lib (News) Inst Hist Res

1852—The poll book, together with the names of the persons . . . that did not vote... Boston: C. Bontoft & Son, [1852]
Alphabetical by qualification. Address. Non-voters. Account of proceedings and election literature.

Gilbert Henry Heathcote Benjamin Bond Cabbell John Alexander Hankey
Thomson Hankey

Bodl Inst Hist Res

1852—The poll book of the Boston parliamentary election... Boston: J. Morton, [1852]
Alphabetical. Occupation and address. Freemen distinguished.

Gilbert Henry Heathcote Benjamin Bond Cabbell John Alexander Hankey
Thomson Hankey

Bodl Inst Hist Res

1856*—Boston election . . . the poll. *Boston, Stamford & Lincolnshire Herald,* [1856]
Alphabetical by candidate and qualification. Address. Non-voters.

Herbert Ingram   William Henry Adams

Brit Lib (News)   Inst Hist Res

1859—Boston election. The poll book... Boston: John Noble, Jr., [1859]
Alphabetical by qualification. Address. Non-voters, distinguishing dead, removed or disqualified. Account of proceedings.

Herbert Ingram   Meaburn Staniland   John Hardwick Hollway

Bodl   Inst Hist Res

1860*—"United we conquer." Boston election, 1860. The poll book... Boston: John Beverley, 1860
Alphabetical by candidate and qualification. Address. Non-voters, distinguishing dead. Account of proceedings.

John Wingfield Malcolm   George Parker Tuxford

Boston Pub Lib   Inst Hist Res

1865—Boston election, 1865. The poll book... Boston: Jas. A. Bontoft, [1865]
Alphabetical by qualification. Address. Non-voters, distinguishing dead, ill, absent or disqualified. Account of proceedings and election literature.

John Wingfield Malcolm   Thomas Parry   Meaburn Staniland

Lincoln Pub Lib   Inst Hist Res

1865—Boston election. The poll book... Boston: J. G. Buck, 1865
Alphabetical by qualification. Address. Non-voters, distinguishing dead, ill, absent or disqualified. Account of proceedings and election literature. Candidates' addresses.

John Wingfield Malcolm   Thomas Parry   Meaburn Staniland

Bodl   Inst Hist Res

1868—Boston election. The poll book... Boston: J. G. Buck, 1868
Alphabetical by qualification. Address. Non-voters distinguished. Account of proceedings and election literature.

John Wingfield Malcolm   Thomas Collins, Jr.   Meaburn Staniland   Thomas Mason Jones

Boston Pub Lib   Inst Hist Res

GRANTHAM

1796—Borough of Grantham. Election, May 28 and 30, 1796. Copy of the poll book. n.p., [1796]
Alphabetical by place of residence. Occupation.

Simon Yorke   George Sutton   Sir William Manners

Lincoln Pub Lib

1818—A collection of all the addresses... Grantham: R. Storr, 1818
Alphabetical. Occupation and place of residence. Election literature.

Sir William Earle Welby   Edward Cust   Felix Thomas Manners   James Hughes

Grantham Pub Lib   Inst Hist Res

1820 (March)—Storr's impartial narrative... Grantham: R. Storr, [1820]
Alphabetical. Occupation and place of residence. Account of proceedings and election literature.

Edward Cust James Hughes Felix Thomas Manners

Grantham Pub Lib Inst Hist Res

[Two editions known.]

1820 (March)—A collection of the addresses... Grantham: S. Ridge, 1820
Alphabetical by place of residence. Occupation. Election literature.

Edward Cust James Hughes Felix Thomas Manners

Grantham Pub Lib Inst Hist Res

1820* (July)—Storr's account of the proceedings... Grantham: R. Storr, 1820
Alphabetical. Occupation and place of residence. Petition documents, account of proceedings and election literature.

Sir Montague Cholmeley Lionel William John Manners

Grantham Pub Lib Inst Hist Res

1826—MDCCCXXVI. Storr's impartial narrative... Grantham: Storr, [1826]
Alphabetical. Occupation and place of residence. Account of proceedings and election literature.

Frederick James Talmarsh Montague John Cholmeley Edward Cust

Grantham Pub Lib Inst Hist Res

1826—A report of the proceedings... Grantham: S. Ridge, 1826
Alphabetical by place of residence. Occupation. Account of proceedings and election literature.

Frederick James Talmarsh Montague John Cholmeley Edward Cust

Grantham Pub Lib Guildhall Lib

1830—Storr's impartial narrative... Grantham: Storr, 1830
Alphabetical. Occupation and place of residence. Supplement alphabetical by place of residence including non-voters. Account of proceedings and election literature.

Glynne Earle Welby Montague John Cholmeley Frederick James Talmarsh

Grantham Pub Lib Inst Hist Res

1830—A list of the poll... Grantham: S. Ridge, 1830
Alphabetical by place of residence. Occupation. Non-voters distinguished. Account of proceedings and election literature.

Glynne Earle Welby Montague John Cholmeley Frederick James Talmarsh

Grantham Pub Lib Guildhall Lib

1831—A collection of all the addresses, squibs... Grantham: R. Storr, 1831
Alphabetical. Occupation and place of residence. List of L10 occupiers, distinguishing freemen.

Glynne Earle Welby James Hughes Algernon Gray Talmash Felix Thomas Talmash

Grantham Pub Lib Inst Hist Res

1831—A narrative of the proceedings... Grantham: Samuel Ridge, 1831
Alphabetical by place of residence. Occupation. Non-voters distinguished. Account of proceedings and election literature.

Glynne Earle Welby   James Hughes   Algernon Gray Talmash   Felix Thomas Talmash

Grantham Pub Lib   Inst Hist Res

1852—Ridge's list of the poll... Grantham: S. Ridge, [1852]
Alphabetical. Occupation and address or place of residence.

Glynne Earle Welby   Lord William Montague Graham   Frederick James Tollemache

Grantham Pub Lib   Inst Hist Res

1852—Grantham election, July 8, 1852. The addresses, squibs... Grantham: Thomas Bushby, [1852]
Alphabetical. Occupation and address or place of residence.
Election literature.

Glynne Earle Welby   Lord William Montague Graham   Frederick James Tollemache

Grantham Pub Lib   Inst Hist Res

1857—Grantham election, March 28, 1857. A summary of the proceedings... Grantham: Thomas Bushby, 1857
Alphabetical. Address. Non-voters. Election literature.

William Earle Welby   Frederick James Tollemache   Lord Montague William Graham

Grantham Pub Lib   Inst Hist Res

1865—Grantham election, July 12th and 13th, 1865. A collection of addresses... Grantham: Lawrence Ridge, [1865]
Alphabetical. Occupation and place of residence. Non-voters.
Election literature.

John Henry Thorold   William Earle Welby   Frederick Tollemache

Grantham Pub Lib   Inst Hist Res

1868*—Grantham election, April 28th, 1868. A collection of the addresses... Grantham: Lawrence Ridge, 1868
Alphabetical. Occupation and place of residence. Account of proceedings and election literature.

Edmund Turnor   Hugh Arthur Henry Cholmeley

Grantham Pub Lib   Inst Hist Res

GREAT GRIMSBY

1818—The poll for the borough... Great Grimsby: T. Squire, [1818]
Poll order. Occupation. Voters for Grant in 1812 now voting against him distinguished.

John Nicholas Fazakerley   Charles Tennyson   John Peter Grant

Lincoln Pub Lib   Brit Lib

1820—A collection of the addresses... Great Grimsby: T. Squire, 1820
Alphabetical, preceded by the corporation. Occupation. Election literature.

Charles Tennyson William Duncombe Samuel Turner John Macpherson Brackenbury

Grimsby Pub Lib Inst Hist Res

1826—The poll for the borough... Grimsby: W. Skelton, [1826]
Alphabetical, preceded by the corporation. Occupation and place of residence. Election literature.

Charles Wood George Fieschi Heneage Sir Thomas Phillipps

Grimsby Pub Lib Inst Hist Res

1830—The poll for the borough... Grimsby: H. Palmer, [1830]
Alphabetical, preceded by the corporation. Occupation.

Charles Wood George Harris George Fieschi Heneage Thomas Challoner

Hull Pub Lib Inst Hist Res

1830—The poll for the election... Grimsby: W. Skelton, [1830]
Alphabetical, preceded by the corporation. Occupation and place of residence. Election literature.

Charles Wood George Harris George Fieschi Heneage Thomas Challoner

Grimsby Pub Lib Inst Hist Res

1831 (May)—The poll for the election... Grimsby: W. Skelton, [1831]
Alphabetical. Occupation and place of residence. Candidates' addresses.

George Harris John Villiers Shelley Rees Howell Gronow Henry William Hobhouse

Grimsby Pub Lib Inst Hist Res

1831* (August)—The poll for the election... Grimsby: W. Skelton, [1831]
Alphabetical, preceded by the corporation. Occupation. Candidates' addresses.

Henry Fitzroy Lord Loughborough H. Bellenden Ker William Maxfield

Grimsby Pub Lib Inst Hist Res

1831* (August)—History of the Grimsby election... Lincoln: E. B. Drury, [1831]
Alphabetical, preceded by the corporation. Occupation. Account of proceedings and election literature.

Henry Fitzroy Lord Loughborough H. Bellenden Ker William Maxfield

Hull Pub Lib Inst Hist Res

1832—The poll for the election... Grimsby: W. Skelton, [1832]
Alphabetical by qualification and place of residence. Address. Non-voters included. Election literature.

William Maxfield Lord Loughborough

Grimsby Pub Lib Inst Hist Res

1832—The poll for the election... Grimsby: H. Palmer, [1832]
Alphabetical by residents and out-voters. Occupation. Non-voters. Election literature.

William Maxfield Lord Loughborough

Grimsby Pub Lib Inst Hist Res

1852—The poll for the election... Grimsby: W. Skelton, 1852
Alphabetical by parish. Occupation, place of residence, nature and situation of qualification. Freemen distinguished. Non-voters included.

Earl of Annesley   Edward Heneage

Grimsby Pub Lib   Inst Hist Res

1852—The poll for the election... Grimsby: W. M. Leigh, 1852
Alphabetical by qualification and parish. Address. Account of proceedings and candidates' addresses.

Earl of Annesley   Edward Heneage

Grimsby Pub Lib   Inst Hist Res

1862*—The poll for the election... Grimsby: George Hickson, 1862
Alphabetical by qualification and parish. Address. Non-voters included. Candidates' addresses.

John Chapman   George Fieschi Heneage

Grimsby Pub Lib   Inst Hist Res

[Two editions known.]

1865—The poll for the electing... Grimsby: M. Hickson, 1865
Alphabetical by qualification and parish. Address. Non-voters included. Candidates' addresses.

John Fildes   John Chapman

Grimsby Pub Lib   Inst Hist Res

1868—The poll for the election... Grimsby: Geo. N. Nutt, [1868]
Alphabetical by qualification and parish. Address. Non-voters included. Candidates' addresses.

George Tomline   John Fildes

Grimsby Pub Lib   Inst Hist Res

LINCOLN

1754—An alphabetical list of the free-men who voted... Lincoln: W. Wood, 1754
Place of residence.

George Monson   John Chaplin   Robert Cracroft

Lincoln Pub Lib

1761—An alphabetical list of the free-men who voted... Lincoln: W. Wood, [1761]
Place of residence.

George Monson   Coningsby Sibthorp   Thomas Scrope

Lincoln Pub Lib

1768—A correct alphabetical list of the free-men who voted... Lincoln: W. Wood & Son, [1768]
Place of residence.

Thomas Scrope   Constantine John Phipps   Robert Vyner

Lincoln Pub Lib

1774—An alphabetical list of the free-men who voted... Lincoln: W. Wood, [1774]
Place of residence.

Lord Lumley   Robert Vyner, Jr.   Thomas Scrope   Humphrey Sibthorp

Lincoln Pub Lib   Bodl

1780—A correct alphabetical list of the free-men who voted... Lincoln: W. Wood, [1780]
Place of residence.

Sir Thomas Clarges   Robert Vyner   Lord Lumley   Thomas Scrope

Lincoln Pub Lib   Bodl

1780—An alphabetical list of freemen... Lincoln: Mary Rose, [1780]
Place of residence.

Sir Thomas Clarges   Robert Vyner   Lord Lumley   Thomas Scrope

Lincs Archives Off   Inst Hist Res

1790—Brooke's alphabetical list of the free-men... Lincoln: W. Brooke, [1790]
Place of residence.

John Fenton Cawthorne   Robert Hobart   George Rawdon

Lincoln Pub Lib

1790—An alphabetical list of the freemen who voted... Lincoln: John Drury, [1790]
Occupation and address or place of residence.

John Fenton Cawthorne   Robert Hobart   George Rawdon

Lincoln Pub Lib   Bodl

[Two editions known.]

1806—An alphabetical list of the freemen... Lincoln: John Drury, [1806]
Occupation and place of residence. Candidates' addresses.

Richard Ellison   John Sullivan   William Monson

Lincoln Pub Lib   Guildhall Lib

1808*—A llist of the freemen who voted... Lincoln: John Drury, [1808]
Poll order. Occupation and place of residence.

Earl of Mexborough   George William Richard Harcourt

Lincoln Pub Lib   Guildhall Lib

1818—An alphabetical list of the freemen who voted... Lincoln: Drury & Sons, 1818
Occupation and place of residence. Account of proceedings.

Coningsby Waldo Sibthorp   Ralph Bernal   Robert Smith

Lincoln Pub Lib   Bodl

1820—The poll for two members... Lincoln: Drury & Son, 1820
Alphabetical. Occupation and place of residence. Election literature.

Coningsby Waldo Sibthorp   Robert Smith   Edward Davies Davenport

Lincoln Pub Lib   Bodl

1826—The poll for two members... Lincoln: Drury & Son, 1826
Alphabetical by place of residence. Occupation.

John Nicholas Fazakerley Charles Delaet Waldo Sibthorp Thomas George Corbett

Lincoln Pub Lib Inst Hist Res

1826—The poll for two members... Lincoln: Hall, 1826
Alphabetical by place of residence. Occupation.

John Nicholas Fazakerley Charles Delaet Waldo Sibthorp Thomas George Corbett

Lincoln Pub Lib Guildhall Lib

1832—The poll for two members... Lincoln: E. B. Drury, 1833
Alphabetical by qualification. Occupation, parish or place of residence. Account of proceedings.

George Fieschi Heneage Edward George Earle Lytton Bulwer
Charles Delaet Waldo Sibthorp

Lincoln Pub Lib Brit Lib

1835—The poll book for members... Lincoln: T. J. N. Brogden, [1835]
Alphabetical by qualification. Occupation of freemen, address of electors. Non-voters included. Election literature.

Charles Delaet Waldo Sibthorp Edward George Earle Lytton Bulwer C. B. Phipps

Lincoln Pub Lib Inst Hist Res

1837—The poll book for members... Lincoln: T. J. N. Brogden, [1837]
Alphabetical by qualification. Occupation and address or place of residence.

Charles Delaet Waldo Sibthorp Edward George Earle Lytton Bulwer Henry Ellis
C. H. Churchill

Lincoln Pub Lib Inst Hist Res

1841—Poll book 1841. A list of the freemen and electors... Lincoln: Charles Brogden, [1841]
Alphabetical by qualification. Occupation and address or place of residence.

Charles Delaet Waldo Sibthorp William Rickford Collett
Sir Edward George Earle Lytton Bulwer Charles Seely

Lincoln Pub Lib Guildhall Lib

1847—A correct list of the poll... Lincoln: John Stainton, [1847]
Alphabetical. Occupation, place of residence, and qualification. Non-voters. Election literature.

Charles Delaet Waldo Sibthorp Charles Seely Sir Edward George Earle Bulwer Lytton
William Rickford Collett

Lincoln Pub Lib Inst Hist Res

1847—Lincoln city election. The poll book... Lincoln: Charles Brogden, [1847]
Alphabetical by qualification and parish. Occupation and place of residence of freemen, address of electors. Non-voters included.

Charles Delaet Waldo Sibthorp Charles Seely Sir Edward George Earle Bulwer Lytton
William Rickford Collett

Lincoln Pub Lib Guildhall Lib

1848*—City of Lincoln election. A correct list of the poll... Lincoln: William H. Bellatti, [1848]
Alphabetical. Address. Account of proceedings.

Thomas Benjamin Hobhouse   L. C. Humfrey

Lincoln Pub Lib

1848*—Lincoln city election. The poll book... Lincoln: Robert Bulman, 1848
Alphabetical by qualification and parish. Occupation and place of residence of freemen, address of electors. Non-voters included. Account of proceedings.

Thomas Benjamin Hobhouse   L. C. Humfrey

Lincoln Pub Lib   Guildhall Lib

1852—Lincoln city election. The poll book... Lincoln: Charles Akrill & C. Keyworth, 1852
Alphabetical by qualification and parish. Occupation and address of freemen, address of electors. Non-voters included. Account of proceedings.

Charles Delaet Waldo Sibthorp   George Fieschi Heneage   Charles Seely

Lincoln Pub Lib   Brit Lib

1852—List of freemen and electors as they voted... Lincoln: Thomas Oxley Brumby, 1852
Alphabetical by polling booth. Occupation and address. Non-voters. Candidates' addresses.

Charles Delaet Waldo Sibthorp   George Fieschi Heneage   Charles Seely

Lincoln Pub Lib   Brit Lib

1857—Lincoln city election. The poll book... Lincoln: C. Akrill, 1857
Alphabetical by qualification and parish. Occupation and address of freemen, address of electors. Non-voters included. Candidates' addresses.

Gervaise Tottenham Waldo Sibthorp   George Fieschi Heneage   John Hinde Palmer

Lincoln Pub Lib   Inst Hist Res

1859—Lincoln city election. The poll book... Lincoln: Edward R. Cousans, [1859]
Poll order by booth. Occupation and address. Freemen distinguished. Non-voters. Account of proceedings.

Gervaise Tottenham Waldo Sibthorp   George Fieschi Heneage   John Hinde Palmer

Lincoln Pub Lib

1859—Lincoln city election. The poll book... Lincoln: Chas. Akrill, 1859
Alphabetical by qualification and parish. Occupation and address of freemen, address of electors. Non-voters included. Account of proceedings.

Gervaise Tottenham Waldo Sibthorp   George Fieschi Heneage   John Hinde Palmer

Lincoln Pub Lib   Inst Hist Res

1862*—Lincoln city election. The poll book... Lincoln: C. Akrill, 1862
Alphabetical by qualification and parish. Occupation and address of freemen, address of electors. Non-voters included. Account of proceedings.

John Bramley-Moore   John Hinde Palmer

Lincoln Pub Lib   Inst Hist Res

1865—Lincoln city election. The poll book... Lincoln: Chas. Akrill, 1865
Alphabetical by qualification and parish. Occupation and address of freemen, address of electors. Account of proceedings.

Charles Seely Edward Heneage John Bramley-Moore

Lincoln Pub Lib Inst Hist Res

STAMFORD

1809*—Narrative of proceedings... Stamford: J. Drakard, 1809
Alphabetical. Occupation. Rejected voters showing parish and voting intentions. Account of proceedings and election literature.

Charles Chaplin Joshua Jepson Oddy

Inst Hist Res

1847—The poll book for the election... Stamford: Robert Bagley, 1847
Alphabetical by parish and qualification. Address. Non-voters included. Account of proceedings and election literature.

Marquess of Granby John Charles Herries John Rolt

Lincoln Pub Lib Brit Lib

Untraced: 1734, 1812, 1830, 1831, 1832

MIDDLESEX

1705—An exact copy of the poll... London, 1705
By parish. A few addresses.

Scorie Barker Sir John Wolstenholme Warwick Lane Hugh Smithson

Chiswick Pub Lib Inst Hist Res

1705—The poll for members... London: Bernard Lintott, 1705
Poll order. Place of freehold.

Scorie Barker Sir John Wolstenholme Warwick Lane Hugh Smithson

Bodl Inst Hist Res

1705—An exact list of the poll... London, 1705
By parish. A few addresses. Votes for Wolstenholme and Barker only.

Scorie Barker Sir John Wolstenholme Warwick Lane Hugh Smithson

Bodl Inst Hist Res

1715—Freeholders names . . . who in the last controverted election voted for Mr. Bertie and Mr. Smithson. 1714
By parish or district. Voters for Bertie and Smithson only.

John Bertie Hugh Smithson Sir John Austen Henry Barker

Guildhall Lib

1768 (March)—The polls at, and since, the late general election... London: J. Swan, 1772
Poll order for by-election of December 1768, with alphabetical appendix of additional voters in the March 1768 general election. Address or place of residence, place, nature and occupier of freehold. Index to both 1768 elections.

John Wilkes George Cooke Sir William Beauchamp Proctor

Guildhall Lib Brit Lib

1768* (December)—The polls at, and since, the late general election... London: J. Swan, 1772
Poll order. Address or place of residence, place, nature and occupier of freehold. Oathtakers distinguished. Index to both 1768 elections.

John Glynn Sir William Beauchamp Proctor

Guildhall Lib Brit Lib

1769*—The polls at, and since, the late general election... London: J. Swan, 1772
Poll order for by-election of December 1768, with alphabetical appedices of additional voters in the March 1768 general election and of voters in the April 1769 by-election not appearing in either of the preceding. Address or place of residence, place, nature and occupier of freehold.

John Wilkes Henry Lawes Luttrell Wiilliam Whitaker

Guildhall Lib Brit Lib

1784—Copy of the poll . . . 1784. [London, 1784]
Alphabetical. Address or place of residence, place, nature and occupier of freehold.

William Mainwaring John Wilkes George Byng

Brit Lib

1802—Copy of the poll... London: E. Rider, 1803
Alphabetical. Address or place of residence, place, nature and occupier of freehold.

George Byng Sir Francis Burdett William Mainwaring

Guildhall Lib Inst Hist Res

1802—A parochial list of the poll... London: W. S. Betham, 1803
Alphabetical by polling booth and parish or district. Address or place of residence, place, nature and occupier of freehold. Index.

George Byng Sir Francis Burdett William Mainwaring

Inst Hist Res

1802—A parochial list (alphabetically arranged) of the poll... London: Brooke & Clarke, 1803
Alphabetical by hundred and parish. Place of residence, place, nature and occupier of freehold. Index.

George Byng Sir Francis Burdett William Mainwaring

Guildhall Lib

LONDON

1710—The poll of the livery-men... London: John Morphew, 1710

Alphabetical by company. Non-voters and objected voters with reasons.

Sir William Withers Sir Richard Hoare Sir George Newland John Cass John Ward
Sir Gilbert Heathcote Sir James Bateman Sir William Asshurst

Guildhall Lib Inst Hist Res

1713—A list of the poll... [London, 1713]

Alphabetical by company. Voters for Withers, Hoare, Cass and Newland only.

Sir William Withers Sir Richard Hoare Sir John Cass Sir George Newland John Ward
Thomas Scawen Robert Heysham Peter Godfrey

Private possession Inst Hist Res

1713—A list of the poll... [Source?]

Alphabetical by company. Voters for Ward, Scawen, Heysham and Godfrey only.

Sir William Withers Sir Richard Hoare Sir John Cass Sir George Newland John Ward
Thomas Scawen Robert Heysham Peter Godfrey

Bodl Inst Hist Res

1722—The poll of the livery-men... London: T. Payne, 1722

Alphabetical by company. Voters rejected at scrutiny distinguished and listed separately. Dubious cases variously distinguished.

Richard Lockwood John Barnard Peter Godfrey Francis Child Humphry Parsons
Robert Heysham

Guildhall Lib

1722— A list of the persons' names... *Freeholder's Journal* Supplement, April 25, April 27, 1722. London: T. Sharpe, [1722]

Alphabetical by company. Voters for Barnard, Godfrey and Heysham only.

Richard Lockwood John Barnard Peter Godfrey Francis Child Humphry Parsons
Robert Heysham

Inst Hist Res

1722—A list of the persons who have polled... [London, 1722]

Alphabetical by company. Voters for Parsons, Child and Lockwood only.

Richard Lockwood John Barnard Peter Godfrey Francis Child Humphry Parsons
Robert Heysham

Private Possession Inst Hist Res

1724*—A list of the persons who have polled for Charles Goodfellow... *Daily Post,* 7 December 1724

Alphabetical by company

Sir Richard Hopkins Charles Goodfellow

Guildhall Lib

1724*—[A list of those who voted for Sir Richard Hopkins . . .] *Daily Journal*, 7 December 1724
Alphabetical by company.

Sir Richard Hopkins Charles Goodfellow

Guildhall Lib

1727—An account of the election... London, 1728
Alphabetical by company. Address. Non-voters.

Sir John Eyles John Barnard Micajah Perry Humphry Parsons Sir John Thompson Richard Lockwood Sir John Williams Sir Richard Hopkins

Guildhall Lib

1768—The poll of the livery... London: John Rivington, 1768
Alphabetical by company. Address.

Thomas Harley Sir Robert Ladbroke William Beckford Barlow Trecothick Sir Richard Glyn John Paterson John Wilkes

Guildhall Lib Inst Hist Res

1773*—A corrected list of the persons who have polled for the Right Hon. Frederick Bull... London: Charles Rivington, 1773
Alphabetical by company. Address.

Frederick Bull John Roberts

Bodl Inst Hist Res

1773*—A list of the persons who have polled for John Roberts... *London Evening Post Extraordinary*, printed for R. Page, [1773]
Alphabetical by company. Address.

Frederick Bull John Roberts

Guildhall Lib

1784—A list of the liverymen . . . who voted for Mr. Alderman Sawbridge and Richard Atkinson... London: W. Lane, [1784]
Alphabetical by candidate and company. Address.

Brook Watson Sir Watkin Lewes Nathaniel Newnham John Sawbridge Richard Atkinson Samuel Smith William Pitt

Bodl Inst Hist Res

1784—A list of the persons who have polled for Richard Atkinson... [London, 1784]
Alphabetical by company. Address.

Brook Watson Sir Watkin Lewes Nathaniel Newnham John Sawbridge Richard Atkinson Samuel Smith William Pitt

Guildhall Lib

1796—The poll for members... London: John Rider, by order of the sheriffs, 1796
Alphabetical. Company, address and day of polling.

William Lushington William Curtis Harvey Christian Combe John William Anderson William Picket Sir Watkin Lewes

Guildhall Lib Inst Hist Res

1837—The city of London poll-book. Election 1837... London: Joseph Rickerby, 1837
Electors by ward and liverymen alphabetical. Qualification or company and place of residence.

Matthew Wood George Grote William Crawford James Pattison John Horsley Palmer

Brit Lib

WESTMINSTER

1749*—A copy of the poll... London: J. Osborn, 1749
Poll order by parish, except for a few votes cast on the first day. Occupation and address.

Lord Trentham Sir George Vandeput

Guildhall Lib Inst Hist Res

1774—A correct copy of the poll... London: Cox & Bigg, 1774
Poll order by parish. Occupation and address.

Earl Percy Lord Thomas Pelham Clinton Viscount Mountmorres Viscount Mahon Humphrey Cotes

Guildhall Lib Inst Hist Res

1780—Copy of the poll... London: W. Richardson, 1780
Alphabetical by parish and street.

Sir George Brydges Rodney Charles James Fox Earl of Lincoln

Guildhall Lib Inst Hist Res

1818—The poll book for electing... London: J. J. Stockdale, 1818
Alphabetical by parish. Occupation and address. Rejected, objected and undetermined voters distinguished.

Sir Samuel Romilly Sir Francis Burdett Sir Murray Maxwell Henry Hunt Douglas Kinnaird John Cartwright

Guildhall Lib Inst Hist Res

1837—Westminster election. A poll taken... London: Cookes & Ollivier, 1837
Alphabetical by parish. Address.

John Temple Leader De Lacey Evans Sir George Murray

Guildhall Lib Inst Hist Res

1841—Westminster election. A poll taken... London: John Ollivier, 1841
Alphabetical by parish. Address.

Henry John Rous John Temple Leader De Lacey Evans

Guildhall Lib Inst Hist Res

LONDON UNIVERSITY

1880—University of London. Parliamentary election: March 1880. List of voters.
London: Eyre & Spottiswodde, for HMSO, [1880]
Alphabetical by candidate.

Robert Lowe Arthur Charles

Brit Lib

MONMOUTHSHIRE

1771*—(By authority). An accurate copy of the poll... Gloucester: R. Raikes, 1771
Alphabetical by hundred. Place of residence and of freehold. Oathtakers distinguished. Rejected voters with reasons included.

John Morgan   Valentine Morris

Newport Pub Lib   Inst Hist Res

1847—The poll book of Monmouthshire... Usk: James Henry Clark, [Two editions known] [1847]
Alphabetical by polling district and parish. Address. Non-voters included. Account of proceedings.

Charles Octavius Swinnerton Morgan   Lord Granville Charles Henry Somerset
Edward Arthur Somerset

Newport Pub Lib   Cardiff Pub Lib   Inst Hist Res

1868—The poll book of Monmouthshire... Usk: J. H. Clark, [1868]
Alphabetical by polling district, parish and qualification. Address. Non-voters included, dead distinguished. Account of proceedings.

Charles Octavius Swinnerton Morgan   Poulett Somerset   Colonel Clifford

Newport Pub Lib   Inst Hist Res

MONMOUTH BOROUGHS

1831—A list of the burgesses... Monmouth: Heath, [1831] [Broadsheet]
Alphabetical by candidate and borough. Occupation.

Benjamin Hall   Marquess of Worcester

Newport Pub Lib   Inst Hist Res

1835—The Monmouth poll book... Monmouth: Merlin Office, 1835
Alphabetical by borough. Occupation and address. Rejected voters with voting intentions.

Benjamin Hall   Joseph Bailey, Jr.

Newport Pub Lib   Inst Hist Res

1852—The Monmouth poll book... Monmouth: *Beacon* Office, 1852
Alphabetical by borough. Occupation and address. Rejected voters with reasons and voting intentions.

Crawshay Bailey   William Schaw Lindsay

Newport Pub Lib   Inst Hist Res

1852—Monmouth borough election, April 1852. The poll book... Newport: W. Pitt, 1852
Alphabetical by borough and qualification. Address. Non-voters included. Account of proceedings.

Crawshay Bailey   William Schaw Lindsay

Newport Pub Lib   Guildhall Lib

1868—Monmouthshire boroughs' election, November 17th, 1868. The poll book... Newport: H. Mullock, 1868
Alphabetical by borough. Address. Lodgers distinguished. Non-voters included. Candidates' addresses.

Sir John William Ramsden | Samuel Homfray

Newport Pub Lib | Inst Hist Res

NORFOLK

1715—A copy of the poll . . . February 18, 1714... Norwich: Henry Cross-grove, 1715
Alphabetical by parish. Place of residence. Alphabetical list of Norwich residents with place of freehold.

Thomas De Grey | Sir Jacob Astley | Sir Ralph Hare | Erasmus Earle

Norwich Pub Lib | Inst Hist Res

1734—A copy of the poll . . . 1734 n.p., [1734]
Alphabetical by parish of residence. Place of freehold. Out-voters by county with place of residence and freehold.

Sir Edmund Bacon | William Wodehouse | William Morden | Robert Coke

Norwich Pub Lib | Inst Hist Res

1768—By permission of the High Sheriff. The poll for knights... Norwich: W. Chase, 1768
Alphabetical by hundred and parish. Place of residence. Index.

Sir Edward Astley | Thomas De Grey | Sir Armine Wodehouse | Wenman Coke

Norwich Pub Lib | Inst Hist Res

1768—A copy of the poll... Norwich: J. Crouse, 1768
Alphabetical by hundred and parish of residence. Place and occupier of freehold. Out-voters by county with place of residence and freehold.

Sir Edward Astley | Thomas De Grey | Sir Armine Wodehouse | Wenman Coke

Norwich Pub Lib | Inst Hist Res

1802—The copy of the poll... Norwich: Stevenson & Matchett, [1802]
Alphabetical by hundred and parish of residence. Place and occupier of freehold. Out-voters by county.

Thomas William Coke | Sir Jacob Henry Astley | John Wodehouse

Norwich Pub Lib | Inst Hist Res

1802—The poll for knights... Norwich: R. Bacon, [1802]
Alphabetical by hundred and parish. Place of residence and occupation. Index distinguishing rejected voters.

Thomas William Coke | Sir Jacob Henry Astley | John Wodehouse

Norwich Pub Lib | Inst Hist Res

1806—The copy of the poll... Norwich: Stevenson & Matchett, [1806]
Alphabetical by hundred and parish of residence. Place and occupier of freehold. Out-voters by county. Account of proceedings.

Thomas William Coke William Windham John Wodehouse

Norwich Pub Lib Inst Hist Res

1806—The poll for knights... Norwich: R. M. Bacon, [1806]
Alphabetical by parish of residence. Place and occupier of freehold. Out-voters alphabetically with place of residence.

Thomas William Coke William Windham John Wodehouse

Norwich Pub Lib Inst Hist Res

1817*—The copy of the poll... Norwich: Stevenson, Matchett & Stevenson, [1817]
[Two editions known] [1817]
Alphabetical by hundred and parish of residence. Place and occupier of freehold. Out-voters by county. Account of proceedings. Report on assessor's decisions on objected votes.

Edmond Wodehouse Edward Roger Pratt

Norwich Pub Lib Inst Hist Res

1817*—The copy of the poll... Norwich: Burks & Kinnebrook, [1817]
Alphabetical by hundred and parish of residence. Place and occupier of freehold. Out-voters by county. Account of proceedings.

Edmond Wodehouse Edward Roger Pratt

Norwich Pub Lib Brit Lib

EAST NORFOLK

1832—Copy of the poll... Norwich: Matchett & Co., 1833
Alphabetical by hundred and parish. Place of residence and qualification.

William Howe Windham George Keppel Nathaniel William Peach
Lord Henry Cholmondeley

Norwich Pub Lib Inst Hist Res

1835—The poll for two knights... Norwich: Matchett, Stevenson & Matchett, 1835
Alphabetical by hundred and parish. Place of residence. Voters on second day distinguished. Non-voters included. Account of proceedings.

Edmond Wodehouse Lord Walpole William Howe Windham Richard Hanbury Gurney

Norwich Pub Lib Inst Hist Res

1835—The poll of the hundred of Diss... Diss: E. E. Abbott, [1835]
Alphabetical by parish. Place of residence. Non-voters included with reasons.

Edmond Wodehouse Lord Walpole William Howe Windham Richard Hanbury Gurney

Inst Hist Res

1837—The poll for two knights... Norwich: Matchett, Stevenson & Matchett, 1837
Alphabetical by hundred and parish of residence. Place of qualification. Out-voters by county. Non-voters included. Account of proceedings.

Edmond Wodehouse Henry Negus Burroughes William Howe Windham
Richard Hanbury Gurney

Norwich Pub Lib Inst Hist Res

1841—The poll for two knights... Norwich: Matchett, Stevenson & Matchett, 1841
Alphabetical by hundred and parish. Place of residence. Non-voters included. Account of proceedings.

Edmond Wodehouse Henry Negus Burroughes Sir William John Henry Browne Folkes

Norwich Pub Lib Inst Hist Res

1858*—East Norfolk election. The poll for a knight... Norwich: Matchett & Stevenson, 1858
Alphabetical by district and parish. Place of residence. Non-voters by parish. Account of proceedings.

Wenman Clarence Walpole Coke Sir Henry Josias Stracey

Norwich Pub Lib Inst Hist Res

1858*—The poll for a knight... Norwich: R. N. Bacon, 1858
Alphabetical by district and parish. Place of residence. Non-voters included. Political history from 1837.

Wenman Clarence Walpole Coke Sir Henry Josias Stracey

Norwich Pub Lib Inst Hist Res

1865—East Norfolk election. The poll for two knights... Norwich: Matchett & Stevenson, 1865
Alphabetical by district and parish. Place of residence. Non-voters by parish. Account of proceedings.

Edward Howes Clare Sewell Read Sir Thomas William Brograve Proctor Beauchamp
Wenman Clarence Walpole

Norwich Pub Lib Inst Hist Res

NORTH NORFOLK

1868—North Norfolk election. The poll for two knights... Beccles: Read Crisp & Moore, 1869
Alphabetical by district, parish and qualification. Place of residence. Non-voters by parish. Account of proceedings.

Frederick Walpole Sir Edmund Henry Knowles Lacon Edmund R. Wodehouse
Robert Thornhagh Gurdon

Norwich Pub Lib Inst Hist Res

SOUTH NORFOLK

1868—South Norfolk election. The poll for two knights... Norwich: Matchett & Stevenson, [1868]
Alphabetical by district, parish and qualification. Place of residence. Non-voters included. Voters in other districts distinguished. Account of proceedings.

Clare Sewell Read   Edward Howes   Henry Lombard Hudson

Norwich Pub Lib   Inst Hist Res

1871*—South Norfolk election. The poll for a knight... Norwich: Stevenson, [1871]
Alphabetical by district, parish and qualification. Place of residence. Non-voters included. Out-voters for each district.

Sir Robert Jacob Buxton   Robert Thornhagh Gurdon

Norwich Pub Lib   Guildhall Lib

WEST NORFOLK

1835—The poll for two knights... Norwich: Matchett, Stevenson & Matchett, 1835
Alphabetical by hundred and parish. Place of residence. Non-voters included. Account of proceedings.

Sir William John Henry Browne Folkes   Sir Jacob Astley   William Bagge

Norwich Pub Lib   Inst Hist Res

1837—The poll for two knights... Norwich: Matchett, Stevenson & Matchett, 1837
Alphabetical by hundred and parish. Place of residence. Non-voters included. Account of proceedings.

William Bagge   William Lyde Wiggett Chute   Sir William John Henry Browne Folkes
Sir Jacob Astley

Norwich Pub Lib   Inst Hist Res

1847—The poll for members... Norwich: Bacon & Kinnebrook, [1847] [Two editions known]
Alphabetical by district and parish. Pairs. Account of proceedings and candidates' addresses.

William Bagge   Edward Keppel Coke   Anthony Hammond
Henry L'Estrange Styleman L'Estrange

Norwich Pub Lib   Brit Lib

1852—The poll for two knights... East Dereham: W. Boyce, 1853
Alphabetical by district and parish. Place of residence. Out-voters for each district with place of qualification. Non-voters included.

William Bagge   George William Pierrepont Bentinck   Anthony Hammond

Norwich Pub Lib   Guildhall Lib

1865—West Norfolk election. The poll... East Dereham: L. E. Hatfield, 1865
Alphabetical by district and parish. Place of residence. Non-voters included, distinguishing dead. Account of proceedings and candidates' addresses.

William Bagge   Thomas De Grey   Sir Willoughby Jones   Brampton Gurdon

Norwich Pub Lib   Brit Lib

GREAT YARMOUTH

1754—The poll for members . . . 1754 n.p., [1754]
Alphabetical. Occupation and place of residence. Family relationships. Voters promised to Fuller who did not vote for him distinguished.

Charles Townshend   Sir Edward Walpole   Richard Fuller   William Browne

Norwich Pub Lib   Inst Hist Res

1777*—The poll for a member... Norwich: W. Chase, 1777
Alphabetical. Occupation and place of residence. Rejected voters.

Charles Townshend   William Beckford

Norwich Pub Lib   Inst Hist Res

1790—The poll for two members... Yarmouth: Downes & March, 1790
Alphabetical. Occupation and place of residence. Rejected voters with reasons.

Charles Townshend   Henry Beaufoy   John Thomas Sandys

Norwich Pub Lib   Inst Hist Res

1795*—The poll for a member... Yarmouth: I. D. Downes, 1795
Alphabetical. Occupation and place of residence.

Stephens Howe   George Anson

Norwich Pub Lib   Guildhall Lib

1796—The poll for two members... Yarmouth: I. D. Downes, 1796
Alphabetical. Occupation and place of residence. Rejected voters with reasons.

William Loftus   Henry Jodrell   Sir John Jervis

Norwich Pub Lib   Inst Hist Res

1807—By permission of the Mayor. The poll for the borough of Great Yarmouth... Yarmouth: J. Keymer, [1807]
Alphabetical. Occupation and place of residence.

Edward Harbord   Stephen Lushington   William Jacob   Abbott Upcher

Norwich Pub Lib   Inst Hist Res

1807—The poll for two members... Yarmouth: P. Forster, [1807]
Alphabetical. Occupation and place of residence.

Edward Harbord   Stephen Lushington   William Jacob   Abbott Upcher

Norwich Pub Lib   Inst Hist Res

1812—The poll for members... Yarmouth: J. Keymer, [1812]
Alphabetical. Occupation and place of residence. Persons voting twice distinguished.

Edmund Knowles Lacon   William Loftus   Giffin Wilson

Norwich Pub Lib   Guildhall Lib

1818—The poll for two members... Yarmouth: C. Sloman, Jr., 1818
Alphabetical. Occupation and place of residence.

Thomas William Anson Charles Edmond Rumbold Edmund Knowles Lacon William Loftus

Norwich Pub Lib Inst Hist Res

1820—The poll for two members... Yarmouth: J. Barnes, 1820
Alphabetical. Occupation and place of residence. Magistrates and council distinguished.

George Anson Charles Edmond Rumbold John Michel Jonas H. Stracey

Norwich Pub Lib Inst Hist Res

1826—The poll for two members... Yarmouth: J. Barnes, 1826
Alphabetical by residents and out-voters. Occupation and place of residence. Candidates' addresses.

Charles Edmond Rumbold George Anson Sir Edmund Knowles Lacon

Norwich Pub Lib Inst Hist Res

1830—The poll for two members... Yarmouth: W. Meggy, 1830
Alphabetical by place of residence. Occupation.

George Anson Charles Edmond Rumbold T. E. Campbell Henry Preston

Norwich Pub Lib Inst Hist Res

1830—The poll for two members... Yarmouth: J. Barnes, 1830
Alphabetical by place of residence. Occupation. Election literature.

George Anson Charles Edmond Rumbold T. E. Campbell Henry Preston

Norwich Pub Lib Guildhall Lib

1831—The poll for two members... Yarmouth: W. Meggy, 1831
Alphabetical. Occupation and place of residence.

George Anson Charles Edmond Rumbold Andrew Colville Henry Bliss

Norwich Pub Lib Inst Hist Res

1832—The poll for two members . . . for the borough... Also the poll of the Yarmouth freeholders for two knights of the shire... Yarmouth: J. Barnes, [1832]
Alphabetical by qualification. Occupation and place of residence of freemen, address of electors. Non-voters distinguished. Tendered votes. County poll alphabetical. Occupation and address. Non-voters distinguished.

Charles Edmond Rumbold George Anson Andrew Colville

Norwich Pub Lib Inst Hist Res

1832—The poll for two members... Yarmouth: W. Meggy, 1832
By qualification. Occupation and place of residence of freemen, address of electors. Non-registered voters distinguished. Tendered votes.

Charles Edmond Rumbold George Anson Andrew Colville

Norwich Pub Lib Inst Hist Res

1835—The poll for two members... Yarmouth: C. Sloman & B. Gooch, [1835]
Alphabetical by qualification. Occupation and place of residence of freemen, address of electors. Tendered votes.

Thomas Baring Winthrop Mackworth Praed George Anson Charles Edmond Rumbold

Norwich Pub Lib Inst Hist Res

1837—The poll for two members... Yarmouth: J. M. Denew, [1837]
Alphabetical by qualification. Occupation and place of residence of freemen, address of electors. Non-registered voters distinguished. Tendered votes.

Charles Edmond Rumbold William Wilshere Thomas Baring Charles S. Gambier

Norwich Pub Lib Inst Hist Res

1838*—The poll for a member... Yarmouth: J. M. Denew, [1838]
Alphabetical by qualification. Occupation and place of residence of freemen, address of electors. Non-registered voters distinguished. Tendered votes. Candidates' addresses.

William Wilshere Thomas Baring

Norwich Pub Lib Inst Hist Res

1841—The poll for two members... Yarmouth: James M. Denew, [1841]
Alphabetical by qualification. Occupation and place of residence of freemen, address of electors. Non-registered voters distinguished.

William Wilshere Charles Edmond Rumbold Thomas Baring Joseph Somes

Norwich Pub Lib Inst Hist Res

1847—The poll for two members... Yarmouth: Sloman, 1847
Alphabetical by qualification. Occupation and place of residence of freemen, address of electors.

Lord Arthur Lennox Octavius Edward Coope Charles Edmond Rumbold
Francis Goldsmid

Norwich Pub Lib Inst Hist Res

1848*—The poll for two members... Great Yarmouth: C. Barber, 1848
Alphabetical by district. Address.

Joseph Sandars Charles Edmond Rumbold Robert John Bagshaw

Norwich Pub Lib Inst Hist Res

1848*—The poll for two members... Yarmouth: Sloman, 1848
Alphabetical by district. Address. Candidates' addresses.

Joseph Sandars Charles Edmond Rumbold Robert John Bagshaw

Norwich Pub Lib Guildhall Lib

1852—The poll for two members... Yarmouth: L. A. Meall, 1852
Alphabetical by district. Address. Non-voters. Candidates' addresses.

Sir Edmund Henry Knowles Lacon Charles Edmond Rumbold
William Torrens McCullagh Sir Charles Napier

Norwich Pub Lib Inst Hist Res

1852—The poll for two members... Yarmouth: J. Cooper, 1852
Alphabetical by district. Address. Non-voters. Candidates' addresses.

Sir Edmund Henry Knowles Lacon Charles Edmond Rumbold
William Torrens McCullagh Sir Charles Napier

Norwich Pub Lib Guildhall Lib

1857—The poll for two members... Yarmouth: L. A. Meall, 1857
Alphabetical by district. Address. Non-voters.

William Torrens McCullagh Edward William Watkin Sir Edmund Henry Knowles Lacon
Charles Smyth Vereker

Norwich Pub Lib Inst Hist Res

1857—The poll for two members... Yarmouth: J. Cooper, 1857
Alphabetical by district. Address. Non-voters, distinguishing dead and absent.

William Torrens McCullagh Edward William Watkin Sir Edmund Henry Knowles Lacon
Charles Smyth Vereker

Norwich Pub Lib Guildhall Lib

1859—The poll for two members... Yarmouth: Wm. Cobb, 1859
Alphabetical by district. Address. Non-voters included, distinguishing dead.

Sir Edmund Henry Knowles Lacon Sir Henry Josias Stracey Edward William Watkin
Adolphus William Young

Inst Hist Res

1859—The poll for two members... Yarmouth: John Cooper, 1859
Alphabetical by district. Address. Non-voters included, dead and absent distinguished. Candidates' addresses.

Sir Edmund Henry Knowles Lacon Sir Henry Josias Stracey Edward William Watkin
Adolphus William Young

Norwich Pub Lib Guildhall Lib

1865—The poll for two members... Yarmouth: John Cooper, 1865
Alphabetical by district. Address. Non-voters, distinguishing dead.

Sir Edmund Henry Knowles Lacon James Goodson Alexander Brogden Philip Vanderbyl

Inst Hist Res

KING'S LYNN

1768—The poll for members... Lynn: J. Garratt, 1768
Poll order. Occupation and place of residence.

Thomas Walpole Sir John Turner Crisp Molineux

Guildhall Lib

1784—The poll for the election... [Lynn:] L Garratt, 1784
Alphabetical. Occupation and place of residence.

Horatio Walpole Crisp Molineux Brigg Price Fountaine

Norwich Pub Lib Inst Hist Res

1822*—A correct copy of the poll... Lynn Regis: E. Mugridge, 1822
Alphabetical. Occupation and place of residence. Account of proceedings.

John Walpole   Sir William John Henry Browne Folkes

King's Lynn Pub Lib   Inst Hist Res

1824*—A correct copy of the poll... Lynn Regis: E. Mugridge, 1824
Alphabetical. Occupation and place of residence. Account of proceedings.

Marquess of Titchfield   Sir William John Henry Browne Folkes

King's Lynn Pub Lib   Inst Hist Res

1826—A copy of the poll... Lynn: E. Mugridge, 1826
Alphabetical. Occupation and place of residence. Account of proceedings. Voters who arrived after the close of the poll.

John Walpole   Lord William Bentinck   Sir William John Henry Browne Folkes

King's Lynn Pub Lib   Inst Hist Res

1835—A correct copy of the poll . . . by John Thew. Lynn: T. Garland, 1835
Alphabetical. Address and qualification. Account of proceedings and election literature.

Lord George Bentinck   Sir Stratford Canning   Sir John Scott Lillie

King's Lynn Pub Lib   Inst Hist Res

1852—A correct copy of the poll... Lynn: Thew & Son, [1852]
Alphabetical. Address. Objected voters distinguished.

Viscount Jocelyn   Lord Stanley   Robert Pashley

Guildhall Lib

1865—The poll taken at the election... King's Lynn: Thew & Son, 1865
Alphabetical by qualification. Address. Non-voters included, dead distinguished.

Lord Stanley   Sir Thomas Fowell Buxton   Frederick Walpole

King's Lynn Pub Lib   Guildhall Lib

1868—The poll taken at the election... King's Lynn: Thew, 1868
Alphabetical by district. Address. Non-voters included.

Lord Stanley   Robert Bourke   Sir Thomas Fowell Buxton

Inst Hist Res

NORWICH

1710—The alphabetical draft of the poll... n.p., [1710]
Alphabetical by parish. Occupation or freehold. Out-voters by place of residence.

Robert Bene   Richard Berney   Waller Bacon   S. Gardiner

Norwich Pub Lib   Inst Hist Res

1715—An alphabetical draught of the poll... of Waller Bacon and Robert Britiss... Norwich: Tho. Goddard, 1716
Alphabetical by parish of residence. Occupation. Freeholders distinguished.

Waller Bacon   Robert Britiss   Richard Berney   Robert Bene

Brit Lib

1715—An alphabetical draught of the poll... of Robert Bene and Richard Berney . . . . Norwich: Tho. Goddard, 1716
Alphabetical by parish of residence. Occupation. Freeholders distinguished.

Waller Bacon   Robert Britiss   Richard Berney   Robert Bene

Brit Lib

1715—An alphabetical draught of the poll... of Waller Bacon and Robert Britiss... The second of February 1714... Norwich: Henry Crossgrove, 1714
Alphabetical by parish of residence. Occupation. Freeholders distinguished.

Waller Bacon   Robert Britiss   Richard Berney   Robert Bene

Norwich Pub Lib   Guildhall Lib

1734—An alphabetical draught of the poll... Norwich: L. Goddard, 1735
Alphabetical by parish of residence. Occupation or freehold and place of residence. Out-voters by London, Norfolk towns and country. Includes February 1735 by-election.

Horatio Walpole   Waller Bacon   Sir Edward Ward   Miles Branthwayt

Norwich Pub Lib   Inst Hist Res

1735*—An alphabetical draught of the polls... Norwich: W. Chase, 1735
Alphabetical by candidate, ward and parish. Occupation or freehold. Out-voters alphabetical by candidate, with occupation or freehold and place of residence. Corporation.

Thomas Vere   Miles Branthwayt

Norwich Pub Lib   Inst Hist Res

1735*—An alphabetical draught of the poll... Norwich: L. Goddard, 1735
Alphabetical by parish of residence. Occupation or freehold and place of residence. Out-voters by London, Norfolk towns and country. Includes 1734 general election.

Thomas Vere   Miles Branthwayt

Norwich Pub Lib   Inst Hist Res

1761—The poll for members... Norwich: William Chase, 1761
Alphabetical by parish of residence. Occupation. Out-voters alphabetical with place of residence.

Harbord Harbord   Edward Bacon   Nockold Tompson   Robert Harvey

Norwich Pub Lib   Inst Hist Res

1768—By permission of the sheriffs. The poll for members... Norwich: W. Chase, [1768]
Alphabetical by parish of residence. Occupation. Out-voters by country and London with place of residence. Freeholders distinguished.

Harbord Harbord Edward Bacon Thomas Beevor

Norwich Pub Lib Inst Hist Res

1768—A copy of the polls... Norwich: J. Crouse, [1768]
Alphabetical by parish of residence and candidate. Occupation. Out-voters by London and country. Freeholders distinguished.

Harbord Harbord Edward Bacon Thomas Beevor

Norwich Pub Lib Guildhall Lib

1780—The poll for members... Norwich: John Crouse, 1780
Alphabetical by parish of residence. Occupation. Out-voters by country and London with place of residence. Freeholders distinguished.

Sir Harbord Harbord Edward Bacon John Thurlow William Windham

Norwich Pub Lib Inst Hist Res

1784—By authority of the sheriffs. The poll for members... Norwich: J. Crouse, [1784]
Alphabetical by parish of residence. Occupation. Out-voters by country and London with place of residence. Freeholders distinguished.

Sir Harbord Harbord William Windham Henry Hobart

Norwich Pub Lib Inst Hist Res

1786*—A copy from the original poll book... Norwich: J. Crouse, [1786]
Alphabetical by parish of residence. Out-voters by country and London with place of residence. Occupation. Freeholders distinguished.

Henry Hobart Sir Thomas Beevor Robert John Buxton

Norwich Pub Lib Inst Hist Res

1786*—The poll for a member... Norwich: Chase, 1786
Alphabetical by parish of residence. Out-voters by hamlets, Yarmouth, country and London with place of residence. Occupation. Freeholders distinguished.

Henry Hobart Sir Thomas Beevor Robert John Buxton

Norwich Pub Lib Inst Hist Res

1787*—The poll for a member... Norwich: Chase, [1787]
Alphabetical by parish of residence. Out-voters by hamlets. Yarmouth, Lynn, country and London with place of residence. Occupation. Freeholders distinguished. 1786 voting.

Henry Hobart Sir Thomas Beevor

Norwich Pub Lib Guildhall Lib

1790—From the sheriffs' books. The poll for members... Norwich: J. Bowen, 1790
Alphabetical by ward and parish of residence. Out-voters by hamlets, Yarmouth, country and London with place of residence. Occupation. Freeholders distinguished.

Henry Hobart   William Windham   Sir Thomas Beevor

Norwich Pub Lib   Inst Hist Res

1794*—The poll for a member... [Norwich:] Richard Bacon, [1794]
Alphabetical by parish of residence. Out-voters by hamlets, Yarmouth, country and London with place of residence. Occupation. Freeholders distinguished.

William Windham   James Mingay

Norwich Pub Lib   Brit Lib

1796—The poll for members... Norwich: R. Bacon & Crouse, Stevenson & Matchett, [1796]
Alphabetical by parish of residence. Out-voters by hamlets, Yarmouth, London and country with place of residence. Occupation. Freeholders distinguished. Candidates' addresses.

Henry Hobart   William Windham   Bartlett Gurney

Norwich Pub Lib   Inst Hist Res

1799*—The poll for a member... Norwich: Stevenson & Matchett and R. Bacon, [1799]
Alphabetical by parish of residence. Out-voters by hamlets, Yarmouth, London, country with place of residence. Occupation. Freeholders distinguished.

John Frere   Robert Fellowes

Norwich Pub Lib   Inst Hist Res

1802—The poll for members... Norwich: Stevenson & Matchett, [1802]
Alphabetical by parish of residence. Out-voters by hamlets, Yarmouth, London and country with place of residence. Occupation. Freeholders distinguished. Candidates' addresses.

Robert Fellowes   William Smith   William Windham   John Frere

Norwich Pub Lib   Inst Hist Res

1802—The poll for members... Norwich: Bacon, [1802]
Alphabetical by parish of residence. Out-voters by hamlets, Yarmouth, London and country with place of residence. Occupation. Freeholders distinguished.

Robert Fellowes   William Smith   William Windham   John Frere

Norwich Pub Lib   Brit Lib

1806—The poll for members... Norwich: Stevenson & Matchett, [1806]
Alphabetical by ward and parish of residence. Out-voters by Yarmouth, London, country with place of residence. Occupation. Freeholders and second day voters distinguished. Account of proceedings.

John Patteson   Robert Fellowes   William Smith

Norwich Pub Lib   Inst Hist Res

1806—The poll for members... Norwich: R. M. Bacon, [1806]
Alphabetical by ward and parish of residence. Out-voters by Yarmouth, London, country with place of residence. Occupation. Freeholders distinguished. Second day voters.

John Patteson Robert Fellowes William Smith

Norwich Pub Lib Brit Lib

1807—The poll for members... Norwich: Stevenson & Matchett, [1807]
Alphabetical by ward and parish of residence. Out-voters by Yarmouth, London, country with place of residence. Occupation. Freeholders distinguished. Account of proceedings and electoral history.

John Patteson William Smith Robert Fellowes

Norwich Pub Lib Inst Hist Res

1812—The poll for members... Norwich: Stevenson & Matchett, [1812]
Alphabetical by parish of residence. Out-voters by Yarmouth, London, country with place of residence. Occupation. Freeholders distinguished. Account of proceedings.

William Smith Charles Harvey John Patteson

Norwich Pub Lib Inst Hist Res

1818—The poll for members... Norwich: Burks & Kinnebrook, [1818]
Alphabetical by parish of residence. Out-voters by Yarmouth, London, country with place of residence. Occupation. Freeholders distinguished. Candidates' addresses.

William Smith Richard Hanbury Gurney Edward Harbord

Norwich Pub Lib Inst Hist Res

1830—The poll for members... Norwich: Bacon & Kinnebrook, [1830]
Alphabetical by parish of residence. Out-voters by district and parish. Occupation. Freeholders distinguished.

Richard Hanbury Gurney Robert Grant Jonathan Peel Sir Charles Ogle

Norwich Pub Lib Inst Hist Res

1832—The register of electors, with the poll... Norwich: Matchett, 1832
Alphabetical by ward, parish and qualification. Address. Non-voters included. Account of proceedings.

Viscount Stormont Sir James Scarlett Richard Hanbury Gurney Henry Bellenden Ker

Norwich Pub Lib Inst Hist Res

1835—The register of electors with the poll... Norwich: Matchett, 1835
Alphabetical by ward, parish and qualification. Address. Non-voters included. Account of proceedings.

Viscount Stormont Robert Campbell Scarlett Edward Vernon Harbord
Frank Offley Martin

Norwich Pub Lib Inst Hist Res

1847—The Norwich poll... Norwich: Stevenson & Kinnebrooke, [1847]
Alphabetical by ward, parish and qualification.

Samuel Morton Peto   Marquess of Douro   John Humphreys Parry

Norwich Pub Lib   Inst Hist Res

1847—The Norwich poll... [Norwich: Stevenson & Matchett, 1852]
Alphabetical by ward, parish and qualification. Blank printed columns for 1852 candidates.

Samuel Morton Peto   Marquess of Douro   John Humphreys Parry

Norwich Pub Lib   Inst Hist Res

1852—[Lacking title page. Begins:] The poll of the city of Norwich election... Norwich: Josiah Fletcher, [1852]
Alphabetical by ward, parish and qualification.

Samuel Morton Peto Edward Warner Marquess of Douro Lothian Sheffield Dickson

Norwich Pub Lib   Inst Hist Res

1854*—Copy of the poll... Norwich: Matchett & Stevenson, [1854]
Alphabetical by ward, parish and qualification. Account of proceedings.

Sir Samuel Bignold   Anthony Hamond

Norwich Pub Lib   Brit Lib

1857—Copy of the poll for members... Norwich: Matchett & Stevenson, [1857]
Alphabetical by ward, parish and qualification. Account of proceedings.

Henry William Schneider   Viscount Bury   Sir Samuel Bignold

Norwich Pub Lib   Inst Hist Res

1857—Copy of the entire register of electors, with the poll... Norwich: *Mercury* Office, [1857]
Alphabetical. Parish. Non-voters included.

Henry William Schneider   Viscount Bury   Sir Samuel Bignold

Norwich Pub Lib   Guildhall Lib

1859—Copy of the entire register . . . with the poll... Norwich: *Mercury* Office, [1859]
Alphabetical. Parish. Non-voters distinguished. Account of proceedings.

Viscount Bury   Henry William Schneider   Sir Samuel Bignold
Charles Manners Lushington

Norwich Pub Lib   Inst Hist Res

1860*—The poll for two members... Norwich: Samuel Daynes, [1860]
Alphabetical by ward, parish and qualification. Non-voters. Account of proceedings and summary of contests since 1832.

Edward Warner   Sir William Russell   William Forlonge   William D. Lewis

Norwich Pub Lib   Inst Hist Res

1865—The poll for two members... Norwich: Samuel Daynes, [1865]
Alphabetical by ward, parish and qualification. Non-voters. Account of proceedings and summary of contests since 1832.

Sir William Russell Edward Warner Augustus Goldsmid Robert Edmond Chester Waters

Norwich Pub Lib Inst Hist Res

1868—The poll for two members... Norwich: Matchett & Stevenson, [1868]
Alphabetical by ward, parish and qualification. Non-voters. Account of proceedings.

Sir Henry Josias Stracey Sir William Russell Jacob Henry Tillett

Norwich Pub Lib Inst Hist Res

1870*—The poll for a member... Norwich: Samuel Daynes, [1870]
Alphabetical by ward, parish and qualification. Non-voters. Account of proceedings.

Jacob Henry Tillett John Walter Huddleston

Norwich Pub Lib Inst Hist Res

1871*—The poll for a member... Norwich: Samuel Daynes, [1871]
Alphabetical by ward, parish and qualification. Non-voters.

Jeremiah James Colman Sir Charles Legard

Norwich Pub Lib Guildhall Lib

NORTHAMPTONSHIRE

1702—A list of the names of the persons... at the last two elections... London, 1705
By hundred and parish. Votes for 1702 and 1705 elections.

Thomas Cartwright Sir Justinian Isham Lord Spencer Sir St. Andrew St. John

Northampton Pub Lib Inst Hist Res

1705—A list of the names of the persons... at the last two elections... London, 1705
By hundred and parish. Votes for 1702 and 1705 elections.

Sir Justinian Isham Thomas Cartwright Lord Mordaunt Sir St. Andrew St. John

Northampton Pub Lib Inst Hist Res

1730*—A copy of the poll for a knight... n.p., [1730] [Two editions known]
By hundred and parish. Place of residence.

Sir Justinian Isham William Hanbury

Northampton Pub Lib Guildhall Lib

1748*—A copy of the poll for a knight... Coventry: James Jopson, 1749
By hundred and parish. Place of residence.

Valentine Knightley William Hanbury

Northampton Pub Lib Inst Hist Res

1806—A copy of the poll... Northampton: Dicey & Sutton, [1806]
By hundred and parish. Place of residence.

Viscount Althorp William Ralph Cartwright Sir William Langham

Northampton Pub Lib Inst Hist Res

1831—A copy of the poll of the freeholders... Northampton: Francis Cordeux, [1831]
Alphabetical by hundred and parish. Occupation, place of residence, nature and occupier of freehold. Index. Supplement contains statistical tables, occupational analysis and out-voters by county and parish of residence.

Viscount Althorp Viscount Milton William Ralph Cartwright Sir Charles Kingsley

Northampton Pub Lib Inst Hist Res

1831—A copy of the poll for two knights... Northampton: T. E. Dicey, 1831
Alphabetical by hundred and parish. Occupation and place of residence. Index.

Viscount Althorp Viscount Milton William Ralph Cartwright Sir Charles Kingsley

Northampton Pub Lib Inst Hist Res

Note: The Dicey edition of the 1831 poll is generally found in *Copies of the polls at the several elections . . . 1702, 1705, 1730, 1745* [sic] *and 1806* (Northampton: Dicey, 1832), which then has an additional half-title reading 'Northamptonshire poll books from 1702 to 1831'. The other poll books in the volume, edited apparently by Beriah Botfield, are not exact reprints of the originals.

NORTH NORTHAMPTONSHIRE

1832—A copy of the poll... Oundle: R. Todd, [1832]
Alphabetical by polling district and parish. Occupation, place of residence and qualification. Index.

Viscount Milton Viscount Brudenell William Hanbury Thomas Tryon

Soc Geneal Inst Hist Res

1832—Copy of the poll . . . printed from the official documents... Kettering: Dash, 1833
Alphabetical by polling district and parish. Place of residence and qualification.

Viscount Milton Viscount Brudenell William Hanbury Thomas Tryon

Northampton Pub Lib Brit Lib

1835*—A copy of the poll, taken at the general election [sic] . . . Northampton: C. S. Adkins, 1836
Alphabetical by polling district and parish. Place of residence. Index.

Thomas Philip Maunsell William Hanbury

Northants County Lib Inst Hist Res

1837—Copy of the poll... Kettering: J. Toller, 1837
Alphabetical by polling district and parish. Place of residence and qualification. Index.

Thomas Philip Maunsell Viscount Maidstone Viscount Milton

Northants County Lib Guildhall Lib

1857*—A copy of the poll... Northampton: Jas. Butterfield, 1858
Alphabetical by polling district and parish. Place of residence. Non-voters.

George Ward Hunt Fitzpatrick Henry Vernon

Brit Lib Guildhall Lib

SOUTH NORTHAMPTONSHIRE

1841—A copy of the poll... Northampton: C. S. Adkins, [1841]
Alphabetical by polling district and parish. Place of residence and qualification. Index.

William Ralph Cartwright   Sir Charles Knightley   Earl of Euston

Northampton Pub Lib   Guildhall Lib

1847—A copy of the poll... Northampton: Jas. Butterfield, [1847]
Alphabetical by polling district and parish. Place of residence and qualification. Index.

Sir Charles Knightley   Richard Henry Howard Vyse   Lord Henley

Northampton Pub Lib   Inst Hist Res

1857—A copy of the poll... Northampton: Jas. Butterfield, [1857]
Alphabetical by polling district and parish. Place of residence and qualification. Index.

Viscount Althorp   Rainald Knightley   Richard Henry Howard Vyse

Northampton Pub Lib   Inst Hist Res

1858*—A copy of the poll... Northampton: Jas. Butterfield, 1858
Alphabetical by polling district and parish. Address or place of residence and qualification. Index.

Henry Cartwright   Lord Henley

Northampton Pub Lib   Guildhall Lib

1865—A copy of the poll... Northampton: Jas. Butterfield, 1865
Alphabetical by polling district and parish. Address or place of residence and qualification. Index.

Sir Rainald Knightley   Henry Cartwright   Lord Frederick Fitzroy

Northants Rec Off   Inst Hist Res

1868—A copy of the poll... Northampton: Stanton & Son, 1869
Alphabetical by polling district, parish and new franchise. Address or place of residence and qualification. Index.

Sir Rainald Knightley   Fairfax William Cartwright   Lord Frederick Fitzroy

Northants Rec Off   Guildhall Lib

1868—A copy of the poll... Northampton: Cordeux & Son, 1869
Alphabetical by polling district, parish and new franchise. Address or place of residence.

Sir Rainald Knightley   Fairfax William Cartwright   Lord Frederick Fitzroy

Northants County Lib   Guildhall Lib

NORTHAMPTON

1727—An account of the poll... London, 1727
By candidate. Place of residence and a few occupations.

George Compton   Edward Montagu   William Wilmer

Northampton Pub Lib   Inst Hist Res

1768—To the worthy electors . . . the poll for members... London, 1768
Alphabetical. Occupation and place of residence.

Sir George Osborn   Sir George Bridges Rodney   Thomas Howe

Northampton Pub Lib Inst Hist Res

1768—To the worthy electors . . . the poll for members... Northampton: Cluer Dicey &Son, [1768]
By candidate. Occupation and place of residence.

Sir George Osborn   Sir George Bridges Rodney   Thomas Howe

Inst Hist Res

1768—A state of the poll . . . in the interest of the Hon. Thomas Howe. Northampton: Cluer Dicey & Son, [1768]
By candidate. Occupation and place of residence. Rejected voters.
Election literature.

Sir George Osborn   Sir George Bridges Rodney   Thomas Howe

Northampton Pub Lib Inst Hist Res

1774—The state of the poll... Northampton: Cluer & Thomas Dicey, 1774
Alphabetical. Occupation and place of residence.

Wilbraham Tollemache   Sir George Robinson   Sir James Langham

Northampton Pub Lib Inst Hist Res

1784—The poll at the last general election... Northampton: T. Dicey & Co., 1784
Alphabetical. Occupation and place of residence.

Lord Compton   Fiennes Trotman   Lord Lucan

Northampton Pub Lib Inst Hist Res

1790—The poll at the general election... Northampton: T. Dicey & Co., 1790
Alphabetical. Occupation and place of residence.

Lord Compton   Edward Bouverie   Robert Manners

Northampton Pub Lib Inst Hist Res

1796—The poll at the general election... Northampton: T. Dicey & Co., 1796
Alphabetical. Occupation and place of residence.

Spencer Perceval   Edward Bouverie   William Walcot, Jr.

Northampton Pub Lib Inst Hist Res

1818—The poll at the election... Northampton: T. E. Dicey & R. Smithson, 1818
Alphabetical. Occupation and place of residence.

Earl Compton   Sir Edward Kerrison   Sir George Robinson

Northampton Pub Lib Inst Hist Res

1820—The poll at the election... Northampton: J. Freeman, [1820]
Alphabetical. Occupation and place of residence.

Sir George Robinson   William Leader Maberley   Earl Compton

Northampton Pub Lib Inst Hist Res

1820—The poll at the election... Northampton: F. Cordeux, 1820
Alphabetical. Occupation and place of residence.
Sir George Robinson William Leader Maberley Earl Compton
Northampton Pub Lib Guildhall Lib

1826—The poll at the election... Northampton: F. Cordeux, 1826
Alphabetical. Occupation and place of residence.
Sir George Robinson William Leader Maberley Sir Robert Henry Gunning
Northampton Pub Lib Inst Hist Res

1826—The poll at the election... Northampton: T. E. Dicey & R. Smithson, 1826
Alphabetical. Occupation and place of residence.
Sir George Robinson William Leader Maberley Sir Robert Henry Gunning
Northampton Pub Lib Brit Lib

1826—The poll at the election... Northampton: J. Freeman, 1826
Alphabetical. Occupation and place of residence.
Sir George Robinson William Leader Maberley Sir Robert Henry Gunning
Northampton Pub Lib Brit Lib

1830—The poll at the election... Northampton: F. Cordeux, 1830
Alphabetical. Occupation and place of residence.
Sir George Robinson Sir Robert Henry Gunning Charles Hill
Northampton Pub Lib Inst Hist Res

1830—The poll at the election... Northampton: J. Freeman, 1830
Alphabetical. Occupation and place of residence. Appendix of votes recorded after the close of the poll.
Sir George Robinson Sir Robert Henry Gunning Charles Hill
Northampton Pub Lib Brit Lib

1831—The poll at the election... Northampton: Frs. Cordeux, 1831
Alphabetical. Occupation and place of residence. Rejected voters with reasons.
Sir George Robinson Sir Robert Henry Gunning Robert Vernon Smith James Lyon
Northampton Pub Lib Inst Hist Res

1831—The poll at the election... Northampton: J. Freeman, 1831
By street. Occupation. Votes recorded after the close of the poll and rejected voters distinguished.
Sir George Robinson Sir Robert Henry Gunning Robert Vernon Smith James Lyon
Northampton Pub Lib Guildhall Lib

1832—The poll at the election... Northampton: J. Freeman, 1833
Alphabetical by parish. Occupation and address.
Robert Vernon Smith Charles Ross George Bainbridge Henry F. Fitzroy
Northants County Lib Inst Hist Res

1835—A copy of the poll... Northampton: J. Freeman, 1835
Alphabetical by parish. Occupation and address.

Robert Vernon Smith   Charles Ross   Charles Hill

Northampton Pub Lib Inst Hist Res

1835—The poll at the election... Northampton: J. Bonham, 1835
Alphabetical by parish. Occupation and address.

Robert Vernon Smith   Charles Ross   Charles Hill

Northampton Pub Lib Guildhall Lib

1837—A copy of the poll... Northampton: C. S. Adkins, [1837]
Alphabetical. Occupation and address.

Robert Vernon Smith   Raikes Currie   Charles Ross

Northampton Pub Lib Inst Hist Res

1837—A copy of the poll... Northampton: Cordeux & Sons, 1837
Alphabetical. Occupation and address.

Robert Vernon Smith   Raikes Currie   Charles Ross

Northampton Pub Lib Guildhall Lib

1837—A copy of the poll... Northampton: J. Freeman, [1837]
Alphabetical. Occupation and address.

Robert Vernon Smith   Raikes Currie   Charles Ross

Northampton Pub Lib Guildhall Lib

1841—Northampton borough election. 1841 . . . by the Committee of the Oak Club... [Northampton, 1841] [Broadsheet]
Alphabetical by party. Occupation and address. Plumpers and cross-voters distinguished.

Robert Vernon Smith Raikes Currie Sir Henry Pollard Willoughby Peter M. McDowall

Northampton Pub Lib Inst Hist Res

1852—A copy of the poll... Northampton: Wm. Stanton, [1852]
Alphabetical by candidate. Occupation and address. Non-voters.

Robert Vernon Smith   Raikes Currie   George Ward Hunt   John Ingram Lockhart

Northampton Pub Lib Inst Hist Res

1859—A copy of the pole... [Northampton: 1859], Broadsheet.
Alphabetical by candidate. Occupation and address. Non-voters, distinguishing dead.

Charles Gilpin   Robert Vernon Smith   James Thompson Mackenzie   Richard Hart

Northampton Pub Lib Inst Hist Res

1865—A copy of the poll... Northampton: Dicey, [1865] [Broadsheet]
Alphabetical by candidate. Occupation and address. Non-voters, distinguishing dead.

Lord Henley   Charles Gilpin   George Frederick Holroyd   Sackville George Stopford

Northampton Pub Lib Inst Hist Res

Untraced: 1852 (Cordeux), 1857

PETERBOROUGH

1835—A copy of the poll... Stamford: Thomas Rawdon, [1835]
Alphabetical by qualification. Occupation and address. Election literature.

John Nicholas Fazakerley Sir Robert Heron Walker Ferrand

Northampton Pub Lib Inst Hist Res

1837—A copy of the poll book... Peterborough: J. S. Clarke, [1837]
Alphabetical by qualification and candidate. Address. Election literature.

John Nicholas Fazakerley Sir Robert Heron W. E. Surtees

Northampton Pub Lib Inst Hist Res

1837—A copy of the poll... Peterborough: T. Chadwell, [1837]
Alphabetical by qualification. Address. Non-voters distinguished.

John Nicholas Fazakerley Sir Robert Heron W. E. Surtees

Northants Rec Off Inst Hist Res

1841—A copy of the poll... Peterborough: T. Chadwell, [1841]
Alphabetical by qualification. Address. Non-voters distinguished.

George Wentworth Fitzwilliam Sir Robert Heron Thomas Gladstone

Northants Rec Off Inst Hist Res

1852 (July)—Copy of the poll... Peterborough: T. Chadwell, [1852]
Alphabetical by qualification. Address. Non-voters, distinguishing dead or "gone to the Diggings." Election literature.

George Wentworth Fitzwilliam Richard Watson John Talbot Clifton

Northampton Pub Lib Inst Hist Res

1852* (December)— Copy of the poll... Peterborough: T. Chadwell, [1852]
Alphabetical by qualification. Address. Non-voters and dead or "gone to the Diggings." distinguished.

George Hammond Whalley George Cornewall Lewis

Northampton Pub Lib Inst Hist Res

[Two editions known]

1852* (December)—Copy of the poll... Peterborough: J. S. Clarke, [1852]
Alphabetical by qualification. Address. Non-voters and dead or "gone to the Diggings." distinguished.

George Hammond Whalley George Cornewall Lewis

Bodl Inst Hist Res

[Same printing as preceding entry with different imprint.]

1853*—Copy of the poll... Peterborough: T. Chadwell, [1853]
Alphabetical by qualification. Address. Non-voters and dead or "gone to the Diggins." distinguished.

George Hammond Whalley Thomson Hankey, Jr.

Northants Rec Off Inst Hist Res

1857—Copy of the poll... Peterborough: J. S. Clarke, [1857]
Alphabetical by qualification. Non-voters included, distinguishing dead. Candidates' addresses.

George Wentworth Fitzwilliam   Thomson Hankey   George Hammond Whalley

Northants Rec Off   Inst Hist Res

1859—Copy of the poll... Peterborough: J. S. Clarke, [1859]
Alphabetical by qualification. Address. Non-voters included, distinguishing dead.

Thomson Hankey   George Hammond Whalley   James Wilde   J. H. Lee Wingfield

Northampton Pub Lib   Inst Hist Res

1865—Copy of the poll... Peterborough: J. S. Clarke, [1865]
Alphabetical by qualification. Address. Non-voters distinguished. Account of proceedings.

George Hammond Whalley   Thomson Hankey   William Wells

Northants Rec Off   Inst Hist Res

1865—General election July 12th, 1865. The poll book... Peterborough: A. Edwards, 1865 (Reprinted from the *Peterborough Times*)
Alphabetical by qualification. Account of proceedings.

George Hammond Whalley   Thomson Hankey   William Wells

Northants Rec Off   Inst Hist Res

1868—Borough of Peterborough. General election... Copy of the poll... arranged by Richard Tow... Peterborough: E. B. Sargeant, [1868]
Alphabetical by parish and qualification. Address. Non-voters included, dead distinguished. Successful candidates' addresses.

William Wells   George Hammond Whalley   Thomson Hankey   William Green
Henry T. Wrenfordsley

Northampton Pub Lib   Inst Hist Res

NORTHUMBERLAND

1723*—The poll at the election of a knight . . . 1722... Newcastle: John White, [1723]
Alphabetical by parish. Place of residence.

William Wrightson   Ralph Jenison

Newcastle Pub Lib   Guildhall Lib

1734—The poll at the election... Newcastle: John White, 1734
Voters for Jenison and Middleton only. Alphabetical by parish. Place of residence.

Ralph Jenison   Sir William Middleton   John Fenwick   William Bacon

Newcastle Univ Lib   Inst Hist Res

1748*—The poll at the election of a knight... 1747-8... Newcastle: John White, 1748
Alphabetical by ward and candidate. Place of residence and freehold.

Lancelet Allgood   Lord Ossulstone

Newcastle Univ Lib   Inst Hist Res

1748*—The poll of the freeholders... n.p., Printed in the year MDCCXLVIII
Alphabetical by ward. Place of residence and freehold. Oathtakers, queried and rejected voters distinguished.

Lancelet Allgood   Lord Ossulston

Bodl   Inst Hist Res

1774—The poll at the election of knights... Newcastle: T. Slack, [1774]
Alphabetical by ward. Place of residence and freehold. Oathtakers and qualifications other than freehold distinguished.

Lord Algernon Percy   Sir William Middleton   Sir John Hussey Delavel   William Fenwick

Newcastle Pub Lib   Brit Lib

1826* (February-March)—The Northumberland poll book... Alnwick: W. Davison, 1826
Alphabetical by ward. Place of residence and freehold. Account of proceedings and election literature. 1748 and 1774 polls and election literature for 1774 included with separate pagination.

Matthew Bell   Henry Thomas Liddell

Newcastle Pub Lib   Inst Hist Res

1826 (June-July)—The poll-book of the contested election... Alnwick: W. Davison, 1827
Alphabetical by ward. Place of residence and place and nature of freehold. Account of proceedings and election literature.

Henry Thomas Liddell   Matthew Bell   Thomas Wentworth Beaumont   Viscount Howick

Newcastle Pub Lib   Inst Hist Res

NORTH NORTHUMBERLAND

1841—The poll book of the contested election... Newcastle-upon-Tyne: John Hernaman, 1841
Alphabetical by polling district and parish or township. Place of residence, address and nature of qualification. Account of proceedings and candidates' addresses. Summary of elections since 1714. Reprints of 1723 and 1734 (successful candidates only) polls.

Lord Ossulston   Addison John Baker Cresswell   Viscount Howick

Newcastle Pub Lib   Inst Hist Res

1847—The poll book of the contested election... Alnwick: W. Davison, 1847
Alphabetical by polling district and parish or township. Place of residence and address and nature of qualification. Account of proceedings and candidates' addresses.

Sir George Grey   Lord Ossulston   Lord Lovaine

Newcastle Pub Lib   Inst Hist Res

1852—The poll book of the contested election... Newcastle-upon-Tyne: John Hernaman, 1852
Alphabetical by polling district and parish or township. Place of residence and address and nature of qualification. Account of proceedings and candidates' addresses. Tenant farmers' requisition to Lord Lovaine.

Lord Lovaine　　Lord Ossulston　　Sir George Grey

Newcastle Pub Lib　Inst Hist Res

SOUTH NORTHUMBERLAND

1832—The poll book of the contested election... Newcastle-upon-Tyne: Hernaman & Perring, 1833
Alphabetical by ward, parish and township. Place of residence and place and nature of qualification. Account of proceedings and election literature.

Thomas Wentworth Beaumont　　Matthew Bell　　William Ord

Newcastle Pub Lib　Inst Hist Res

1852—The poll book of the contested election... Newcastle-upon-Tyne: John Hernaman, 1852
Alphabetical by polling district and parish or township. Address and place and nature of qualification. Account of proceedings and candidates' addresses.

Wentworth Blackett Beaumont　　Henry George Liddell　　George Ridley

Newcastle Pub Lib　Inst Hist Res

1852—The poll book of the contested election... Newcastle-upon-Tyne: M. & M. W. Lambert, 1852
Alphabetical by polling district and parish or township. Address and place and nature of qualification. Account of proceedings and candidates' addresses. Non-voters.

Wentworth Blackett Beaumont　　Henry George Liddell　　George Ridley

Inst Hist Res　Guildhall Lib

BERWICK-ON-TWEED

1820*—A copy of the poll-book... Berwick: H. Richardson, 1820
Poll order by candidate. Occupation and place of residence.

Sir Francis Blake　　James Balfour

Brit Lib

1847—[List of persons who voted]. *Berwick & Kelso Warder,* 7 August 1847
Alphabetical by qualification. Address.

Matthew Forster　　John Campbell Renton　　W. H. Miller

Brit Lib (News)　Inst Hist Res

1852—Poll for the Berwick election. *Berwick & Kelso Warder,* 16 July 1852
Alphabetical by candidate. Qualification.

Matthew Forster　John Stapleton　John Campbell Renton　Richard Hodgson

Brit Lib (News)　Inst Hist Res

1859 (May)—[The poll]. *Berwick Advertiser,* 7 May 1859
Alphabetical. Occupation.

Charles William Gordon Ralph Anstruther Earle Dudley Coutts Marjoribanks
John Stapleton

Brit Lib (News) Inst Hist Res

1859*(August)—A report of the poll as taken... *Berwick Advertiser,* 27 August 1859
Alphabetical by candidate. Occupation and address.

Dudley Coutts Marjoribanks Richard Hodgson

Brit Lib (News) Inst Hist Res

1863*—The borough election. The polling. *Berwick Advertiser,* 11 July 1863
Alphabetical by polling booth and qualification. Address.

William Walter Cargill Alexander Mitchell

Brit Lib (News) Inst Hist Res

1865—List of voters polled. *Berwick Advertiser,* 14 and 21 July 1865
By candidate. Occupation, address and qualification.

Dudley Coutts Marjoribanks Alexander Mitchell William Walter Cargill J. Hubback

Brit Lib (News) Inst Hist Res

1868—Polling at Berwick election... *Berwick Warder,* 27 November 1868
Alphabetical by polling booth. Address.

Viscount Bury John Stapleton W. Carpenter Richard Hodgson

Brit Lib (News) Inst Hist Res

NEWCASTLE-UPON-TYNE

1722—The poll at the election... Newcastle: John White, [1722]
By company and candidate.

William Carr Sir William Blackett William Wirghtson

Newcastle Pub Lib Inst Hist Res

1734—The poll at the election... Newcastle: John White, 1734
Alphabetical by company and candidate.

Walter Blackett Nicholas Fenwick William Carr

Newcastle Pub Lib Inst Hist Res

1741—The poll at the election... Newcastle: J. White, 1741
Alphabetical by company and candidate.

Walter Blackett Nicholas Fenwick Matthew Ridley William Carr

Newcastle Pub Lib Inst Hist Res

1741—The poll at the election... Newcastle: W. Cuthbert, [1741]
Alphabetical by company and candidate.

Walter Blackett Nicholas Fenwick Matthew Ridley William Carr

Newcastle Pub Lib Brit Lib

1774—The poll at the election... Newcastle: T. Saint, 1774
Alphabetical by company and candidate.

Sir Walter Blackett Sir Matthew White Ridley Constantine John Phipps Thomas Delavel

Newcastle Pub Lib Inst Hist Res

1774—The burgesses' poll at the late election... Newcastle: printed for the editor, [1774]
Alphabetical. Company, place of residence and order of polling. Account of proceedings and regulation of the poll.

Sir Walter Blackett Sir Matthew White Ridley Constantine John Phipps Thomas Delavel

Newcastle Pub Lib Inst Hist Res

[Two editions known]

1777*—The polling at the election... Newcastle: T. Angus, [1777]
Alphabetical. Company and place of residence.

Sir John Trevelyan Andrew Robinson Bowes

Newcastle Pub Lib Inst Hist Res

1780—The poll at the election... Newcastle: T. Saint, 1780
Alphabetical. Company and place of residence. Oathtakers distinguished.

Sir Matthew White Ridley Andrew Robinson Bowes Thomas Delaval

Newcastle Pub Lib Inst Hist Res

1820—The poll at the election... Newcastle: George Angus for Emerson Charnlet, 1820
Alphabetical. Company and place of residence. Account of proceedings.

William Scott Sir Matthew White Ridley Cuthbert Ellison

Newcastle Pub Lib Inst Hist Res

1832—The poll book of the free burgesses... Newcastle: William Boag, 1833
Alphabetical by qualification. Occupation and address.

Sir Matthew White Ridley John Hodgson Charles Attwood

Newcastle Pub Lib Inst Hist Res

1835—The poll book of the electors... Newcastle: J. Blackwell, 1835
Alphabetical. Address and qualification.

Sir Matthew White Ridley William Ord John Hodgson James Aytoun

Newcastle Pub Lib Inst Hist Res

1836*—The poll taken at the election... Newcastle: T. & J. Hodgson, 1836
Alphabetical by candidate. Address. Freemen distinguished.

John Hodgson Christopher Blackett

Newcastle Pub Lib Brit Lib

1837—The poll taken at the election... Newcastle: T. & J. Hodgson, 1837
Alphabetical. Address. Freemen distinguished.

William Ord John Hodgson Hinde Charles John Bigge John Blenkinsopp Coulson Augustus Harding Beaumont

Newcastle Pub Lib Inst Hist Res

1847—The poll taken at the election... Newcastle: *Newcastle Advertiser* Office, 1847
Alphabetical by qualification. Address.

William Ord Thomas Emerson Headlam Richard Hodgson

Newcastle Pub Lib Inst Hist Res

1852—[Title page missing. Begins:] Newcastle election 1852. Poll book... Newcastle: M. & M. W. Lambert, [1852]
Alphabetical by candidate. Address. Freemen distinguished.

John Fenwick Burgoyne Blackett Thomas Emerson Headlam William Henry Watson

Newcastle Pub Lib Inst Hist Res

1859 (April)—The poll books of the Newcastle elections... Newcastle-upon-Tyne: M. Benson, 1859
Alphabetical by qualification and parish. Address. Votes for general election and June by-election.

Thomas Emerson Headlam George Ridley Peter Alfred Taylor

Newcastle Pub Lib Guildhall Lib

1859* (June)—The poll books of the Newcastle elections... Newcastle-upon-Tyne: M. Benson, 1859
Alphabetical by qualification and parish. Address. Votes for general election and June by-election.

Thomas Emerson Headlam William Cuthbert

Newcastle Pub Lib Guildhall Lib

1860*—The poll book of the Newcastle election... Newcastle-upon-Tyne: Horn & Story, [1860]
Alphabetical by qualification and parish. Address.

Somerset Archibald Beaumont Peter Carstairs

Newcastle Soc Antiquaries Inst Hist Res

TYNEMOUTH

1852—Poll for North Shields election, July 8, 1852. *North & South Shields Gazette*, 16 July 1852 [Broadsheet]
Alphabetical by township and candidate. Non-voters and dead.

Hugh Taylor Ralph William Grey

Tynemouth Pub Lib Guildhall Lib

1861*—Poll for Tynemouth election... *North & South Shields Gazette*, 25 April 1861
Alphabetical by candidate and district. Address.

Richard Hodgson   Arthur Otway

Brit Lib (News) Inst Hist Res

Untraced: 1837

NOTTINGHAMSHIRE

1722—A copy of the poll... Nottingham: Anne Ayscough, [1722]
Alphabetical by place of residence. Out-voters by county and parish. Place of freehold.

William Levinz   Francis Willoughby   Sir Robert Sutton   Viscount Howe

Nottingham Pub Lib Inst Hist Res

NORTH NOTTINGHAMSHIRE

1832—An alphabetical list of the freeholders... Nottingham: Richard Sutton, 1833
Address, place and nature of qualification. Account of proceedings.

Viscount Lumley   Thomas Holdsworth   John Gilbert Cooper-Gardiner

Nottingham Pub Lib Inst Hist Res

1872*—Poll book of North Notts. election... Nottingham: T. Forman, [1872]
Alphabetical by polling district and parish. Address or place of residence.

George Edmund Milnes Monckton   Robert Laycock

Nottingham Pub Lib Inst Hist Res

SOUTH NOTTINGHAMSHIRE

1846*—South Nottinghamshire election, 1846. The poll book... Newark-upon-Trent: W. Tomlinson, [1846]
Alphabetical by polling district and booth. Place of residence. Account of proceedings.

Thomas Blackborne Thoroton Hildyard   Earl of Lincoln

Nottingham Pub Lib Inst Hist Res

1851*—A full and impartial report of the proceedings... including . . . the poll... Nottingham: T. Forman, [1851]
Alphabetical by polling district and parish. Place of residence. Non-voters included. Account of proceedings.

William Hodgson Barrow   Viscount Newark

Nottingham Pub Lib Inst Hist Res

EAST RETFORD

1831—Borough of East Retford and Hundred of Bassetlaw. The poll for burgesses... Retford: Benjamin Dewhirst, 1831
Alphabetical by division and parish of residence. Occupation and place of freehold.

Granville Harcourt Vernon   Viscount Newark   Arthur Duncombe

Nottingham Pub Lib Inst Hist Res

1831—The poll, with proceedings, speeches, etc.... Retford: F. Hodson, 1831
Alphabetical. Occupation and place of residence. Burgesses distinguished. Account of proceedings.

Granville Harcourt Vernon   Viscount Newark   Arthur Duncombe

Nottingham Pub Lib Inst Hist Res

NEWARK

1780—Newark election. Alphabetical list of the poll... Newark: James Tomlinson, [1780]
A few occupations and addresses. Non-voters.

Sir Henry Clinton   Lord George Sutton   Robert Foster

Newark Pub Lib Inst Hist Res

1790—An alphabetical list of the poll... Newark: D. Holt, [1790]
Occupation. Rejected voters distinguished.

William Crosbie   John Manners Sutton   William Paxton

Newark Pub Lib Guildhall Lib

1796—An alphabetical list of the poll... Newark: S. & J. Ridge, [1796]
Address. Rejected voters with reasons. Non-voters.

Thomas Manners Sutton   Mark Wood   William Paxton

Newark Pub Lib Inst Hist Res

1826—Election for the borough of Newark. The poll book... Newark: Hage, [1826]
Alphabetical. Occupation and address. Election literature.

Henry Willoughby   Sir William Henry Clinton   Samuel Ellis Bristowe

Newark Pub Lib Inst Hist Res

1826—An alphabetical list of the poll... Newark: S. & J. Ridge, [1826]
Address.

Henry Willoughby   Sir William Henry Clinton   Samuel Ellis Bristowe

Newark Pub Lib Inst Hist Res

1829*—An alphabetical list of the poll... Newark: Ridge, [1829]
Occupation and address.

Michael Thomas Sadler   Thomas Wilde

Newark Pub Lib Inst Hist Res

1829*—Particulars of Newark election .. list of the poll... Newark: Hage, [1829]
Alphabetical by street. Occupation. Non-voters included. Account of proceedings and election literature.

Michael Thomas Sadler   Thomas Wilde

Newark Pub Lib Inst Hist Res

1830—The Newark poll book... Newark: H. & J. Hage, [1830]
Alphabetical. Occupation and address. Non-voters distinguished.

Henry Willoughby   Michael Thomas Sadler   Thomas Wilde

Newark Pub Lib Inst Hist Res

1830—A report of the speeches... also an alphabetical list of the poll... Newark: S. & C. Ridge, 1830
Occupation and address. Rejected and non-voters distinguished. Account of proceedings and election literature.

Henry Willoughby   Michael Thomas Sadler   Thomas Wilde

Newark Pub Lib Inst Hist Res

1831—Newark election. The poll book... Newark: Henry & John Hage, [1831]
Alphabetical. Occupation and address. Objected, rejected and non-voters distinguished.

Thomas Wilde   William Farnworth Handley   Sir Roger Greisley

Leicester Univ Lib Inst Hist Res

1832—Newark election. The poll book... Newark: Eliza Hage, 1833
Alphabetical. Occupation and address. Rejected and non-voters distinguished.

William Ewart Gladstone   William Farnsworth Handley   Thomas Wilde

Newark Pub Lib Inst Hist Res

1840*—The poll book, containing a report of the speeches... Newark: J. Wells, [1840]
Alphabetical. Address. Non-voters distinguished. Account of proceedings and election literature.

Thomas Wilde   Frederick Thesiger

Nottingham Pub Lib Inst Hist Res

1840*—Newark election, 1840. The poll book... Newark: J. Bridges, [1840]
Alphabetical by qualification. Address. Non-voters distinguished. Account of proceedings and election literature.

Thomas Wilde   Frederick Thesiger

Nottingham Pub Lib Inst Hist Res

1841—Newark election. The poll book... Newark: J. Wells, [1841]
Alphabetical. Address. Objected and non-voters distinguished.

William Ewart Gladstone   Lord John Manners   Thomas Benjamin Hobhouse

Newark Pub Lib Inst Hist Res

1847—Newark election, 1847. An alphabetical list of the poll... Newark: C. & W. Ridge, [1847]
Alphabetical by qualification. Address. Dead and non-voters distinguished.

John Henry Manners Sutton   John Stuart   George Hussey Packe

Newark Pub Lib   Inst Hist Res

1852—Newark election, 1852. A correct list of the poll... Newark: J. Perfect, 1852
Alphabetical by qualification. Address. Dead and non-voters distinguished.

Granville Edward Harcourt Vernon   John Henry Manners Sutton
Marcus Merryweather Turner

Newark Pub Lib   Inst Hist Res

1859—Newark election, 1859. A correct list of the poll... Newark: James Perfect, 1859
Alphabetical by qualification. Address. Dead and non-voters distinguished.

Grosvenor Hodgkinson   John Handley   Earl of Lincoln

Newark Pub Lib   Inst Hist Res

1868—Newark election, 1868. The poll book... Newark: Tomlinson & Whiles, 1868
Alphabetical by qualification. Address. Non-voters included. Account of proceedings.

Grosvenor Hodgkinson   Edward Denison   Philip Handley

Newark Pub Lib   Inst Hist Res

1870*—Newark election, 1870. The poll book... Newark: Tomlinson & Whiles, 1870
Alphabetical by qualification. Address. Non-voters included.

Samuel Boteler Bristowe   William Campbell Sleigh   Sir George Grey

Newark Pub Lib   Inst Hist Res

NOTTINGHAM

1754—An alphabetical list of the burgesses... Nottingham: Samuel Cresswell, 1754
By resident, London and country. Occupation and address or place of residence. Some tenants of out-voters. Freeholders distinguished. Non-voters.

Viscount Howe   Sir Willoughby Aston   John Plumtre

Nottingham Pub Lib   Inst Hist Res

1754—A copy of a poll of the burgesses... Nottingham: Tho. Collyer, 1754
Poll order. Occupation and address or place of residence. Some tenants of out-voters. Freeholders distinguished. Index.

Viscount Howe   Sir Willoughby Aston   John Plumtre

Nottingham Pub Lib   Inst Hist Res

1774—An exact list of the burgesses... Nottingham: George Burbage, for S. Cresswell and G. Burbage, 1774
Alphabetical by resident, London and country. Occupation and address or place of residence. Freeholders distinguished. Non-voters.

Sir Charles Sedley   William Howe   Lord Edward Bentinck

Nottingham Pub Lib   Inst Hist Res

1780—An alphabetical list of the burgesses... Nottingham: T. Wheatcroft, [1780]
Occupation and address. Parliamentary and council elections.

Robert Smith   Daniel Parker Coke   John Cartwright

Nottingham Pub Lib Inst Hist Res

1796—An alphabetical list of the burgesses... Nottingham: C. Sutton, [1796]
Occupation and address or place of residence.

Robert Smith   Daniel Parker Coke   Peter Crompton

Nottingham Pub Lib Inst Hist Res

1802—An alphabetical list of the burgesses... Nottingham: C. Sutton, [1802]
Occupation and address. Remarks on the rioting and letter from the mayor and sheriffs.

Sir John Borlase Warren   Joseph Birch   Daniel Parker Coke

Nottingham Pub Lib Inst Hist Res

1802—An alphabetical list of the burgesses... Nottingham: J. Dunn, [1802]
Occupation and address.

Sir John Borlase Warren   Joseph Birch   Daniel Parker Coke

Nottingham Pub Lib Inst Hist Res

1803*—A complete alphabetical list of the 2525 burgesses... Nottingham: Harrod & Turner, 1803
Occupation and address. Freeholders distinguished. Mottoes on candidates' flags.

Daniel Parker Coke   Joseph Birch

Nottingham Pub Lib Inst Hist Res

1803*—An alphabetical list of the burgesses... Nottingham: C. Sutton, [1803]
By resident and out-voters. Occupation and address. Freeholders distinguished. Account of proceedings.

Daniel Parker Coke   Joseph Birch

Nottingham Pub Lib Inst Hist Res

1803*—A correct list of burgesses... Nottingham: J. Dunn, [1803]
Poll order. Occupation and address. Freeholders distinguished. Index.

Daniel Parker Coke   Joseph Birch

Nottingham Pub Lib Inst Hist Res

1806—An alphabetical list of the burgesses... Nottingham: Burbage & Stretton, [1806]
Occupation and address. Freeholders distinguished.

Daniel Parker Coke   John Smith   Joseph Birch

Nottingham Pub Lib Inst Hist Res

1806—An alphabetical list of the burgesses... Nottingham: J. Dunn, [1806]
Occupation and address. Freeholders distinguished.

Daniel Parker Coke   John Smith   Joseph Birch

Nottingham Pub Lib Inst Hist Res

1806—An alphabetical list of the burgesses... Nottingham: Sutton & Fowler, [1806]
By resident and out-voters. Occupation and address.
Freeholders distinguished.

Daniel Parker Coke John Smith Joseph Birch

Nottingham Pub Lib Inst Hist Res

1812—An alphabetical list of the burgesses... Nottingham: J. Dunn, C. Sutton & H. Barnett, [1812]
By resident and out-voters. Occupation and address.
Freeholders distinguished.

John Smith Lord Rancliffe Richard Arkwright Dr. Crompton Joseph Birch

Nottingham Pub Lib Inst Hist Res

1818—An alphabetical list of the burgesses... Nottingham: H. Barnett & G. Stretton, [1818]
By resident and out-voters. Occupation and address. Freeholders distinguished. Remarks on the political state of the borough.

Joseph Birch Lord Rancliffe Thomas Assheton Smith

Nottingham Pub Lib Inst Hist Res

1818—An alphabetical list of the burgesses... Nottingham: Sutton, [1818]
By resident and out-voters. Occupation and address. Freeholders distinguished. Remarks on the political state of the borough.

Joseph Birch Lord Rancliffe Thomas Assheton Smith

Nottingham Pub Lib Guildhall Lib

1818—A list of the burgesses... Nottingham: Sutton & Son, 1818
Poll order. Occupation and address. Freeholders distinguished.

Joseph Birch Lord Rancliffe Thomas Assheton Smith

Nottingham Pub Lib Inst Hist Res

1820—An alphabetical list of the burgesses... Nottingham: Sutton, [1820]
Occupation and address. Freeholders distinguished. Account of proceedings.

Joseph Birch Thomas Denman Thomas Assheton Smith Lancelot Rolleston

Nottingham Pub Lib Inst Hist Res

1820—A list of the burgesses... Nottingham: Sutton, 1820
Poll order. Occupation and address. Freeholders distinguished. Account of proceedings.

Joseph Birch Thomas Denman Thomas Assheton Smith Lancelot Rolleston

Nottingham Pub Lib Inst Hist Res

1826—An alphabetical list of the burgesses... Nottingham: Sutton, [1826]
Occupation and address. Freeholders distinguished. Account of proceedings.

Joseph Birch Lord Rancliffe John Smith Wright George Hopkinson

Nottingham Pub Lib Inst Hist Res

1826—An alphabetical list of the burgesses... Nottingham: G. Stretton, 1826
By resident and out-voters. Occupation and address. Freeholders and honorary burgesses distinguished.

Joseph Birch   Lord Rancliffe   John Smith Wright   George Hopkinson

Nottingham Pub Lib Inst Hist Res

1830—An alphabetical list of the burgesses... Nottingham: Richard Sutton, [1830]
Occupation and address. Freeholders distinguished. Account of proceedings.

Thomas Denman   Sir Ronald Crawford Ferguson   Thomas Bailey

Nottingham Pub Lib Inst Hist Res

1832—An alphabetical list of the burgesses... Nottingham: Richard Sutton, [1832]
Occupation, address and qualification. Account of proceedings.

Sir Ronald Crawford Ferguson   Viscount Duncannon   James Edward Gordon

Nottingham Univ Lib Inst Hist Res

1841*—An alphabetical list of the burgesses... Nottingham: R. Allen, [1841]
By ward and out-voters. Occupation and address. Non-voters.

John Walter   George Gerard de Hochepied Larpent

Nottingham Univ Lib Inst Hist Res

1842*—Nottingham elections, 1842 and 1843. An alphabetical poll book... Nottingham: *Journal* Office, 1843
By ward and out-voters. Occupation, address and qualification. Voting for 1842 and 1843 by-elections.

John Walter   Joseph Sturge

Nottingham Pub Lib Inst Hist Res

1843*—Nottingham elections, 1842 and 1843. An alphabetical poll book... Nottingham: *Journal* Office, 1843
By ward and out-voters. Occupation, address and qualification. Voting for 1842 and 1843 by-elections.

Thomas Gisborne, Jr.   John Walter, Jr.

Nottingham Pub Lib Inst Hist Res

1847—An alphabetical list of the burgesses... Nottingham: R. Allen, [1847]
By ward and out-voters. Address and a few occupations. Non-voters included.

John Walter   Feargus O'Connor   Thomas Gisborne   Sir John Cam Hobhouse

Nottingham Pub Lib Inst Hist Res

1852—An alphabetical list of the burgesses... Nottingham: R. Sutton, [1852]
By ward and out-voters. Occupation and address.

Edward Strutt   John Walter   Charles Sturgeon

Nottingham Pub Lib Inst Hist Res

1857—Poll sheets of the Nottingham election… *Nottingham Review* Supplement, 3 April 1857
Alphabetical by ward. Occupation and address.

Charles Paget John Walter Ernest Jones

Brit Lib (News) Inst Hist Res

1859—Poll sheets of the Nottingham election… *Nottingham Review* Supplement, 6 May 1859
Alphabetical by ward. Occupation and address.

Charles Paget John Mellor Thomas Bromley Ernest Jones

Brit Lib (News) Inst Hist Res

1861*—Nottingham election. The poll lists. *Nottingham Daily Guardian,* 28 December 1861
Alphabetical by ward. Occupation and address.

Sir Robert Juckes Clifton Earl of Lincoln

Brit Lib (News) Inst Hist Res

1865—Poll sheet of Nottingham election. *Nottingham Daily Guardian* Extraordinary edition, 12 July 1865. Nottingham: T. Forman, [1865]
Alphabetical by ward. Occupation and address.

Samuel Morley Sir Robert Juckes Clifton Charles Paget Alfred George Marten

Nottingham Pub Lib Inst Hist Res

1866*—[The name of every voter who polled . . .] *Nottingham Review,* 18 May 1866
Alphabetical by ward. Address.

Ralph Bernal Osborne Viscount Amberley Sir George Samuel Jenkinson H. Cossham D. Faulkner

Brit Lib (News) Inst Hist Res

1868—Poll book of the Nottingham election, 17 November 1868. Nottingham: *Daily Guardian,* [1868]
Alphabetical by ward and out-voters. Address.

Sir Robert Juckes Clifton Charles Ichabod Wright Charles Seely, Jr. Peter William Clayden Ralph Bernal Osborne

Nottingham Pub Lib Inst Hist Res

1869*—Poll book of Nottingham election, 15 June 1869. Nottingham: *Daily Guardian,* [1869]
Alphabetical by ward and out-voters. Address.

Charles Seely, Jr. William Digby Seymour

Nottingham Pub Lib Inst Hist Res

OXFORDSHIRE

1754—A copy of the poll... Oxford: the Theatre, 1754
Alphabetical by hundred. Place of residence, place, nature and occupier of freehold. Oath-takers noted. Queried voters distinguished.

Viscount Wenman   Sir James Dashwood   Viscount Parker   Sir Edward Turner

Bodl Inst Hist Res

1754—The poll of the freeholders... Oxford: W. Jackson, 1754
Alphabetical by hundred and parish. Place of residence, nature and occupier of freehold. Queried voters distinguished.

Viscount Wenman   Sir James Dashwood   Viscount Parker   Sir Edward Turner

Bodl Inst Hist Res

1826—The copy of the poll... Oxford: H. Slatter and Haldon & Lowndes, 1826
Alphabetical by hundred and parish. Place of residence, nature and occupier of freehold. Oath-takers distinguished. Index.

William Henry Ashhurst   John Fane   George Frederick Stratton

Bodl Inst Hist Res

1830—The copy of the poll... Oxford: W. Baxter, 1830
Alphabetical by hundred and parish. Place of residence, nature and occupier of freehold. Index.

John Fane   Lord Norreys   Sir George Dashwood

Bodl Guildhall Lib

1831—The copy of the poll... Oxford: W. Baxter, 1831
Alphabetical by hundred and parish. Place of residence, nature and occupier of freehold. Index.

George Harcourt   Richard Weyland   Lord Norreys

Bodl Inst Hist Res

1837—The poll of the electors... Oxford: Henry Slatter, 1837
Alphabetical by hundred and parish. Place of residence and nature of qualification. Index.

Lord Norreys   George Granvile Harcourt   Thomas Augustus Wolstenholme Parker
Thomas Stonor

Bodl Inst Hist Res

1862*—The poll of the electors... Oxford: Henry Groom, 1862
Alphabetical by polling district and parish. Address.

John William Fane   Sir Henry William Dashwood

Bodl Guildhall Lib

BANBURY

1835—A copy of the poll... Banbury: William Potts, [1835]
Alphabetical by candidate and district. Address. Non-voters.

Henry William Tancred   Edward Lloyd Williams

Bodl Inst Hist Res

1837—The poll taken for the election... Banbury: J. G. Rusher, [1837]
Alphabetical by candidate. Occupation and address. Tendered votes and non-voters, distinguishing dead and removed. Present or former councillors and other local officials distinguished.

Henry William Tancred   Henry Tawney

Bodl Inst Hist Res

1841—1841. List of the persons whose names are upon the register . . . with the poll... Banbury: J. G. Rusher, [1841]
Alphabetical. Occupation and address. Non-voters, distinguishing dead and removed.

Henry William Tacred   Hugh Holbech   Henry Vincent

Bodl Inst Hist Res

1847—A copy of the poll... Banbury: William Potts, [1847]
Alphabetical by candidate. Address. Non-voters, distinguishing dead.

Henry William Tancred   James Macgregor

Bodl Inst Hist Res

1847—1847. List of persons... with the poll... Banbury: J. G. Rusher, [1847]
Alphabetical. Occupation and address. Non-voters included, distinguishing dead and absent.

Henry William Tancred   James Macgregor

Bodl Inst Hist Res

1859* (February)—The Banbury poll book, 1859. Poll of the electors... Rusher, [1859]
Alphabetical by candidate. Occupation, address, and poor rate assessment. Non-voters.

Bernhard Samuelson   John Hardy   Edward Miall

Banbury Pub Lib Inst Hist Res

1859* (February)—The Banbury and Neithrop register of electors, 1865... [Banbury, 1865]
By street. Shows voting in both 1859 elections.

Bernhard Samuelson   John Hardy   Edward Miall

Banbury Pub Lib Inst Hist Res

1859 (April)—The Banbury and Neithrop register of electors, 1865... [Banbury, 1865]
By street. Shows voting in both 1859 elections.

Sir Charles Eurwicke Douglas   Bernhard Samuelson

Banbury Pub Lib Inst Hist Res

1865—Copy of the poll of the electors of Banbury... [Banbury, 1865] [Broadsheet]
Alphabetical by candidate. Address. Non-voters.

Bernhard Samuelson Charles Bell Sir Charles Eurwicke Douglas

Banbury Pub Lib Inst Hist Res

OXFORD

1768—A true copy of the poll... Oxford: W. Jackson, 1768
Alphabetical. Occupation and parish. Queried voters distinguished.

George Nares William Harcourt William Craven Sir James Cotter

Bodl Guildhall Lib

1790*—A true copy of the poll... Oxford: Palmer, [1790]
Alphabetical. Occupation and parish.

Arthur Annesley George Ogilvie

Bodl Inst Hist Res

1796*—The poll of the freemen... Oxford: Mercury Press, 1796
Alphabetical. Occupation and parish.

Henry Peters Francis Burton Arthur Annesley

Bodl Inst Hist Res

1802—The poll of the freemen... Oxford: Slatter & Munday, 1802
Alphabetical. Occupation and parish or place of residence. Non-voters.

John Atkyns Wright Francis Burton John Ingram Lockhart

Bodl Inst Hist Res

1806—The poll of the freemen... Oxford: Slatter & Munday, 1806
Alphabetical. Occupation and parish or place of residence. Non-voters.

Francis Burton John Atkyns Wright John Ingram Lockhart

Bodl Inst Hist Res

1812—The poll of the freemen... Oxford: Munday & Slatter, 1812
Alphabetical by residents and out-voters. Occupation and parish or place of residence. Members of council including non-voters.

John Atkyns Wright John Ingram Lockhart George Eden Henry Roper Curson

Bodl Inst Hist Res

1818—The poll of the freemen... Oxford: Munday & Slatter, 1818
Alphabetical by residents and out-voters. Occupation and parish or place of residence. Members of council including non-voters.

John Atkyns Wright Frederick St. John John Ingram Lockhart

Bodl Inst Hist Res

1820—The poll of the freemen... Oxford: Munday & Slatter, 1820
Alphabetical by residents by parish and out-voters. Occupation and address or place of residence.

Charles Wetherell John Ingram Lockhart Frederick St. John

Bodl Inst Hist Res

1826—The poll of the freemen... Oxford: J. Munday, 1826
Alphabetical. Occupation and parish or place of residence.
John Ingram Lockhart William Hughes Hughes James Haughton Langston
Bodl Inst Hist Res

1830—The poll of the freemen... Oxford: H. Cooke, 1830
Alphabetical. Occupation and parish or place of residence. Members of the council distinguished.
John Ingram Lockhart James Haughton Langston William Hughes Hughes
Bodl Inst Hist Res

1832—The poll of the freemen and electors... Oxford: Jacob, 1832
Alphabetical by qualification. Occupation and address or place of residence.
James Haughton Langston Thomas Stonor William Hughes Hughes
Sir Charles Wetherell
Bodl

1835—The poll of the freemen and electors... Oxford: W. Graham, 1835
Alphabetical. Occupation and address.
William Hughes Hughes Donald Maclean Thomas Stonor
Bodl Inst Hist Res

1837—The poll of the freemen and non-freemen electors... Oxford: J. Munday, Jun., 1837
Alphabetical by qualification and parish. Occupation and parish or place of residence of freemen, address of electors. Non-voters.
Donald Maclean William Erle William Hughes Hughes
Bodl Inst Hist Res

1841—The poll of the freemen and electors... Oxford: Vincent, 1841
Alphabetical by qualification and parish. Occupation and address or place of residence.
James Haughton Langston Donald Maclean Neil Malcolm
Bodl

1841—List of the electors... *Oxford University, City and County Herald* Supplement 16 October 1841
Alphabetical by candidate. Occupation and address.
James Haughton Langston Donald Maclean Neil Malcolm
Oxford Pub Lib Inst Hist Res

1868—The poll of the freemen and electors... Oxford: *Oxford Chronicle* Co., 1868
Alphabetical by parish and out-voters. Occupation and address. Freemen distinguished. Lodgers at the end of each parish.
Edward Cardwell William Vernon Harcourt James Parker Deane
Bodl Inst Hist Res

OXFORD UNIVERSITY

1722—A true copy of the poll... 1721... Oxford: Clarendon Printing House, 1722
Alphabetical by college. Recent additions, residents and non-residents not in the books, those not of any foundation and holders of honorary degrees distinguished. Queried voters distinguished, showing decision.

William Bromley   George Clarke   William King

Bodl Inst Hist Res

1737*—An exact account of the poll... London: L. Gilliver & J. Clarke, [1737]
Alphabetical by college, candidate and degree. Non-voters within each college.

William Bromley   Robert Trevor

Bodl Inst Hist Res

1750*—A true copy of the poll... London: R. Baldwin, Jr., [1750]
By college. Queried voters distinguished. Papers circulated concerning the university representation.

Sir Roger Newdigate   Robert Harley   Sir Edward Turner

Bodl Inst Hist Res

1768—An authentic copy of the poll... Oxford: Clarendon Press, 1768
By college. Queried voters distinguished.

Sir Roger Newdigate   Francis Page   Charles Jenkinson   George Hay

Bodl Inst Hist Res

1806—An authentic copy of the poll... Oxford: Clarendon Press, 1806
By college. Queried voters distinguished.

Sir William Scott   Charles Abbot   Richard Heber

Bodl Inst Hist Res

1821*—An authentic copy of the poll... Oxford: Clarendon Press, 1821
Poll order by college and degree.

Richard Heber   Sir John Nicholl

Bodl Brit Lib

1829*—An authentic copy of the poll... Oxford: Clarendon Press, 1829
By college.

Sir Robert Harry Inglis   Robert Peel

Bodl Inst Hist Res

1847—An authentic copy of the poll... Oxford: University Press, 1847
By college.

Sir Robert Harry Inglis   William Ewart Gladstone   Charles Gray Round

Bodl Inst Hist Res

1852—An authentic copy of the poll... Oxford: University Press, 1852
By college. Fellows distinguished. Pairs.

Sir Robert Harry Inglis   William Ewart Gladstone   Robert Bullock Marsham

Bodl Inst Hist Res

1853*—An authentic copy of the poll... Oxford: University Press, 1853
Poll order by college and degree.

William Ewart Gladstone   Dudley Montagu Perceval

Bodl Brit Lib

1853*—A copy of the poll... London: W. Clowes, [1853]
Alphabetical by college and candidate. Pairs. Perceval's London and Oxford committees.

William Ewart Gladstone   Dudley Montagu Perceval

Bodl Inst Hist Res

1853*—Oxford University election, January z4-20, 1853... Oxford: I. Shrimpton, [1853]
Pairs alphabetically by college.

William Ewart Gladstone   Dudley Montagu Perceval

Bodl Brit Lib

1859*—An authentic copy of the poll... Oxford: University Press, 1859
Alphabetical by college. Fellows distinguished.

William Ewart Gladstone   Marquess of Chandos

Bodl Inst Hist Res

1865—An authentic copy of the poll... Oxford: Clarendon Press, 1865
Alphabetical by college. Voters in person distinguished.

Sir William Heathcote   Gathorne Hardy   William Ewart Gladstone

Bodl Brit Lib

[Two editions known]

1878*—An authentic copy of the poll... Oxford: Clarendon Press, 1878
Alphabetical by college. Fellows and voters in person distinguished.

John Gilbert Talbot   Henry John Stephen Smith

Bodl Inst Hist Res

RUTLAND

1710—The poll (taken October 16, 1710)... Stamford: in St. Martins, 1710
By parish. Place of residence.

John Noel   Lord Finch   Richard Halford   Philip Sherard

Bodl Inst Hist Res

1841—County of Rutland, 1841. Poll book of the election... Oakham: Cunnington, [1841]
Alphabetical by hundred and parish. Address. Non-voters, dead and disqualified distinguished.

Gilbert John Heathcote   William Henry Dawnay   Charles George Noel

Bodl   Guildhall Lib

Untraced: 1722, 1754

SHROPSHIRE

1713—A true copy of the poll... n.p., 1714
Poll order by booth. Place of residence and of freehold. Index.

Viscount Newport   John Kynaston   Sir John Astley

Shrewsbury Pub Lib

1831—A correct alphabetical list of the freeholders... Shrewsbury: John Eddowes, [1831]
Alphabetical. Occupation and place of residence. Tendered votes, distinguishing rejected.

Sir Rowland Hill   John Cressett Pelham   William Lloyd   John Mytton

Shrewsbury Pub Lib

NORTH SHROPSHIRE

1832—Shropshire election, Northern Division. List of the electors... Shrewsbury: John Watton, 1833
Alphabetical by polling booth. Occupation and address. Tendered voters included.

Sir Rowland Hill   John Cotes   William Ormesby Gore

Shrewsbury Pub Lib

1868—21st November 1868. Poll book... Shrewsbury: Leake & Evans, 1868
Alphabetical by polling district, parish and qualification. Non-voters included.

John Ralph Ormesby Gore   Viscount Newport   Richard George Jebb

Shrewsbury Pub Lib

SOUTH SHROPSHIRE

1865—18th July 1865. Poll book... Shrewsbury: J. O. Sandford, [1865]
Alphabetical by polling district and parish. Non-voters included.

Robert Jasper More   Percy Egerton Herbert   Sir Baldwin Leighton

Shrewsbury Pub Lib   Inst Hist Res

1865—South Shropshire elections, 1865 and 1868... Copy of the polls... London: Haverson & Martin, [1868]
Alphabetical by polling district and parish. Non-voters included. Voters not on the register in 1868 omitted.

Robert Jasper More   Percy Egerton Herbert   Sir Baldwin Leighton

Shropshire Rec Off   Guildhall Lib

1868—23rd November 1868. Poll book of the South Shropshire election... Shrewsbury: J. O. Sandford, [1868]
Alphabetical by polling district, parish and qualification. Non-voters included.

Percy Egerton Herbert Edward Corbett Robert Jasper More

Shropshire Rec Off Guildhall Lib

1868—South Shropshire elections, 1865 and 1868... Copy of the polls... London: Haverson & Martin, [1868]
Alphabetical by polling district and parish. Non-voters included. Voters not on the register in 1868 omitted.

Percy Egerton Herbert Edward Corbett Robert Jasper More

Shropshire Rec Off Guildhall Lib

BRIDGNORTH

1837—The poll for the election of members... Ironbridge: Walter, [1837]
Alphabetical by qualification and parish. Occupation and address of freemen, address of electors.

Thomas Charlton Whitmore Charles Hanbury Tracy Robert Pigot

Shrewsbury Pub Lib

1847—The official copy of the poll book... Bridgnorth: Gitton, [1847]
Alphabetical. Occupation and address.

Thomas Charlton Whitmore Sir Robert Pigot Sir John Easthope

Shrewsbury School Inst Hist Res

1865—Copy of the poll book... Bridgnorth: W. J. Rowley, [1865]
Alphabetical by qualification and parish. Address. Non-voters included, distinguishing dead.

John Pritchard Sir John Acton Henry Whitmore

Bodl Inst Hist Res

LUDLOW

1865—An alphabetical list of the poll... Ludlow: R. Jones, [1865]
Alphabetical by qualification. Address. Non-voters.

George Herbert Windsor Windsor Clive John Edmund Severne Sir William Yardley

Soc Gen

1868—An alphabetical list of the poll... Ludlow: R. Jones, [1868]
Alphabetical by qualification and parish. Address. Non-voters.

George Herbert Windsor Windsor Clive Sir William Yardley

Shrewsbury Pub Lib

SHREWSBURY

1734—A list of persons that voted for Sr. Richard Corbett, Bart. and William Kinaston, Esq.... n.p., 1734, [Broadsheet]
Alphabetical. Occupation and address. New burgesses distinguished.
William Kinaston Richard Corbett John Mytton Richard Lyster
Shrewsbury Pub Lib Inst Hist Res

1768—A list of burgesses who voted for the Right Hon. Lord Clive and Noel Hill, Esq.... n.p., [1768] [Broadsheet]
Alphabetical. Occupation and address. Voters for Hill and Pulteney. Plumpers for Hill and for Pulteney, voters for Clive and Pulteney and doubtful voters distinguished.
Noel Hill Lord Clive William Pulteney
Shrewsbury Pub Lib

1768—A list of burgesses who voted for William Pulteney... Salop: Stafford Pryce 1768, [Broadsheet]
Alphabetical. Occupation and address. Rejected voters for Pulteney.
Noel Hill Lord Clive William Pulteney
Shrewsbury Pub Lib

1774—List of the burgesses and freemen burgesses... n.p., [1774] [Broadsheet]
Alphabetical. Occupation and address. Rejected voters.
Lord Clive Charlton Leighton William Pulteney
Shrewsbury Pub Lib

1796—A correct alphabetical list of the burgesses... Shrewsbury: J. & W. Eddowes, 1796
Occupation and address. Tendered votes.
Sir William Pulteney William Hill John Hill
Shrewsbury Pub Lib Inst Hist Res

1806—Shrewsbury election. Alphabetical list of the voters... T. Wood, [1806]
Occupation and address. Tendered votes.
William Hill Henry Grey Bennett Thomas Jones
Shrewsbury Pub Lib Inst Hist Res

1806—A correct alphabetical list of the burgesses... Shrewsbury: J. & W. Eddowes, [1806]
Occupation and address. Tendered votes.
William Hill Henry Grey Bennett Thomas Jones
Shrewsbury Pub Lib

1807—A correct alphabetical list of the burgesses... J. & W. Eddowes, [1807]
Occupation and address. Tendered votes.
William Hill Thomas Jones Henry George Bennett
Inst Hist Res

1807—The poll for the borough of Shrewsbury... T. Wood, [1807]
Alphabetical. Occupation and address. Tendered votes.

William Hill | Thomas Jones | Henry George Bennett

Shrewsbury Pub Lib Inst Hist Res

1812—A correct alphabetical list of the burgesses... William Eddowes, [1812]
Occupation and address. Tendered votes.

Henry Grey Bennett | Sir Rowland Hill | Benjamin Benyon

Shropshire Rec Off Inst Hist Res

1812—A correct alphabetical list of the burgesses... Shrewsbury: Waidson, [1812]
Occupation and address. Tendered votes. Additional list of voters on the last day after Benyon's withdrawal.

Henry Grey Bennett | Sir Rowland Hill | Benjamin Benyon

Shrewsbury Pub Lib Inst Hist Res

1814*—Correct alphabetical lists of the burgesses... Shrewsbury: W. Eddowes, 1814
By candidate. Occupation and address. Tendered votes.

Richard Lyster | Benjamin Benyon

Shrewsbury Pub Lib Inst Hist Res

1819*—Correct alphabetical lists of the burgesses... Shrewsbury: W. Eddowes, 1819
By candidate. Occupation and address. Tendered votes.

John Mytton | Panton Corbett

Shrewsbury Pub Lib Inst Hist Res

1819*—Pollbook, 1819. Correct alphabetical lists of the burgesses... Shrewsbury: T. Howell, [1819]
By candidate. Occupation and address. Tendered votes. Account of proceedings.

John Mytton | Panton Corbett

Shrewsbury Pub Lib

1826—A correct alphabetical list... Shrewsbury: W. & J. Eddowes, [1826]
Occupation and address. Tendered and rejected votes. List of voters after Boycott's withdrawal.

Panton Corbett | Robert Aglionby Slaney | Thomas Boycott

Shrewsbury Pub Lib Inst Hist Res

1826—A correct alphabetical list... Shrewsbury: T. Howell, [1826]
Occupation and address. Tendered votes.

Panton Corbett | Robert Aglionby Slaney | Thomas Boycott

Shrewsbury Pub Lib

1830—A correct alphabetical list of the burgesses... Shrewsbury: W & J. Eddowes, [1830]
Occupation and address. Tendered votes.

Richard Jenkins | Robert Aglionby Slaney | Panton Corbett

Shrewsbury Pub Lib Inst Hist Res

1831—A correct alphabetical list of the burgesses... Shrewsbury: John Eddowes, [1831]
Occupation and address. Tendered votes.

Robert Aglionby Slaney Richard Jenkins Thomas Boycott Richard Potter

Shrewsbury Pub Lib Inst Hist Res

1832—A correct alphabetical list of the electors... Shrewsbury: John Eddowes, 1833
Occupation and address. New electors distinguished. Non-voters.

Sir John Hanmer Robert Aglionby Slaney John Cressett Pelham

Shropshire Rec Off Inst Hist Res

1835—A correct alphabetical list of the electors... Shrewsbury: John Eddowes, 1835
Occupation and address. New electors distinguished. Non-voters.

Sir John Hanmer John Cressett Pelham Robert Aglionby Slaney

Shropshire Rec Off Inst Hist Res

1837—A correct alphabetical list of the electors... Shrewsbury: Richard Davies, 1837
Occupation and address. Non-voters. Tendered and rejected votes.

Richard Jenkins Robert Aglionby Slaney John Cressett Pelham Francis Dashwood

Shrewsbury Pub Lib

1837—[Title page missing. Begins:] 'Electors who voted at the borough election... [Shrewsbury: 1837]
Alphabetical. Occupation and address. Non-voters, distinguishing removed. Tendered and rejected votes.

Richard Jenkins Robert Aglionby Slaney John Cressett Pelham Francis Dashwood

Inst Hist Res

1841—A correct alphabetical list of the electors... Shrewsbury: Richard Davies, 1841
Occupation and address. Tendered and rejected votes. Non-voters.

George Tomline Benjamin Disraeli Sir Love Parry Christopher Temple

Shrewsbury Pub Lib Inst Hist Res

1847—A correct alphabetical list of the electors... Shrewsbury: Richard Davies, 1847
Occupation and address. Non-voters.

Edward Holmes Baldock Robert Aglionby Slaney George Tomline

Shrewsbury Pub Lib Inst Hist Res

1847—E. & J. Edwards's alphabetical list of the electors... Shrewsbury: E. & J. Edwards, 1847
Occupation and address. Non-voters.

Edward Holmes Baldock Robert Aglionby Slaney George Tomline

Shropshire Rec Off Guildhall Lib

1852—Alphabetical list of the electors... Shrewsbury: Pearson & Rutland, [1852]
Occupation and address. Non-voters and dead.

George Tomline Edward Holmes Baldock Augustin Robinson

Shrewsbury Pub Lib Inst Hist Res

1857—Shrewsbury borough election, Saturday, 28th March, 1857... Shrewsbury: Watton, [1857], Broadsheet
Alphabetical by candidate. Occupation and address.
George Tomline Robert Aglionby Slaney John Walter Huddleston R. Phibbs
Shrewsbury School Inst Hist Res

1857—List of voters at Shrewsbury borough election... Shrewsbury: *Shrewsbury Journal* Office, 1857 [Broadsheet]
Alphabetical by candidate. Occupation and address. Non-voters.
George Tomline Robert Aglionby Slaney John Walter Huddleston R. Phibbs
Shrewsbury School Inst Hist Res

1862*—List of voters for the borough... Reprinted from Eddowes's *Shrewsbury Journal,* 11 June 1862 [Broadsheet]
Alphabetical by candidate. Occupation and address. Non-voters.
Henry Robertson Richard Banner Oakeley Henry Atkin
Shrewsbury School Inst Hist Res

1862*—List of voters at the Shrewsbury borough election... *Shrewsbury Chronicle* Supplement, 6 June 1862
Alphabetical by candidate. Occupation and address. Non-voters.
Henry Robertson Richard Banner Oakeley Henry Atkin
Shrewsbury Pub Lib

1862*—List of voters at Shrewsbury borough election... Shrewsbury: Watton, [1862], Broadsheet
Alphabetical by candidate. Occupation and address. Non-voters.
Henry Robertson Richard Banner Oakeley Henry Atkin
Manchester Pub Lib

1868—Shrewsbury borough election... poll book... Shrewsbury: J. Watton, 1868
Alphabetical by candidate. Occupation and address. Non-voters.
William James Clement James Figgins Robert Crawford
Shrewsbury Pub Lib Inst Hist Res

1870*—Shrewsbury borough election... Shrewsbury: Richard Davies, [1870]
Alphabetical by polling booth. Address. Non-voters by qualification with occupation and address.
Douglas Straight Charles Cecil Cotes
Shrewsbury Pub Lib Inst Hist Res

WENLOCK

1832—An alphabetical list of the electors... Wakefield: J. Stanfield, 1835
Alphabetical by qualification and parish. Place of residence of burgesses.
George Cecil Weld Forester James Milnes Gaskell Matthew Bridges
Guildhall Lib

1835—An alphabetical list of the electors... Ironbridge: Walter, 1835
Alphabetical by qualification and parish.
George Cecil Weld Forester James Milnes Gaskell Sir William Somerville
Guildhall Lib

BATH

1832—The Bath poll: being a list of names... Bath: J. Weston, 1833
Alphabetical by parish. Address. Non-voters distinguished.
Charles Palmer John Arthur Roebuck H. W. Hobhouse
Bath Pub Lib Inst Hist Res

1835—The Bath poll: being a list of names... Bath: C. Duffield, 1835
Alphabetical by parish. Address. Non-voters distinguished.
Charles Palmer John Arthur Roebuck Henry Daubeny
Bath Pub Lib Guildhall Lib

1837—The Bath poll: being a list of names... Bath: C. Duffield, 1837
Alphabetical by parish. Address. Non-voters distinguished.
Viscount Powerscourt William Heald Ludlow Bruges Charles Palmer
John Arthur Roebuck
Bath Pub Lib Inst Hist Res

1837—The Bath reform poll book... Bath: Samuel Gibbs, [1837]
Alphabetical by parish. Address. Non-voters included, distinguishing dead and removed. Aldermen and councillors. Votes in 1832 and 1835.
Viscount Powerscourt William Heald Ludlow Bruges Charles Palmer
John Arthur Roebuck
Bath Pub Lib Inst Hist Res

1841—The Bath poll book... Bath: W. Pocock, 1841
Alphabetical. Occupation and address. Non-voters included, distinguishing dead and removed.
Viscount Duncan John Arthur Roebuck William Heald Ludlow Bruges
Viscount Powerscourt
Bath Pub Lib Guildhall Lib

1841—The Bath reform poll book... Bath: Samuel Gibbs, [1841]
Alphabetical by parish. Address. Non-voters included, distinguishing dead and removed. Aldermen and councillors. Votes in 1832, 1835 and 1837.
Viscount Duncan John Arthur Roebuck William Heald Ludlow Bruges
Viscount Powerscourt
Bath Pub Lib nst Hist Res

1847—The Bath poll book... Bath: W. Pocock, 1847
Alphabetical. Occupation and address. Non-voters included, distinguishing dead.
Lord Ashley Viscount Duncan John Arthur Roebuck
Bath Pub Lib Inst Hist Res

1847—The Bath Liberal poll book... Bath: S. Gibbs, [1847]
Alphabetical. Address. Non-voters included, distinguishing dead. Aldermen and councillors. Votes in 1841.

Lord Ashley Viscount Duncan John Arthur Roebuck

Bath Pub Lib Inst Hist Res

1851*—The poll-book of the Bath election... Bath: S. Hayward & M. A. Pocock, 1851
Alphabetical by candidate. Occupation and address. Non-voters.

George Treweeke Scobell W. Sutcliffe

Bath Pub Lib Inst Hist Res

1852—The Bath poll book... Bath: R. E. Peach; S. Hayward, 1852
Alphabetical by parish. Occupation and address. Non-voters distinguished.

George Treweeke Scobell Thomas Phinn William Whateley

Bath Pub Lib Inst Hist Res

1855*—The Bath poll-book... Bath: R. E. Peach, 1855
Alphabetical by candidate. Occupation, address and poor rate assessment. Non-voters.

William Tite William Whateley

Bath Pub Lib Inst Hist Res

1857—The Bath poll book... Bath: R. E. Peach, 1857
Alphabetical. Address. Non-voters distinguished.

Sir Arthur Hallam Elton William Tite Arthur Edwin Way

Bath Pub Lib Inst Hist Res

1859—The Bath poll book... Bath: R. E. Peach, 1859
Alphabetical by parish. Address. Non-voters distinguished.

William Tite Arthur Edwin Way Thomas Phinn

Bath Pub Lib Inst Hist Res

1859—Bath election, 1859. The names... n.p., [1859]
Alphabetical by parish. Address. Non-voters included, distinguishing dead.

William Tite Arthur Edwin Way Thomas Phinn

Soc Geneal Inst Hist Res

1868—The Bath poll book... Bath: S. Hayward & R. E. Peach, 1868
Alphabetical by parish. Occupation and address. Non-voters distinguished.

William Tite Donald Dalrymple James Macnaghton Hogg

Bath Pub Lib Inst Hist Res

BRIDGWATER

1754—A list of the electors... Bristol: E. Farley, [1754]
Alphabetical by candidate. Occupation. Non-voters.

Earl of Egmont Robert Balch George Dodington

Bridgwater Pub Lib Inst Hist Res

1780—A list of the electors... William Cass, [1780], Broadsheet
Alphabetical. Occupation. Rejected voters. Those active in opposition to Poulett and those promised to Poulett or Acland who voted for their opponents distinguished.

Ann Poulett Benjamin Allen John Acland Charles James Fox

Bridgwater Pub Lib Inst Hist Res

1790—A list of the electors... n.p., [1790] [Broadsheet]
Alphabetical. Occupation. Non-voters.

Vere Poulett John Langston Lord Perceval

Bridgwater Pub Lib Inst Hist Res

1802—A list of the electors... Bridgwater: Cass, [1802], Broadsheet
Alphabetical. Occupation. Rejected and non-voters.

Jefferys Allen George Pocock John Agnew John Harcourt

Bridgwater Pub Lib Inst Hist Res

1806—A list of the electors... Bridgwater: J. Poole, [1806] [Broadsheet]
Alphabetical. Occupation. Non-voters.

Vere Poulett John Langston John Hudleston William Thornton

Bridgwater Pub Lib Inst Hist Res

1807—A list of the electors... Bridgwater: Cass, [1807] Broadsheet
Alphabetical. Occupation. Non-voters.

William Thornton George Pocock Vere Poulett

Bridgwater Pub Lib Inst Hist Res

1818—A list of the electors... Bridgwater: J. Binning, [1818] [Broadsheet]
Alphabetical. Occupation. Rejected and non-voters.

William Astell George Pocock John Hudder Moggridge Edward Parkins

Bridgwater Pub Lib Inst Hist Res

1818—A list of the electors... Bridgwater: J. Poole, [1818] [Broadsheet]
Alphabetical. Occupation. Rejected, objected and non-voters.

William Astell George Pocock John Hudder Moggridge Edward Parkins

Bridgwater Pub Lib Inst Hist Res

1826—List of the electors... Bridgwater: Poole & Son, [1826] [Broadsheet]
Alphabetical. Occupation. Rejected and non-voters.

William Astell Charles Kemeys Kemeys Tynte Sir Colin Campbell

Bridgwater Pub Lib Inst Hist Res

1831—1831. Bridgwater election. A list of the electors... Bridgwater: Awbrey, [1831] [Broadsheet]
Alphabetical. Occupation. Non-voters.

Charles Kemeys Kemeys Tynte William Astell Henry Shirley

Bridgwater Pub Lib Inst Hist Res

1831—List of the electors... Bridgwater: Quiers, [1831] [Broadsheet]
Alphabetical. Occupation. Rejected and non-voters.

Charles Kemeys Kemeys Tynte William Astell Henry Shirley

Bridgwater Pub Lib Inst Hist Res

1835—A list of the electors... Bridgwater: C. Faun, [1835] [Broadsheet]
Alphabetical. Occupation. Non-voters.

Charles Kemeys Kemeys Tynte John Temple Leader Henry Broadwood
Francis Mountjoy Martyn

Bridgwater Pub Lib Inst Hist Res

1837* (May)—A list of the electors... Bridgwater: Charles Faun, [1837] [Broadsheet]
Alphabetical. Occupation. Disqualified and non-voters.

Henry Broadwood Richard Brinsley Sheridan

Bridgwater Pub Lib Inst Hist Res

1841—A list of the electors... Bridgwater: Faun, [1841] [Broadsheet]
Alphabetical. Occupation. Disqualified and non-voters.

Henry Broadwood Thomas Seaton Forman Edward Simcoe Drewe Augustin Robinson

Bridgwater Pub Lib Inst Hist Res

1847—A list of the electors... Bridgwater: C. Faun, [1847] [Broadsheet]
Alphabetical. Occupation. Non-voters, distinguishing dead.

Charles John Kemeys Tynte Henry Broadwood Stephen Gaselee

Bridgwater Pub Lib Inst Hist Res

1847—A list of the electors... Bridgwater: S. West, [1847] [Broadsheet]
Alphabetical. Occupation. Non-voters, distinguishing dead.

Charles John Kemeys Tynte Henry Broadwood Stephen Gaselee

Bridgwater Pub Lib Inst Hist Res

1852—A list of the electors... Bridgwater: Chas. Faun, [1852] [Broadsheet]
Alphabetical. Occupation. Non-voters.

Charles John Kemeys Tynte Brent Spencer Follett John Clavell Mansel Lord Henley
Alexander William Kinglake

Bridgwater Pub Lib Inst Hist Res

1852—A list of the electors... Bridgwater: S. West, [1852] [Broadsheet]
Alphabetical. Occupation. Non-voters.

Charles John Kemeys Tynte Brent Spencer Follett John Clavell Mansel Lord Henley
Alexander William Kinglake

Bridgwater Pub Lib Inst Hist Res

1857—A list of the electors... Bridgwater: C. Faun, [1857] [Broadsheet]
Alphabetical. Occupation. Non-voters.

Charles John Kemeys Tynte Alexander William Kinglake Brent Spencer Follett

Bridgwater Pub Lib Inst Hist Res

1865—A list of the electors... Bridgwater: Chas. Faun, [1865] [Broadsheet]
Alphabetical by qualification. Address. Non-voters.

Henry Westropp   Alexander William Kinglake   Sir John Villiers Shelley

Bridgwater Pub Lib   Inst Hist Res

1865—A list of the electors... Bridgwater: Archibald Graham, [1865] [Broadsheet]
Alphabetical. Occupation. Non-voters.

Henry Westropp   Alexander William Kinglake   Sir John Villiers Shelley

Bridgwater Pub Lib   Inst Hist Res

1866* (June)—A list of the electors... Bridgwater: Chas. Faun, [1866] [Broadsheet]
Alphabetical. Occupation. Non-voters.

George Patton   Walter Bagehot

Bridgwater Pub Lib   Inst Hist Res

1866* (July)—A list of the electors... Bridgwater: Chas. Faun, [1866] [Broadsheet]
Alphabetical. Occupation. Non-voters.

Philip Vanderbyl   George Patton

Bridgwater Pub Lib   Inst Hist Res

TAUNTON

1853*—Taunton election, 3rd May 1853 *Somerset County Herald & Great Western Advertiser,* 14 May 1853
Alphabetical by candidate. Occupation and address. Non-voters.

Sir John William Ramsden   Henry Badcock

Brit Lib (News)   Inst Hist Res

WELLS

1765—The poll taken at the town-hall... n.p., [1765]
By candidate, rival polls being held at the town hall and the assize court. Qualification, including previous votes accepted from freemen by servitude.

Peter Taylor   Robert Child

Brit Lib

STAFFORDSHIRE

1747—A copy of a poll... n.p., [1747]
By hundred and parish. Place of residence, nature and occupier of freehold. Oath-takers distinguished.

Sir Walter Wagstaff Bagott   William Leveson Gower   John Crew, Jr.
Sir Richard Wrottesley

William Salt Lib   Inst Hist Res

NORTH STAFFORDSHIRE

1832—A copy of the poll... Newcastle-under-Lyme: W. H. Hyde, 1833
Alphabetical by hundred and parish. Place of residence. Non-voters included.

Sir Oswald Mosley   Edward Buller   Jesse Watts Russell

William Salt Lib Inst Hist Res

1837—A copy of the poll... Newcastle-under-Lyme: W. H. Hyde, 1837
Alphabetical by hundred and parish. Address. Non-voters included.

William Bingham Baring   Edward Buller   Sir Oswald Mosley

William Salt Lib Guildhall Lib

1865—The poll book: showing how each voter polled... Hanley: Keates & Ford, 1865
Alphabetical by polling district and parish. Address. Non-voters included.

Edward Buller   Charles Bowyer Adderley   Viscount Ingestre

Stoke Pub Lib Guildhall Lib

SOUTH STAFFORDSHIRE

1835*—A copy of the poll... Rugeley: J. T. Walters, 1835
Alphabetical by polling place and parish. Place of residence. Non-voters included.

Sir Francis Lyttleton Holyoake Goodricke   George Anson

William Salt Lib Inst Hist Res

WEST STAFFORDSHIRE

1868—1868. The poll for two knights... compiled . . . by Edward Fernie... London: Spottiswoode & Co., [1869]
Alphabetical by polling district, parish and qualification. Address. Non-voters distinguished. Index.

Smith Child   Hugo Francis Meynell Ingram   William Orme Foster
Henry Wentworth Hodgetts Foley

William Salt Lib Guildhall Lib

LICHFIELD

1747—The poll taken for representatives... Birmingham: T. Aris for R. Bailey, Lichfield, [1747]
Alphabetical. Occupation and place of residence. Rejected voters.

Richard Leveson Gower Thomas Anson Sir Lister Holte George Venables Vernon

Staffs Rec Off Inst Hist Res

1799*—The poll for a member... Lichfield: M. Morgan, [1799]
Poll order. Place of residence, place, nature, occupier and grantor of qualification. Rejected voters distinguished with notes. Notes on a few other voters.

Sir John Wrottesley   Sir Nigel Bowyer Gresley

William Salt Lib Inst Hist Res

1799*—The poll, taken for a representative... n.p., [1799]
Poll order by candidate. Place of residence, place, nature, occupier and grantor of qualification. Rejected voters not included.

Sir John Wrottesley   Sir Nigel Bowyer Gresley

Staffs Rec Off Inst Hist Res

1835—A statement of the poll (alphabetically arranged)... Lichfield: W. Morgan, [1835]
Occupation, address and qualification. Rejected voters included.

Sir George Anson   Sir Edward Dolman Scott   Francis Finch

Lichfield Pub Lib Inst Hist Res

NEWCASTLE-UNDER-LYME

1734—A copy of the poll... n.p., [1734]
Alphabetical. Occupation.

Baptist Leveson Gower   John Lawton   John Ward   Edwaard Sneyd

Newcastle Pub Lib Inst Hist Res

1774—A copy of the poll... Newcastle: James Smith, 1774
Alphabetical. Occupation, address and paternity in some cases. Capital burgesses distinguished.

Viscount Chewton   Sir George Hay   Clement Kinnersley

Newcastle Pub Lib Inst Hist Res

1790—A copy of the poll... Newcastle: J. Smith, [1790]
Alphabetical. Occupation, address and paternity in some cases. Capital burgesses distinguished.

Sir Archibald Macdonald John Leveson Gower Thomas Fletcher Clement Kinnersley

1792*—An alphabetical copy of the poll... Newcastle: James Smith, [1792]
Occupation, address and paternity in some cases. Capital burgesses distinguished.

William Egerton   Thomas Fletcher

Newcastle Pub Lib Inst Hist Res

1793*—An alphabetical copy of the poll... Newcastle: James Smith, [1793]
Alphabetical. Occupation. Address or paternity in some cases. Capital burgesses distinguished. Rejected and objected voters.

Sir Francis Ford   Thomas Fletcher

Staffs Rec Off Inst Hist Res

1802—An alphabetical copy of the poll... Newcastle: Smith, [1802]
Occupation. Address or paternity in some cases. Capital burgesses distinguished. Rejected voters with reasons and intentions.

Edward Wilbraham Bootle   Sir Robert Lawley   Oliver Beckett   Joseph James

Staffs Rec Off Inst Hist Res

1807—A copy of the poll (in alphabetical order)... Newcastle: C. Chester, 1807
Occupation. Capital burgesses and independent voters distinguished. Remarks on many voters, including details of property held under Lord Stafford. Rejected voters with intentions.

Edward Wilbraham Bootle James Macdonald John Fenton Boughley Fletcher
Joseph Minet

Newcastle Pub Lib Inst Hist Res

1812—A copy of the poll... Newcastle: C. Chester, 1812
Alphabetical. Occupation and paternity in some cases. Capital burgesses distinguished. Rejected voters with reasons and intentions.

Earl Gower Sir John Fenton Boughey Edward Wilbraham Bootle

William Salt Lib Inst Hist Res

1812—An alphabetical copy of the poll... Newcastle: Smith, [1812]
Occupation and paternity in some cases. Capital burgesses distinguished. Rejected voters with reasons and intentions.

Earl Gower Sir John Fenton Boughey Edward Wilbraham Bootle

Newcastle Pub Lib Guildhall Lib

1815*—A copy of the poll... Newcastle: Chester, [1815]
Alphabetical. Occupation and paternity in some cases. Capital burgesses distinguished. Rejected voters with reasons and intentions. Account of proceedings.

Sir John Chetwode Robert John Wilmot

William Salt Lib Inst Hist Res

1818—An alphabetical copy of the poll... Newcastle: J. Smith, [1818]
Occupation and paternity in some cases. Capital burgesses distinguished. Rejected voters with reasons and intentions. Voters who intended to poll for Kinnersley and Wilmot.

William Shepherd Kinnersley Robert John Wilmot Sir John Fenton Boughey

Newcastle Pub Lib Inst Hist Res

1820—An alphabetical copy of the poll... Newcastle: James Smith, [1820]
Occupation and paternity in some cases. Capital burgesses distinguished. Rejected voters with reasons and intentions.

William Shepherd Kinnersley Robert John Wilmot Timothy Yeates Brown

Newcastle Pub Lib Inst Hist Res

1823*—An alphabetical copy of the poll... Newcastle: James Smith, [1823]
Occupation and paternity in some cases. Capital burgesses distinguished. Rejected voters with reasons and intentions.

John Evelyn Denison Richard Edensor Heathcote

William Salt Lib Inst Hist Res

1830—An alphabetical copy of the poll... Newcastle: J. Bayley, [1830]
Occupation and paternity in some cases. Capital burgesses distinguished. Rejected and objected voters with reasons and intentions.

Richardson Borradaile William Henry Miller Edmund Peel John Evelyn Denison

William Salt Lib Inst Hist Res

1831—An alphabetical copy of the poll... Newcastle: J. Bayley, [1831]
By candidate. Occupation and paternity in some cases. Capital burgesses distinguished. Rejected and objected voters with reasons and intentions.

Edmund Peel William Henry Miller Josiah Wedgwood

Newcastle Pub Lib Inst Hist Res

1831—An alphabetical copy of the poll... Newcastle: W. H. Hyde, [1831]
By candidate. Occupation and paternity in some cases. Capital burgesses distinguished. Rejected and objected voters with reasons and intentions.

Edmund Peel William Henry Miller Josiah Wedgwood

William Salt Lib Inst Hist Res

1832—An alphabetical copy of the poll... Newcastle-under-Lyme: W. H. Hyde, 1832
Occupation for old voters. Address for new voters.

William Henry Miller Sir Henry Pollard Willoughby Edmund Peel

William Salt Lib Inst Hist Res

1832—An alphabetical copy of the poll... Newcastle-under-Lyme: J. Bayley, 1832
Occupation and qualification. Paternity in some cases. Non-voters.

William Henry Miller Sir Henry Pollard Willoughby Edmund Peel

William Salt Lib Guildhall Lib

1835—An alphabetical copy of the poll... Newcastle-under-Lyme: W. H. Hyde, [1835]
Occupation for old voters. Address for new voters.

Edmund Peel William Henry Miller Sir Henry Pollard Willoughby

William Salt Lib Inst Hist Res

1837—An alphabetical copy of the poll... Newcastle-under-Lyme: W. H. Hyde, 1837
Occupation and qualification.

William Henry Miller Spencer Horsey de Horsey Richard Badnall

Newcastle Pub Lib Guildhall Lib

1841—An alphabetical copy of the poll... Newcastle-under-Lyme: Hyde & Crewe, 1841
Occupation for old voters. Address for new voters.

Edmund Buckley John Quincey Harris William Henry Miller

William Salt Lib Inst Hist Res

1865—Newcastle-under-Lyme borough election, 1865... Birmingham: Martin Billing, [1865]
Alphabetical. Address. Non-voters included.
William Shepherd Allen   Edmund Buckley   John Ayshford Wise
Newcastle Pub Lib   Inst Hist Res

Untraced: 1842, 1857

STAFFORD

1780—A poll for the election... n.p., [1780]
Alphabetical.
Edward Monckton   Richard Brinsley Sheridan   Richard Whitworth
Andrew John Drummond
William Salt Lib   Guildhall Lib

1790—(By permission of the Mayor.) A poll... Boden, [1790]
Alphabetical preceded by the corporation. Paternity in some cases.
Edward Monckton   Richard Brinsley Sheridan   George Townsend Sloper
Benjamin Bond Hopkins
William Salt Lib   Inst Hist Res

1807—[Title page missing. Begins:] Poll. [Stafford, 1807]
Alphabetical preceded by the corporation. Paternity in some cases.
Edward Monckton   Richard Mansell Philipps   Sir Oswald Mosley
William Salt Lib   Inst Hist Res

1812—A poll for the election... Stafford: J. Drewry, [1812]
Poll order. Paternity in some cases.
Ralph Benson   Thomas Wilson   Richard Brinsley Sheridan
William Salt Lib   Inst Hist Res

1818—A poll for the election... Stafford: J. Drewry, 1818
Poll order. Paternity in some cases.
Benjamin Benyon   Samuel Homfray   Colin Macaulay
William Salt Lib   Guildhall Lib

1826—A poll for the election... Stafford: J. Drewry, 1826
Poll order. Paternity in some cases. Corporation and disputed votes distinguished.
Richard Ironmonger   Ralph Benson   John Campbell
William Salt Lib   Inst Hist Res

1830—A poll for the election... Stafford: J. Drewry, 1830
Poll order. Paternity in some cases.
Thomas Gisborne   John Campbell   Thomas Hawkes
William Salt Lib   Inst Hist Res

1831—A poll for the election... Stafford: J. Drewry, 1831
Poll order. Paternity in some cases.

John Campbell Thomas Gisborne Thomas Hawkes

William Salt Lib Inst Hist Res

1832—A poll for the election... Stafford: J. Drewry, 1832
Poll order by booth. Separate list of electors.

William Fawkener Chetwynd Rees Howell Gronow William Blount

William Salt Lib Inst Hist Res

1835—A poll for the election... Stafford: J. Drewry, 1835
Poll order by booth.

Francis Lyttleton Holyoake Goodricke William Fawkener Chetwynd Robert Farrand
Rees Howell Gronow Sir Charles Wolseley

William Salt Lib Inst Hist Res

1837—A poll for the election... Stafford: J. & W. Drewry, 1837
Poll order by booth.

William Fawkener Chetwynd Robert Farrand William Bingham Baring William Blount

William Salt Lib Guildhall Lib

1841—The poll for the election... Stafford: Edward Dawson, [1841]
Alphabetical by qualification. Address. Non-voters included.

Swynfen Thomas Carnegie Edward Buller William Holmes

William Salt Lib Inst Hist Res

1847—The poll for the election... Stafford: Edward Dawson, [1847]
Alphabetical. Address.

David Urquhart Thomas Sidney Swynfen Thomas Carnegie John Lee James A. Gordon

William Salt Lib Inst Hist Res

1852—Borough of Stafford. The poll for the election... Stafford: Hill & Halden, 1852
Alphabetical by polling booth. Address.

John Ayshford Wise Arthur Otway John Bourne James Cook Evans

William Salt Lib Inst Hist Res

1857—Borough of Stafford. The poll for the election... Stafford: Hill & Halden, 1857
Alphabetical by polling booth. Address.

John Ayshford Wise Viscount Ingestre Frederick Cadogan

William Salt Lib Inst Hist Res

1859—Borough of Stafford. The poll for the election... Stafford: Hill & Halden, 1859
Alphabetical by qualification. Address.

John Ayshford Wise Thomas Salt, Jr. Thomas Sidney H. R. Addison

William Salt Lib Inst Hist Res

1860*—Boroough of Stafford. The poll for the election... Stafford: Hill & Halden, 1860
Alphabetical by polling booth. Address.

Thomas Sidney   Lord Sandon

William Salt Lib Inst Hist Res

1865—The poll for the election... Stafford: Joseph Halden, 1865
Alphabetical. Address. Separate lists of plumpers.

Michael Arthur Bass   Walter Meller   Henry Davis Pochin

William Salt Lib Brit Lib

1868—The poll for two burgesses... Stafford: Joseph Halden, [1869]
Alphabetical by polling booth and qualification. Address. Non-voters distinguished. Voting in 1868. Analysis of 1865, 1868 and 1869 elections and of the "test ballot" held prior to the 1869 election.

Henry Davis Pochin   Walter Meller   R. C. Chaumes

William Salt Lib Inst Hist Res

1869*—The poll for two burgesses...compiled by Edward Fernie, Secretary to the Staffordshire Central Conservative Association...Stafford: Edward Dawson, [1869]
Alphabetical by qualification. Address. Non-voters distinguished.

Thomas Salt, Jr.   Reginald Arthur James Talbot   Thomas William Evans
Benjamin Whitworth

William Salt Lib Inst Hist Res

1869*—The poll for two burgesses... Stafford: Joseph Halden, [1869]
Alphabetical by polling booth and qualification. Address. Non-voters distinguished. Voting in 1868. Analysis of 1865, 1868 and 1869 elections and of the "test ballot" held prior to the 1869 election.

Thomas Salt, Jr.   Reginald Arthur James Talbot   Thomas William Evans
Benjamin Whitworth

William Salt Lib Inst Hist Res

STOKE-UPON-TRENT

1832—A list of the electors, and how they polled... Hanley: T. Allbut, 1833
Alphabetical by district. Nature and address of qualification. Non-voters included.

Josiah Wedgwood John Davenport Richard Edensor Heathcote George Miles Mason

William Salt Lib Inst Hist Res

1837—A list of the electors... Hanley: T. Allbut, 1837
Alphabetical by parish and township. Nature and address of qualification. Non-voters included, distinguishing disputed, tendered, rejected and removed.

William Taylor Copeland John Davenport Matthew Bridges Francis Cynric Sheridan

Guildhall Lib

1841—A list of the electors, and how they polled... Hanley: T. Allbut & Son, 1841
Alphabetical by parish and district. Nature and address of qualification. Non-voters included.

John Lewis Ricardo William Taylor Copeland Frederic Dudley Ryder

Stoke Pub Lib Inst Hist Res

1847—A list of the electors, and how they polled... Hanley: T. Allbut & Son, 1847
Alphabetical by district. Address. Non-voters included.

John Lewis Ricardo William Taylor Copeland Thomas Piers Healey

Inst Hist Res

1859—A list of the electors, and how they polled...Hanley: Allbut & Daniel, 1859
Alphabetical by district. Address. Non-voters included.

John Lewis Ricardo William Taylor Copeland Samuel Pope

Stoke Pub Lib Inst Hist Res

1862*—A list of the electors, and how they polled...Hanley: Allbut & Daniel, 1862
Alphabetical by district. Address. Non-voters included.

Henry Riversdale Grenfell Alexander James Beresford Beresford Hope William Shee

Stoke Pub Lib Inst Hist Res

1865—A list of the electors, and how they polled...Hanley: Allbut & Daniel, 1865
Alphabetical by district. Address. Non-voters included.

Alexander James Beresford Beresford Hope Henry Riversdale Grenfell George Melly

Stoke Pub Lib Inst Hist Res

1865—The poll book for the borough... Hanley: Keates & Ford, 1865
Alphabetical by district. Address. Non-voters included.

Alexander James Beresford Beresford Hope Henry Riversdale Grenfell George Melly

Stoke Pub Lib Inst Hist Res

1868*—The poll book for the borough... Hanley: J. Keates, 1868
Alphabetical by district. Address. Non-voters included.

George Mally Colin Minton Campbell

Stoke Pub Lib Inst Hist Res

TAMWORTH

1761—A true copy of the poll... Birmingham & Tamworth: James Sketchley, [1761]
Alphabetical. Occupation.

Viscount Villiers Sir Robert Burdett Simon Luttrell

Tamworth Pub Lib Guildhall Lib

[1818]

1837—A correct copy of the poll... Tamworth: J. Thompson, 1837
By street or parish. Occupation. Non-voters.

Sir Robert Peel Edward Henry A'Court John Townshend

Guildhall Lib

1841—A correct copy of the poll... Tamworth: J. Thompson, 1841
By street or parish. Occupation. Non-voters, disqualified and removed.
Sir Robert Peel   Edward Henry A'Court   John Townshend
William Salt Lib   Guildhall Lib

1868—A copy of the poll...Tamworth: Sadler, [1868]
Poll order by booth. Address.
Sir Robert Peel   Sir Henry Lytton Bulwer   John Peel
Tamworth Pub Lib   Inst Hist Res

1872*—1872. The poll for a member...London: M'Corquodale, [1872]
Alphabetical by township. Address. Non-voters distinguished.
Robert William Hanbury   Sir Robert Spencer Robinson
Tamworth Pub   Inst Hist Res

SUFFOLK

1702—A true and exact list of the names...London, 1702
By candidate and parish.
Earl of Dysart   Sir Dudley Cullum   Sir Robert Davers   Samuel Barnardiston
Bury St. Edmunds Pub Lib   Inst Hist Res

1705—A copy of the poll...n.p., [1705]
By parish.
Sir Robert Davers   Earl of Dysart   Sir Dudley Cullum   Sir Samuel Barnardiston
Soc Geneal   Inst Hist Res

1710—A copy of the poll...London: John Barber, 1711
By parish.
Sir Thomas Hanmer   Sir Robert Davers   Sir Philip Parker
Bury St. Edmunds Pub Lib   Inst Hist Res

1727—A copy of the poll...Ipswich: John Bagnall, 1727
By parish. Place of residence.
Sir Jermyn Davers   Sir William Barker   John Holt
Suffolk Rec Off   Inst Hist Res

1784—The poll for knights of the shire... Ipswich: C. Punchard, 1784
Alphabetical by place of residence. Place of freehold.
Sir John Rous   Joshua Grigsby   Sir Thomas Charles Bunbury
Suffolk Rec Off   Inst Hist Res

1790—The poll for knights of the shire... Ipswich: G. Jermyn, 1790
Alphabetical by place of residence. Place of freehold.
Sir Thomas Charles Bunbury   Sir John Rous   Sir Gerard William Vanneck
Suffolk Rec Off   Inst Hist Res

1830—The poll for knights of the shire... Ipswich: John Raw, [1830]
Alphabetical by hundred and parish of residence. Place of freehold.

Sir Henry Charles Bunbury   Charles Tyrell   Sir Thomas Sherlock Gooch

Suffolk Rec Off   Inst Hist Res

EAST SUFFOLK

1832—By permission of the High Sheriff. The poll book... Ipswich: S. Piper, [1832]
Alphabetical by polling district and parish. Place of residence and qualification.

Lord Henniker   Robert Newton Shawe   Sir Charles Broke Vere

Suffolk Rec Off   Inst Hist Res

1835—By permission of the High Sheriff. The poll book... Halesworth: T. Tippell, 1835
Alphabetical by polling district and parish. Place of residence and qualification.

Lord Henniker   Sir Charles Broke Vere   Robert Newton Shawe

Suffolk Rec Off   Inst Hist Res

1841—The poll for members... Ipswich: F. Pawsey, [1841]
Alphabetical by polling district and parish. Place of residence.

Lord Henniker   Sir Charles Broke Vere   Alexander Shafto Adair

Suffolk Rec Off   Brit Lib

1843*—The poll for a member... Ipswich: F. Pawsey, [1843]
Alphabetical by polling district and parish. Place of residence.

Lord Rendlesham   Alexander Shafto Adair

Suffolk Rec Off   Brit Lib

1859—The poll for members... Ipswich: J. Haddock, 1859
Alphabetical by polling district and parish. Place of residence.

Lord Henniker   Sir Fitzroy Kelly   Alexander Shafto Adair

Suffolk Rec Off   Inst Hist Res

1868—The poll for members... Ipswich: Henry Knights, [1868]
Alphabetical by polling district, parish and qualification. Place of residence. Non-voters included.

John Major Henniker-Major   Frederick Snowden Corrance   Alexander Shafto Adair
Thomas Sutton Western

Suffolk Rec Off   Guildhall Lib

WEST SUFFOLK

1832—The poll book for the western division... Bury: T. C. Newby, [1832]
Alphabetical by polling district. Place of residence.

Charles Tyrell   Sir Hyde Parker   Harry Spencer Waddington

Suffolk Rec Off   Brit Lib

1859—The poll for two members... Bury St. Edmunds: T. F. Lucia, [1859]
Alphabetical by polling district and parish. Place of residence. Non-voters.

Earl Jermyn   Windsor Parker   Philip Bennet

Suffolk Rec Off Guildhall Lib

1868—The poll for the western division... Bury St. Edmunds: T. F. Lucia, [1868]
Alphabetical by polling district and parish. Place of residence. Non-voters.

Windsor Parker   Lord Augustus Henry Charles Hervey   Charles Lamport

Suffolk Rec Off Guildhall Lib

ALDEBURGH

1812—Copy of the poll... Halesworth: T. Tippell, [1812]
Poll order. Occupation, place of residence and qualification. Tendered votes.

Lord Dufferin   Andrew Strahan   James Cranborne Strode   Justinian Casamajor

Suffolk Rec Off Inst Hist Res

BURY ST. EDMUNDS

1832—The poll for members... Bury St. Edmunds: W. B. Frost, [1832] [Broadsheet]
Alphabetical by parish. Address.

Lord Charles Fitzroy   Earl Jermyn   Francis King Eagle

Suffolk Rec Off Inst Hist Res

1832—An account of the proceedings at the election... Bury St. Edmunds: Walter B. Frost, 1833
Alphabetical by parish. Address. Non-voters. Account of proceedings and election literature.

Lord Charles Fitzroy   Earl Jermyn   Francis King Eagle

Suffolk Rec Off Brit Lib

1835—The poll for members... Bury St. Edmunds: W. B. Frost, [1835] [Broadsheet]
Alphabetical by parish. Address.

Earl Jermyn   Lord Charles Fitzroy   Charles James Fox Bunbury

Suffolk Rec Off Inst Hist Res

1835—Proceedings at the election... and the poll... Bury: Gedge & Barker, [1835]
Alphabetical by parish. Address. Non-voters. Account of proceedings.

Earl Jermyn   Lord Charles Fitzroy   Charles James Fox Bunbury

Suffolk Rec Off Brit Lib

1837—The poll for members... Bury St. Edmunds: W. B. Frost, 1837
Alphabetical by parish. Address. Non-voters distinguished. Claimants to vote. Dead and removed

Lord Charles Fitzroy   Earl Jermyn   Charles James Fox Bunbury
Frederick George Calthorpe

Suffolk Rec Off Inst Hist Res

1841—The poll of the borough election... Bury St. Edmunds: S. Gross, [1841]
Alphabetical by ward. Address. Non-voters included.

Earl Jermyn   Lord Charles Fitzroy   Horace Twiss   R. G. Alston

Suffolk Rec Off Inst Hist Res

1847—Borough of Bury St. Edmunds. The poll at the election... Bury St. Edmunds: G. Tyson, [1847]
Alphabetical by parish. Address. Non-voters distinguished. Dead.

Earl Jermyn   Edward Herbert Bunbury   Horace Twiss

Suffolk Rec Off Inst Hist Res

1847—Poll at the Bury election... *Bury & Norwich Post,* 18 August 1847
Alphabetical by candidate. Address. Non-voters.

Earl Jermyn   Edward Herbert Bunbury   Horace Twiss

Brit Lib (News) Inst Hist Res

1852 (July)—The poll for the borough... Bury St. Edmunds: G. Thompson, 1852
Alphabetical by parish. Occupation and address. Non-voters distinguished.

Earl Jermyn   John Stuart   Edward Herbert Bunbury

Norwich Pub Lib Guildhall Lib

1852 (July)—The poll for the borough... *Bury & Norwich Post,* 11 July, 1852
Alphabetical by candidate. Address. Non-voters.

Earl Jermyn   John Stuart   Edward Herbert Bunbury

Brit Lib (News) Inst Hist Res

1852* (December)—The poll for the borough... *Bury & Norwich Post,* 7 December 1852
Alphabetical by candidate and parish. Address. Non-voters.

James Henry Porteus Oakes   Joseph Alfred Hardcastle

Brit Lib (News) Inst Hist Res

1857—The poll for the borough... Bury St. Edmunds: Barker, [1857]
Alphabetical by candidate. Address. Non-voters.

Earl Jermyn   Joseph Alfred Hardcastle   James Henry Porteus Oakes

Suffolk Rec Off Inst Hist Res

1857—The poll for the borough... *Bury & Norwich Post* Supplement, 31 March 1857
Alphabetical by candidate. Address. Non-voters.

Earl Jermyn   Joseph Alfred Hardcastle   James Henry Porteus Oakes

Brit Lib (News) Inst Hist Res

1859—The poll for the borough... *Bury & Norwich Post,* 31 May 1859
Alphabetical by candidate. Address. Non-voters.

Lord Alfred Hervey   Joseph Alfred Haardcastle   Sir Robert Jacob Buxton

Brit Lib (News) Inst Hist Res

1865—The poll for the borough... *Bury & Norwich Post,* 18 July 1865
Alphabetical by candidate. Address. Non-voters.

Joseph Alfred Hardcastle   Edward Greene   Lord Alfred Hervey

Brit Lib (News) Inst Hist Res

1868—The poll for the borough... *Bury & Norwich Post* Supplement, 17 November 1868
Alphabetical by candidate. Address. Non-voters.

Edward Greene   Joseph Alfred Hardcastle   Edward Herbert Bunbury

Suffolk Rec Off Inst Hist Res

IPSWICH

1741—The poll for members... Ipswich: W. Craighton, 1741
Alphabetical.

Edward Vernon   Samuel Kent   Knox Ward

Guildhall Lib

1741—A supplement to the poll... Ipswich: W. Craighton, 1741
Alphabetical lists of non-voters and those abroad. Freemen admitted 11 May 1741. Voters with corporation or government places with notes.

Edward Vernon   Samuel Kent   Knox Ward

Inst Hist Res Guildhall Lib

1768—The poll for members... Ipswich: E. Craighton & W. Jackson, 1768
Alphabetical. Occupation or place of residence in a few cases. Objected voters distinguished. Rejected voters with reasons.

Thomas Staunton William Wollaston Wilbraham Tollemache Edward Holden Cruttenden

Suffolk Rec Off Inst Hist Res

1780—The poll for members... Ipswich: Shave & Jackson, [1780]
Alphabetical. Occupation or place of residence in a few cases. Disputed and rejected voters distinguished.

Thomas Staunton   William Wollaston   Joshua Grigby   William Middleton

Suffolk Rec Off Guildhall Lib

1784—The poll for members... Ipswich: C. Punchard, [1784]
Alphabetical. Council distinguished.

William Middleton   John Cator   Charles Alexander Crickitt

Bodl Inst Hist Res

1784*—The poll for a member... Ipswich: Charles Punchard, [1784]
Alphabetical. Council distinguished.

Charles Alexander Crickitt   Robert Thornton

Inst Hist Res

1790—The poll for members... Ipswich: G. Jermyn, [1790]
Alphabetical. Council distinguished.

Sir John Hadley D'Oyley Charles Alexander Crickitt William Middleton
George Rochfort

Suffolk Rec Off Inst Hist Res

1806—The poll for members... Ipswich: A. Dorkin, [1806]
Alphabetical. Council distinguished.

Richard Wilson Robert Stopford Robert Alexander Crickitt John Gibbons

Suffolk Rec Off Inst Hist Res

1807—The poll for members... Ipswich: A. Dorkin, 1807
Alphabetical. Council distinguished. Wilson and Bennett's address.

Sir Home Popham Robert Alexander Crickitt Richard Wilson
Richard Henry Alexander Bennett

Suffolk Rec Off Guildhall Lib

1807—The poll for members... Ipswich: John Bransby, 1807
Alphabetical. Council distinguished.

Sir Home Popham Robert Alexander Crickitt Richard Wilson
Richard Henry Alexander Bennett

Suffolk Rec Off Brit Lib

1818—The poll for members... Ipswich: A. Dorkin, 1818
Alphabetical. Council distinguished. Rejected voters. Crickitt and Newton's address.

Robert Alexander Crickitt William Newton Henry Baring Sir William Bolton

Suffolk Rec Off Inst Hist Res

1818—The poll for members... Ipswich: J. Raw, 1818
Alphabetical. Council distinguished. Baring's address.

Robert Alexander Crickitt William Newton Henry Baring Sir William Bolton

Suffolk Rec Off Guildhall Lib

1820—The poll for members... Ipswich: Cowell, [1820]
Alphabetical. Council distinguished. Rejected voters. Electoral history since 1818 and account of proceedings.

William Haldimond Thomas Barrett Lennard Robert Alexander Crickitt John Round

Suffolk Rec Off Inst Hist Res

1820—The poll for members... Ipswich: A. Dorkin, [1820]
Alphabetical. Council distinguished. Rejected voters. Poll order. Crickitt and Round's addresses.

William Haldimond Thomas Barett Lennard Robert Alexander Crickitt John Round

Suffolk Rec Off Guildhall Lib

1826—The poll for members... Ipswich: A. Dorkin, [1826]
Alphabetical. Occupation and place of residence in a few cases. Rejected voters with reasons. Addresses of Mackinnon and Dundas and findings of the petition committee which returned them.

William Haldimond Robert Torrens Charles Mackinnon Robert Adam Dundas

Suffolk Rec Off Inst Hist Res

1831—The poll for members... Ipswich: S. H. Cowell, [1831]
Alphabetical. Place of residence. Voters who arrived after the poll closed.

James Morrison Rigby Wason Charles Mackinnon Robert Fitzroy

Suffolk Rec Off Inst Hist Res

1832—The pollbook for members... Ipswich: S. Piper, [1832]
Alphabetical by qualification and parish. Occupation. Addresses of Morrison and Wason.

James Morrison Rigby Wason Edward Goulburn Fitzroy Kelly Charles Mackinnon

Suffolk Rec Off Inst Hist Res

1835 (January)—The poll for members... Ipswich: R. Deck, 1835
Alphabetical by qualification and parish. Occupation and address. Tendered votes. Address of Kelly and Dundas.

Fitzroy Kelly Robert Adam Dundas Rigby Wason James Morrison

Suffolk Rec Off Inst Hist Res

1835* (June)—The poll for members... Ipswich: S. H. Cowell, [1835]
Alphabetical by qualification and parish. Occupation.

James Morrison Rigby Wason H. G. Broke William Holmes

Suffolk Rec Off Inst Hist Res

1839*—The poll for a member... Ipswich: A. Dorkin, 1839
Alphabetical by occupation. Address. Cochrane's address.

Sir Thomas John Cochrane Thomas Milner Gibson

Suffolk Rec Off Inst Hist Res

1841—The poll for members... Ipswich: F. Pawsey, [1841]
Alphabetical by occupation. Address. Index.

Rigby Wason George Rennie Fitzroy Kelly John Charles Herries

Suffolk Rec Off Guildhall Lib

1842* (June)—The poll of the Ipswich borough election... Ipswich: Stephen Piper, 1842
Alphabetical by qualification, candidate and parish. Non-voters, pairs and removed voters with party allegiance.

Earl of Desart Thomas Gladstone Thomas Gisborne George Moffatt John Nicholson

Inst Hist Res

1842* (August)—The poll for members... Ipswich: F. Pawsey, [1842]
Alphabetical by occupation. Address. Index.

John Neilstone Gladstone Sackville Lane Fox D. Thornbury Henry Vincent John Nicholson

Suffolk Rec Off Guildhall Lib

1847—The poll for members... Ipswich: Hunt & Son, 1847
Alphabetical by qualification and parish. Occupation and address. Non-voters included without occupation. Addresses of Cobbold and Gladstone.

John Chevalier Cobbold Hugh Edward Adair John Neilstone Gladstone Henry Vincent

Suffolk Rec Off Inst Hist Res

[Two editions known]

1847—The poll of the Ipswich borough election... Ipswich: S. Piper, [1847]
Alphabetical by qualification and groups of parishes.

John Chevalier Cobbold Hugh Edward Adair John Neilstone Gladstone Henry Vincent

Suffolk Rec Off Guildhall Lib

1852—The poll for members... Ipswich: R. Deck, [1852]
Alphabetical by qualification and parish. Occupation and address. Non-voters included without occupation. Pairs.

John Chevalier Cobbold Hugh Edward Adair Samuel Bateson Thomas Benjamin Hobhouse

Inst Hist Res

1852—The poll for the election... Ipswich: S. Piper, [1852]
Alphabetical by qualification and parish. Occupation and address. Non-voters, distinguishing dead. Pairs. Addresses of Adair and Hobhouse.

John Chevalier Cobbold Hugh Edward Adair Samuel Bateson Thomas Benjamin Hobhouse

Suffolk Rec Off Guildhall Lib

1857—The poll for the election... Ipswich: S. H. Cowell, [1857]
Alphabetical by qualification and parish. Occupation and address. Non-voters included. Addresses of Adair and Marshman.

John Chevalier Cobbold Hugh Edward Adair John C. Marshman Henry John Selwin

Suffolk Rec Off Inst Hist Res

1859—The poll for the election... Ipswich: E. F. Barber, [1859]
Alphabetical by qualification and parish. Occupation and address. Non-voters included. Addresses of Cobbold and Selwin.

John Chevallier Cobbold Hugh Edward Adair Henry John Selwin John King

Suffolk Rec Off Inst Hist Res

1859—The poll for the election... Ipswich: Alfred Piper, [1859]
Alphabetical by qualification and parish. Occupation and address. Non-voters included. Adair's address.

John Chevallier Cobbold Hugh Edward Adair Henry John Selwin John King

Suffolk Rec Off Guildhall Lib

1865—The poll for the election... Ipswich: Scoggins & Parker, [1865]
Alphabetical by qualification and parish. Occupation and address. Non-voters included without occupation. Addresses of Adair and West.

Hugh Edward Adair John Chevallier Cobbold Henry Wyndham West W. Tidmas

Suffolk Rec Off Inst Hist Res

1865—The poll for the election... Ipswich: W. Spalding, [1865]
Alphabetical by qualification and parish. Occupation and address. Non-voters included without occupation.

Hugh Edward Adair John Chevallier Cobbold Henry Wyndham West W. Tidmas

Suffolk Rec Off Inst Hist Res

[Same printing as preceding entry with reversal of candidates on title page and omission of addresses of candidates.]

1868—The poll for the election... Ipswich: Rees & Gripper, 1869
Alphabetical by qualification and parish. Occupation and address. Non-voters included without occupation.

Hugh Edward Adair Henry Wyndham West John Chevallier Cobbold

Suffolk Rec Off Inst Hist Res

SUDBURY

1826—The poll for members... Sudbury: Burkitt & Goldsmith, 1826
Alphabetical. Occupation and place of residence.

John Wilks Bethel Walrond Charles Ogilvy

Private Possession

1828*—The poll for a member... Sudbury: G. W. Fulcher, 1828
Alphabetical. Occupation, place of residence and poll order.

John Norman Macleod John Abel Smith

Private Possession

1828*—The poll for a member... Sudbury: Burkitt & Goldsmith, 1828
Alphabetical. Occupation, place of residence and poll order.

John Norman Macleod John Abel Smith

Private Possession

[Same printing as preceding entry with different imprint.]

1831—The poll for members... Sudbury: W. Goldsmith, 1831
Alphabetical. Occupation, place of residence and poll order.

Sir John Benn Walsh Digby Cayley Wrangham William Windham

Private Possession

1832—The poll for members... Ballingdon: William Hill, 1832
Alphabetical by qualification. Occupation and place of residence. Tendered votes.

Michael Angelo Taylor Sir John Benn Walsh Digby Caley Wrangham John Bagshaw

Private Possession

1832—The poll for members... Sudbury: G. W. Fulcher, 1832
Alphabetical by qualification. Occupation and place of residence. Speeches after the poll.

Michael Angelo Taylor Sir John Benn Walsh Digby Caley Wrangham John Bagshaw

Private Possession

1834*—The poll for a member... Ballingdon: W. Hill, 1834
Alphabetical. Occupation, address or place of residence and qualification. Non-voters distinguished.

Sir Edward Barnes John Bagshaw

Private Possession

1835—The poll for members... Sudbury: J. Brackett, 1835
Alphabetical. Occupation, address and qualification. Tendered votes. Non-voters. Voters split between parties. Voters polled after Barnes and Stephens had declined the contest. Analysis of promised votes for Bagshaw and Smith.

John Bagshaw Benjamin Smith Sir Edward Barnes Stephens Lyne Stephens

Private Possession

1837 (July)—The poll for two members... Sudbury: G. W. Fulcher, [1837]
Alphabetical by qualification. Address and nature of qualification. Non-voters included.

Sir Edward Barnes Sir John James Hamilton W. A. Smith T. E. M. Turton

Private Possession

1837* (December)—The poll for a member... Sudbury: G. W. Fulcher, [1837]
Alphabetical. Address and patrimony.

Joseph Bailey, Jr. James Morrison

Private Possession

1838*—The poll for a member... Sudbury: G. W. Fulcher, [1838]
Alphabetical by qualification. Address and nature of qualification. Non-voters distinguished.

Sir John Benn Walsh John Bagshaw

Private Possession

1841—The poll for members...

Sudbury: J. Large, 1841
Alphabetical by qualification. Address and patrimony. Non-voters distinguished.

Frederick Villiers David Ochterlony Dyce-Sombre David Jones Charles Taylor
Private Possession

SURREY

1705—The poll for knights... London: Sam. Crouch, 1705
By hundred and parish. Place of residence. Voters for Harvey who did not vote in the previous election, supposed leaseholders and those supposed not to be freeholders distinguished.

Sir Richard Onslow Sir William Scawen Edward Harvey
Guildford Pub Lib Inst Hist Res

1710—The poll for knights... London, 1710
By hundred and parish. Place of residence.

Sir Francis Vincent Heneage Finch Sir Richard Onslow Sir William Scawen
Guildford Pub Lib Inst Hist Res

1719*—The poll for a knight... London, 1720
By hundred and parish. Place of residence.

John Walter Sir Francis Vincent
Minet Pub Lib Inst Hist Res

1774—A poll for knights... Guildford: J. Russell, 1774
By hundred and parish. Place of residence.

Sir Francis Vincent James Scawen Sir Joseph Mawbey
Guildford Pub Lib Inst Hist Res

1775*—Copy of the poll... London: Thomas Harrison & Samuel Brooke, 1775
Poll order by hundred. Place of residence and place, occupier and sometimes nature of freehold.

Sir Joseph Mawbey William Norton Sir Francis Vincent
Guildford Pub Lib Inst Hist Res

1780—Copy of the poll... Guildford: J. Russell, 1780
By hundred and parish. Place of residence and owner or occupier of freehold.

Sir Joseph Mawbey Augustus Keppel Thomas Onslow
Guildford Pub Lib Inst Hist Res

1826—Surrey election 1826. A list of freeholders... Dorking: Edward Langley, 1826
Poll order by hundred. Place of residence, place, nature and occupier of freehold.

William Joseph Denison George Holme Sumner Charles Nicholas Pallmer
Minet Pub Lib Inst Hist Res

EAST SURREY

1865—East Surrey, 1865. A list of the persons... London: Joseph Causton, [1865]
By polling district and booth. Address.

Peter John Locke King   Charles Buxton   William Brodrick   Henry William Peck

Minet Pub Lib   Inst Hist Res

WEST SURREY

1835—West Surrey election. The poll... Guildford: G. W. & J. Russell, 1835
Alphabetical by hundred and parish. Address or place of residence. Non-voters included.

William Joseph Denison   Charles Barclay   Henry Lawes Long

Guildford Pub Lib   Brit Lib

1837—West Surrey election. A list of the electors... [Godalming: Richard Stedman, printer, 1837]
Alphabetical by hundred and parish. Address or place of residence. Non-voters included.

William Joseph Denison   George James Perceval   Henry Lawes Long

Guildford Pub Lib   Inst Hist Res

1849*—West Surrey election. 1849. A list of the electors... Guildford: G. W. & J. Russell, [1849]
Alphabetical by polling district and parish. Address or place of residence. Non-voters included.

William John Evelyn   Richard Wyatt Edgell

Guildford Pub Lib   Inst Hist Res

1852—West Surrey election. 1852. A list of the electors... Guildford: G. W. & J. Russell, [1852]
Alphabetical by polling district and parish. Address or place of residence. Non-voters included.

William John Evelyn   Henry Drummond   C. B. Challoner

Guildford Pub Lib   Inst Hist Res

1857—West Surrey election, 1857. A list of the electors... Guildford: Gardner & Stent, [1857]
Alphabetical by polling district and parish. Address or place of residence. Non-voters included.

John Ivatt Briscoe   Henry Drummond   Henry Currie

Guildford Pub Lib   Inst Hist Res

1868—West Surrey election, 1868. A list of the electors... Guildford: William Stent, [1868]
Alphabetical by polling district, parish and qualification. Address. Non-voters included.

George Cubitt   John Ivatt Briscoe   Frederick Pennington

Guildford Pub Lib   Guildhall Lib

GUILDFORD

1790—De Guldeforde. A true state of the poll and proceedings... Guildford: A. Martin, 1790
Poll order. Occupation, address and qualification. Non-voters by parish, also other scot and lot payers and those omitted from the poor rate books. Full interrogation of objected voters. Poll for churchwardens. Account of proceedings.

Thomas Onslow George Sumner Chapple Norton

Guildford Pub Lib Inst Hist Res

1835—A correct account of the poll at the election... Guildford: G., W. & H. Russell, [1835]
Alphabetical by candidate. Occupation and address. Non-voters.

James Mangles Charles Baring Wall Robert Alfred Cloyne Austen

Guildford Pub Lib Inst Hist Res

1841—A correct account of the poll... Guildford: G. W. & J. Russell, [1841]
Alphabetical by candidate. Occupation and address. Non-voters.

Ross Donnelly Mangles Charles Baring Wall J. Yorke Scarlett Henry Currie

Guildford Pub Lib Brit Lib

1847—A list of the voters... Guildford: E. Andrews, 1847
Alphabetical by candidate. Occupation and address. Non-voters.

Henry Currie Ross Donnelly Mangles Thomas Lyon Thurlow

Guildford Pub Lib Inst Hist Res

1852—A correct account of the poll... Guildford: G., W. & J. Russell, [1852]
Alphabetical by candidate and parish. Address. Non-voters.

Ross Donnelly Mangles James Bell Thomas Lyon Thurlow

Guildford Pub Lib Inst Hist Res

1857—A correct account of the poll... Guildford: Gardner & Stent, [1857]
Alphabetical by candidate and parish. Address. Non-voters.

Ross Donnelly Mangles William Bovill James Bell

Guildford Pub Lib Inst Hist Res

1858*—A correct account of the poll... Guildford: Gardner & Stent, [1858]
Alphabetical by candidate and parish. Address. Non-voters, distinguishing dead.

Guildford Onslow William John Evelyn

Guildford Pub Lib Guildhall Lib

1865—A correct account of the poll... Guildford: W. Stent, [1865]
Alphabetical by candidate and parish. Occupation and address. Non-voters.

Guildford Onslow William Bovill William Willmer Pocock

Guildford Pub Lib Inst Hist Res

1866*—A correct account of the poll... Guildford: W. Stent, [1866]
Alphabetical by candidate and parish. Occupation and address. Non-voters.

Richard Garth   William Willmer Pocock

Guildford Pub Lib Inst Hist Res

1868—A correct account of the poll... Guildford: W. Stent, [1868]
Alphabetical by candidate and parish. Occupation and address. Non-voters.

Guildford Onslow   Richard Garth

Guildford Pub Lib Inst Hist Res

SUSSEX

1734—A poll taken... London: John Coles, 1734
Alphabetical by parish. Place of residence.

Henry Pelham   James Butler   Sir Cecil Bishop   John Fuller

Brighton Pub Lib Inst Hist Res

1774—The poll for knights... Lewes: William Lee, 1775
By rape. Place of residence, place, nature and occupier of freehold. Oath-takers distinguished. Index by rape.

Lord George Henry Lennox   Sir Thomas Spencer Wilson   Sir James Peachey

Brighton Pub Lib Inst Hist Res

1820—An account of the Sussex election... including the poll book... Chichester: W. Mason, [1820]
Alphabetical by rape and parish. Place of residence. Account of proceedings and election literature.

Walter Burrell   Edward Jeremiah Curteis   Charles Compton Cavendish

Brighton Pub Lib Inst Hist Res

1820—Sussex election, 1820. The poll for knights... Lewes: J. Baxter, [1820]
By rape. Place of residence, place, nature and occupier of freehold. Rejected voters and oath-takers distinguished. Index by east and west divisions. Account of proceedings.

Walter Burrell   Edward Jeremiah Curteis   Charles Compton Cavendish

Brighton Pub Lib Inst Hist Res

EAST SUSSEX

1832—East Sussex, 1832. List of the registered electors... Lewes: Baxter, 1833
Alphabetical by parish of residence. Place of qualification. Out-voters by county. Non-voters and voters on the second day distinguished. Index.

Charles Compton Cavendish   Herbert Barratt Curteis   George Darby

Brighton Pub Lib Inst Hist Res

1837—East Sussex election. List of the registered electors... Lewes: R. W. Lower; Brighton: W. Leppard, 1837
Alphabetical by polling district and parish of residence. Place of qualification. Out-voters by county. Non-voters distinguished. Index.

George Darby   Charles Compton Cavendish   Augustus Elliott Fuller
Herbert Barratt Curteis

Brighton Pub Lib   Guildhall Lib

1837—East Sussex, 1837. A list of the registered electors... Lewes: Baxter & Son, 1837
Alphabetical by polling district and parish. Place of residence, place and nature of qualification. Non-voters and voters on the second day distinguished. Addresses of Darby and Fuller. Index.

George Darby   Charles Compton Cavendish   Augustus Elliott Fuller
Herbert Barratt Curteis

East Sussex Rec Off   Inst Hist Res

WEST SUSSEX

1837—A poll taken before George Palmer... Chichester: William Hayley Mason, 1837
Alphabetical by polling district. Place of residence and parish of qualification.

Lord John George Lennox   Earl of Surrey   Henry Wyndham

West Sussex Rec Off   Guildhall Lib

BRIGHTON

1832—A poll taken by Mr. Samuel Ridley... Brighton: W. Fleet, [1832]
Alphabetical. Occupation and address. Tendered votes.

Isaac Newton Wigney   George Faithfull   George Richard Pechell   William Crawford
Sir Adolphus John Dalrymple

Brighton Pub Lib   Guildhall Lib

1835—Published by authority. A poll taken by George Gwynne... Brighton: W. Leppard, [1835]
Alphabetical. Occupation and address.

George Richard Pechell   Isaac Newton Wigney   Sir Adolphus John Dalrymple
George Faithfull

Brighton Pub Lib   Guildhall Lib

1837—Published by authority. A poll taken... Brighton: R. D. Buckoll, printed by W. Leppard, [1837]
Alphabetical by district. Occupation and address.

George Richard Pechell   Sir Adolphus John Dalrymple   Isaac Newton Wigney
George Faithfull

Brighton Pub Lib   Inst Hist Res

1841—Published by authority. A poll taken... Brighton: R. D. Buckoll, printed by W. Leppard, [1841]
Alphabetical by district. Occupation and address. Non-voters distinguished.

George Richard Pechell Isaac Newton Wigney Sir Adolphus John Dalrymple Charles Brooker

Brighton Pub Lib Inst Hist Res

1841—A classified list of those electors who voted for Sir A. J. Dalrymple... Brighton: Henry S. King, [1841]
Alphabetical by occupation and district. Address.

George Richard Pechell Isaac Newton Wigney Sir Adolphus John Dalrymple Charles Brooker

Brighton Pub Lib Inst Hist Res

1842*—Published by authority. A poll taken... Brighton: R. D. Buckoll, printed by W. Leppard, [1842]
Alphabetical by district. Occupation and address.

Lord Alfred Hervey Summers Harford Charles Brooker

Brighton Pub Lib Inst Hist Res

1847—Published by authority. A poll taken... Brighton: Edwin Wright, printed by Levy Emanuel Cohen, [1847]
Alphabetical by district. Address.

George Richard Pechell Lord Alfred Hervey William Coningham

Brighton Pub Lib Inst Hist Res

1852—Published by authority. A poll taken... Brighton: W. J. Taylor & Edwin Wright, 1852
Alphabetical by district. Address. Non-voters distinguished.

Sir George Richard Pechell Lord Alfred Hervey John Salisbury Trelawny John Ffooks

Brighton Pub Lib Inst Hist Res

1857—Published by authority. A poll taken . . . carefully arranged by Edwin Wright... Brighton: H. Trussell, 1857
Alphabetical by district. Address. Non-voters distinguished.

Sir George Richard Pechell William Coningham Lord Alfred Hervey

Brighton Pub Lib Inst Hist Res

1859—1859. A poll taken... compiled by Edwin eWright... Brighton: H. Trussell, [1859]
Alphabetical by district and candidate. Address. Non-voters.

Sir George Richard Pechell William Coningham Sir Allan Macnab

Brighton Pub Lib Inst Hist Res

CHICHESTER

[1734]

1784—A poll taken at the Guildhall... Chichester: D. Jacques, [1784]
Poll order. Occupation and address.

George White Thomas   Thomas Steele   William Smith

Brit Lib

1823*—A poll taken at the Guildhall... Chichester: William Mason, 1823
Alphabetical. Occupation and parish. Corporation distinguished. Rejected voters. Non-voters, distinguishing poor and including women occupiers of rateable property. Account of proceedings.

William Stephen Poyntz   Sir Godfrey Webster

Guildhall Lib

1826—An account of the proceedings... including the poll book... Chichester: W. Mason, [1826]
Alphabetical. Occupation and parish. Rejected voters included. Corporation and freemen distinguished. Account of proceedings and election literature.

Lord John George Lennox   William Stephen Poyntz   Sir Godfrey Webster

Sussex Archaeol Soc   Guildhall Lib

1830—Proceedings at the contested election... including . . . copy of the poll book... Chichester: J. Hackman, 1830
Alphabetical. Occupation and parish of residence. Freemen distinguished. Account of proceedings of Chichester and Sussex elections.

Lord George Lennox   John Smith   Charles Sinclair Cullen

Brit Lib

1831—A poll taken at the city of Chichester... Chichester: Williams & Pullinger, [1831]
Alphabetical. Occupation and parish of residence. Rejected voters distinguished.

Lord Arthur Lennox   John Abel Smith   Sir Godfrey Webster

Brit Lib

1837—Chichester contested election. The poll taken . . . with an introduction by the hard-working man. Chichester: J. Hackman, [1837]
Alphabetical by candidate. Occupation and parish of residence. Account of proceedings and candidates' addresses.

John Abel Smith   Lord Arthur Lennox   John Morgan Cobbett

Brit Lib

[Two editions known]

HASTINGS

1722—A state of the poll... *A collection of advertisements, letters and papers... relating to the last elections at Westminster and Hastings.* (London, 1722), pp. 53-54
By candidate.

Sir William Ashburnham Archibald Hutcheson John Pulteney

Bodl Inst Hist Res

1868—Poll book of the Hastings election... Hastings: Parsons & Cousins, [1868]
Alphabetical by parish and qualification. Non-voters and dead distinguished.

Thomas Brassey Frederick North Somerset G. Calthorpe Clement Arthur Thruston

Guildhall Lib

Untraced: 1865

LEWES

1734—A poll taken by Tho. Friend and James Reeve... London: W. Russ, 1734
Alphabetical. Occupation. Objected voters admitted to the poll distinguished. Twenty-four rejected voters for Garland and Sergison compared with similar cases allowed to vote for the Pelhams.

Thomas Pelham Thomas Pelham Nathaniel Garland Thomas Sergison

Soc Geneal Inst Hist Res

1734—An exact state of the poll... London: J. Wilford, 1734
Poll order. Justification by the constables of the admission of objected voters and preface defending their conduct of the poll.

Thomas Pelham Thomas Pelham Nathaniel Garland Thomas Sergison

East Sussex Rec Off Guildhall Lib

1768—A poll taken by Samuel Ollive... Lewes: William Lee, 1768
Poll order. Occupation in a few cases.

Thomas Hampden Thomas Hay Thomas Miller

Sussex Archaeol Soc Inst Hist Res

1774—A poll taken by Edmund Davey... Lewes: William Lee, 1774
Poll order. Occupation. Objected voters distinguished.

Sir Thomas Miller Thomas Hay John Trevor William Kempe

Sussex Archaeol Soc Inst Hist Res

1780—A poll taken by William Hammond... Lewes: William Lee, 1780
Poll order. Occupation. Objected voters distinguished. Non-voters.

Henry Pelham Thomas Kemp Thomas Hay

Sussex Archaeol Soc Inst Hist Res

1790—A poll taken by John Wimble and George Grantham... Lewes: W. & A. Lee, 1790
Poll order. Occupation. Rejected and objected voters distinguished. Non-voters.

Henry Pelham — Thomas Kemp — Henry Shelley, Jr.

Sussex Archaeol Soc — Guildhall Lib

1796—A poll taken by Thomas Read and Henry Pawson... Lewes: W. & A. Lee, 1796
Poll order. Occupation. Objected voters distinguished. Rejected voters and non-voters.

Thomas Kemp — John Cressett Pelham — William Green

East Sussex Rec Off — Guildhall Lib

1802—A poll taken by George Grantham... Lewes: W. & A. Lee, 1803
Poll order. Occupation. Rejected voters included. Rejected voters who made a second attempt, voters rejected on scrutiny, voters admitted on scrutiny. Non-voters.

Lord Francis Godolphin Osborne — Henry Shelley — Thomas Kemp

East Sussex Rec Off — Inst Hist Res

1812—Borough of Lewes—to wit. A poll... Lewes: W. & A. Lee, [1812]
Poll order. Occupation and parish of residence. Rejected voters distinguished. Non-voters.

Thomas Read Kemp — George Shiffner — James Scarlett

East Sussex Rec Off — Inst Hist Res

1812—A poll taken by Mr. Thomas Woolgar and Mr. William Figg... Lewes: John Baxter, 1812
Alphabetical. Occupation. Rejected and non-voters.

Thomas Read Kemp — George Shiffner — James Scarlett

Guildhall Lib

1816*—Borough of Lewes—to wit. A poll taken... Lewes: J. Baxter, [1816]
Poll order. Occupation and parish of residence. Rejected voters included. Index.

Sir John Shelley — James Scarlett

East Sussex Rec Off — Guildhall Lib

1818—A poll taken by Mr. Wm. Smart and Mr. Thos. Whiteman... Lewes: J. Baxter, [1818]
Poll order. Occupation and address. Rejected voters included. Non-voters. Index.

Sir John Shelley — George Shiffner — Thomas Erskine

Sussex Archaeol Soc — Inst Hist Res

1826—Lewes election, 1826. A poll taken... Lewes: W. Lee, 1826
Poll order. Occupation and parish. Rejected voters included and also listed separately with reasons. Index.

Thomas Read Kemp | Sir John Shelley | Alexander Donovan

Sussex Archaeol Soc Inst Hist Res

1830—Borough of Lewes. A poll taken... Lewes: W. Lee, 1830
Alphabetical. Occupation, address and day of polling. Rejected and non-voters included. New electors since 1826 distinguished.

Thomas Read Kemp | Sir John Shelley | Alexander Donovan

Sussex Archaeol Soc Inst Hist Res

1830—Borough of Lewes. A poll taken by Benjamin Ridge, Esq. and Mr. G. Bailey... Lewes: J. Baxter, 1830
Alphabetical. Occupation, address and day of polling. Rejected and non-voters included. New electors since 1826 distinguished.

Thomas Read Kemp | Sir John Shelley | Alexander Donovan

Guildhall Lib

1830—Borough of Lewes. A poll taken by Messrs. Benjamin Ridge and George Bailey. Lewes: J. Baxter, 1830
Alphabetical. Occupation and address. Rejected voters included with reasons. Non-voters.

Thomas Read Kemp | Sir John Shelley | Alexander Donovan

Guildhall Lib

1835—Borough of Lewes. List of registered electors... Lewes: R. W. Lower, 1835
Alphabetical. Occupation, address, polling booth and order of voting. Non-voters included. Addresses other than those acting as qualification distinguished. Objected voters distinguished.

Sir Charles Richard Blunt | Thomas Read Kemp | Henry Fitzroy

Sussex Archaeol Soc Inst Hist Res

1835—A poll taken by Mr. George Bailey... Lewes: Baxter, 1835
Alphabetical by polling booth. Occupation. Voters on the second day distinguished. Non-voters, removed and dead. Fitzroy's nomination speech and letter to his supporters after the election.

Sir Charles Richard Blunt | Thomas Read Kemp | Henry Fitzroy

Inst Hist Res

1837* (April)—A poll taken by Mr. Plumer Verrall... Lewes: Baxter & Son, [1837]
[Two broadsheets in cover]
Alphabetical by candidate and parish. Occupation and place of residence. Non-voters.

Henry Fitzroy | John Easthorpe

Sussex Archaeol Soc Guildhall Lib

1837 (July)—Borough of Lewes. A poll taken by Mr. Plumer Verrall...Lewes: R. W. Lower, 1837
Poll order by booth. Occupation and place of residence. Objected voters distinguished. Index.

Sir Charles Richard Blunt Henry Fitzroy Thomas Brand William Lyon

East Sussex Rec Off Guildhall Lib

1837 (July)—A poll taken by Mr. Plumer Verrall...Lewes: Baxter & Son, [1837]
Alphabetical by parish. Occupation and place of residence. Non-voters.

Sir Charles Richard Blunt Henry Fitzroy Thomas Brand William Lyon

Guildhall Lib

1841—A poll taken by Mr. Nehemiah Wimble... Lewes: Baxter & Son, [1841]
Alphabetical. Occupation and address. Non-voters distinguished.

Henry Fitzroy Viscount Cantilupe Howard Elphinstone Summers Harford

Sussex Archaeol Soc Guildhall Lib

1841—The Lewes Conservative list . . . [and] The Lewes Whig list... Lewes: Baxter & Son, [1841] [Broadsheet]
Alphabetical by candidate and occupation.

Henry Fitzroy Viscount Cantilupe Howard Elphinstone Summers Harford

Guildhall Lib

1847—A poll taken by Mr. Benjamin Flint & Mr. John Hilton... Lewes: Geo. P. Bacon, 1847
Alphabetical. Address. Non-voters distinguished.

Henry Fitzroy Robert Perfect John Godfrey Bellinger Hudson Lord Henry Loftus

East Sussex Rec Off Guildhall Lib

1859—A poll taken by Mr. Richard Lambe and Mr. Charles Parsons... Lewes: Geo. P. Bacon, 1859
Alphabetical. Address. Non-voters distinguished.

Henry Fitzroy Henry Bouverie William Brand Sir Charles William Blunt
Richard Paul Amphlett

East Sussex Rec Off Guildhall Lib

1865—A poll taken by Mr. Henry S. Gorringe... Lewes: *East Sussex News,* 1865
Alphabetical. Address. Non-voters distinguished.

Henry Bouverie William Brand Lord Pelham William Langham Christie
Sir Alfred Frederick Adolphus Slade

East Sussex Rec Off Inst Hist Res

1868—A poll taken by Mr. James Broad... Lewes: Farncombe & Bates, 1869
Alphabetical. Address. Non-voters distinguished. Those polling to the wrong pollclerk for Christie distinguished.

Lord Pelham William Langham Christie

East Sussex Rec Off Inst Hist Res

NEW SHOREHAM

1807—The poll taken at New Shoreham... Lewes: W. & A. Lee, 1808
By parish. Place of residence.
Sir Charles Merrik Burrell   Timothy Shelley   Cecil Bishop
Guildhall Lib

NEW SHOREHAM AND BRAMBER

1841—An account of the proceedings... including . . . copy of the poll book... Worthing: C. Cook, [1841]
Alphabetical by polling district and parish. Place of residence. Non-voters distinguished. Account of proceedings.
Sir Charles Merrik Burrell   Charles Goring   Lord Edward Howard
Sussex Archaeol Soc Inst Hist Res

1865—Copy of the poll book... Worthing: Paine, [1865]
Alphabetical by polling district and parish. Non-voters included.
Stephen Cave   Sir Percy Burrell   James Hannen
West Sussex Rec Off Inst Hist Res

RYE

1832—[Title page missing. Begins:] List of persons who voted... Rye: H. P. Clark, [1832]
Alphabetical.
Herbert Curteis   De Lacy Evans
Brit Lib

1868—1868. The poll for a baron... Rye: L. Parsons, 1868
Alphabetical by parish. Address. Non-voters included, distinguishing disqualified.
John Stewart Hardy   William Jones Loyd
Sussex Archaeol Soc Inst Hist Res

WARWICKSHIRE

1774—The poll of the freeholders... Coventry: J. W. Piercy; Warwick: J. Sharp, 1775
Alphabetical by hundred and parish. Place of residence. Index.
Thomas George Skipwith   Sir Charles Holte   John Mordaunt
Birmingham Pub Lib Inst Hist Res

1820*—The poll of the freeholders... Birmingham: T. Knott, Jr., 1820
Alphabetical by hundred and parish. Place of residence.
Francis Lawley   Richard Spooner
Birmingham Pub Lib Inst Hist Res

NORTH WARWICKSHIRE

1832—The poll for the election... Rugby: Rowell & Son, 1833
Alphabetical by polling district and parish. Place of sresidence. Tendered votes.

Sir Eardley Eardley Wilmot   William Stratford Dugdale   Dempster Heming

Birmingham Pub Lib Guildhall Lib

1835—The poll for the election... Coventry: W. Reader, 1835
Alphabetical by polling district and parish. Address.

Sir Eardley Eardley Wilmot   William Stratford Dugdale   Arthur Francis Gregory

Birmingham Pub Lib Guildhall Lib

1837—The poll for the election... Birmingham: Knott, Hawker & Coburn, [1837]
Alphabetical by polling district and parish. Address.

William Stratford Dugdale   Sir Eardley Eardley Wilmot   Sir Gray Skipwith
Charles Holte Bracebridge

Birmingham Pub Lib Guildhall Lib

SOUTH WARWICKSHIRE

1832—A statement of the poll... Stratford: W. Barnacle, [1833]
Alphabetical by hundred and parish. Place of residence.

Sir Gray Skipwith   Sir George Philips   Evelyn John Shirley

Birmingham Pub Lib Inst Hist Res

[Two editions were published]

1836*—A statement of the poll... Warwick: John Merridew, [1836]
Alphabetical by hundred and parish. Place of residence.

Evelyn John Shirley   Sir Gray Skipwith

Birmingham Pub Lib Inst Hist Res

1865—Poll book, South Warwickshire election, 1865, by Henry Mills. Warwick: H. T. Cooke, 1865
Alphabetical by polling district and parish. Non-voters distinguished.

Henry Christopher Wise   Sir Charles Mordaunt   Viscount Duncan

Birmingham Pub Lib Guildhall Lib

1865—South Warwickshire election. Copy of the poll books. *Royal Leamington Spa Courier & Warwickshire Standard,* 5 August 1865
Alphabetical by parish. Place of residence or address.

Henry Christopher Wise   Sir Charles Mordaunt   Viscount Duncan

Brit Lib (News) Inst Hist Res

1868—Poll book, South Warwickshire election, 1868, by H. Mills. Warwick: H. T. Cooke & Son, 1869
Alphabetical by polling district, parish and qualification. Non-voters distinguished.

Henry Christopher Wise John Hardy Sir Robert North Collie Hamilton Lord Hyde

Birmingham Pub Lib Inst Hist Res

BIRMINGHAM

1837—Birmingham election, 1837. The poll book... Birmingham: F. B. S. Flindell, 1837
Alphabetical by candidate. Address.

Thomas Attwood Joshua Scholefield A. G. Stapleton

Birmingham Pub Lib Inst Hist Res

1841—List of votes recorded at the late election. [Mounted list from a newspaper, 1841]
Alphabetical by candidate. Address.

George Frederick Muntz Joshua Scholefield Richard Spooner

Birmingham Pub Lib Inst Hist Res

COVENTRY

1741—A true list of such persons as voted... Coventry, 1741
Alphabetical. Ward or place of residence.

Earl of Euston William Grove John Neale

Bodl Inst Hist Res

1747*—An alphabetical list of the poll... Coventry: S. Brooks, 1748
Ward or place of residence. Brief summary of proceedings.

Samuel Greatheed Robert Bird

Birmingham Pub Lib Inst Hist Res

1761—An alphabetical list of the poll... Coventry: T. Luckman, [1761]
Ward or place of residence.

James Hewitt Andrew Archer William Grove

Birmingham Pub Lib Inst Hist Res

1761—An alphabetical list of the poll... to represent the city of C***** in Parliament. London: Moses Right, 1761
Alphabetical by ward. Out-voters alphabetical with place of residence. Dubious voters allowed distinguished with remarks.

James Hewitt Andrew Archer William Grove

Coventry Pub Lib Inst Hist Res

1768*—A correct copy of the poll... London: J. Jones, [1768]
Alphabetical by ward for each letter. Out-voters by place of residence. London alphabetical.

Sir Richard Glyn Thomas Nash

Coventry Pub Lib Inst Hist Res

1774—An alphabetical list of the poll... Coventry: J. W. Piercy, [1774]
Ward or place of residence.

Edward Roe Yeo | Walter Waring | Thomas Green

Coventry Pub Lib Inst Hist Res

1774—A complete copy of the poll... Coventry: J. Jones, [1774]
Ward or place of residence.

Edward Roe Yeo | Walter Waring | Thomas Green

Coventry Pub Lib Inst Hist Res

1780—A correct copy of the poll... Coventry: R. Bird, [1780]
Alphabetical by ward. Out-voters by place of residence. Voters disqualified by the House of Commons Committee with occupations.

Sir Thomas Hallifax | Thomas Rogers | Edward Roe Yeo

Coventry Pub Lib Inst Hist Res

1790—A correct copy of the poll... Coventry: J. W. Piercy, [1790]
Alphabetical. Ward. Out-voters by place of residence. Voters for Bird promised to Eardley and Wilmot distinguished. Two addresses of support to Eardley and Wilmot.

Lord Eardley | John Wilmot | William Wilberforce Bird

Coventry Pub Lib Inst Hist Res

1802—A correct copy of the poll... Coventry: J. Turner, [1802]
Alphabetical by ward or place of residence.

Francis William Barlow | Nathaniel Jefferys | William Wilberforce Bird | Peter Moore

Coventry Pub Lib Inst Hist Res

1803*—A correct copy of the poll... Coventry: J. Turner, [1803]
Alphabetical. Ward. Out-voters alphabetical by place of residence.

Peter Moore | George F. Stratton

Coventry Pub Lib Inst Hist Res

1818—A correct copy of the poll... Coventry: J. Turner, 1818
Alphabetical. Ward. Out-voters alphabetical by place of residence.

Peter Moore | Edward Ellice | Joseph Butterworth

Coventry Pub Lib Inst Hist Res

1820—A correct copy of the poll... Coventry: W. Rotherham, 1820
Alphabetical. Ward. Out-voters by place of residence, London alphabetical.

Edward Ellice | Peter Moore | William Cobbett | H. J. Close

Coventry Pub Lib Inst Hist Res

1833*—A correct copy of the poll... Coventry: Rollason & Reader, 1833
Alphabetical. Ward and qualification. Out-voters alphabetical by place of residence.

Edward Ellice | Morgan Thomas | John Cobbett

Coventry Pub Lib Inst Hist Res

1835—A correct copy of the poll... Coventry: W. Reader, 1835
Alphabetical by ward or place of residence. Qualification.

William Williams Edward Ellice Morgan Thomas

Coventry Pub Lib Guildhall Lib

1837—A correct copy from the sheriff's books, of the poll... Coventry: W. Edwards, 1837
Alphabetical by ward or place of residence. Qualification.

Edward Ellice William Williams Morgan Thomas John David Hay Hill John Bell

Coventry Pub Lib Inst Hist Res

1837—A correct copy of the poll... Coventry: Stephen Knapp, 1837
Alphabetical by ward or place of residence. Qualification. Non-voters.

Edward Ellice William Williams Morgan Thomas John David Hay Hill John Bell

Coventry Pub Lib Inst Hist Res

1841—A correct copy from the sheriff's books of the poll... Coventry: Knapp & Pearce, [1841]
Alphabetical by ward or place of residence. Qualification.

William Williams Edward Ellice Thomas Weir

Coventry Pub Lib Inst Hist Res

1847—A correct copy of the poll... Coventry: Joseph Tomkinson, 1847
Alphabetical by ward or place of residence. Qualification.

Edward Ellice George James Turner William Williams

Coventry Pub Lib Inst Hist Res

1851*—A correct copy of the poll... Coventry: Stephen Knapp, [1851]
Alphabetical by ward or place of residence. Qualification.

Charles Geach Edward Strutt

Coventry Pub Lib Inst Hist Res

1857—Taunton and Sons authorised copy of the poll... Coventry: Taunton & Son, [1857]
Alphabetical by ward or place of residence.

Edward Ellice Sir Joseph Paxton John Mellor Morgan Treherne
Robert Joseph Phillimore

Coventry Pub Lib Inst Hist Res

1859—Taunton's authorised list of polled and unpolled voters... Coventry: W. F. Taunton, [1859]
Alphabetical by ward or place of residence. Non-voters included with reasons.

Edward Ellice Sir Joseph Paxton Morgan Treherne

Coventry Pub Lib Inst Hist Res

1863*—Taunton's list of polled and unpolled voters... Coventry: W. F. Taunton, [1863]
Alphabetical by ward or place of residence. Non-voters included with reasons.

Morgan Treherne   Arthur Wellesley Peel

Coventry Pub Lib Inst Hist Res

1865* (June)—Lewin's correct copy of the poll... Coventry: A. Lewin, 1865
Alphabetical by ward or place of residence. Non-voters included. Votes for June and July elections.

Henry William Eaton   Thomas Mason Jones

Coventry Pub Lib Guildhall Lib

1865 (July)—Lewin's correct copy of the poll... Coventry: A. Lewin, 1865
Alphabetical by ward or place of residence. Non-voters included. Votes for June and July elections.

Morgan Treherne Henry William Eaton Edward Fordham Flower Thomas Mason Jones

Coventry Pub Lib Guildhall Lib

1867*—Civitas Coventriae. Taunton's authorised list of polled and unpolled voters... Coventry: W. Fred. Taunton, [1867]
Alphabetical by ward or place of residence. Non-voters included with reasons.

Henry Mather Jackson   William Busfield Ferrand

Coventry Pub Lib Inst Hist Res

1868* (March)—Civitas Coventriae. Taunton's authorised list of polled and unpolled voters... Coventry: W. Fred. Taunton, [1868]
Alphabetical by ward or place of residence. Non-voters included with reasons.

Samuel Carter   Alexander Staveley Hill

Coventry Pub Lib Inst Hist Res

1868 (November)—Civitas Coventriae. Astill's authorised list of polled and unpolled voters... Coventry: Astill's Machine Offices, [1868]
Alphabetical by ward or place of residence. Non-voters included. Oath takers distinguished.

Henry William Eaton Alexander Staveley Hill Henry Mather Jackson Samuel Carter

Coventry Pub Lib Inst Hist Res

Untraced: 1790 (Rollason), 1826

WARWICK

1784—The poll of the burgesses... Warwick: J. Sharp, [1784]
Alphabetical. Occupation and address. Signatories of address to the King distinguished. Non-voters.

Charles Francis Greville   Robert Ladbroke   William Holbech

Guildhall Lib

1792*—The poll of the burgesses... Warwick: J. Sharp, [1792]
Alphabetical. Occupation and address. Non-voters.
George Villiers Robert Knight
Bodl Inst Hist Res

1831—The poll of the burgesses... Warwick: John Merridew & W. Rose, [1831]
Alphabetical. Occupation and address. Rejected voters with reasons. Non-voters.
John Tomes Edward Bolton King Sir Charles John Greville
Warwicks Rec Off Inst Hist Res

1831—The poll of the burgesses... Warwick: E. Heathcote, 1831
Poll order. Occupation and address. Rejected voters included. Non-voters. Index.
John Tomes Edward Bolton King Sir Charles John Greville
Warwicks Rec Off Guildhall Lib

1832—The poll of the burgesses.. Warwick: W. Rose, [1832]
Alphabetical with separate list under each letter for St. Nicholas parish. Occupation, nature and situation of qualification. Non-voters and tendered votes.
Sir Charles John Greville Edward Bolton King John Tomes
Warwicks Rec Off Inst Hist Res

1835—The poll of the burgesses... Warwick: E. Heathcote, 1835
Alphabetical. Occupation and address. Non-voters and dead distinguished. Tendered votes.
Sir Charles John Greville Edward Bolton King John Halcomb
Modern Records Centre, Warwick Univ Inst Hist Res

1837—The poll of the burgesses... Warwick: E. Heathcote, 1837
Alphabetical by parish. Occupation and address. Non-voters distinguished.
William Collins Sir Charles Dugdale Edward Bolton King
Warwicks Rec Off Inst Hist Res

1852—The poll taken... Warwick: W. G. Perry, 1852
Alphabetical by parish. Address. Non-voters distinguished.
George William John Repton Edward Greaves John Mellor
Warwicks Rec Off Inst Hist Res

1865—The poll taken... Warwick: Joseph F. Squires, 1865
Alphabetical by parish. Address. Non-voters distinguished.
George William John Repton Arthur Wellesley Peel Edward Greaves
Warwicks Rec Off Inst Hist Res

1868—Authenticated copy of the poll... Warwick: R. Spennell, [1868]
Alphabetical by parish. Address. Non-voters included.

Arthur Wellesley Peel   Edward Greaves   William R. Cremer

Warwicks Rec Off Inst Hist Res

[Two editions known]

WESTMORLAND

1768—The poll for knights... Kendal: James Ashburner, [1768]
Alphabetical by ward and township. Place of residence. Oath-takers distinguished. Rejected voters.

John Robinson   Thomas Fenwick   John Upton

Inst Hist Res

1774—The poll for knights... Kendal, [1774]
Alphabetical by ward. Place of residence and of freehold.

Sir James Lowther   Sir Michael Le Fleming   Thomas Fenwick

Bodl Inst Hist Res

1818—The poll for knights... Kendal: Airey & Bellingham, 1818
Alphabetical. Place of residence and of freehold.

Viscount Lonsdale   Henry Cecil Lonsdale   Henry Brougham

Cumbria County Lib Guildhall Lib

1818—Correct edition. The poll for knights... Kendal: R. Lough, [1818]
Alphabetical by ward and township. Place of residence. Oath-takers distinguished. Appendix of those prevented from voting for Brougham.

Viscount Lonsdale   Henry Cecil Lonsdale   Henry Brougham

Carlisle Pub Lib Inst Hist Res

1820—The poll for knights... Kendal: John Kilner, [1820]
Alphabetical by ward. Place of residence and of freehold. Votes remaining undecided.

Viscount Lonsdale   Henry Cecil Lonsdale   Henry Brougham

Carlisle Pub Lib Inst Hist Res

1820—The poll for knights... Kendal: Richard Lough, [1820]
Alphabetical by ward and township. Place of residence. Oath-takers distinguished. Votes remaining undecided and main cases dealt with by the assessor.

Viscount Lonsdale   Henry Cecil Lonsdale   Henry Brougham

Carlisle Pub Lib Guildhall Lib

1826—The poll for knights... Kendal: Tyras Redhead, [1826]
Alphabetical by ward. Place of residence and of freehold.

Viscount Lonsdale   Henry Cecil Lonsdale   Henry Brougham

Carlisle Pub Lib Inst Hist Res

1826—The poll for knights... Kendal: Richard Lough, [1826]
Alphabetical by ward and township. Place of residence. Votes remaining undecided.

Viscount Lonsdale   Henry Cecil Lonsdale   Henry Brougham

Cumbria County Lib Guildhall Lib

ISLE OF WIGHT

1832—The poll of the electors... Newport: Robert Squire, 1833
Poll order. Occupation and place of residence. Non-voters alphabetical by hundred with parish of qualification and place of residence.

Sir Richard Godin Simeon   Alexander Glynn Campbell

Carisbrooke Castle Museum Inst Hist Res

1835—The poll of the electors... Newport: W. W. Yelf, [1835]
Alphabetical by district and candidate. Occupation and place of residence. Rejected, paired, dead and non-voters. Unregistered tenders.

Sir Richard Godin Simeon   George Henry Ward

Isle of Wight Rec Off Inst Hist Res

Untraced: 1852, 1857, 1859, 1865, 1870

NEWPORT

1832—The poll of the electors... Newport: H. Caplen, 1832
Poll order and alphabetical. Occupation and address. Non-voters. Objected and rejected voters.

John Heywood Hawkins   William Henry Ord   Sir James Willoughby Gordon

Carisbrooke Castle Museum Inst Hist Res

1835—The poll of the electors... Newport: Yelf & Co., [1835]
Alphabetical by candidate. Occupation and address. Rejected and non-voters.

William Henry Ord   John Heywood Hawkins   Sir James Willoughby Gordon
William John Hamilton

Isle of Wight Rec Off Inst Hist Res

1841—The poll of the electors... Newport: W. W. Yelf, 1841
Alphabetical. Address. Non-voters included.

Charles Wykeham Martin William John Hamilton Thomas Gisborne William John Blake

Carisbrooke Castle Museum Inst Hist Res

1852—The poll of the electors... Wootton: Henry Brannon, 1852
Alphabetical by candidate and parish. Occupation and address. Non-voters.

William Biggs William Nathaniel Massey W. H. C. Plowden Charles Wykeham Martin

Brit Lib

1857*—The poll of the electors… published by order of the committee for conducting the election of Charles Seely
Alphabetical by candidate and parish. Occupation and address. Non-voters by parish.

Robert William Kennard — Charles Seely

Carisbrooke Castle Museum — Inst Hist Res

1865—The poll of the electors… Newport: W. Blake, 1865
Alphabetical by parish. Address. Non-voters included.

Charles Wykeham Martin — Robert William Kennard — Auberon Herbert

Isle of Wight Rec Off — Inst Hist Res

Untraced: 1847, 1859, 1870

WILTSHIRE

1705—A true copy of the poll… London, 1705
By parish.

Sir Richard Howe — Robert Hide — William Ash — Sir Edward Ernle

Devizes Museum — Inst Hist Res

1772*—The poll of the freeholders… Salisbury: E. Easton, 1772
By parish. Place of residence.

Ambrose Goddard — Henry Herbert

Wilts Rec Off — Inst Hist Res

1818—The poll for the election… Salisbury: Brodie & Dowding, [1818]
By polling booth, hundred and parish. Place of residence.

Paul Methuen — William Pole Tylney Long Wellesley — John Benett

Devizes Museum — Inst Hist Res

1819*—The poll of the freeholders… by G. Butt… Salisbury: Brodie & Dowding, [1819]
Alphabetical by polling booth, hundred and parish. Occupation, place of residence, nature and occupier of freehold, voting in 1818. Tendered, rejected and withdrawn voters and oath-takers distinguished. Index of surnames.

John Benett — John Dugdale Astley

Devizes Museum — Inst Hist Res

SOUTH WILTSHIRE

1865—A copy of the poll… Salisbury: *Wiltshire County Mirror* Office, [1865]
Alphabetical by polling district and parish. Address or place of residence. Non-voters included, distinguishing dead.

Lord Henry Thynne — Thomas Fraser Grove — Frederick Henry Bathurst

Devizes Museum — Guildhall Lib

CHIPPENHAM

1841—Chippenham general election. The poll for the election... Chippenham: J. Noyes, [1841]
Alphabetical. Occupation. Non-voters.
Joseph Neeld   Henry George Boldero   William John Lysley
Wilts Archaeol Soc Inst Hist Res

1865—A poll for the election... Chippenham: George Noyes, [1865]
Alphabetical. Occupation. Non-voters.
Sir John Neeld   Gabriel Goldney   William John Lysley
Wilts Archaeol Soc Inst Hist Res

1868—The poll at the Chippenham election... Chippenham: G. Noyes, [1868]
Alphabetical by candidate and parish. Address. Non-voters.
Gabriel Goldney   Sir George Young
Wilts Archaeol Soc Inst Hist Res

CRICKLADE

1831—The poll of the freeholders and other electors... Highworth: Joseph Ricketts, [1831]
Alphabetical by hundred and parish of residence. Occupation, place, nature and occupier of property. Queried and rejected voters and oath-takers distinguished. Out-voters by place of residence. Index.
Robert Gordon   Thomas Calley   P. P. Bouverie
Swindon Pub Lib Inst Hist Res

1859—The poll book of the election... Cirencester: C. H. Savory, [1859]
Alphabetical by district and parish. Place of residence. Non-voters included.
Ambrose Lethbridge Goddard   Lord Ashley   Sir John Neeld
Wilts Archaeol Soc Inst Hist Res

1865—Cricklade election. *North Wilts Herald,* 22 July and 29 July 1865
Alphabetical by district and parish. Non-voters distinguished.
Ambrose Lethbridge Goddard   Daniel Gooch   Lord Eliot
Brit Lib (News) Inst Hist Res

1868—Poll book of the Cricklade election... Swindon: J. H. Piper, [1868]
Alphabetical by district and parish. Address. Non-voters distinguished.
Frederick William Cadogan   Sir Daniel Gooch   Ambrose Lethbridge Goddard
Wilts Archaeol Soc Inst Hist Res

DEVIZES

1844*—A list of persons who polled. *Devizes & Wiltshire Gazette,* 15 February 1844
Alphabetical by candidate. Occupation and address.
William Heald Ludlow Bruges   Christopher Temple
Brit Lib (News) Inst Hist Res

1857—Devizes election. *Wiltshire Independent,* 9 April 1857
Alphabetical by candidate. Occupation and address. Non-voters.
Simon Watson Taylor Christopher Darby Griffith John Neilson Gladstone
Brit Lib (News) Inst Hist Res

1859—Devizes election... Poll lists. *Wiltshire Independent* Supplement, 5 May 1859
Alphabetical by candidate. Occupation. Non-voters and dead.
John Neilson Gladstone Christopher Darby Griffith Simon Watson Taylor
Brit Lib (News) Inst Hist Res

1863*—The poll. *Wiltshire Independent,* 19 February 1863
Alphabetical by candidate. Non-voters.
William Wells Addington John Webb Probyn Israel Abrahams
Brit Lib (News) Inst Hist Res

1868—List of voters... *Wiltshire Independent,* 26 November 1868
Alphabetical by candidate. Address. Non-voters.
Sir Thomas Bateson John Webb Probyn Christopher Darby Griffith
Brit Lib (News) Inst Hist Res

1868—The poll. *Devizes & Wiltshire Gazette,* 26 November 1868
Alphabetical by candidate. Address. Non-voters.
Sir Thomas Bateson John Webb Probyn Christopher Darby Griffith
Brit Lib (News) Inst Hist Res

SALISBURY

1765*—A true and exact copy of the poll... *Public Advertiser,* 11 February 1765
By candidate. Non-voters.
Samuel Eyre Peter Bathurst
Brit Lib (News) Inst Hist Res (Typescript)

1843*—The poll of the election of a member... *Salisbury & Wiltshire Herald,* 2 December 1843
Alphabetical by candidate. Address. Non-voters.
John Henry Campbell E. P. Bouverie
Brit Lib (News) Inst Hist Res

1853*—Election for the borough of Salisbury. *Salisbury & Winchester Journal* Supplement, 19 November 1853
Alphabetical by candidate. Non-voters.
Edward Pery Buckley Julius Roberts
Brit Lib (News) Inst Hist Res

1865—Salisbury election—poll list... *Wiltshire County Mirror,* 2 August 1865
Alphabetical by candidate. Address. Non-voters.
Matthew Henry Marsh Edward William Terrick Hamilton John Chapman
Brit Lib (News) Inst Hist Res

1868—Salisbury election—poll list. *Wiltshire County Mirror,* 2 December 1868
Alphabetical by candidate. Non-voters.

John Alfred Lush   Edward William Terrick Hamilton   Granville Richard Ryder

Brit Lib (News)   Inst Hist Res

WORCESTERSHIRE

1715—A copy of the poll... taken the second and third days of February, in the year 1714... Worcester: S. Bryan, 1715
By parish. Place of residence.

Sir John Pakington 1970   Thomas Vernon 1802   Samuel Pytts 1676

Guildhall Lib

1741—A copy of the poll... n.p., 1741
By parish. Place of residence.

Edmund Lechmere 2309   Edmund Pytts 2120   Lord Deerhurst 1930
George Lyttleton 1412

Hereford & Worcs Rec Off   Inst Hist Res

WEST WORCESTERSHIRE

1835—West Worcestershire. The poll taken... Worcester: Chalk & Hall, 1835
Alphabetical by division and parish. Address. Non-voters included.

Henry Beauchamp Lygon   Henry Jefferies Winnington   John Somerset Pakington

Soc Geneal   Inst Hist Res

KIDDERMINSTER

1849*—Poll book of the Kidderminster election... Kidderminster: George Friend, 1849
Alphabetical by candidate. Occupation and address. Non-voters, paired and dead.

John Best   Thomas Gisborne

Kidderminster Pub Lib   Inst Hist Res

1865—[Title page missing. Begins:] 'List of persons who voted for Albert Grant, Esquire...
Alphabetical by candidate. Address.

Albert Grant   Luke White

Kidderminster Pub Lib   Inst Hist Res

WORCESTER

1741—A correct copy of the poll... n.p., 1741
Alphabetical by parish. Out-voters by county and parish.

Thomas Winnington   Samuel Sandys   John Ravenhill

Private possession   Inst Hist Res

1747—An alphabetical copy of the poll... n.p., 1747
By parish. Out-voters by county and parish. Occupation.

Thomas Vernon Thomas Winford Robert Tracy

Guildhall Lib

1761—An alphabetical copy of the poll... Worcester: H. Berrow, 1761
By parish. Out-voters by county and parish. Occupation. Queried voters and unfulfilled promises to Boulton and Walsh distinguished.

Henry Crabb Boulton John Walsh Robert Tracy

Bodl Inst Hist Res

1841—A copy of the poll... Worcester: *Guardian* Office, [1841]
Alphabetical. Occupation, address and qualification. Non-voters, distinguishing tendered voters and dead. Account of proceedings and candidates' addresses.

Sir Thomas Wilde Joseph Bailey Robert Hardy

Birmingham Pub Lib Inst Hist Res

1852—Worcester city election. *Berrow's Worcester Journal,* 29 July, 5 August, 12 August, 19 August, 1852
By polling booth. Address.

William Laslett Osman Richards J. W. Huddleston

Brit Lib (News) Inst Hist Res

1865—Copy of the poll... Worcester: Knight & Co., [1865]
Alphabetical by polling booth. Address.

Alexander Clunes Sherriff Richard Padmore James Levick

Birmingham Pub Lib Inst Hist Res

1868—City of Worcester election, November 17, 1868. Poll book. Worcester: *Journal* Office, [1868]
Alphabetical by district, parish and qualification. Address. Non-voters included.

William Laslett Alexander Clunes Sherriff Thomas Rowley Hill Sir Francis Lycett

Birmingham Pub Lib Guildhall Lib

YORKSHIRE

1734—Alphabetically dige[sted] original poll books... Newcastle-upon-Tyne: John White, 1734
By place of freehold. Place of residence. Voters for Wynne and Turner only.

Sir Myles Stapleton Cholmley Turner Edward Wortley Montagu Sir Rowland Wynne

Castle Howard Archives Inst Hist Res

1742*—The poll for a representative... York: Ward & Chandler, 1742
Alphabetical by candidate and place of residence. Place of freehold.

Cholmley Turner George Fox

York Pub Lib Inst Hist Res

1742*—The poll for the county of York... York: John Jackson, [1742]
Alphabetical. Place of residence and of freehold. Rejected voters with reasons.

Cholmley Turner George Fox

Sheffield Pub Lib Guildhall Lib

1807—County of York. The poll for knights... York: T. Wilson & R. Spence, 1807
Alphabetical by wapentake and township of residence. Occupation and place of freehold. Out-voters, including Hullshire and York, by county and parish. Record of proceedings.

William Wilberforce Viscount Milton Henry Lascelles

York Pub Lib Inst Hist Res

YORKSHIRE EAST RIDING

1837—Poll book for the East Riding of Yorkshire... Beverley: John Kemp, [1837]
Alphabetical by district and parish. Place of residence.

Richard Bethell Henry Broadley Paul Beilby Thompson

Humberside County Lib Inst Hist Res

[A separate issue of the Hedon District section is also known.]

1868—1868. East-Riding election. The poll... Driffield: George Robert Jackson, 1869
Alphabetical by polling district, township and qualification. Address.

Christopher Sykes William Henry Harrison Broadley B. B. Haworth

York Pub Lib Inst Hist Res

YORKSHIRE WEST RIDING

1835*—West Riding election. The poll for a knight... Wakefield: John Stanfield, 1835
Alphabetical by polling district and township. Address. Non-voters included. Tendered and non-registered voters. Account of proceedings.

Viscount Morpeth John Stuart Wortley

Sheffield Pub Lib Inst Hist Res

1835*—The poll book: being a list... Sheffield: Robert Leader, [1835]
Alphabetical by township. Sheffield District only. Non-voters at end of each township. Account of proceedings.

Viscount Morpeth John Stuart Wortley

Sheffield Pub Lib Inst Hist Res

1835*—West Riding election. The poll book... Sheffield: G. Ridge, [1835]
Alphabetical by township. Sheffield only. Address and nature of qualification. Non-voters included.

Viscount Morpeth John Stuart Wortley

Sheffield Pub Lib Inst Hist Res

1837—West Riding election. The poll... Leeds: George Crosby, 1838
Alphabetical by polling district and township. Address. Non-voters included. Account of proceedings.

Viscount Morpeth Sir George Strickland John Stuart Wortley

Sheffield Pub Lib Inst Hist Res

1841—West Riding election. The poll... Wakefield: John Stanfield, 1841
Alphabetical by polling district and township. Address. Occupiers distinguished. Non-voters included. Account of proceedings. Tendered and non-registered votes.

John Stuart Wortley Edmund Beckett Denison Viscount Morpeth Viscount Milton

Sheffield Pub Lib Inst Hist Res

1848*—West Riding election. The poll for a knight... Leeds: D. I. Roebuck, 1849
Alphabetical by polling district and township. Address. Non-voters included, distinguishing dead. Account of proceedings.

Edmund Beckett Denison Sir Culling Eardley Eardley

Sheffield Pub Lib Inst Hist Res

1848*—West Riding election 1848. The poll for a knight... Leeds: Crosby, 1849
Alphabetical by polling district and township. Address. Non-voters included, distinguishing dead. Account of proceedings.

Edmund Beckett Denison Sir Culling Eardley Eardley

Huddersfield Pub Lib

1859—West Riding election. The poll book... Wakefield: Stanfield & Son, 1859
Alphabetical by polling district and township. Address. Candidates' addresses and summary of proceedings.

Sir John William Ramsden Frank Crossley James Stuart Wortley

Dewsbury Pub Lib Inst Hist Res

YORKSHIRE WEST RIDING (EAST)

1868—West Riding election, Eastern Division. The poll book... Leeds: Edward Baines & Sons, 1869
Alphabetical by polling district, township and qualification. Address. Non-voters included.

Christopher Beckett Davison Joshua Fielden Harry Stephen Thompson Isaac Holden

Leeds Pub Lib Guildhall Lib

YORKSHIRE WEST RIDING (SOUTH)

1865—The poll for the Southern Division... Wakefield: J. Robinson, 1866
Alphabetical by polling district and township. Address. Candidates' addresses.

Viscount Milton Henry Frederick Beaumont Christopher Beckett Denison
Walter Spencer Stanhope

Sheffield Pub Lib Guildhall Lib

1868—The poll of the Southern Division of the West Riding... Wakefield: Alfred W. Stanfield, 1869
Alphabetical by polling district, township and qualification. Address. Candidates' addresses.
Viscount Milton Henry Frederick Beaumont Walter Spencer Stanhope Lewis Randle Starkey
Dewsbury Pub Lib Guildhall Lib

BEVERLEY

1774—A copy of the poll, in alphabetical order... Hull: J. Ferraby, [1774]
Occupation of residents and place of residence of out-voters.
Sir James Pennyman George Forster Tufnel Sir Charles Thompson
Beverley Pub Lib Inst Hist Res

1784—A copy of the poll (in alphabetical order)... Hull: J. Ferraby, [1784]
Occupation and place of residence.
Sir James Pennyman Sir Christopher Sykes Evelyn Anderson
Beverley Pub Lib Inst Hist Res

1790—Copy of the poll (in alphabetical order)... Hull: J. Ferraby, [1790]
Occupation and place of residence.
John Hall Wharton Sir James Pennyman William Egerton
Beverley Pub Lib Inst Hist Res

1799*—A copy of the poll (in alphabetical order)... Beverley, 1799
Occupation and place of residence.
John Bacon Sawrey Morritt John Hall Wharton
Guildhall Lib

1802—A copy of the poll (in alphabetical order)... Beverley: M. Turner, [1802]
Occupation and place of residence.
John Wharton Napier Christie Burton John Bacon Sawry Morritt
Beverley Pub Lib Inst Hist Res

1802—A copy of the poll (in alphabetical order)... Beverley: W. Rawson, [1802]
Occupation and place of residence.
John Wharton Napier Christie Burton John Bacon Sawry Morritt
Guildhall Lib

1806—A copy of the poll (arranged in alphabetical order)... Hull: Robert Peck, 1806
Occupation and place of residence.
John Wharton Richard Vyse Napier Christie Burton
Beverley Pub Lib Inst Hist Res

1807—A copy of the poll (arranged in alphabetical order)... Beverley: M. Turner, 1807
Occupation and place of residence.

Howard Vyse John Wharton Philip Staples

Humberside County Lib Inst Hist Res

1812—A copy of the poll (arranged in alphabetical order)... Hull: B. Tate [1812]
Occupation and place of residence.

John Wharton Charles Forbes William Beverley

Beverley Pub Lib Inst Hist Res

1818—A copy of the poll... Beverley: T. Procter, [1818]
Alphabetical. Occupation and place of residence.

John Wharton Robert Christie Burton Dymoke Wells William Beverley

Beverley Pub Lib Inst Hist Res

1820—A copy of the poll... Beverley: T. Procter, [1820]
Alphabetical. Occupation and place of residence.

George Lane Fox John Wharton Robert Christie Burton

Beverley Pub Lib Inst Hist Res

1820—A copy of the poll... Beverley: printed for J. Ramsden, [1820]
Alphabetical. Occupation and place of residence.

George Lane Fox John Wharton Robert Christie Burton

Humberside County Lib Inst Hist Res

[Same printing as preceding entry with different imprint.]

1826—A copy of the poll... Beverley: M. Turner, [1826]
Alphabetical. Occupation and place of residence.

John Stewart Charles Harrison Batley John Wharton

Humberside County Lib Inst Hist Res

1826—A copy of the poll... Beverley: W. B. Johnson, [1826]
Alphabetical. Occupation and place of residence.

John Stewart Charles Harrison Batley John Wharton

Beverley Pub Lib Inst Hist Res

1830—A copy of the poll... Beverley: G. Scaum, [1830]
Alphabetical. Occupation and place of residence.

Henry Burton Daniel Sykes Capel Cure

Beverley Pub Lib Inst Hist Res

1831—A copy of the poll... Hull: W. Stephenson, 1831
Alphabetical. Occupation and place of residence.

William Marshall Henry Burton Charles Winn

Beverley Pub Lib Inst Hist Res

1832—A copy of the poll... Hull: John Hutchinson, [1832]
Alphabetical by qualification. Occupation and address.
Charles Langdale Henry Burton Charles Winn
Beverley Pub Lib Inst Hist Res

1835—A copy of the poll... Beverley: John Kemp, 1835
Alphabetical by qualification. Occupation, address and polling place. Non-voters and dead.
James Weir Hogg Henry Burton Joseph Sykes
Beverley Pub Lib Inst Hist Res

1835—A copy of the poll... Beverley: James Ramsden, 1835
Alphabetical by qualification. Occupation, address and polling place.
James Weir Hogg Henry Burton Joseph Sykes
Humberside County Lib Inst Hist Res

[Same printing as preceding entry with different imprint.]

1837—A copy of the poll... Beverley: John Kemp, 1837
Alphabetical by qualification. Occupation and address. Non-voters and dead.
James Weir Hogg George Lane Fox James Clay George Rennie
Beverley Pub Lib Inst Hist Res

1840*—A copy of the poll... Beverley: John Kemp, 1840
Alphabetical by qualification. Occupation and address. Non-voters and dead.
Sackville Lane Fox Thomas Lamie Murray
Beverley Pub Lib Inst Hist Res

1841—A copy of the poll... Beverley: John Kemp, 1841
Alphabetical by qualification. Occupation and address. Non-voters and dead.
John Towneley James Weir Hogg Sackville Lane Fox
Beverley Pub Lib Inst Hist Res

1841—A copy of the poll... Beverley: James Ramsden, 1841
Alphabetical by qualification. Occupation and address. Non-voters and dead.
John Towneley James Weir Hogg Sackville Lane Fox
Hull Pub Lib Inst Hist Res

1847—A copy of the poll... Beverley: John Kemp, 1847
Alphabetical by qualification. Occupation and address. Tendered votes, non-voters and dead.
Sackville Lane Fox John Towneley Sir Isaac Lyon Goldsmid
Humberside County Lib Inst Hist Res

1847—A copy of the poll... Beverley: W. B. Johnson, 1847
Alphabetical by qualification. Occupation and address. Tendered votes, non-voters and dead.
Sackville Lane Fox John Towneley Sir Isaac Lyon Goldsmid
Beverley Pub Lib Inst Hist Res

1847—A copy of the poll... Beverley: John Green, 1847
Alphabetical by qualification. Occupation and address. Tendered votes, non-voters and dead.
Sackville Lane Fox John Towneley Sir Isaac Lyon Goldsmid
Hull Univ Lib Guildhall Lib

1852—A copy of the poll... Beverley: M Ellis, 1853
Alphabetical by qualification. Occupation and address. Non-voters and dead.
Francis Charles Lawley William Wells Edward Auchmuty Glover
Beverley Pub Lib Inst Hist Res

1854*—A copy of the poll... Beverley: M. Ellis, 1854
Alphabetical by qualification. Occupation and address. Non-voters, distinguishing dead.
Arthur Gordon Edward Hastings
Beverley Pub Lib Inst Hist Res

1857*—A copy of the poll... Beverley: Kemp & Son, 1857
Alphabetical by qualification. Occupation and address. Non-voters and dead.
Henry Edwards William Wells
Beverley Pub Lib Inst Hist Res

1859—A copy of the poll... Beverley: John Green, 1859
Alphabetical by qualification. Occupation and address. Non-voters and dead.
Ralph Waters Henry Edwards James Robert Walker Edward Auchmuty Glover
Humberside County Lib Inst Hist Res

1859—A copy of the poll... Beverley: Kemp & Son, 1859
Alphabetical by qualification. Occupation and address. Non-voters and dead.
Ralph Waters Henry Edwards James Robert Walker Edward Auchmuty Glover
Beverley Pub Lib

1860*—A copy of the poll... Beverley: J. Kemp & Son, 1860
Alphabetical by qualification. Occupation and address. Non-voters and dead.
James Robert Walker Henry Gillet Gridley
Beverley Pub Lib Inst Hist Res

1865—A copy of the poll... Beverley: John Green, 1865
Alphabetical by qualification. Occupation and address. Non-voters and dead.
Henry Edwards Christopher Sykes David Deady Keane
Beverley Pub Lib Inst Hist Res

1868—Copy of the poll... Beverley: J. Ward, 1869
Alphabetical by qualification and parish or township. Address. Non-voters included.

Sir Henry Edwards   Edmund Hegan Kennard   M. C. Maxwell   Anthony Trollope

Humberside County Lib   Inst Hist Res

1868—A copy of the poll... Beverley: Kemp & Son, 1868
Alphabetical by qualification and parish or township. Address. Non-voters and dead.

Sir Henry Edwards   Edmund Hegan Kennard   M. C. Maxwell   Anthony Trollope

Beverley Pub Lib   Inst Hist Res

BRADFORD

1835—Bradford borough election, January 12, 1835. The poll book... Bradford: John Dale, 1835
Alphabetical by township. Occupation and nature and situation of qualification. Non-voters and rejected voters included.

John Hardy   Ellis Cunliffe Lister   George Hadfield

Bradford Pub Lib   Inst Hist Res

1837—Bradford borough election. July 27, 1837. The poll book... Bradford: John Dale, 1837
Alphabetical by township. Nature and situation of qualification. Non-voters and rejected voters included.

Ellis Cunliffe Lister   William Busfield   John Hardy   William Busfield, Jr.

Bradford Pub Lib   Inst Hist Res

1841 (June)—Bradford borough election, June 30th, 1841. The poll book... Bradford: E. A. W. Taylor, 1841
Alphabetical by township. Nature and situation of qualification. Non-voters and rejected voters included.

John Hardy   Ellis Cunliffe Lister   William Busfield

Bradford Pub Lib   Inst Hist Res

1841 (June)—Bradford borough elections... June 30th and September 15th, 1841. The poll book... Bradford: John Dale, 1841
Alphabetical by township. Nature and situation of quallification. Non-voters included. Pairs. Votes for both elections.

John Hardy   Ellis Cunliffe Lister   William Busfield

Bradford Pub Lib   Inst Hist Res

1841 (September)—Bradford borough elections... June 30th and September 15th, 1841. The poll book... Bradford: John Dale, 1841
Alphabetical by township. Nature and situation of quallification. Non-voters included. Pairs. Votes for both elections.

William Busfield   William Wilberforce

Bradford Pub Lib   Inst Hist Res

1847—Bradford borough election, July 30, 1847. The poll book... Bradford: C. Stanfield, 1847
Alphabetical by township. Place of qualification. Non-voters included.

William Busfield Thomas Perronet Thompson Henry Wickham Wickham John Hardy

Bradford Pub Lib Inst Hist Res

1852—Bradford borough election, July 7th, 1852. The poll book... Bradford: John Dale, 1852
Alphabetical by township. Nature and situation of qualification. Non-voters included.

Robert Milligan Henry Wickham Wickham Thomas Perronet Thompson

Bradford Pub Lib Inst Hist Res

1852—Bradford borough election, July 7th, 1852. The poll book... Bradford: C. Stanfield, 1852
Alphabetical by township. Address of qualification. Non-voters and dead included.

Robert Milligan Henry Wickham Wickham Thomas Perronet Thompson

Bradford Pub Lib Inst Hist Res

1859—Bradford borough election, April 30th, 1859. The poll book...
Alphabetical by township. Address of qualification. Non-voters included.

Henry Wickham Wickham Titus Salt Alfred Harris

Bradford Pub Lib Inst Hist Res

1867*—The poll book, 1867. Bradford: W. Cooke, [1867]
Alphabetical by township. Address.

Matthew William Thompson Edward Miall

Bradford Pub Lib Inst Hist Res

1867*—Bradford election. The poll... *Bradford Times*, 19 October 1867
Alphabetical by township. Address.

Matthew William Thompson Edward Miall

Brit Lib (News) Inst Hist Res

1868—The Bradford poll book... Bradford: C. Denton, 1869
Alphabetical by ward, district and qualification. Address. Non-voters included. Votes for general election and 1869 by-election.

William Edward Forster Henry William Ripley Edward Miall

Bradford Pub Lib Inst Hist Res

1869*—The Bradford poll book... Bradford: C. Denton, 1869
Alphabetical by ward, district and qualification. Address. Non-voters included. Votes for general election and 1869 by-election.

Matthew William Thompson Edward Miall

Bradford Pub Lib Inst Hist Res

HALIFAX

1832—Halifax borough election... the poll book... Halifax: H. T. Rogers, 1833
Alphabetical by borough and townships. Address. Non-voters.

Rawdon Briggs, Jr. Charles Wood Michael Stocks James Stuart Wortley

Guildhall Lib

1835—Halifax borough election, January 5th, 1835. The poll book... Halifax: Hartley & Walker, 1835
Alphabetical by borough and townships. Occupation and address. Non-voters, tendered votes and rejected voters with reasons.

Charles Wood James Stuart Wortley Edward Protheroe

Halifax Pub Lib Inst Hist Res

[Two editions known]

1837—Halifax borough election, July 25th, 1837. The poll book... Halifax: Hartley & Walker, 1837
Alphabetical. Occupation and address. Voters entered twice and rejected voters. Non-voters.

Edward Protheroe Charles Wood James Stuart Wortley

Halifax Pub Lib Inst Hist Res

1841—Halifax borough election, July 1841. The poll book... Halifax: J. Hartley, 1841
Alphabetical by borough and townships. Address. Non-voters, removed and dead. Rejected voters.

Edward Protheroe, Jr. Charles Wood Sir George Sinclair

Halifax Pub Lib Inst Hist Res

1847—Halifax borough election, July 29th, 1847. The poll book... Halifax: J. Hartley & Son, 1847
Alphabetical by borough and townships. Address. Dead and non-voters.

Henry Edwards Sir Charles Wood Edward Miall Ernest Jones

Halifax Pub Lib Inst Hist Res

1847—Halifax borough election. The poll book... Halifax: Nicholson & Wilson, 1847
Alphabetical by borough and townships. Occupation and address. Dead and non-voters with address only.

Henry Edwards Sir Charles Wood Edward Miall Ernest Jones

Halifax Pub Lib Inst Hist Res

1852—Halifax borough election. The poll book... Halifax: William Nicholson, [1852]
By borough and townships. Occupation and address. Non-voters and dead with address only.

Sir Charles Wood Frank Crossley Henry Edwards Ernest Jones

Halifax Pub Lib Inst Hist Res

1853*—Halifax borough election, January 3rd, 4th, and 5th, 1853. The poll book... Halifax: William Nicholson, [1853]
Alphabetical by borough and townships. Occupation and address. Non-voters and dead.

Sir Charles Wood   Henry Edwards

Halifax Pub Lib Inst Hist Res

1857—Halifax borough election, March 27 & 28, 1857. The poll book... Halifax: William Nicholson, [1857]
Alphabetical by borough and townships. Address. Non-voters and dead.

Frank Crossley   Sir Charles Wood   Henry Edwards

Halifax Pub Lib Inst Hist Res

Untraced: 1832 (Lister)

HEDON

1802—A copy of the poll... Hull: J. Ferraby, 1802
Alphabetical. Occupation and place of residence.

George Johnstone   Christopher Saville   Peter Everitt Mestaer   Randle Jackson

Humberside Rec Off Inst Hist Res

1818—A copy of the poll... Hull: Robert Peck, 1818
Alphabetical. Occupation and place of residence.

Edmund Turton   Robert Farrand   Anthony Browne

Guildhall Lib

1820—A copy of the poll (in alphabetical order)... Hull: Widow Peck, 1820
Occupation and place of residence.

John Baillie   Robert Farrand   Benjamin Shaw

Humberside County Lib Inst Hist Res

1826—A copy of the poll... Hedon: Wilkinson & Vanderkiste, [1826]
Alphabetical. Occupation and place of residence.

John Baillie   Robert Farrand   Thomas Hyde Villiers

Hull Pub Lib Inst Hist Res

HUDDERSFIELD

1834*—Borough of Huddersfield. A copy of the poll... Leeds: Bingley & Hobson, 1834
By candidate and occupation. Address. Non-electors who subscribed to Wood's expenses.

Joseph Wood   Michael Thomas Sadler   John Blackburn

Huddersfield Pub Lib

1837*—A copy of the poll... Leeds: Joshua Hobson, 1837
Alphabetical by candidate and occupation. Address. Non-voters. Voters pledged to Oastler who did not vote for him distinguished.

Edward Ellice, Jr. Richard Oastler

Huddersfield Pub Lib Inst Hist Res

1847—Huddersfield election. The poll... Huddersfield: Edward Clayton, [1847]
Alphabetical by candidate and occupation. Address. Voters for Stansfield pledged to Cheetham distinguished.

William Rookes Crompton Stansfield John Cheetham

Brit Lib

1852—Huddersfield election, July 8th, 1852. List of the poll... Huddersfield: William Pratt, [1852] [Broadsheet]
Alphabetical by candidate. Occupation and address. Voters for Stansfield who promised neutrality distinguished. Voters for Stansfield pledged to Willans listed separately.

William Rookes Crompton Stansfield William Willans

Huddersfield Museum Inst Hist Res

1857—Poll list of the Huddersfield election, March 28, 1857. [Huddersfield, 1857] [Broadsheet]
Alphabetical by street. Non-voters included.

Edward Akroyd Richard Cobden

Huddersfield Museum Inst Hist Res

1868* (March)—Huddersfield election, 1868. List of persons who voted... Huddersfield: G. Whitehead, [1868]
Alphabetical by candidate. Address. Non-voters, distinguishing dead.

Edward Aldam Leatham W. Campbell Sleigh

Huddersfield Pub Lib Inst Hist Res

Untraced: 1859, 1865

KINGSTON-UPON-HULL

1774—A copy of the poll... Hull: J. Rawson for T. Williamson, [1774]
Alphabetical. Occupation and place of residence.

Lord Robert Manners David Hartley Thomas Shirley

Hull Pub Lib Guildhall Lib

1780—A copy of the poll (in alphabetical order)... Hull: J. Rawson for T. Williamson, [1780]
Occupation and place of residence.

William Wilberforce Lord Robert Manners David Hartley

Hull Pub Lib Inst Hist Res

1784—A copy of the poll... Hull: G. Ferraby, [1784]
Alphabetical. Occupation and place of residence.

William Wilberforce Samuel Thornton David Hartley

Hull Pub Lib Inst Hist Res

1796—A copy of the poll... Hull: W. Rawson, [1796]
Alphabetical. Occupation and place of residence.

Sir Charles Turner Samuel Thornton Walter Spencer Stanhope

Hull Pub Lib Inst Hist Res

1802—A copy of the poll (in alphabetical order)... Hull: J. Ferraby, 1802
Occupation and place of residence. Non-burgesses polled.

Samuel Thornton John Staniforth William Joseph Denison William Bell

Hull Pub Lib Inst Hist Res

1806—A copy of the poll... Hull: Robert Peck, 1806
Alphabetical. Occupation and place of residence.

John Staniforth William Joseph Denison Samuel Thornton

Hull Pub Lib Guildhall Lib

1812—A copy of the poll... Hull: John Perkins, 1812
Alphabetical. Occupation and place of residence. Election literature.

John Staniforth George William Denys Viscount Mahon

Hull Pub Lib Inst Hist Res

1818—A copy of the poll (alphabetically arranged)... Hull: William Ross, 1818
Occupation and place of residence.

John Mitchell James Robert George Graham John Staniforth

Hull Pub Lib Inst Hist Res

1818—Extract from the poll... Hull: Topping & Dawson, [1818]
Occupation and place of residence.

John Mitchell James Robert George Graham John Staniforth

Hull Pub Lib Guildhall Lib

1826—A copy of the poll... Hull: William Ross, 1826
Alphabetical. Occupation and place of residence.

Augustus John O'Neill Daniel Sykes Charles Pelham Villiers

Hull Pub Lib Inst Hist Res

1830—A copy of the poll... Hull: Rodford & Stephenson, 1830
Alphabetical. Occupation and place of residence.

George Schonswar William Batty Wrightson Thomas Gisborne Burke

Hull Pub Lib Guildhall Lib

1832—A copy of the poll... Hull: Goddard & Brown, 1832
Alphabetical by polling booth. Address. Tendered votes. Those voting twice distinguished.

Matthew Davenport Hill   William Hutt   David Carruthers   James Acland

Hull Pub Lib Guildhall Lib

1832—Reformers' copy. The poll book... Hull: Peck & Smith, 1832
Alphabetical by polling booth. Address. Tendered votes.

Matthew Davenport Hill   William Hutt   David Carruthers   James Acland

Hull Pub Lib Inst Hist Res

1832—Acland's comparative poll book... Hull: James Acland, 1835
Alphabetical. Address and qualification. Non-voters included. Shows party voted for in 1832, January 1835 and June 1835.

Matthew Davenport Hill   William Hutt   David Carruthers   James Acland

Hull Pub Lib Inst Hist Res

1835 (January)—A copy of the poll... Hull: Goddard & Brown, 1835
Alphabetical by candidate. Address. Tendered votes.

David Carruthers   William Hutt   Matthew Davenport Hill

Leeds Pub Lib Inst Hist Res

1835 (January)—The poll-book, as taken... Hull: Wm. Stephenson, 1835
Alphabetical by ward and qualification. Address and day of voting. Tendered votes and non-voters.

David Carruthers   William Hutt   Matthew Davenport Hill

Hull Pub Lib Inst Hist Res

1835 (January)—Acland's comparative poll book... Hull: James Acland, 1835
Alphabetical. Address and qualification. Non-voters included. Shows party voted for in 1832, January 1835 and June 1835.

David Carruthers   William Hutt   Matthew Davenport Hill

Hull Pub Lib Inst Hist Res

1835* (June)—The poll-book, as taken... Hull: Wm. Stephenson, 1835
Alphabetical. Address. Tendered votes.

Thomas Perronet Thompson   Humphrey St. John Mildmay

Hull Pub Lib Inst Hist Res

1835* (June)—Acland's comparative poll book... Hull: James Acland, 1835
Alphabetical. Address and qualification. Non-voters included. Shows party voted for in 1832, January 1835 and June 1835.

Thomas Perronet Thompson   Humphrey St. John Mildmay

Hull Pub Lib Inst Hist Res

1837—By authority of the sheriff. A copy of the poll book... Hull: Goddard & Brown, 1837
Alphabetical by polling booth. Occupation and address. Tendered votes.

William Wilberforce   Sir Walter Charles James   William Hutt   Benjamin Ward

Hull Pub Lib   Inst Hist Res

1841—The poll book, as taken... Hull: William Stephenson, 1841
Alphabetical. Address. Tendered votes.

Sir John Hanmer   Sir Walter Charles James   James Clay   Thomas Perronet Thompson

Hull Pub Lib   Inst Hist Res

1847—The poll-book, as taken... compiled and arranged by J. Stark... Hull: Michael Charles Peck, 1847
Alphabetical. Address and qualification. Non-voters included, distinguishing dead and those at sea.

Matthew Talbot Baines   James Clay   James Brown

Hull Pub Lib   Inst Hist Res

1852—The poll-book, as taken... compiled and arranged by J. Stark... Hull: Stephenson, Plaxton & Co., 1852
Alphabetical. Address, qualification and booth. Non-voters included, distinguishing dead.

James Clay   Viscount Goderich   John Bramley Moore   Charles Lennox Butler

Hull Pub Lib   Guildhall Lib

1854*—The poll-book, as taken... Hull: Stephenson, Plaxton & Co., 1854
Alphabetical. Address, qualification and booth. Non-voters included.

William Digby Seymour   William Henry Watson   Samuel Auchmuty Dickson

Hull Pub Lib   Guildhall Lib

1857—The poll book, as taken... Hull: J. B. Dimbleby, 1857
Alphabetical by parish and qualification. Address and booth. Non-voters included, distinguishing dead.

James Clay   Lord Ashley   Lord William Maclean Compton   William Digby Seymour

Hull Pub Lib   Guildhall Lib

1859 (April)—The poll book, as taken at the two elections... Hull: William Kirk [1859]
Alphabetical by parish and qualification. Address. Non-voters included. Voting for general election and August 1859 by-election.

James Clay   Joseph Hoare   John Harvey Lewis

Hull Pub Lib   Guildhall Lib

1859* (August)—The poll book, as taken at the two elections... Hull: William Kirk [1859]
Alphabetical by parish and qualification. Address. Non-voters included. Voting for general election and August 1859 by-election.

Joseph Somes   John Harvey Lewis

Hull Pub Lib   Guildhall Lib

1865—The poll book, as taken... Hull: John Montgomery, [1865]
Alphabetical by district or parish. Address and qualification. Non-voters included, distinguishing dead.

James Clay   Charles Morgan Norwood   Joseph Somes   Joseph Hoare

Hull Pub Lib Guildhall Lib

1868—The poll book, as taken... Hull: John Montgomery, 1869
Alphabetical by parish or township and by qualification within each letter. Address.

Charles Morgan Norwood   James Clay   Henry John Atkinson   Robert Baxter

Hull Pub Lib Inst Hist Res

Untraced: 1724, 1747, 1754, 1768

KNARESBOROUGH

1841—Borough of Knaresborough. The poll on the election... Knaresborough: G. Wilson, 1841
Alphabetical. Occupation and address. Separate list of plumpers.

Andrew Lawson   William Busfield Ferrand   Charles Sturgeon

Guildhall Lib

LEEDS

1832—The poll book of the Leeds borough election... Leeds: Hernaman & Perring, 1833
Alphabetical by township. Address and nature of qualification. Non-voters included.

John Marshall, Jr.   Thomas Babington Macaulay   Michael Thomas Sadler

Leeds Pub Lib Inst Hist Res

1834*—The poll book of the Leeds borough election... Leeds: R. Perring, 1834
Alphabetical by township. Occupation and address. Non-voters included, distinguishing dead, removed and rejected. Note on proceedings.

Edward Baines   Sir John Beckett   Joshua Bower

Leeds Pub Lib Inst Hist Res

1835—The poll book of the Leeds borough election... Leeds: R. Perring, 1835
Alphabetical by township. Nature and address of qualification. Non-voters included, distinguishing dead and removed.

Sir John Beckett   Edward Baines   William Brougham

Leeds Pub Lib Guildhall Lib

1837—The poll book of the Leeds borough election... Leeds: R. Perring, 1837
Alphabetical by township. Nature and address of qualification. Non-voters included, distinguishing dead and removed.

Edward Baines   Sir William Molesworth   Sir John Beckett

Leeds Pub Lib Guildhall Lib

1841—The poll book of the Leeds borough election... Leeds: J. Swallow, 1841
Alphabetical by township. Nature and address of qualification. Non-voters included, distinguishing dead and removed.

William Beckett William Aldam, Jr. Joseph Hume Lord Jocelyn

Leeds Pub Lib Inst Hist Res

1847—The poll book of the Leeds borough election... Leeds: T. W. Green, 1847
Alphabetical by township. Nature and address of qualification. Non-voters included, distinguishing dead.

William Beckett James Garth Marshall Joseph Sturge

Leeds Pub Lib Inst Hist Res

1852—The poll book of the Leeds borough election... Leeds: D. I. Roebuck, 1853
Alphabetical by ward and township. Address.

Sir George Goodman Matthew Talbot Baines Robert Hall Thomas Sidney

Leeds Pub Lib Inst Hist Res

1857 (March)—Poll book of the Leeds borough election... Leeds: C. Kemplay, 1857
Alphabetical. Address. Non-voters included.

Matthew Talbot Baines Robert Hall John Remington Mills

Leeds Pub Lib Inst Hist Res

1857* (June)—The poll book of the Leeds borough election... Leeds: H. W. Walker, 1857
Alphabetical by ward and township. Address.

George Skirrow Beecroft John Remington Mills

Leeds Pub Lib Inst Hist Res

1859—Poll book of the Leeds borough election... Leeds: David Green, [1859]
Alphabetical by ward and township. Address. Non-voters, pairs and dead distinguished.

Edward Baines George Skirrow Beecroft William Edward Forster

Leeds Pub Lib Inst Hist Res

1865—Poll book of the Leeds borough election... Leeds: C. Kemplay, 1865
Alphabetical. Address. Non-voters included.

George Skirrow Beecroft Edward Baines Viscount Amberley

Leeds Pub Lib Guildhall Lib

1868—The poll book of the Leeds borough election... Leeds: Edwd. Baines & Sons, 1868
Alphabetical by ward and division. Address.

Edward Baines Robert Meek Carter William St. James Wheelhouse
Sir Andrew Fairbairn A. Duncombe

Leeds Pub Lib Guildhall Lib

PONTEFRACT

1852—Polling book of the election... Pontefract: William Edward Bownas, 1852
Alphabetical by township. Non-voters included.

Richard Monckton Milnes Benjamin Oliveira William David Lewis

Bodl Inst Hist Res

1857—Polling book of the election... Pontefract: William Edward Bownas, 1857
Alphabetical by township and qualification.

Richard Monckton Milnes William Wood Benjamin Oliveira

Bodl Guildhall Lib

1859—Polling book of the election... Pontefract: William Edward Bownas, 1859
Alphabetical by township and qualification.

Richard Monckton Milnes William Overend Hugh Culling Eardley Childers

Bodl Inst Hist Res

1860*—Polling book of the election... Pontefract: William Edward Bownas, 1860
Poll order by booth.

Hugh Culling Eardley Childers Samuel Waterhouse

Bodl Inst Hist Res

1865—Polling book of the election... Pontefract: Richard Holmes, 1865
Alphabetical by township and qualification.

Hugh Culling Eardley Childers Samuel Waterhouse William Macarthur

Bodl Inst Hist Res

1868—A full and accurate poll book... Pontefract: Richard Holmes, 1868
Alphabetical by polling district and township. Qualification. Non-voters distinguished. Tendered votes. Account of proceedings.

Hugh Culling Eardley Childers Samuel Waterhouse C. M. Gaskell

Bodl Inst Hist Res

RIPON

1832—A copy of the poll... Ripon: Thomas Procter, 1832
Alphabetical by qualification. Tendered votes with address and non-voters.

Thomas Kitchingman Staveley Joshua Samuel Crompton Sir Charles James Dalbiac
William Markham

Bodl Inst Hist Res

1832—Ripon election. The poll for two burgesses... Ripon: E. Langdale, 1832
Alphabetical by qualification. Address. Tendered and non-voters.

Thomas Kitchingman Staveley Joshua Samuel Crompton Sir Charles James Dalbiac
William Markham

Guildhall Lib

1868—A copy of the poll... Ripon: G. Parker, [1868]
Alphabetical by district. Address.

Lord John Hay G. A. Cayley

Guildhall Lib

SCARBOROUGH

1835—A complete list of voters... Scarborough: C. R. Todd, 1835
Alphabetical by township. Address. Non-voters included, distinguishing dead and absent.

Sir Frederick William Trench Sir John Vanden Bempde Johnstone Sir George Cayley

Reading Univ Lib Inst Hist Res

1835—Bye's list of voters... Scarborough: J. Bye, 1835
Alphabetical. Occupation and differing 1832 votes. Non-voters. Members of the corporation, tenants of the corporation or of its individual members, new voters and objected voters distinguished. Remarks on the election.

Sir Frederick William Trench Sir John Vanden Bempde Johnstone Sir George Cayley

Scarborough Pub Lib Inst Hist Res

1837—Ainsworth's list of voters... Scarborough: J. Ainsworth & Sons, 1837
Alphabetical by qualification and township. Address. Speeches at a dinner for Style's friends.

Sir Frederick William Trench Sir Thomas Charles Style
Sir John Vanden Bempde Johnstone

Bodl Inst Hist Res

1852—A report of the speeches... and a list of the voters... Scarborough: J. Ainsworth & Sons, 1852
Alphabetical by qualification and township. Non-voters, distinguishing absent and disqualified. Account of proceedings and election literature.

Sir John Vanden Bempde Johnstone Earl of Mulgrave George Frederick Young

Scarborough Pub Lib Inst Hist Res

1857*—Return of the polling. *Scarborough Times and Weekly List of Visitors,* 19 December, 26 December 1857, 2 January, 9 January 1858
Poll order by booth. Address.

John Dent Dent George John Cayley

Brit Lib (News) Inst Hist Res

1859—The list of the voters... *Scarborough Times and Weekly List of Visitors,* 7 May, 14 May 1859
Alphabetical by township.

William Denison Sir John Vanden Bempde Johnstone John Dent Dent
George John Cayley

Brit Lib (News) Inst Hist Res

1860*—The list of the voting... *Scarborough Times and Weekly List of Visitors*, 4 February 1860
Poll order by booth. Address.

John Dent Dent J. M. Caulfield

Brit Lib (News) Inst Hist Res

1860*—Scarborough election. *Scarborough Gazette*, 9 February 1860
Alphabetical by candidate.

John Dent Dent J. M. Caulfield

Brit Lib (News) Inst Hist Res

1865—A list of the voters... *Scarborough Gazette*, 25 July 1865
Alphabetical.

Sir John Vanden Bempde Johnstone John Dent Dent George John Cayley

Brit Lib (News) Inst Hist Res

SHEFFIELD

1832—The poll book: containing a correct list... Sheffield: A. Whitaker, 1833
Alphabetical by township. Address. Non-voters included.

John Parker Samuel Bailey Thomas Asline Wood James Silk Buckingham

Sheffield Pub Lib Inst Hist Res

1835—The poll book: containing the proceedings... Sheffield: George Ridge, [1835]
Alphabetical by township. Address. Non-voters included. Account of proceedings.

John Parker James Silk Buckingham Samuel Bailey

Sheffield Pub Lib Inst Hist Res

1852—The poll book of the Sheffield election... Sheffield: Leader, [1852]
Alphabetical by township. Address. Non-voters included.

John Arthur Roebuck George Hadfield John Parker William Overend

Sheffield Pub Lib Inst Hist Res

1857—The poll book of the Sheffield election...
Alphabetical by township. Address. Non-voters included.

John Arthur Roebuck George Hadfield William Overend

Sheffield Pub Lib Inst Hist Res

WAKEFIELD

1835—A revised and corrected list of the electors... Wakefield: R. Hurst, 1835
Alphabetical by candidate. Address.

Daniel Gaskell William Sebright Lascelles

Wakefield Pub Lib Guildhall Lib

1835—The poll book for the borough of Wakefield... Wakefield: Richard Nichols, 1835
Alphabetical by township. Address. Rejected voters included.

Daniel Gaskell — William Sebright Lascelles

Guildhall Lib

1837—Wakefield borough election... The poll book... Wakefield: Thomas Nichols & Son, [1837]
Alphabetical by candidate. Occupation and address. Non-voters, rejected, disqualified and dead.

William Sebright Lascelles — Daniel Gaskell

Wakefield Pub Lib   Guildhall Lib

1837—The poll book for the borough of Wakefield. Wakefield: John Stanfield, 1837
Alphabetical. Nature and address of qualification. Non-voters included. Rejected voters and dead distinguished. Answers of queried voters. Separate lists of voters disqualified, dead or abroad.

William Sebright Lascelles — Daniel Gaskell

Guildhall Lib

1841—Wakefield borough election, July 2nd 1841. The poll book... Wakefield: Thomas Nichols, [1841]
Alphabetical by candidate. Address. Non-voters, dead, rejected and disqualified.

Joseph Holdsworth — William Sebright Lascelles

Wakefield Pub Lib   Inst Hist Res

1841—Wakefield borough election, July 2nd 1841. The poll book... Wakefield: Stanfield & Palmer, [1841]
Alphabetical by candidate. Address. Non-voters, dead, rejected and disqualified.

Joseph Holdsworth — William Sebright Lascelles

Guildhall Lib

1852—Wakefield borough election, July 9, 1852. The poll book... Wakefield: Charles Hicks, 1852
Alphabetical by candidate. Nature and address of qualification. Non-voters.

George Sandars — William Henry Leatham

Wakefield Pub Lib   Inst Hist Res

1862*—Poll book of the Wakefield borough election... Wakefield: J. Robinson, 1862
Alphabetical. Occupation, address and 1859 voting. Non-voters, rejected and dead. Electoral history and chronology from 1859.

Sir John Charles Dalrymple Hay — Richard Smethurst

Wakefield Pub Lib   Inst Hist Res

1865—Poll book of the Wakefield borough election... Wakefield: J. Robinson, 1866
Alphabetical. Occupation, address and votes cast since 1835. Voters on the 1832 register distinguished. Non-voters, dead and tendered voters. Electoral history and account of proceedings.

William Henry Leatham   Sir John Charles Dalrymple Hay

Wakefield Pub Lib   Inst Hist Res

1868—[List of the poll] *Wakefield Express* Supplement, 21 November 1868
Alphabetical by candidate. Address. Non-voters.

Somerset Archibald Beaumont   Thomas Kemp Sanderson

Brit Lib (News)   Inst Hist Res

Untraced: 1847, 1852 (Robinson), 1859

YORK

1741—The poll for members... York: John Jackson, [1741]
Alphabetical. Occupation and address or place of residence.

Edward Thompson   Godfrey Wentworth   Sir John Lister Kaye   Sir William Milner

Inst Hist Res

1741—The poll for the election... York: John Gilfillen & William Shaw, [1741]
Alphabetical. Occupation and address or place of residence.

Edward Thompson   Godfrey Wentworth   Sir John Lister Kaye   Sir William Milner

Leeds Pub Lib   Guildhall Lib

1758*—The poll for a member... York: John Jackson, [1758]
Alphabetical. Occupation and address or place of residence.
Election literature.

William Thornton   Robert Lane

York Pub Lib   Inst Hist Res

1774—The poll for members... York: F. Jackson & N. Nickson, 1774
Alphabetical. Occupation and address or place of residence. Address to Cavendish and Turner.

Charles Turner   Lord John Cavendish   Martin Bladen Hawke

York Pub Lib   Inst Hist Res

1784—The state of the poll... York: W. Blanchard, [1784]
Alphabetical. Occupation and address or place of residence.

Viscount Galway   Richard Slater Milnes   Lord John Cavendish   Sir William Milner

York Pub Lib   Guildhall Lib

1807—City of York election, 1807. The state of the poll... London: W. Flint, 1807
Alphabetical by first letter. Occupation and address or place of residence.

Sir William Mordaunt Milner   Sir Mark Masterman Sykes   Lawrence Dundas

Bodl   Inst Hist Res

1807—Pick's edition of the state of the poll... York: W. Pick, 1807
Alphabetical. Occupation and address or place of residence. Rejected and postponed voters with reasons. Voters since dead. Surviving freemen who polled in the 1758, 1774 and 1784 elections showing votes. Account of elections from 1713.

Sir William Mordaunt Milner   Sir Mark Masterman Sykes   Lawrence Dundas

York Pub Lib   Inst Hist Res

1818—The poll for members... York: Thomas Wilson for T. Sotheran, [1818]
Alphabetical. Occupation and address or place of residence. Account of proceedings. Record of elections since 1713 and obituaries of past members.

Lawrence Dundas   Sir Mark Masterman Sykes   William Bryan Cooke

York Pub Lib   Inst Hist Res

1820—The poll for members... York: Thomas Wilson for T. Sotheran, [1820]
Alphabetical. Occupation and address or place of residence. Account of proceedings.

Lawrence Dundas   Marmaduke Wyvill   Lord Howden

York Pub Lib   Inst Hist Res

1830—The poll for members... York: H. Bellerby, [1830]
Alphabetical. Occupation and address or place of residence. Rejected voters with reasons. Account of proceedings.

Samuel Adam Bayntun   Thomas Dundas   Edward Robert Petre

York Pub Lib   Inst Hist Res

1832—The poll for members... York: H. Bellerby, 1833
Alphabetical. Occupation and address. Rejected voters. Non-voters.

Edward Robert Petre   Samuel Adlam Bayntun   John Henry Lowther   Thomas Dundas

York Pub Lib   Guildhall Lib

1832—The poll for members... York: printed for the election committee of the Hon. Edward Petre, [1832]
Alphabetical by parish. Address. Prefatory statement.

Edward Robert Petre   Samuel Adlam Bayntun   John Henry Lowther   Thomas Dundas

York Pub Lib   Guildhall Lib

1835—The poll for members... York: H. Bellerby, 1835
Alphabetical. Occupation and address.

John Henry Lowther   John Charles Dundas   Charles Francis Barkley

York Pub Lib   Guildhall Lib

1837—York city election. The poll for members...
Alphabetical. Occupation and address.

John Henry Lowther   John Charles Dundas   David Francis Atcherley

Humberside Rec Off   Inst Hist Res

1841—The poll for members… York: H. Bellerby, [1841]
Alphabetical. Occupation and address. Account of proceedings.
John Henry Lowther Henry Redhead Yorke David Francis Atcherley
York Pub Lib Inst Hist Res

1852—The poll book: a record of the votes… York: John Brown, [1852]
Alphabetical. Occupation and address. Rejected voters. Prefatory review.
John George Smyth William Mordaunt Edward Milner Henry Vincent
York Pub Lib Inst Hist Res

1857—The poll book: a record of the votes… York: John Brown, [1857]
Alphabetical. Address.
Joshua Proctor Brown-Westhead John George Smyth Malcolm Lewin
York Pub Lib Inst Hist Res

1859—The poll book: a record of votes… York: John Brown, [1859]
Alphabetical by candidate. Address.
Joshua Proctor Brown-Westhead John George Smyth Austin Henry Layard
York Pub Lib Guildhall Lib

[Two editions known]

1865—The poll book: a record of the votes… York: John Brown, [1865]
Alphabetical. Address. Prefatory review.
James Lowther George Leeman Joshua Proctor Brown-Westhead
York Pub Lib Inst Hist Res

1868—The poll book: a record of the votes… York: John Sampson, [1868]
Alphabetical. Address.
James Lowther Joshua Proctor Brown-Westhead John Hall Gladstone
York Pub Lib Inst Hist Res

SCOTLAND AND WALES

CROMARTY

1790—[List of freeholders who voted] *A View of the Political State of Scotland at the Last General Election* (Edinburgh: Mundell & Son, 1790), pp. 74-75
By candidate. Place of residence or occupation.

Duncan Davidson Alexander Brodie

Natl Lib Scot Inst Hist Res

DUMFRIESSHIRE

1790—[List of freeholders who voted] *A View of the Political State of Scotland at the Last General Election* (Edinburgh: Mundell & Son, 1790), pp. 82-83
By candidate. Place of residence or occupation in preceding roll of freeholders.

Sir Robert Lawrie John Johnston

Natl Lib Scot Inst Hist Res

1868—List of electors . . . showing state of voting... Glasgow: City Steam Printing Works, [1869]
Alphabetical by district and parish. Address. Non-voters included. Voting for 1868 general election and for 1869 by-election.

Sir Sydney Hedley Waterlow George Gustavus Walker

Soc Geneal

1868—Analysis of the poll books... Glasgow: Robert Anderson, 1869
By district, parish and candidate. Address. Non-voters.

Sir Sydney Hedley Waterlow George Gustavus Walker

Soc Geneal

1869*—List of electors . . . showing state of voting... Glasgow: City Steam Printing Works, [1868]
Alphabetical by district and parish. Address. Non-voters included. Voting for 1868 general election and for 1869 by-election.

George Gustavus Walker Sir Sydney Hedley Waterlow

Soc Geneal

EDINBURGH

1847—List of voters... who voted for Mr. Charles Cowan. Edinburgh: T. Constable, [1847]
Alphabetical by district. Address, religious denomination and candidate for whom second vote cast. Proprietors distinguished.

Charles Cowan William Gibson Craig Thomas Babington Macaulay Peter Blackburne

Edinburgh Pub Lib Inst Hist Res

1852—List of the electors... corrected after Appeal Court 1854, shewing the voting... [Edinburgh, 1854]
By district and street. Occupation and qualification. Non-voters and those enrolled by Conservatives since the last election distinguished.

Thomas Babington Macaulay Charles Cowan Duncan McLaren Thomas Charles Bruce Alexander Campbell

Edinburgh Pub Lib Inst Hist Res

GLASGOW

1832—Glasgow electors: list of the names... who voted... Glasgow: Muir, Gowans, 1832
Alphabetical by district. Address and occupation.

James Ewing James Oswald Sir Daniel Keyte Sandford John Crawford John Douglas Joseph Dixon

Natl Lib Scot Inst Hist Res

LINLITHGOWSHIRE

1790—[List of freeholders who voted] *A View of the Political State of Scotland at the Last General Election* (Edinburgh: Mundell & Son, 1790), pp. 133-136
By candidate. Place of residence or occupation in preceding roll of freeholders.

John Hope Sir William Augustus Cuninghame

Natl Lib Scot Inst Hist Res

ORKNEY

1790—[List of freeholders who voted] *A View of the Political State of Scotland at the Last General Election* (Edinburgh: Mundell & Son, 1790), pp. 142-144
By candidate. Place of residence or occupation in preceding roll of freeholders.

John Balfour Thomas Dundas

Natl Lib Scot Inst Hist Res

PERTHSHIRE

1790—[List of freeholders who voted] *A View of the Political State of Scotland at the Last General Election* (Edinburgh: Mundell & Son, 1790), pp. 154-159
By candidate. Place of residence or occupation.

James Murray John Drummond

Natl Lib Scot Inst Hist Res

RENFREWSHIRE

1790—[List of freeholders who voted] *A View of the Political State of Scotland at the Last General Election* (Edinburgh: Mundell & Son, 1790), pp. 165-167
By candidate. Place of residence or occupation.

John Shaw Stewart Alexander Cuninghame

Natl Lib Scot Inst Hist Res

1832—Red and black list of electors... shewing how they voted... n.p., [1833]
Alphabetical by candidate and parish. Place of residence and occupation. Non-voters. Account of proceedings.

Sir Michael Shaw Stewart R. Cunninghame Bontine

Mitchell Lib, Glasgow Inst Hist Res

ROXBURGHSHIRE

1780—[List of freeholders who voted] *Minutes of a Meeting of the Freeholders of the County of Roxburgh...* [Jedburgh, 1780], pp. 64-66
By candidate. Place of residence and occupation.

Sir Gilbert Elliot Lord Robert Ker

Natl Lib Scot Inst Hist Res

1790—[List of freeholders who voted] *A View of the Political State of Scotland at the Last General Election* (Edinburgh: Mundell & Son, 1790), pp. 174-177

Sir George Douglas John Rutherford

Natl Lib Scot Inst Hist Res

STIRLINGSHIRE

1790—[List of freeholders who voted] *A View of the Political State of Scotland at the Last General Election* (Edinburgh: Mundell & Son, 1790), pp. 183-185
By candidate. Place of residence or occupation in preceding roll of freeholders.

Sir Thomas Dundas Sir Alexander Campbell

Natl Lib Scot Inst Hist Res

SUTHERLAND

1790—[List of freeholders who voted] *A View of the Political State of Scotland at the Last General Election* (Edinburgh: Mundell & Son, 1790)
By candidate. Place of residence or occupation in preceding roll of freeholders.

James Grant Robert Bruce Aeneas McLeod

Natl Lib Scot Inst Hist Res

CARMARTHENSHIRE

1868—A list of the electors in the Carmarthen polling district, shewing how they voted. Carmarthen: William Spurrell, 1869
Alphabetical by parish and qualification. Place of residence and place and nature of property. Non-voters included.

Edward John Sartoris John Jones H. L. Puxley David Pugh

Natl Lib Wales Inst Hist Res

MONTGOMERYSHIRE BOROUGHS

1847—The poll of the borough of Welch-pool... Welshpool: Robert Owen, [1847] Alphabetical by division. Address and occupation. Non-voters. Voters for Pugh promised to Cholmondley or to be neutral distinguished.

Hugh Cholmondley David Pugh

Natl Lib Wales Inst Hist Res

Index